Critical Essays on
Wallace Stevens

Critical Essays on Wallace Stevens

Steven Gould Axelrod
Helen Deese

G. K. Hall & Co. • Boston, Massachusetts

Library of Congress Cataloging in Publication Data

   Critical essays on Wallace Stevens.

   (Critical essays on American literature)
   Includes index.
   1. Stevens, Wallace, 1879-1955—Criticism and interpretation.
I. Axelrod, Steven Gould, 1944-   . II. Deese, Helen. III. Series.
PS3537.T4753Z624   1988   811'.52   88-5245
ISBN 0-8161-8886-6

This publication is printed on permanent durable acid-free paper
MANUFACTURED IN THE UNITED STATES OF AMERICA

CRITICAL ESSAYS ON AMERICAN LITERATURE

This series seeks to anthologize the most important criticism on a wide variety of topics and writers in American literature. Our readers will find in various volumes not only a generous selection of reprinted articles and reviews but original essays, bibliographies, manuscript sections, and other materials brought to public attention for the first time. This volume contains a balanced historical record of critical reaction to one of America's most important poets, Wallace Stevens. The book contains both a sizable gathering of early reviews and a broad selection of more recent scholarship. Among noted early reviewers are Harriet Monroe, F. O. Matthiessen, Marianne Moore, Frank Kermode, and Irving Howe. There are reprinted essays by Northrop Frye, Harold Bloom, Frank Lentricchia, Fredric Jameson, and J. Hillis Miller. In addition to an extensive introduction by Steven Gould Axelrod and Helen Deese that describes both Stevens's career and critical reactions to it, there are also new essays by Claudia Yukman and Paul Douglass and an important revised essay by Lawrence Kramer. We are confident that this book will make a permanent and significant contribution to American literary study.

JAMES NAGEL, GENERAL EDITOR

Northeastern University

CONTENTS

Essays

INTRODUCTION

Wallace Stevens:
The Critical Reception

I. Reviews

Wallace Stevens's reviewers were divided from the beginning. Negative reviewers assumed that Stevens's poetry lacked significant content: His technical skills may be superb, but his poetry falls short of intellectual seriousness and evades political concerns. Positive reviewers, conversely, discovered in his texts illumination about the human faculties, the physical world, and the mind/reality interplay that makes poetry possible. These would seem to be highly serious matters.

Ironically, Stevens's first widely noticed poems were initiated by the bloodiest political disaster up to that time: the first World War. In her review of *Harmonium*, included in this volume, Harriet Monroe tells the story of Stevens's late submission of a set of poems for *Poetry*'s "War Number" (November 1914).[1] Despite their lateness, she published four of them, all she had space for. These poems, entitled "Phases," are neither a call to arms nor a denunciation of war's cruelty, but they do concern an abstracted figure of the soldier at war. The only contemporaneous review we have of these four poems is a brief comment by an Irish-American poet, Shaemas O'Sheel, who gained some renown as the author of an Irish war poem, "They Went Forth to Battle, But They Always Fell." Writing for *Minaret*, a journal that considered itself a rival of *Poetry*, O'Sheel assessed *Poetry* as well as Stevens's poems. He condemned the entire "War Number," citing the first quatrain of Stevens's "Phases" as an "excellent example," of poetry that is "untruthful, and nauseating to read."[2]

Stevens continued to contribute regularly to *Poetry* as well as to Alfred Kreymborg and Walter Arensberg's more consciously radical journal, *Others*. The first poem he gave to Kreymborg was "Peter Quince at the Clavier," a poem that immediately became a favorite of anthologists. The month after O'Sheel's adverse comment on "Phases," George Soule, reviewing an anthology in which Stevens was represented, found pleasure in Stevens's style: "Delicate and fantastic is 'Peter Quince at the Clavier' . . . ; it has at least momentary charm."[3] And then in June 1916, reviewing *Others*, Max Michelson, a poet who contributed frequently to *Poetry*, agreed, in a similarly backward-running sentence, that "Graceful as the tilting of a bird is the greater part of 'Peter Quince,' in spite of some slight technical defects in the construction."[4]

Because Stevens did not publish a book-length collection until *Harmonium* in 1923, comments on his early poetry occur almost entirely in reviews of anthologies. One anthology, *The New Era in American Poetry*, because it deliberately neglected Stevens and other poets of the avant-garde while conferring favor on earnest poets named Oppenheim, Giovannitti, Wood, and Brody, sparked a spirited quarrel between its editor, Louis Untermeyer, a poet himself, and Conrad Aiken, another poet. Aiken, in a scathing review, observed that "the critic of poetry who is also a poet is apt to be the most interesting and the most unreliable of critics."[5] The poet-critic is unreliable because he is "vitally concerned with the success or failure of this or that particular strain of work." Aiken went on to accuse Untermeyer of favoring "poetry with a [politically correct] message," while condemning poetry that seemed to suggest a doctrine of "art for art's sake." Aiken alleged that "when poetry is in the Fletcher-Bodenheim-Stevens vein he grants its skillful use of word color, but is distressed by its apparent emptiness."

In the same issue of the *New Republic*, Untermeyer wrote a spirited reply that only confirmed Aiken's allegation.[6] The true artist, Untermeyer wrote, "is concerned chiefly with what he has to say. His manner of expression is usually fortuitous and always secondary. . . . The over-nice preoccupation with shades, the elaborate analysis of a spent emotion, the false emphasis on half-lights or a novel technique lead inevitably to The Yellow Book, to the mere verbal legerdemain of the Pound-Stevens-Arensberg-Others" concept of poetry. Untermeyer went on to insist that what the poet should say must be affirmative: "No major art has ever existed and . . . no art-work has survived that has not been built on faith." Misreading both Robert Frost and Edwin Arlington Robinson, Untermeyer pointed to those poets as exemplars of the art that is "a glorified communication, a sharing of life."

Over the years, many of Stevens's reviewers were themselves poets, some distinguished, some less so. Most, like Aiken and Untermeyer, were vitally concerned with the success or failure of certain strains of poetry. Other reviewers applied political or moral criteria to the poetry, as determined by their own ideology. Only a few shaken realists, such as Eda Lou Walton, Robert Lowell, Delmore Schwartz, and R. P. Blackmur, overcame their inevitable biases and saw Stevens's poems as structures that, in violating preconceived paradigms, encompassed an imaginative new beginning.

During the period before *Harmonium*, Stevens also turned his attention to the theater, with ultimately unhappy results. In 1916, he wrote *Three Travelers Watch a Sunrise*, which won *Poetry*'s $100 prize for a short play. (William Carlos Williams called it "Arriet's prize" in his letter of congratulation.[7]) Buoyed by this success, Stevens wrote two additional pieces at the behest of the Wisconsin Players: *Carlos among the Candles*, a dramatic monologue, and *Bowl, Cat and Broomstick*. The Wisconsin Players staged *Carlos* on a program with three other short plays in New York on 20 October 1917. The two brief reviews that survive are harsh. The anonymous reviewer for the *New York Times* wrote that "*Carlos among the Candles* is a brief monologue by Wallace Stevens, intended neither for the stage nor the library."[8] Ralph Block in the *New York Tribune* complained that the play's process "appears to be to say something that has no meaning at all with all the bearing of significance, recalling what Alice said . . . about the sound and not the sense being the most important."[9] Although scheduled for a two-week run, *Carlos* was taken off the program after the first night.

The Wisconsin Players staged *Bowl, Cat and Broomstick* a few nights after the *Carlos* disaster. Walter Pach, who designed the set for the piece, characterized it, according to Samuel French Morse, as a "book review."[10] We have no reviews beyond Pach's remark, but Stevens never published the play. Harriet Monroe printed the prize-winning *Three Travelers* in the July 1916 issue of *Poetry*, and Stevens sent her *Carlos* for the December 1917 issue. He included none of his plays in *Collected Poems*, and *Bowl* did not even make *Opus Posthumous*.[11]

Three Travelers was performed on 13 February 1920 in New York at the Provincetown Playhouse. We have no reviews of the single performance, which Stevens did not attend. He wrote to Harriet Monroe that

> I was in New York while they were doing the play but did not have an opportunity to see it or even to see anyone to make inquiries. So much water has gone under the bridge since the thing was written that I have not the curiosity even to read it to see how it looks at this late date.[12]

Joan Richardson, Stevens's biographer, believes that in 1916 and 1917 when he wrote *Three Travelers* and *Carlos* (she does not mention *Bowl*), Stevens "was as interested in the theater as he was in poetry—perhaps even more so. It was the terrible reaction of the audience and critics to the production of *Carlos among the Candles* that accounted for his turning away from theater, just as a few years later, after the reception of *Harmonium*, he turned away from poetry."[13] Stevens, however, understood that he had written essentially nondramatic works, especially in *Carlos*. To his set designer, Bancel La Farge, he had written, "My intention is not to produce a dramatic effect but to produce a poetic effect."[14] *Carlos*, by design, was a poem made visible, metaphor given physical form. After the disaster, Stevens wrote to Harriet Monroe that "a theatre without action or characters ought to be within the range of human interests. . . . Why not?"[15] Stevens was probably right that his texts ought to be stageable, and the answer to his question—"Why not?"—should refer to time and the audience. He was a few decades ahead of his age. Audiences today might receive his plays as rich instances of scripted performance art.

Although, like Henry James, Stevens harbored a keen theatrical interest, the embarrassing response to his productions induced the emotionally "fragile" writer[16] to return from the stage to the printed text. After much reluctance, Stevens signed a contract with Knopf to publish a collection of his poetry. He delivered the manuscript of *Harmonium* to his editor, Carl Van Vechten, in November of 1922, but as late as 17 July he wrote to Van Vechten that he felt "frightfully uncertain about a book."[17]

When *Harmonium* appeared in 1923,[18] it received sympathetic reviews from Harriet Monroe and Marianne Moore, though Monroe seems to have understood Stevens as a more sanguine poet than he is: "The bleak despairs of lesser men visit him not at all."[19] Moore astutely noted the "achieved remoteness" of Stevens's imagination, adding that it "takes refuge" in a "riot of gorgeousness."[20] She praised "Sunday Morning" and other poems, yet observed that although "Mr. Stevens is never inadvertently crude, one is conscious . . . of a deliberate bearishness—a shadow of acrimonious, unprovoked contumely."

Among the negative reviewers, Mark Van Doren, writing in the *Nation*, concluded that Stevens's wit "is tentative, perverse, and superfine; and it will never be popular."[21] Edmund Wilson, in the *New Republic*, made the common division between sense and style: "Even when you do not know what he is saying, you know that he is saying it well."[22] He opined that Stevens, who is so observant and fanciful, "seems to have emotion neither in abundance nor in intensity." In his review, reprinted in this volume, Louis Untermeyer expressed skepticism that the author of *Harmonium* "even cares to communicate in a tongue familiar to the reader."[23] He concluded that "this conscious aesthete 'at war with reality' achieves little beyond an amusing preciosity."

More perceptive were Matthew Josephson and John Gould Fletcher. They ranked Stevens among the best of contemporary poets, yet both suggested the need for an extended range in any subsequent collection. Josephson, in a review included here, identified two principal qualities in Stevens's poetry.[24] One side is "exotic . . . so that we have a poetry of sensuousness," a poetry that can only grow "more intimate and scandalous" if pursued. The other side exhibits "a mathematical, a *metaphysical* quality." Poems of this latter sort, such as "Thirteen Ways of Looking at a Blackbird" and "Anecdote of the Jar," will be "spell-binding for hundreds of years." Josephson hoped that in the future Stevens would emphasize this metaphysical dimension.

Fletcher, like Untermeyer, characterized Stevens as an aesthete, but for Fletcher the term was not necessarily derogatory: "The careful reader . . . can readily ascertain that Mr. Stevens is definitely out of tune with life and with his surroundings, and is seeking an escape into a sphere of finer harmony between instinct and intelligence."[25] Because of his honesty, Stevens stands "head and shoulders" above the internationally famous aesthetes like Eliot, the Sitwells, and Valéry. Fletcher even defended Stevens's "obscurity" as deriving from "a wealth of meaning and allusion." Still, Fletcher warned that the poet faced "a clear choice of evils: he must either expand his range to take in more of human experience, or give up writing altogether. 'Harmonium' is a sublimation which does not permit a sequel."

A sequel was indeed long in coming. During the five or six years after *Harmonium*, Stevens apparently wrote only two poems, both in 1924: "Sea Surface Full of Clouds" and "Red Loves Kit."[26] Perhaps the mixed nature of the reviews together with the lack of sales discouraged him. Probably Gorham Munson's derisive essay in the *Dial*, two years after *Harmonium*, further troubled him. We know that he saw the essay, and we can assume that he read at least part of it. On 19 November 1925, he wrote to Marianne Moore, the *Dial*'s editor: "Sometime ago *The Dial* sent me Gorham Munson's note in your November number. I ought to have thanked you, and Munson too; but there are a lot of things one ought to do."[27] Stevens said no more on the subject, but the "thanks" to Munson must surely have been ironic.

Munson gave Stevens a pejorative name—dandy—that was to haunt him ever after. The name imposed on the poet a caricature even more trivial than Untermeyer's "conscious aesthete." Munson wrote that Stevens had mastered the two elements that constitute "the impeccability of the dandy . . . correctness and elegance."[28] The correctness resides in his absorption of "the teachings of the academy," while the elegance manifests itself in "his fabulous vocabulary." But the true object of Munson's sarcasm was not Stevens's craft but what Munson took to be his indifference to the political and social pain of the era:

> Mr. Stevens . . . appears to sit comfortably in the age, to enjoy a sense of security, to be conscious of no need of fighting the times. The world is a gay and bright phenomenon, and he gives the impression of feasting on it without misgiving.

Munson described the tranquility he detested in Stevens as the "well-fed and well-booted dandyism of contentment."

If Munson and the generally disheartening response to *Harmonium* did not upset Stevens's "tranquility," something else did. Between August 1924, when "Red Loves Kit" appeared in the *Measure*, and 16 April 1930, when "The Sun This March" appeared in the *New Republic*, Stevens published no poetry. His letters reveal that he received many requests from editors, but he repeatedly replied that his home life—a baby born in 1924— and his business left him no time for writing. Stevens later reflected on this poetically fallow period in a much-quoted letter to Ronald Lane Latimer:

> A good many years ago, when I really was a poet in the sense that I was all imagination, and so on, I deliberately gave up writing poetry because, much as I loved it, there were too many other things I wanted not to make an effort to have them. . . . I didn't like the idea of being bedeviled all the time about money and I didn't for a moment like the idea of poverty, so I went to work like anybody else and kept at it for a good many years.[29]

Certainly, in those years Stevens worked diligently at the Hartford Accident and Insurance Company, and in February 1934 he was named a vice president of the firm. His position there as a lawyer in the surety division was so vital to his pattern of living that he avoided retirement long after he had passed the company's normal retirement age. Even in his final illness in 1955, he appeared daily at his desk until he entered the hospital for the last time. Those years from 1924 to the early 1930s did change the material status of his family from modest to comfortable. In 1932, he was able to move his family from a noisy, rented duplex to the pleasant home in which he and Elsie lived for the rest of their lives.

Still, one feels that more than the need for professional and monetary success underlay his prolonged poetic silence. Very likely he had been stung by the response to *Carlos* and *Harmonium*. Moreover, as John Gould Fletcher had recommended, he may have been looking for the means and material to "expand his range" in poetry, while meditating on the place of the imagination in human experience.

In 1931, Knopf reissued *Harmonium* with fourteen poems added and three dropped.[30] The "dandy" appellation became the easy tag of the lazy reviewer: The anonymous writer for the *Bookman* advised that Stevens's "restrained good taste errs, as he himself admits, on the side of foppishness, like that of Beau Brummell"; and Raymond Larsson judged Stevens to be a "beau with a muff" whose character was "the dandy's."[31] Eda Lou Walton, on the other hand, sharply disputed Munson's characterization in her review of *Harmonium*'s new edition.[32] She pointed out that "in the deliberate deflation of the emotions . . . [Stevens] has chosen to explore every mood, with full realization of its several anti-moods; he has chosen to build up the vision, only to prick it." Stevens's poems demonstrate that "the disassociation of the emotions lies . . . within the very inception of the emotion itself." She concluded with sharp irony that because of Stevens's iconoclastic perception of emotional duality and fluidity, he "has been called a 'dandy.'"

The epithet of "dandy" persisted among reviewers and critics for decades, though transformed to "hedonist" in the more analytical discourse of Yvor Winters. In his 1943 essay, "Wallace Stevens, or the Hedonist's Progress," Winters contended that "Sunday Morning," which he believed to be a great poem in many ways, propounds the poet's fundamental ideas.[33] Winters was disturbed that those ideas do not give primacy to the intellect among human faculties, or to orthodox Christian beliefs among concepts of divinity. He complained that Stevens's philosophy releases him "from all the restraints of Christianity, and . . . his hedonism is so fused with Romanticism as to be merely an elegant variation on that somewhat inelegant System of Thoughtlessness" (p. 119). Although capable of reading Stevens's text with great perception, Winters used "hedonism" as Munson had used "dandyism," not to describe but to estrange and to suppress.

Stevens summoned up the personal and creative resources to publish a new poetry collection in 1935, *Ideas of Order*.[34] It was widely and, for the most part, sensitively reviewed. F. O. Matthiessen, in a review reprinted here, judged the poems to mark an advance: "Mr. Stevens has brought his talents to an expression that is at once precise and opulent. One is tempted to say that this is the nearest approach to major poetry being made in this country today."[35] Howard Baker related Stevens's poetry to Freudian thought: "Psychoanalysis probably gave an emphasis to Stevens's psychical symbols, and perhaps encouraged the use to some extent of 'free association' of ideas rather than strict logic" (p. 381).[36] Marianne Moore, in a review reprinted here, praised Stevens's art of "proprieties," while Theodore Roethke ambivalently observed that "the times and a ripened maturity have begun to stiffen Mr. Stevens' rhetoric."[37]

There was, however, one notorious review that immortalized its writer and energized the poet—Stanley Burnshaw's "Turmoil in the Middle Ground" in *New Masses*,[38] which is reprinted here. Louis Martz, writing two decades later, said that Burnshaw wrote "with considerable acuteness, though with a condescending tone."[39] That statement still seems fair today, though at least one section of Burnshaw's review expressed more derision than condescension. He termed *Harmonium* "the kind of verse that people concerned with the murderous world collapse can hardly swallow today except in tiny doses." He judged that "it is verse that Stevens can no longer write. His harmonious cosmos is suddenly screeching with confusion. *Ideas of Order* is the record of a man who, having lost his footing, now scrambles to stand up and keep his balance."

Stevens read the review and wrote about his reaction in a letter to Latimer on 9 October 1935: "The review in *Masses* was a most interesting review, because it placed me in a new setting. I hope I am headed left, but there are lefts and lefts, and certainly I am not headed for the ghastly left of *Masses*."[40] Three weeks later, he again wrote to Latimer:

> You will remember that Mr. Burnshaw applied the point of view of the practical Communist to *Ideas of Order*; in "Mr. Burnshaw and the Statue" I have tried to reverse the process: that is to say, to apply the point of view of a poet to communism.[41]

In this instance, a reviewer had spurred Stevens not to silence but to poetry. By November, Stevens wrote that "Mr. Burnshaw and the Statue" was ready for publication: "It is simply a general and rather vaguely poetic justification of leftism: to the extent that the Marxians are raising Cain with the peacocks and the doves, nature has been ruined by them."[42]

Now Stevens's most prolific period of writing began. "Mr. Burnshaw and the Statue" grew into *Owl's Clover*, which Latimer's Alcestis Press published in fall of 1936.[43] Stevens was never happy with *Owl's Clover*. He revised and cut the poem for his next Knopf collection—*The Man with the Blue Guitar*—and left it out of *The Collected Poems* altogether. It was Stevens's only work in which he deliberately tried to apply his own "sort of poetry" to "what one reads in the papers," and he called the result "rather boring."[44]

Ruth Lechlitner, writing in *New York Herald Tribune Books*, thought that the result seemed confused:

> By recognizing the importance of political and social change but refusing to admit the desirability of the union of the mass in an "orderly life," Stevens is obviously open to attack from the left. . . . He is aware that his is the philosophical liberal attitude; that he ironically admits his confusion and the anomaly of his position ("my old boat goes round on a crutch") is a point in his favor, but scarcely helps in resolving contradictions.[45]

Latimer sent a copy of the notice to Stevens, who hyperbolically replied that "we are all much disturbed about a possible attack from the Left; I expect the house to be burned down almost any moment."[46] Other reviewers, however, admired "Owl's Clover." Robert Fitzgerald, reviewing *The Man with the Blue Guitar*, wrote that "Owl's Clover" exemplified "the luxuriant thoroughness of Stevens's mind. The subject is the decline of the west."[47]

After *The Man with the Blue Guitar* appeared in 1937, Delmore Schwartz remarked, in a review included in this volume, that beneath the "baroque decoration" of Stevens's poetry, "we are confronted with a mind of the utmost seriousness, aware and involved in the most important things in our lives"; Hi Simons observed that between 1935 and 1937 the recognition of the poet's "greatness" had become general.[48] When Stevens's next collection was published—*Parts of a World* in 1942[49]—the *New Yorker* and *Time* both reviewed it. Although Louise Bogan complained that he was becoming progressively more "philosophic, closed in, and obscure," *Time*'s reviewer was more sympathetic to a poet who "spent his normal working hours disguised as a lawyer-employee of Hartford Accident and Indemnity Co."[50] Now in his sixties, Stevens accelerated his pace of writing. He published *Notes toward a Supreme Fiction* in 1942, *Esthétique du Mal* in 1945, and *Transport to Summer* in 1947.[51] In seminal reviews (both reprinted here), R. P. Blackmur accurately explained the three movements of "Notes toward a Supreme Fiction," while Louis Martz observed of *Transport to Summer* that Stevens, "having mastered one mode," was developing "in new directions, impelled by a growing vision."[52]

Reviewing *Transport to Summer* for the *Nation*, Robert Lowell responded fully to the poetic power he found in the volume. Lowell's own poetry was developing in a distinctively different direction from that of Stevens, though it would arguably come around to Stevens at the end.[53] Unlike Lowell's poetry of the 1940s, Stevens's was abstract, removed from external pressures, playful, calm—a pleasure to the contemplative mind and ear rather than a goad to fury. Yet Lowell resisted the impulse to promote his own strain of poetry at the expense of his colleague's. Nor did he wish to serve in an antiromantic crusade, like Winters's, or in a political attack, like Burnshaw's. It is true that Lowell's review begins with a genuflecting bob to the antihedonists and also to the Marxists:

> Perhaps Stevens is too much the leisured man of taste. As with Santayana, one feels that the tolerance and serenity are a little too blandly appropriated, that a man is able to be an imagination and the imagination able to be disinterested and urbane only because it is supported by industrial slaves.[54]

But when Lowell goes on to discuss the poems more specifically, his evaluation becomes formalist. Although he finds "Notes toward a Supreme Fiction" to be "sloppy, idiosyncratic, and repetitious," he thinks that the best poems in *Transport to Summer* are "as good as anyone is writing in English" (incidentally echoing Randall Jarrell's comment about Lowell's own poetry).[55] He calls "No Possum, No Sop, No Taters" "subtle in its rhythms and perceptions" and praises "Dutch Graves in Bucks County" for its "tremendous feeling, pathos and power" and "the magnificence of its rhetoric and resonance." Finally, he judges "Esthétique du Mal" to be "as good and important a poem as T. S. Eliot's *Four Quartets* or *Ash Wednesday*" and "more in the grand manner than any poetry since Yeats's."

Lowell's emphasis on form derived from the New Criticism, in which he had been well schooled. Many of the best reviewers of Stevens's last books were close readers in the New Critical mode. M. L. Rosenthal's review of *Three Academic Pieces* (1947) was in effect a brief explication.[56] Joseph Bennett's more extensive review of Stevens's next collection, *The Auroras of Autumn* (1950), analyzed prosody and images.[57] William Van O'Connor's review of the same volume, reprinted here, is a thematic study, placing Stevens within the American tradition.[58] In 1951, when Stevens was seventy-two, Knopf published his only collection of essays, *The Necessary Angel*.[59] In their reviews, Richard Eberhart and Bernard Heringman both gave this text the close attention they would give to poetry.[60]

Finally, in 1954, a year before his death, Stevens assembled his canon in *The Collected Poems of Wallace Stevens*.[61] To most reviewers, Stevens's importance now seemed apparent. Randall Jarrell, in a review reprinted here, wrote that the book contains "the poetry of one of the greatest living poets. . . . Some of these cool, clear, airy poems, which tower above us in the dazzling elegance, the 'minute brilliance,' of yachts or clouds, ought to be sailing over other heads many centuries from now."[62]

Both Delmore Schwartz and Hayden Carruth focused their discussion on Stevens's language, which they believed had significance in the poetic tradition as well as within Stevens's enclosed fictive world. Schwartz predicted that Stevens's "inventions, his discoveries, his long labor in the orchards of the imagination will directly affect other poets more and more in the future."[63] Carruth concluded that "in the texts themselves, the language is the only constant ratification of our sense of the poet's opulent invention."[64]

Adverse commentary, however, continued to appear. Donald Davie, for example, revived Winters's strictures and reflected a widespread British resistance to Stevens. *The Collected Poems*, he wrote, prove "the point of Yvor Winters' verdict that from *Harmonium*, despite its technical flaws, there could be no way forward." In fact, Davie continued, there was "one development that Winters did not forsee: the poetry could thereafter live on its own fat, gnaw its own vitals, conduct a running commentary on itself."[65]

Stevens died at seventy-five in August 1955. *Opus Posthumous*, edited by Samuel French Morse, appeared two years later, and the *Letters*, edited by the poet's daughter, Holly Stevens, appeared nine years after that.[66] Irving Howe's review of *Opus Posthumous*, reprinted here, provided an excellent survey of the poet's career and a fine commentary on the poems.[67] Hilton Kramer's review of the *Letters* temperately sought to explain, if not explain away, Stevens's sometimes distasteful social attitudes.[68] Many of the other notices were restrained and of minor interest. But when *Opus Posthumous* and *The Necessary Angel* were published in Great Britain, Henry Reed wrote a review (reprinted here) containing an appropriate final comment on the reception that Stevens's poetry had received:

> This is the poet who has often been called a dandy and a hedonist: the terms have not always been consciously dismissive: but they do in fact belittle him, even if indulgently. For the idiosyncracies of Stevens' thought and expression are not merely endearing perversities: a man who pleads his agnosticism so earnestly must be taken seriously, even if he does so with elegance, humour and calm.[69]

II. Criticism

If the reviews published during Stevens's lifetime haphazardly raised issues of dandyism, hedonism, social responsibility, intelligibility, thematic significance, and formal unity, the criticism published since his death has been a good deal more systematic and analytical. Raising many of the same issues, though often reformulating them, critics and scholars have engaged in an impressively productive dialogue about texts and about critical methodology.

We may divide the criticism into three broad categories: explicative and stylistic studies, interpretations employing history as a cognitive model, and interpretations employing philosophy as a cognitive model. The quantity and quality of critical texts in the third category have been especially remarkable. Stevens's discourse and philosophical interpretation have developed a symbiosis. On the one hand, Stevens's poems have given this mode of interpretation some of its most convincing proof-texts. On the other hand, since philosophically oriented literary theory, ranging from phenomenology to deconstruction, has been on the cutting edge for the last quarter century, it has been able to transform Stevens from a relatively minor byline in the Pound / Eliot era into the central figure in the modern canon, a poet with an era of his own. Over the last three decades, then, philosophical criticism and Stevens's reputation have come a long way together. Whether the poet's standing can survive a paradigm shift, whether the current turn to New Historicism, Marxism, psychoanalysis, feminism, and new biography will adversely affect his prestige: these questions currently remain open to speculation.

During Stevens's lifetime, his poetry generated a small number of significant essays by R. P. Blackmur (1932), Hi Simons (1940, 1945, 1946), Yvor Winters (1943), Marius Bewley (1949), Randall Jarrell (1951), Roy Harvey Pearce (1951), Sister Bernetta Quinn (1952), and Samuel French Morse (1952).[70] One book-length study appeared, William Van O'Connor's now-obsolete introduction, *The Shaping Spirit* (1950).[71] In the decade and a half following Stevens's death in 1955, however, criticism entered a cycle of boom and greater boom. This period comprised a major new stage in the critical appropriation of Stevens. By 1964, Joseph Riddel observed that although "there is not yet a Wallace Stevens 'industry,'" his rise in esteem "portends one."[72] Even as Riddel wrote, the cottage industry was becoming a multinational conglomerate.

Of the numerous explications that appeared, three stand out. Frank Kermode's *Wallace Stevens* (1960) was the first distinguished example of the genre.[73] Kermode takes his readers on a quick tour of all of Stevens's poetry and prose, elucidating formal and thematic subtleties, locating the poems among the greatest British and French texts of the last two centuries, and taking evident pleasure in Stevens's intellectual and verbal mastery. Believing that "no poet ever wrote so fixedly from within the human head" (p. 20), he focuses on Stevens's power of world-making and word-making. Kermode provides an erudite and coherent overview, while exuding his exhilaration at being able to ratify a new poetic genius in the canon.

Less elegant but more methodical is Ronald Sukenick's *Wallace Stevens: Musing the Obscure* (1967), still the novice reader's best possible companion to Stevens's texts.[74] Although this book has not been influential on other critics, who either ignore it or dismiss it as a trot, it has the great value of succinctly explaining the mysteries of Stevens's discourse, of reducing its resistance to the intelligence. Sukenick tends to simplify what is complex and rigidify what is fluid, and he programmatically commits what used to be called the heresy of paraphrase. Yet these are the vices of his virtue. For the reader who needs help, this book offers its services in an efficient form.

Helen Vendler's explication of Stevens's longer poems, *On Extended Wings* (1969), is at once more ambitious and more problematic than Sukenick's book.[75] Frequently quoted by other Stevens critics, it unquestionably brings much to light. Yet its influence has not been entirely benign. Wishing to prevent Stevens and his readers from being violated by an idea, Vendler labors to isolate the poet's "experiments in style" (p. 10) from all intellectual contexts. She idealizes poetic language as nonreferential and poetic texts as autonomous—putting a positive spin on what Mikhail Bakhtin called "sealed-off utterance."[76] This approach anesthetizes Stevens's texts against both history and philosophy, despite the poet's contrary intentions.

The majority of the critical work written in the 1960s adhered to the traditional historical model of criticism, studying the poems from the standpoint of the literary past or the poet's chronological development. Five books in this mode remain vital.

Frank Doggett's *Stevens' Poetry of Thought* (1966) discusses the poet's philosophical concerns from the perspective of an intellectual historian.[77] Doggett emphasizes the importance of ideation for Stevens, without detaching the poet's concepts from the language and fictions in which he embeds them. The critic shows Stevens appropriating philosophy for aesthetic contemplation, using it to "evoke an inner discourse" that merges thinking with feeling (p. viii). Juxtaposing Stevens with Bergson, William James, Schopenhauer, Whitehead, and especially Santayana, Doggett exposes the poet's pained awareness of the self's estrangement from external reality and his consequent effort to envision a "world burgeoning in the flow of consciousness" (p. 201), a world that continually shifts as the self shifts. Transcending the limits of New Critical epistemology, this study reveals that Stevens's poetry was not simply stylistically distinguished but intellectually powerful as well.

A species of literary biography, Robert Buttel's *Wallace Stevens: The Making of Harmonium* (1967) studies Stevens's poetic development from the immaturity of his undergraduate pieces to the creative mastery of *Harmonium*.[78] Buttel shows Stevens absorbing such diverse traditions and innovations as Romanticism, Victorianism, Elizabethan comedy, French irony, Symbolism, Imagism, and Modernist art. Buttel insists that Stevens's thematic intensity—his exaltation in the power of the imagination, his awareness of the "fullness of an earthly life circumscribed by negation" (p. 148)—underlies his stylistic experimentation and contributes to his artistic triumph. An analysis of the way Stevens synthesized his influences and transcended their limitations, this book, like Doggett's, makes an enduringly significant contribution to our understanding.

Daniel Fuchs's *The Comic Spirit of Wallace Stevens* (1963) discusses Stevens's comic sense in such poems as "The Comedian as the Letter C," "The Man on the Dump," and "Esthétique du Mal," often with perception, but without a systematic presentation of comedy's genealogy or types.[79] Eugene Paul Nassar's *Wallace Stevens: An Anatomy of Figuration* (1965) helpfully collocates the poet's recurrent figures of mind, disorder, order, and change, while unanalytically denying that biographical information might provide a legitimate sphere of critical reference.[80] James Baird's *The Dome and the Rock* (1968) also collocates recurrent images and themes.[81] It describes Stevens's individual lyrics as a single "dome" memorializing his "shaping power" (p. 324). Although Baird advocates that criticism become a transparency that permits poetry to comment on itself, we would err in regarding the elaborated structure he describes as a construction of the poetry alone and not of the critic.

In addition, five books containing important chapters on Stevens appeared during this period.[82] Roy Harvey Pearce's *The Continuity of American Poetry* (1961) examines Stevens's developing dialectic of mind and world, portraying him as a culmination of the "Adamic" mode of American poetry (p. 377). Northrop Frye's *Fables of Identity* (1963) contains a canonical essay (reprinted in this volume) defining mythic and structural elements in Stevens's poetry. L. S. Dembo's *Conceptions of Reality in Modern American Poetry* (1966) focuses on the poet's aesthetic transformations of reality. Louis Martz's *Poem of the Mind* (1966) portrays Stevens as a late and secular member of the meditative line of John Donne. Frank Lentricchia's *The Gaiety of Language* (1968) portrays Stevens and Yeats as coinheritors of French symbolism.

There were also two influential anthologies of essays: Marie Borroff's *Wallace Stevens: A Collection of Critical Essays* (1963), which contains substantial essays by such critics as Harold Bloom, Ralph J. Mills, Riddel, Pearce, and Martz; and Roy Harvey Pearce and J. Hillis Miller's *The Act of the Mind* (1965), a collection of new, sophisticated essays by Bernard Heringman, Michel Benamou, Mac Hammond, Richard Macksey, Denis Donoghue, Doggett, Buttel, Morse, Pearce, Miller, Vendler, and Riddel.[83]

Finally, two texts appeared in the 1960s that adhered to an innovative philosophical model of criticism: Joseph Riddel's *The Clairvoyant Eye* and J. Hillis Miller's *Poets of Reality*. Although both writers revealed ideas and themes also present in such mainstream critics as Doggett and Pearce, Riddel and especially Miller did so in a different critical vocabulary, one that established them not as traditional critic-historians but as something new to our English departments (though hardly to our culture): critic-philosophers.

Although Riddel quite accurately claims that in *The Clairvoyant Eye* (1967) he tries "to see Stevens' poems in their historical and philosophical perspective" (p. vi), it is the philosophical perspective that predominates and that gives his discourse distinction.[84] He focuses on Stevens's acts of "continuous self-creation" in his poetry (p. 272). Although this thesis is not remarkable in itself, the subtlety and comprehensiveness of its working-out is. Riddel shows beyond dispute that Stevens offers us the mind's process rather than finished products, and that the poet found satisfaction not in the results of his poetic acts but in the activity itself. Riddel's introduction and first chapter comprise a superior presentation of Stevens's poetics. Juxtaposing Stevens with Coleridge, Emerson, Valéry, Eliot, Williams, Whitehead, and especially Santayana and Bergson, he almost convinces us of his premise that "philosophy may illuminate aspects of Stevens's poetics. But only his poetry illuminates philosophy" (p. 41). The five following chapters proceed chronologically through the poet's volumes, from *Harmonium* through *The Auroras of Autumn*. Treating Stevens's poems individually rather than as a cross-referential Grand Poem, these chapters provide an advanced guide to the poetry. But it is Riddel's "Afterword" that contains the heart of his argument: that existential phenomenology can affix its beam on Stevens's texts with remarkable efficacy. Influenced by Georges Poulet and Roy Harvey Pearce, this chapter emphasizes Stevens's evolving effort "to *be* in the act of the mind" (p. 273), an endeavor that inevitably produced an imaginative space bounded in every direction by nothingness.

Miller's chapter on Stevens in *Poets of Reality* (1965), partially reprinted here, represents a more thoroughgoing phenomenological reading of Stevens's texts than Riddel attempts, and a more decisive and successful break from the conventions of historicism and New Critical explication.[85] Miller does not proceed through Stevens's canon chronologically but suspends all of the poet's poems, lines, and phrases on a single phenomenological plane, virtually ignoring the formal boundaries precious to the New Criticism and the temporal distinctions essential to historicism. Miller reconstructs Stevens's oeuvre to make it tell a narrative of individual man's fall from an illusory union with mankind, nature, and God to the reality of fragmented consciousness, indifferent nature, and a vanished deity. He then describes the poet's compensatory exertion to achieve a "flittering," numinous conjoining of the imagination with that new reality (p. 282). This chapter remains exemplary of Stevens criticism at its most original and creative. Together with *The Clairvoyant Eye* and the essays by Macksey, Pearce, and Benamou in *The Act of the Mind*, it inaugurated a perspective revolution that would carry Stevens to the heights of esteem in ensuing years.

Riddel and Miller would continue to play leading roles in the burgeoning field of philosophical criticism, but as the decade turned, so did their theory turn. In the early 1970s, both critics assumed a poststructuralist stance, which replaced the discourse of presence with a discourse on discourse, exchanging phenomenology's landscape of empty reality for deconstruction's tropic of slippery language. If, as Pearce has suggested, Stevens's poems oscillate between "the reality which is unchanging and unchangeable, perdurably out there" and "the mind which not only wills but makes its knowledge,"[86] criticism has oscillated analogously, between presenting a "clairvoyant eye" on "reality" and presenting a "metaphoric staging" of the "linguistic moment" (to borrow titles from Riddel and Miller's pre- and post-1970 discourse). Phenomenology had been demystified, stripped of its metaphysics, turned fully around so that the notion that "reality is part of the mind," which Miller had earlier dismissed as a "momentary hallucination,"[87] now was understood as the only idea about reality that was *not* hallucinatory. The problematic of Stevens criticism remained constant, but the perspective had reversed itself: not the thing itself but tropes about the thing; the only impossibility was not to live in a linguistic world.

Riddel explained and exemplified his new position in a series of essays, including the one reprinted here, "The Climate of Our Poems" (1983).[88] Riddel no longer aspired to fix Stevens as an object but rather performed a verbal dance that acknowledged its own status as an uncentered play of difference. He argued that *The Clairvoyant Eye*, whatever its innovations, had been trapped within Stevens's romantic coordinates of imagination and reality, which only the new rhetoric could escape. He now interpreted such poems as "Esthétique du Mal," "Notes toward a Supreme Fiction," "The Auroras of Autumn," and "Credences of Summer" as being about the scene of writing, the inescapable "play of tropes."[89] Riddel as poststructuralist does not intend to deny meaning but to disrupt the illusion of closure. Critiquing his own discourse along with that of other commentators, he figures a Stevens hard at work interrogating his own language.

Miller collected the most important of his post-1970 essays on Stevens in *The Linguistic Moment* (1985).[90] Miller begins unpromisingly by asserting that "all right-thinking readers will come to agree with what I have to say if they go on thinking about my poems long enough" (p. xx)— heavy pressure from any critic but almost bizarre coming from one who believes that language at best is only a thin splint over an abyss. Nonetheless, when Miller gets down to business he provides one of the most able demonstrations of deconstruction—and the most provocative reading of "The Rock"—yet in print. He wishes to stress interpretive "uncertainty": the moments when language becomes opaque, when solid "ground" turns into an abyss before our eyes (p. 396). Beginning with a brilliant discussion of "The Rock's" key word "cure," which he shows to have multiple incompatible meanings and etymologies, he proceeds to discover a labyrinth of incongruent parallelisms, shifting scenes, dissolving selves, and finally catachreses revealing that linguistic referentiality is but a trope, that the "literal" is simply a supreme fiction (p. 420). The poem disappears into what Miller calls the *mise en abyme* of poetry. Despite the perhaps tongue-in-cheek assurance of the critic's aim to convince all "right-thinking" readers, *The Linguistic Moment*, when juxtaposed with the substantially incompatible *Poets of Reality*, exposes the *mise en abyme* of criticism: its tendency to give way beneath the heft of proliferating, contradictory meanings.

Among more recent deconstructive analyses, Michael Beehler's *T. S. Eliot, Wallace Stevens and the Discourses of Difference* (1987) exposes not the play of difference between Eliot and Stevens, as Miller and Pearce have done, but the play of difference within their texts.[91] Drawing on Peirce, Nietzsche, and Derrida, Beehler portrays Stevens's writing as an invented world of differentially constituted signs, a "machine of language" rather than a reflection or expression of the poet's self (p. 50). His analysis focuses attention on the elements of instability, the metaphoric detours, the polyphony of echoes, and the meta-metaphorics in the poet's theater of trope.

A less coherent study, Paul Bové's *Destructive Poetics: Heidegger and American Poetry* (1980) catches itself in a contradiction between presence and difference, epistemology and language.[92] Nonetheless, it provides some authentic insights: for example, that Stevens does not engage in a failed quest for center, as many critics have thought, but rather employs the quest metaphor against itself, aware from the outset that a center does not exist, that all such structures are fictions.

Other noteworthy contributions to the philosophic enterprise include Michel Benamou's Mallarméan "Displacements of Parental Space" (1977); Richard Kuhns's Cartesian "Metaphor as Plausible Inference in Poetry and Philosophy" (1979); Joseph Kronick's Derridean "Of Parents, Children, and Rabbis" (1982), which is included in this volume; Charles Altieri's post-Derridean "Wallace Stevens' Metaphors of Metaphor" (1983); Steven Shaviro's Nietzschean "'That Which is Always Beginning'" (1985), also included here; passages in books by Gerald Bruns and Thomas Weiskel; and essays by Terrance King, R. D. Ackerman, Ellwood Johnson, and Patricia Parker.[93]

In a sense, the culminating work of philosophically oriented criticism up to this time is Harold Bloom's *Wallace Stevens: The Poems of Our Climate* (1977),[94] a chapter of which is reprinted here. Bloom is the only major critic to attempt to resolve the language / history antithesis that has regulated critical discourse on Stevens over the last fifteen years. His synthesis, a "diachronic rhetoric" (p. 388), reunites language with literary history and the poet's will, though it continues to put social, political, and economic history to one side. Bloom's theoretical first chapter, among the most brilliant and coherent portrayals of American poetry ever composed, places Stevens in an Emerson-Whitman-Dickinson tradition of "surprise," a term Bloom uses to imply an "ecstasy," a sudden manifestation of the poet's "Will-to-Power over anteriority and the interpretation of his own poem" (pp. 5-6). Succeeding chapters bring together psychology and rhetoric as aids in the close reading of all of Stevens's poems, beginning with those in *Harmonium* and ending with the final lyrics. Bloom believes that the poems of 1942-55 represent Stevens's major phase, with "Notes toward a Supreme Fiction" and "The Auroras of Autumn" standing as the very greatest achievements.

Bloom's final, theoretical chapter conducts a dialogue with deconstruction on poetic rhetoric. Rather than considering poems as purely linguistic structures, he views them as instances of "the will to utter within a tradition of uttering," and as images of the "war between text and intentions" (pp. 393, 396). Taking into account Stevens's motives as well as the differential character of language, Bloom discovers strange relations previously unimaginable yet subsequently undismissable. His critical myth has such power that it may have had the ironic effect of discouraging further philosophical and developmental study, leaving the way clear, again most ironically, for exactly the sorts of skeptical and materialist criticism to which it stands in staunchest opposition.

A small number of stylistic and explicative studies also appeared in the 1970s and 1980s. Marie Borroff in *Language and the Poet* (1979) provides the first truly precise description of Stevens's style.[95] She reveals the poet's proclivity toward contrastive, foregrounded, scholarly, sacred, and playful words, and his avoidance of the colloquial. Focusing on diction, this study represents an initial, welcome step toward a truly rigorous analysis of Stevens's language system. In a complementary and more theoretical fashion, Jacqueline Vaught Brogan's *Stevens and Simile* (1986) traces the way that Stevens allowed two competing conceptions of language—one realist and the other deconstructive—to interact simultaneously in his texts.[96] David Walker's brilliant rhetorical study, *The Transparent Lyric: Reading and Meaning in the Poetry of Stevens and Williams* (1984), interprets poems by both Stevens and Williams as centering on the reading experience itself rather than on any prior subject matter.[97] Of the books of explication, Rajeev Patke's *The Long Poems of Wallace Stevens* (1985) supplies genuinely new insights into Stevens's seven long poems, while Susan B. Weston's *Wallace Stevens: An Introduction to the Poetry* (1977) is helpful but perhaps, after Sukenick, superfluous.[98]

Although they were no longer at the center of a diamond, studies adhering to the historical model of criticism abounded in the 1970s and 1980s. For one thing, old paradigms die hard—sometimes they even endure and prevail. For another, the materials for historicist analysis became increasingly accessible during this period. As we have seen, Holly Stevens's generous selection of Stevens's letters appeared in 1966. In the mid-1970s, the Huntington Library acquired and made available to scholars an enormous collection of Stevensiana; and the *Wallace Stevens Journal* commenced publication. In 1977, Holly Stevens published *Souvenirs and Prophecies*, an annotated assemblage of her father's early journals.[99] Six years later, Peter Brazeau published *Parts of a World: Wallace Stevens Remembered*, an annotated collection of oral reminiscences by friends of the poet.[100] Finally, in 1986, Joan Richardson's biography, *Wallace Stevens: The Early Years*, appeared.[101] Often brilliant, sometimes unconvincing, always fact-filled and valuable, this book brings to fruition twenty years of growing knowledge about the poet. It will certainly foster the revival of interest already under way in the interrelations between Stevens's art and his life.

Of the historically oriented critical books that have appeared since 1970, three stand out in importance. The first is A. Walton Litz's developmental study, *Introspective Voyager* (1972), which, along with Buttel's earlier work, remains a classic of diachronic analysis, an exemplary historicist text.[102] Litz extracts Stevens's poems from their arrangement in books, and studies them in the order of their composition. He thus reads them as "contemporary documents" rather than as finished sections of a single grand poem (p. viii). Furthermore, Litz redirects attention from the later poems to the earlier ones. He shows that the poems written between 1914 and 1923 constitute a voyage of discovery, a long process of experimentation yielding such masterpieces as "Sunday Morning," "Le Monocle de Mon Oncle," and "The Comedian as the Letter C," for all of which he supplies canonical readings. He contends that Stevens began to consolidate his gains in 1934, while in the poems of 1937-55 he achieved a final turning from external pressures to self-reference. Litz concludes that each of Stevens's phases produced great "sustaining fictions" that make the poverty of our lives "bearable for a moment" (p. 295).

In *Wallace Stevens: Imagination and Faith* (1974), Adalaide Kirby Morris convincingly argues that Stevens's poetry centers on his successful search for an alternative to religion.[103] In Stevens's mind, the imagination came to assume divine attributes, allowing human beings to recognize the earth as a place of harmony and grace. Morris's first two chapters examine the poet's ambivalent attitudes toward Christianity and his ultimate substitution of the "chapel of breath"—poetry—for what he contemptuously termed the "deaf-mute" church. Her last two chapters describe the ways in which Stevens's theory of poetry approaches a theology: a faith in the redemption to be gained from "the imagination's love for the world" (p. 188). Morris presents a Stevens who transcends his reputation for dandyism, hedonism, and epistemological or linguistic play. This Stevens, for all his interiority and verbal ingenuity, comes to us as an exuberant prophet, bearing news of how to live, what to do.

Milton J. Bates's work of biographical criticism, *Wallace Stevens: A Mythology of Self* (1985), is the first book to make full use of the manuscript materials collected at the Huntington Library.[104] A product of meticulous scholarship, it provides the most accessible and coherent overview of the poet's career to date. Interpretively, however, it has several limitations. For one thing, it skims lightly over the surface of Stevens's troubled emotional life. In describing the poet's disastrous marriage, for example, Bates at first denies that anything was "truly amiss" (p. 66), and then concedes that the marriage was unhappy without dwelling on the topic. The conventions of polite biography may be speaking through Bates at such moments; but his evasiveness may also result from a genuine lack of interest in psychological issues, a disinclination to reflect any theory of self whatever. In a similar way, Bates's comments on Stevens's poetry generally avoid risk or distinction. He situates himself in a happy, pre-lapsarian world in which "the meaning of the poems can be determined, and without elaborate theoretical apparatus" (p. x). This book provides a beautifully researched, commonsensical portrait of Stevens—with all the strengths and weaknesses that commonsense understandings usually possess.

A number of more specialized studies also merit attention. Diane Wood Middlebrook's *Walt Whitman and Wallace Stevens* (1974) helpfully outlines the two poets' "shared theory of poetry" deriving from Coleridge and Emerson (p. 17).[105] Charles Berger's *Forms of Farewell* (1985) portrays the poems of Stevens's last decade as enacting a tripartite elegiac "plot" of apocalypse, counterapocalypse, and leavetaking.[106] George Lensing's informative *Wallace Stevens: A Poet's Growth* (1986) covers some of the same ground as Bates's study, with a narrower focus on the poet's self-instructions, self-appraisals, compositional procedures, and ways of presenting his work to his readers.[107]

Other valuable critical statements include Helen Regueiro's *The Limits of Imagination* (1976), which posits that Stevens's imagination ultimately aims to undercut "its own validity" (p. 211); Frank Doggett's *Wallace Stevens: The Making of the Poem* (1980), which concisely studies the theories, sources, and attributes of the poet's creativity; David La Guardia's *Advance on Chaos* (1983), which places Stevens's concept of the imagination in the tradition of Emerson and William James; Leonora Woodman's *Stanza My Stone* (1983), which argues, contra most other commentators, that Stevens was "a deeply religious poet whose work is as consistent and systematic as any rigorous reader might wish" (p. 4); Helen Vendler's brief *Wallace Stevens: Words Chosen Out of Desire* (1984), notable for its depiction of Stevens as a poet of passion and notable also for the critic's belated acknowledgment that "the historical and cultural bases of poetry are important to it" (p. 80); R. J. Leggett's *Wallace Stevens and Poetic Theory* (1987), which discusses the influence of I. A. Richards, Charles Mauron, and Henri Focillon; John N. Serio's "'The Comedian' as the Idea of Order in *Harmonium*" (1976); Marjorie Perloff's classic study "Pound / Stevens: Whose Era?" (1982); Martha Strom's "Wallace Stevens' Revisions of Crispin's Journal" (1982), reprinted here; Eleanor Cook's "Riddles, Charms, and Fictions in Wallace Stevens" (1983), also reprinted here; incidental comments in historicist books by M. H. Abrams, Frank Lentricchia (reprinted here), and Lawrence Kramer (expanded for inclusion here); and essays by Roy Harvey Pearce, Lisa M. Steinman, and Nancy Prothro.[108]

In the mid-1980s, the romance of history reformulated and reasserted itself in the interpretive community. As a result, a de-idealizing strain emerged in the American reception of Stevens for virtually the first time since his death. The most obvious example of this new tendency was the publication of Albert Gelpi's consensus-disturbing collection of essays, *Wallace Stevens: The Poetics of Modernism* (1985), whose dominant mood contrasts sharply with that of an earlier, more establishmentarian anthology, Doggett and Buttel's indicatively titled *Wallace Stevens: A Celebration* (1980).[109] Gelpi himself inaugurates the skeptical temper of his collection with a masterful essay that tests Stevens's conception of the imagination against that of William Carlos Williams, concluding that the former poet runs "the risks of escapism" (p. 14). Gerald Bruns, in a brilliant historical and dialogical analysis, finds that Stevens is primarily motivated by "the fear and repression of alien voices" (p. 35). In a frontal assault, Marjorie Perloff paints a powerful picture of Stevens as literary troglodyte and social reactionary—though surely Robert Buttel was right to demur that "unintended irony arises" when Perloff unfavorably contrasts Stevens to Pound, considering the latter's "sick politics" during the war.[110] Other essays in the volume, such as Alan Golding's and Michael Davidson's fine discussions of Stevens's influence on other poets, make more traditional, positive assessments, but the inclusion of negative evaluations, based largely on historical and ethical grounds, marks a significant shift in critical opinion.

The shift is even more pronounced in two essays written by Marxist critics. In an essay reprinted in this volume called "Wallace Stevens" (1984), Fredric Jameson dismisses Stevens as a poet of linguistic richness but "inner hollowness" (p. 11)—a creator of semiautonomous symbolic constructs that appropriate Third World materials in the manner of commodity capitalism.[111] In a more nuanced analysis, "Patriarchy Against Itself" (1987), Frank Lentricchia discusses Stevens's economic and sexual marginality as a young man and his developing strategy of writing a critique of capitalism "at a safe distance; critique that could not function as intervention and trigger of social change" (p. 751).[112] Taken together, the essays by Gelpi, Bruns, Perloff, Jameson, and Lentricchia indicate that a new, more severe phase of interpretation of Stevens may have begun.

In his essay in the Gelpi collection, Bruns asks the most resonant question in Stevens criticism today: "What happens to our reading of Stevens's poetry when the problem of how the mind links up with reality is no longer of any concern to us?"[113] That human beings have always manifested at least a modicum of interest in the mind / reality problem suggests one preliminary response to Bruns's question. That Stevens treats many topics beyond that of mind and reality suggests another. But we must leave the ultimate answer to readers of the commentaries collected in this book—and to all those who listen to Stevens's elusive, evasive, euphonious fictive music as it plays across the torrents of time and consciousness.

STEVEN GOULD AXELROD
University of California, Riverside

HELEN DEESE
Mount Saint Mary's College

Notes

1. Harriet Monroe, "Comment: A Cavalier of Beauty," *Poetry* 23 (March 1924):322-27.

2. Shaemas O'Sheel, "Chicago Poets and Poetry," *Minaret* 1 (February 1916):26-27; quoted in *Wallace Stevens: The Critical Heritage*, ed. Charles Doyle (London: Routledge & Kegan Paul), 25-26.

3. George Soule, "Public Verse," *New Republic* 6 (25 March 1916):223.

4. Max Michelson, "The Radicals," *Poetry* 8 (June 1916):152.

5. Conrad Aiken, "The Ivory Tower—I," *New Republic* 19 (10 May 1919):58-59.

6. Louis Untermeyer, "The Ivory Tower—II," *New Republic* 19 (10 May 1919):61.

7. Letter of William Carlos Williams to Wallace Stevens, 8 June 1916, *Wallace Stevens Journal* 3 (Fall 1979):72-73.

8. "Wisconsin Players Here," *New York Times*, 22 October 1917, 13.

9. Ralph Block, Theater Review, *New York Tribune*, 22 October 1917, 9.

10. Samuel French Morse, "A Note on 'Bowl, Cat and Broomstick,'" *Wallace Stevens Journal* 2 (Spring 1978):10-12.

11. *Bowl, Cat and Broomstick* was printed first in *Quarterly Review* in Summer 1969 and then in Holly Stevens's edition of Stevens's poems, *The Palm at the End of the Mind*, in 1971. Both versions, however, lacked one page of Stevens's manuscript. Samuel French Morse supplied the missing page in the *Wallace Stevens Journal*, 2 (Spring 1978):10-12. According to Morse, Stevens had "little to say about the play."

12. *The Letters of Wallace Stevens*, ed. Holly Stevens (New York: Knopf, 1981), 216.

13. Joan Richardson, *Wallace Stevens, A Biography: The Early Years, 1879-1923* (New York: Morrow, 1986), 481.

14. *Letters*, 200.

15. Ibid., 203.

16. Richardson, *Biography*, 481.

17. *Letters*, 228.

18. Wallace Stevens, *Harmonium* (New York: Knopf, 1923).

19. Monroe, "Cavalier of Beauty," 322-27.

20. Marianne Moore, "Well-Moused Lion," *Dial* 76 (January 1924):84-91.

21. Mark Van Doren, "Poets and Wits," *Nation* 117 (10 October 1923):400.

22. Edmund Wilson, "Wallace Stevens and E. E. Cummings," *New Republic* 38 (19 March 1924):102-3.

23. Louis Untermeyer, "Among the New Books: Five American Poets," *Yale Review* n.s. 14 (October 1924):159-60.

24. Matthew Josephson, Review of *Harmonium*, *Broom* 5 (November 1923):236-37.

25. John Gould Fletcher, "The Revival of Aestheticism," *Freeman* 8 (19 December 1923):355-56.

26. *Letters*, 242.

27. Ibid., 246.

28. Gorham Munson, "The Dandyism of Wallace Stevens," *Dial* 79 (November 1925):413-17.

29. *Letters*, 320.

30. Wallace Stevens, *Harmonium* [second edition] (New York: Knopf, 1931).

31. *Bookman* 74 (October 1931):207-8; Raymond Larsson, "The Beau as Poet," *Commonweal* 15 (6 April 1932):640-41.

32. Eda Lou Walton, *Nation* 133 (9 September 1931):263-64.

33. Yvor Winters, "Wallace Stevens, or the Hedonist's Progress," *The Anatomy of Nonsense* (Norfolk, Conn.: New Directions, 1943), 88-119.

34. Wallace Stevens, *Ideas of Order* (New York: Alcestis Press, 1935; New York: Knopf, 1936).

35. F. O. Matthiessen, "Society and Solitude in Poetry," *Yale Review* n.s. 25 (Spring 1936):605-7.

36. Howard Baker, "Wallace Stevens and Other Poets," *Southern Review* 1 (Autumn 1935):373-96.

37. Marianne Moore, Review of *Ideas of Order*, *Criterion* 15 (January 1936):307-9; Theodore Roethke, Review of *Ideas of Order*, *New Republic* 87 (15 July 1936):304-5.

38. Stanley Burnshaw, "Turmoil in the Middle Ground," *New Masses* 17 (1 October 1935):41-42.

39. Louis Martz, "Wallace Stevens: The World as Meditation," *Yale Review* n.s. 47 (Summer 1958):324.

40. *Letters*, 286.

41. Ibid., 289.

42. Ibid., 294-95.

43. Wallace Stevens, *Owl's Clover* (New York: Alcestis Press, 1936).

44. *Letters*, 308.

45. Ruth Lechlitner, "Imagination as Reality," *New York Herald Tribune Books*, 6 December 1936, 40.

46. *Letters*, 313.

47. Robert Fitzgerald, "Thoughts Revolved," *Poetry* 51 (December 1937):153-57.

48. Wallace Stevens, *The Man with the Blue Guitar* (New York: Knopf, 1937); Delmore Schwartz, "New Verse," *Partisan Review* 4 (February 1938):49-52; Hi Simons, "Vicissitudes of Reputation, 1914-1940," *Harvard Advocate* 126 (December 1940):8-10, 34-44.

49. Wallace Stevens, *Parts of a World* (New York: Knopf, 1942).

50. Louise Bogan, *New Yorker* 18 (10 October 1942):73-74; *Time* 40 (2 November 1942):103-4.

51. Wallace Stevens, *Notes toward a Supreme Fiction* (Cummington, Mass.: Cummington Press, 1942); Wallace Stevens, *Esthétique du Mal* (Cummington, Mass.: Cummington Press, 1945); Wallace Stevens, *Transport to Summer* (New York: Knopf, 1947).

52. R. P. Blackmur, "An Abstraction Blooded," *Partisan Review* 10 (May-June 1943):297-300; Louis L. Martz, "New Books in Review," *Yale Review* n.s. 37 (December 1947):339-41.

53. See Steven Gould Axelrod, *Robert Lowell: Life and Art* (Princeton: Princeton University Press, 1978), 184-86, 204-7, 214-18, 226.

54. Robert Lowell, "Imagination and Reality," *Nation* 164 (5 April 1947):400-2.

55. Randall Jarrell, "From the Kingdom of Necessity," *Poetry and the Age* (New York: Vintage, 1953), 198-99.

56. Wallace Stevens, *Three Academic Pieces* (Cummington, Mass.: Cummington Press, 1947); M. L. Rosenthal, "Two Modern Poets on their Art: Three Academic Pieces," *New York Herald Tribune Weekly Book Review*, 9 May 1948, 21.

57. Wallace Stevens, *The Auroras of Autumn* (New York: Knopf, 1950); Joseph Bennett, "Five Books, Four Poets," *Hudson Review* 4 (Spring 1951):134-37.

58. William Van O'Connor, Review of *The Auroras of Autumn*, *Poetry* 77 (November 1950):109-12.

59. Wallace Stevens, *The Necessary Angel* (New York: Knopf, 1951; London: Faber and Faber, 1960).

60. Richard Eberhart, "The Stevens Prose," *Accent* 12 (Spring 1952):122-25; Bernard Heringman, "The Critical Angel," *Kenyon Review* 14 (Summer 1952):520-23. Frank Kermode reviewed the volume some years after its American publication but before it had been published in Great Britain: "The Gaiety of Language," *Spectator* 201 (3 October 1958):454-55.

61. Wallace Stevens, *Collected Poems* (New York: Knopf, 1954; London: Faber and Faber, 1955).

62. Randall Jarrell, "Very Graceful Are the Uses of Culture," *Harper's* 209 (November 1954):100.

63. Delmore Schwartz, "In the Orchards of the Imagination," *New Republic* 131 (1 November 1954):16-18.

64. Hayden Carruth, "Without the Inventions of Sorrow," *Poetry* 85 (February 1955):288-93.

65. Donald Davie, Review of *Collected Poems*, *Shenandoah* 6 (Spring 1965):62-64.

66. Wallace Stevens, *Opus Posthumous* (New York: Knopf, 1957; London: Faber and Faber, 1959); *Letters of Wallace Stevens* (New York: Knopf, 1966; London: Faber and Faber, 1967).

67. Irving Howe, "Another Way of Looking at the Blackbird," *New Republic* 137 (4 November 1957):16-19.

68. Hilton Kramer, "A Man in his Thoughts," *New Leader* 49 (5 December 1966):18.

69. Henry Reed, Review of *The Necessary Angel* and *Opus Posthumous*, *Listener* 63 (14 April 1960):675-76.

70. R. P. Blackmur, "Examples of Wallace Stevens," *Hound and Horn* 5 (Winter 1932):223-55; Hi Simons, "'The Comedian as the Letter C': Its Sense and Significance,"

Southern Review 5 (Winter 1940):453-68; Hi Simons, "The Genre of Wallace Stevens," *Sewanee Review* 53 (Autumn 1945):566-79; Hi Simons, "Wallace Stevens and Mallarmé," *Modern Philology* 43 (May 1946):235-59; Winters, "Hedonist's Progress," 88-119; Marius Bewley, "The Poetry of Wallace Stevens," *Partisan Review* 16 (September 1949):895-915; Randall Jarrell, "Reflections on Wallace Stevens," *Partisan Review* 18 (May-June 1951): 335-44; Roy Harvey Pearce, "Wallace Stevens: The Life of the Imagination," *PMLA* 66 (September 1951):561-82; Bernetta Quinn, "Metamorphosis in Wallace Stevens," *Sewanee Review* 60 (Spring 1952):230-52; Samuel French Morse, "The Motive for Metaphor," *Origin V* 2 (Spring 1952):3-65.

71. William Van O'Connor, *The Shaping Spirit: A Study of Wallace Stevens* (Chicago: Regnery, 1950).

72. Joseph Riddel, "The Contours of Stevens Criticism," *The Act of the Mind: Essays on the Poetry of Wallace Stevens*, eds. Roy Harvey Pearce and J. Hillis Miller (Baltimore: Johns Hopkins University Press, 1965), 243.

73. Frank Kermode, *Wallace Stevens* (Edinburgh and London: Oliver and Boyd, 1960).

74. Ronald Sukenick, *Wallace Stevens: Musing the Obscure* (New York: New York University Press, 1967).

75. Helen Hennessy Vendler, *On Extended Wings: Wallace Stevens' Longer Poems* (Cambridge: Harvard University Press, 1969).

76. Mikhail Bakhtin, "Discourse in the Novel," *The Dialogic Imagination* (Austin: University of Texas Press, 1981), 296.

77. Frank Doggett, *Stevens' Poetry of Thought* (Baltimore: Johns Hopkins University Press, 1966).

78. Robert Buttel, *Wallace Stevens: The Making of Harmonium* (Princeton: Princeton University Press, 1967).

79. Daniel Fuchs, *The Comic Spirit of Wallace Stevens* (Durham: Duke University Press, 1963).

80. Eugene Paul Nassar, *Wallace Stevens: An Anatomy of Figuration* (Philadelphia: University of Pennsylvania Press, 1965).

81. James Baird, *The Dome and the Rock: Structure in the Poetry of Wallace Stevens* (Baltimore: Johns Hopkins University Press, 1968).

82. Roy Harvey Pearce, *The Continuity of American Poetry* (Princeton: Princeton University Press, 1961); Northrop Frye, *Fables of Identity: Studies in Poetic Mythology* (New York: Harcourt, Brace and World, 1963); L. S. Dembo, *Conceptions of Reality in Modern American Poetry* (Berkeley and Los Angeles: University of California Press, 1966); Louis Martz, *Poem of the Mind* (New York: Oxford University Press, 1966); Frank Lentricchia, *The Gaiety of Language: An Essay on the Radical Poetics of W. B. Yeats and Wallace Stevens* (Berkeley and Los Angeles: University of California Press, 1968).

83. Marie Borroff, ed., *Wallace Stevens: A Collection of Critical Essays* (Englewood Cliffs, N.J.: Prentice-Hall, 1963); Roy Harvey Pearce and J. Hillis Miller, eds., *The Act of the Mind: Essays on the Poetry of Wallace Stevens* (Baltimore: Johns Hopkins University Press, 1965).

84. Joseph Riddel, *The Clairvoyant Eye: The Poetry and Poetics of Wallace Stevens* (Baton Rouge: Louisiana State University Press, 1965).

85. J. Hillis Miller, *Poets of Reality: Six Twentieth Century Writers* (Cambridge: Harvard University Press, 1965).

86. Roy Harvey Pearce, "Wallace Stevens: The Last Lesson of the Master," *Act of the Mind*, 126.

87. Miller, *Poets of Reality*, 257.

88. Joseph Riddel, "Interpreting Stevens," *Boundary 2* 1 (Fall 1972):79-97; Joseph Riddel, "Bloom—A Commentary—Stevens," *Wallace Stevens Journal* 1 (Fall-Winter 1977):111-19; Joseph Riddel, "Metaphoric Staging," *Wallace Stevens: A Celebration*, eds.

Frank Doggett and Robert Buttel (Princeton: Princeton University Press, 1980), 308-38; Joseph Riddel, "Juda Becomes New Haven," *Diacritics* 10 (Summer 1980):17-34; Joseph Riddel, "The Climate of Our Poems," *Wallace Stevens Journal* 7 (Fall 1983):59-75.

89. Riddel, "Climate of Our Poems," 71.

90. J. Hillis Miller, *The Linguistic Moment: From Wordsworth to Stevens* (Princeton: Princeton University Press, 1985).

91. Michael Beehler, *T. S. Eliot, Wallace Stevens and the Discourses of Difference* (Baton Rouge: Louisiana State University Press, 1987).

92. Paul Bové, *Destructive Poetics: Heidegger and Modern American Poetry* (New York: Columbia University Press, 1980).

93. Michel Benamou, "Displacements of Parental Space: American Poetry and French Symbolism," *Boundary 2* 5 (Winter 1977):471-86; Richard Kuhns, "Metaphor as Plausible Inference in Poetry and Philosophy," *Philosophy and Literature* 3 (Fall 1979):225-38; Joseph Kronick, "Of Parents, Children, and Rabbis: Wallace Stevens and the Question of the Book," *Boundary 2* 10 (Spring 1982):125-54; Charles Altieri, "Wallace Stevens' Metaphors of Metaphor: Poetry as Theory," *American Poetry* 1 (Fall 1983):27-48; Steven Shaviro, "'That Which Is Always Beginning': Stevens' Poetry of Affirmation," *PMLA* 100 (March 1985):220-33; Gerald Bruns, *Modern Poetry and the Idea of Language* (New Haven: Yale University Press, 1974); Thomas Weiskel, *The Romantic Sublime* (Baltimore: Johns Hopkins University Press, 1976); Terrance King, "The Semiotic Poetry of Wallace Stevens," *Semiotica* 23 (1978):77-98; R. D. Ackerman, "Desire, Distance, Death: Stevens' Meditative Beginnings," *Texas Studies in Literature and Language* 25 (Winter 1983):616-31; Ellwood Johnson, "Wallace Stevens' Transforming Imagination," *Wallace Stevens Journal* 8 (Spring 1984):28-38; Patricia A. Parker, "The Motive for Metaphor: Stevens and Derrida," *Wallace Stevens Journal* 7 (Fall 1983):76-88.

94. Harold Bloom, *Wallace Stevens: The Poems of Our Climate* (Ithaca: Cornell University Press, 1977).

95. Marie Borroff, *Language and the Poet: Verbal Artistry in Frost, Stevens, and Moore* (Chicago: University of Chicago Press, 1979).

96. Jacqueline Vaught Brogan, *Stevens and Simile: A Theory of Language* (Princeton University Press, 1986).

97. David Walker, *The Transparent Lyric: Reading and Meaning in the Poetry of Stevens and Williams* (Princeton: Princeton University Press, 1984).

98. Rajeev S. Patke, *The Long Poems of Wallace Stevens* (Cambridge, Eng.: Cambridge University Press, 1985); Susan B. Weston, *Wallace Stevens: An Introduction to the Poetry* (New York: Columbia University Press, 1977).

99. Holly Stevens, *Souvenirs and Prophecies: The Young Wallace Stevens* (New York: Knopf, 1977).

100. Peter Brazeau, *Parts of a World: Wallace Stevens Remembered* (New York: Random House, 1983).

101. Joan Richardson, *Wallace Stevens: The Early Years 1879-1923* (New York: Morrow, 1986).

102. A. Walton Litz, *Introspective Voyager: The Poetic Development of Wallace Stevens* (New York: Oxford University Press, 1972).

103. Adalaide Kirby Morris, *Wallace Stevens: Imagination and Faith* (Princeton: Princeton University Press, 1974).

104. Milton J. Bates, *Wallace Stevens: A Mythology of Self* (Berkeley and Los Angeles: University of California Press, 1985).

105. Diane Wood Middlebrook, *Walt Whitman and Wallace Stevens* (Ithaca: Cornell University Press, 1974).

106. Charles Berger, *Forms of Farewell: The Late Poetry of Wallace Stevens* (Madison: University of Wisconsin Press, 1985).

107. George Lensing, *Wallace Stevens: A Poet's Growth* (Baton Rouge: Louisiana State University Press, 1986).

108. Helen Regueiro, *The Limits of Imagination: Wordsworth, Yeats, and Stevens* (Ithaca: Cornell University Press, 1976); Frank Doggett, *Wallace Stevens: The Making of the Poem* (Baltimore: Johns Hopkins University Press, 1980); David M. La Guardia, *Advance on Chaos: The Sanctifying Imagination of Wallace Stevens* (Hanover: University Press of New England, 1983); Leonora Woodman, *Stanza My Stone: Wallace Stevens and the Hermetic Tradition* (West Lafayette, Ind.: Purdue University Press, 1983); Helen Vendler, *Wallace Stevens: Words Chosen Out of Desire* (Knoxville: University of Tennessee Press, 1984); B. J. Leggett, *Wallace Stevens and Poetic Theory: Conceiving the Supreme Fiction* (Chapel Hill: University of North Carolina Press, 1987); John N. Serio, "'The Comedian' as the Idea of Order in *Harmonium*," *PLL* 12 (Winter 1976):87-104; Marjorie Perloff, "Pound/Stevens: Whose Era?," *New Literary History* 13 (Spring 1982):485-514; Martha Strom, "Wallace Stevens' Revisions of Crispin's Journal: A Reaction Against the 'Local,'" *American Literature* 54 (May 1982):258-76; Eleanor Cook, "Riddles, Charms, and Fictions in Wallace Stevens," *Centre and Labyrinth*, ed. Eleanor Cook, et al. (Toronto: University of Toronto Press, 1983), 227-44; M. H. Abrams, *Natural Supernaturalism: Tradition and Revolution in Romantic Literature* (New York: Norton, 1971); Frank Lentricchia, *After the New Criticism* (Chicago: University of Chicago Press, 1980); Lawrence Kramer, *Music and Poetry: The Nineteenth Century and After* (Berkeley and Los Angeles: University of California Press, 1984); Roy Harvey Pearce, "Toward Decreation: Stevens and the ' Theory of Poetry,' " *Wallace Stevens: A Celebration*, ed. Frank Doggett and Robert Buttel (Princeton: Princeton University Press, 1980), 286-307; Lisa M. Steinman, "A Dithering of Presences: Style and Language in Stevens' Essays," *Contemporary Literature* 21 (Winter 1980):111-17; Nancy W. Prothro, "'On the Edge of Space': Wallace Stevens' Last Poems," *New England Quarterly* 57 (September 1984):347-58.

109. Albert Gelpi, ed., *Wallace Stevens: The Poetics of Modernism* (Cambridge, Eng.: Cambridge University Press, 1985); Frank Doggett and Robert Buttel, eds., *Wallace Stevens: A Celebration* (Princeton: Princeton University Press, 1980).

110. Robert Buttel, Review of *Wallace Stevens: The Poetics of Modernism*, *Journal of Modern Literature* 13 (November 1986):542.

111. Fredric Jameson, "Wallace Stevens," *New Orleans Review* 11 (Spring 1984):10-19.

112. Frank Lentricchia, "Patriarchy Against Itself—The Young Manhood of Wallace Stevens," *Critical Inquiry* 13 (Summer 1987):742-86.

113. Gerald Bruns, "Stevens without Epistemology," *Wallace Stevens: The Poetics of Modernism*, ed. Albert Gelpi, 24.

Reviews

Comment: A Cavalier of Beauty
[*Harmonium*]
Harriet Monroe*

Sometimes a book comes to us which moves the editor to reminiscence and reflection. Now that certain poets have marked a decade of history in our pages, it may be permissible to indulge the mood and consider what they stand for and how far they have gone. Among books of recent arrival, such an one is Vachel Lindsay's *Collected Poems*; another is Miss Millay's *Harp-weaver*; a third is Wallace Stevens' *Harmonium*; and there are others.

As this is the first time Mr. Stevens has issued a volume and thereby challenged the world to write about him, he shall be the first in a very irregular editorial series. His book reminds me of a day nine-and-a-half years ago when the World War was still new, and we were preparing for the printer our *War Number* of November, 1914. We had selected for it thirteen poems of war from the seven-hundred-and-thirty-seven submitted in competition for our one-hundred-dollar prize, and had even paged up the proof, when a new and irresistible claimant arrived, and we had to squeeze out two more pages for a group of *Phases*, by one Wallace Stevens, a name then unfamiliar. Under this necessary two-page limit, we could accept only four of the six or seven battle-sketches he sent us, and to this day the others have never seen the light of print. Indeed, even the beautiful one about "fallen Winkle," the fourth in Poetry's group, is not included in this volume, although its author reluctantly permitted *The New Poetry* to reprint it.

For Mr. Stevens is the most abstemious of poets. It is the unwritten poem in his mind which interests him—the old ones, once they are registered in some magazine, may go fluttering down the wind like dead leaves. For nearly a decade his admirers pleaded in vain for a book, and at last they feel lucky to get one at all, even though they scan it in vain for *Three Travellers Watch a Sunrise, Carlos Among the Candles*, and many a briefer poem which any other poet would be proud to claim. The future collector of Mr. Stevens' complete works will have to pay a fancy price for certain back numbers of Poetry and *Others*. Meantime, *Harmonium*

*Reprinted from *Poetry* 23 (March 1924):322-27, by permission of Dr. and Mrs. Edwin S. Fetcher of St. Paul, Minn.

contains most of our favorites, besides a few new poems of high importance.

One gets a stronger flavor of personality from a one-man show than from any mixed exhibition, and there was never a more flavorously original poetic personality than the author of this book. If one seeks sheer beauty of sound, phrase, rhythm, packed with prismatically colored ideas by a mind at once wise and whimsical, one should open one's eyes and ears, sharpen one's wits, widen one's sympathies to include rare and exquisite aspects of life, and then run for this volume of iridescent poems.

I should like to take my copy to some quiet sea-flung space in Florida, where a number of the poems were written. The sky, perhaps, is cobalt, with mauve-white clouds; the sea is sapphire, flicking into diamonds under the wind; the sand is a line of purplish rose, and there are pink and yellow parasols on the beach. And here is a poet undaunted by all this splendor, a poet as sure of delight as nature herself, as serenely receptive of beauty. The bleak despairs of lesser men visit him not at all—his philosophy embraces the whole fantastic miracle of life, a miracle so wild and strange that man, confronting it, must feel the enormous humor of his lordly pose, and take refuge in

> The magnificent cause of being,
> The imagination, the one reality
> In this imagined world.

For the philosopher and the satirist temper the poet's rage in Wallace Stevens. Whether he ever writes his masterpiece or not—and that is always uncertain through the turmoil of conflicting claims which besets us all today—he is of the race of the great humorists, using the word in its most profound sense, the sense in which Cervantes, Shakespeare, Synge, Lincoln may be counted as great humorists. In such men agony sinks into depths dark, hidden and unconfessed. The hard black stone is there, but laughter washes over it, covers it up, conceals it. Tragedy is comedy with such men—they are aware of the laughter of the gods and the flaming splendor of man's fight against it. This poet is one of them; his book, however incomplete as yet, is haughty with their lineage.

Always, in his lightest play of whimsicalities as well as in his most splendid assertions of beauty, one feels this deeper note, this sense of ultimate vanities and ecstasies contending, in the human atom, against infinities that threaten it with doom. The play of whimsicalities may seem a mere banter of word-bubbles, as in *Ordinary Women*; the assertions of beauty may be as magical in pomp of color and sound as *Le Monocle de Mon Oncle*, which lifts to our thirsty lips

> This luscious and impeccable fruit of life—

or as *The Paltry Nude*, moving forever

> Across the spick torrent, ceaselessly,
> Upon her irretrievable way—

but in either extreme of lovely or whimsical utterance one feels the larger rhythms, one measures the poet's sweep by spaces beyond our earthly inches.

Perhaps *The Comedian as the Letter C* is the most complete assertion of cosmic humor which Mr. Stevens has as yet confessed to the world. It is at least the presentment, probably more or less autobiographical, of the predicament of man in general, or of highly sensitized man—let us say the artist—in particular, as he tries to live gloriously, and finds his soul caught in the meshes of life's allurements. Many poets have made a tragedy of this situation, shouting their agonies of rebellion and despair in more or less effective verse. Mr. Stevens is perhaps more keenly inspired in making of it a comedy searching and profound, a comedy whose azure laughter ripples almost inaudibly over hushed and sombre depths.

His little human unit—this "Socrates of snails," this "wig of things," this "sovereign ghost,"

> This connoisseur of elemental fate,
> Aware of exquisite thought—

in short, this Crispin, who was "washed away by magnitude," is he not our modern exemplar of frustration, as Don Quixote was in his day?

> Against his pipping sounds a trumpet cried
> Celestial sneering boisterously.

And as he sails into the blue southern sea,

> How many poems he denied himself
> In his observant progress, lesser things
> Than the relentless contact he desired!

He is in search of "a sinewy nakedness"—this Crispin poet-man;

> He gripped more closely the essential prose,
> As being, in a world so falsified,
> The one integrity for him.

But alas, he finds himself settling down:

> Crispin dwelt in the land, and dwelling there,
> Slid from his continent by slow recess
> To things within his actual eye, alert
> To the difficulty of rebellious thought
> When the sky is blue.

And so he falls into "a nice shady home," into bewildered marital allegiances, into parental loyalties to four daughters, bluet-eyed,

> Leaving no room upon his cloudy knee,
> Prophetic joint, for its diviner young.

Thus enmeshed, what is a puzzled prophet to do?

> Should he lay by the personal, and make
> Of his own fate an instance of all fate?
> What is one man among so many men?
> What are so many men in such a world?
> Can one man think one thing and think it long?
> Can one man be one thing and be it long?

So the poet in Crispin comes to a bad end:

> So deep a sound fell down
> It was as if the solitude concealed
> And covered him and his congenial sleep.
> So deep a sound fell down it grew to be
> A long soothsaying silence down and down.

We must hope that the poem is not strictly autobiographical, that Mr. Stevens, unlike his baffled hero, will get his story uttered—to such a degree at least, as may be within the reach of poor mortality. For this poet, like a super-sensitized plate, is aware of color-subtleties and sound-vibrations which most of us do not detect, and of happiness in fine degrees which most of us do not attain. He derives, so far as one may trace the less obvious origins, from no one; but like Napoleon he may say, "*Je suis ancêtre!*" for shoals of young poets derive from him. Quite free of literary allegiances to period or place, he distils into a pure essence the beauty of his own world. And beauty's imperishable perfection among shifting mortal shows is the incongruity at the heart of life which this poet accepts with the kind of serene laughter that covers pain.

Among the New Books:
Five American Poets
[*Harmonium*]

Louis Untermeyer*

. . . The really reticent poet of this quintet is Wallace Stevens. His is a reticence which results in determined obscurity, an obscurity of intention as well as an uncertainty of communication. There are, in fact, many pages in "Harmonium" which lead one to doubt whether its author even cares to communicate in a tongue familiar to the reader; he is preoccupied with language as color or contrasting sound-values, scarcely as a medium for registering degrees of emotion. Moreover, what Stevens spreads before us is less like a canvas and more like a color-palette. The book abounds in arrangements like:

*Reprinted with permission from the *Yale Review*, n.s. 14 (October 1924):159-60.

> Pierce, too, with buttresses of coral air
> And purple timbers,
> Various argentines,
> Embossings of the sky.

Or, more brilliantly:

> In Yucatan, the Maya sonneteers,
> In spite of hawk and falcon, green toucan
> And jay, still to the night-bird made their plea,
> As if raspberry tanagers in palms,
> High up in orange air, were barbarous.

Nor are these exotically splashed lines without a certain sonority. Although Stevens displays an almost childish love of alliteration and assonance (one can only smile indulgently at "Chieftan Iffucan of Azcan in caftan" or "Gloomy grammarians in golden gowns") he strikes out splendid phrases. That autobiographical confession of withdrawal ("The Comedian as the Letter C") is alert with such witty precisions as "Crispin, the lutanist of fleas," "this auditor of insects," "the florist asking aid from cabbages . . . the blind man as astronomer." Both "Sunday Morning" and "Peter Quince at the Clavier" attain a verbal elegance that far surpasses Stevens's more habitual dexterities. But for the most part, this conscious aesthete "at war with reality" achieves little beyond an amusing preciosity; he luxuriates in an ingeniously distorted world. Even his titles—which deliberately add to the reader's confusion by having little or no connection with most of the poems—are typical: "The Emperor of Ice Cream," "The Paltry Nude Starts on a Spring Voyage," "Frogs Eat Butterflies. Snakes Eat Frogs. Hogs Eat Snakes. Men Eat Hogs." For all its word-painting, there is little of the human voice in these glittering lines, and so, lacking the spell of any emotion, "Harmonium" loses both itself and its audience. It has much for the eye, something for the ear, but nothing for that central hunger which is at the heart of all the senses.

[Review of *Harmonium*]   Matthew Josephson[*]

A singular breed of Sensitive Plants begins to flourish in the severe climate of America. Some, revolted by its moral and economic bars, may have fled to voice their bitter protest. Wallace Stevens remains. Oblivious to all elements, save the natural beauty which puzzles and humors and holds him, and for which he returns the music of his words.

One side of him is exotic: colors are richer, sounds are sharper in him than in other minds or in the real existence which the mass mind accepts. So

[*]Reprinted with permission from *Broom* 5 (November 1923):236-37.

that we have the poetry of sensuousness, a poetry which depends chiefly upon its exotic spirit to hold us, as in Banal Sojourn:

> The sky is a blue gum streaked with rose. The trees are black.
> The grackles crack their throats of bone in the smooth air.
> Moisture and heat have swollen the garden into a slum of bloom.
> Pardie! Summer is like a fat beast, sleepy in mildew. . . .

Yet, the fallacy of this manner, even in its most admirable and sympathetic exponent, is that it must go on being more and more *strange*. The cultured sensuousness of Mr. Stevens in his next book would have to be more and more intimate and scandalous, *ad absurdum*. I stress this side of his production because it has influenced many of his younger contemporaries, and in them, at least, leads to pretense, and murkiness.

On the other hand there is a mathematical, a *metaphysical* quality in certain of these poems which is entertaining in the highest sense. Poems such as Thirteen Ways of Looking at a Blackbird, or The Cuban Doctor, or Anecdote of the Jar, The Worms at Heaven's Gate, will be spell-binding for hundreds of years. The Jar is as finished and simple as any of the perfect Landor fragments:

> I placed a jar in Tennessee,
> And round it was upon a hill.
> It made the slovenly wilderness
> Surround that hill.
>
> The wilderness rose up to it,
> And sprawled around no longer wild.
> The jar was round upon the ground
> And tall and of a port in air.
>
> It took dominion everywhere.
> The jar was gray and bare.
> It did not give of bird or bush,
> Like nothing else in Tennessee.

The method of this is more impoverished, there is more under-emphasis than over-ripeness, and yet it has the geometrical interest of a piece of modern abstract painting. In the vein of The Jar Mr. Stevens strikes absolutely fresh qualities in poetry, and with the authority of a superb virtuoso. Stevens, Williams (Wm. Carlos), Marianne Moore, Cummings, and one or two others alone have such cultured hands. One more perfect thing must be quoted (The Worms at Heaven's Gate):

> Out of the tomb, we bring Badroulbadour,
> Within our bellies, we her chariot.
> Here is an eye. And here are, one by one,
> The lashes of that eye and its white lid.
> Here is the cheek on which that lid declined,
> And, finger after finger, here, the hand,

The genius of that cheek. Here are the lips,
The bundle of the body and the feet.

Out of the tomb we bring Badroulbadour.

It is, of course, Miltonic blank verse. The marching rhythms are made with the severity and precision of Baudelaire and Rimbaud. Otherwise, there are two sensational feats: the nonsense-name, "Badroulbadour"; the use of the word "declined."

This first book of Mr. Stevens contains the groups of poems which aroused such interest when published in magazines. They are in many manners, and as a book serve to isolate an extraordinary personality, a man who is in turn shy, child-like, sensuous, sophisticated, discursive, who blushes for his sentiments, who is possessed of boundless curiosity. It is to be hoped that this curiosity will cause him yet to break loose in those directions (mathematical, metaphysical) for which his personality is most singularly fitted.

Society and Solitude in Poetry
[*Ideas of Order*]
F. O. Matthiessen*

. . . But of the poets at hand the one whose lines yield both the sense of strong individual life and a mature apprehension of actual society is Wallace Stevens in his "Ideas of Order." In building around such ideas, the best of these poems mark an advance over his previous volume, "Harmonium." They seem more robustly integrated; there is no longer the *dandyisme* of "Le Monocle de mon Oncle," or the slightly affected traces as in the elaborate language of "The Comedian as the Letter C." But there has been no waning in the lusty joy of his senses, or in the acute perception that discovered "Thirteen Ways of Looking at a Blackbird," or in what has always been his outstanding gift, the subtle resilient modulations of his rhythm. As a result his poems do not make statements about life; they create for the reader an illusion of sharing in a complete experience. When Mr. Stevens comments on the present state of the world, you are not given Mr. Jeffers's melodramatic vision of all mankind plunging down the hill to a darkened sea, or the romantic utopian dawn of the current revolutionists. Instead, "Sad Strains of a Gay Waltz" notes the emptiness that has crept into conventional forms of thought and feeling, and the stirring of the immense suppressed energies that are rising beyond those forms, and comes to this conclusion:

*Reprinted with permission from the *Yale Review* 25 (Spring 1936):605-07.

> Too many waltzes have ended. Yet the shapes
> For which the voices cry, these, too, may be
> Modes of desire, modes of revealing desire.
>
> Too many waltzes—The epic of disbelief
> Blares oftener and soon, will soon be constant.
> Some harmonious skeptic soon in a skeptical music
>
> Will unite these figures of men and their shapes
> Will glisten again with motion, the music
> Will be motion and full of shadows.

Beneath the haunting expert cadence of these lines Mr. Stevens is passionately concerned with human proportion. He does not rush to any easy extreme; he envisages life not merely as change but as continuity. Both "grief" and "grievance" unite to cause the shudder that is produced by "Dance of the Macabre Mice" when the silhouette of the statue of the Founder of the State is suddenly seen in the dead of winter to be swarming with black forms. Likewise, in "Re-statement of Romance," in "How to Live. What to Do," or in the complex "Idea of Order at Key West," which has music for its subject as well as for its effect, Mr. Stevens has brought his talents to an expression that is at once precise and opulent. One is tempted to say that this is the nearest approach to major poetry being made in this country to-day. At the very least, it is the one fully ripened book of poems to have originated here within the past year, the only one that would lend great distinction to a Pulitzer prize.

[Review of *Ideas of Order*]   Marianne Moore[*]

Poetry is an unintelligible unmistakable vernacular like the language of the animals—a system of communication whereby a fox with a turkey too heavy for it to carry, reappears shortly with another fox to share the booty, and Wallace Stevens is a practised hand at this kind of open cypher. With compactness beyond compare and the *forte agitato* competence of the concert room, he shows one how not to call joy satisfaction, and how one may be the epic one indites and yet be anonymous; how one may have "mighty Fortitudo, frantic bass" while maintaining one's native rareness in peace. Art is here shown to be a thing of proprieties, of mounting "the thickest man on thickest stallion-back"; yet a congruence of opposites as in the titles, Sad Strains of a Gay Waltz, and A Fish-scale Sunrise. Meditation for the fatalist is a surrender to "the morphology of regret"—a drowning in one's welter of woes, dangers, risks, obstacles to inclination. Poetry viewed

[*]Reprinted with permission of Viking Penguin Inc. from *Criterion* 15 (January 1936):307-09.

morphologically is "a finikin thing of air," "a few words tuned and tuned and tuned and tuned"; and "the function of the poet" is "sound to stuff the ear"; or—rather—it is "particles of order, a single majesty"; it is "our unfinished spirits realized more sharply in more furious selves." Art is both "rage for order" and "rage against chaos." It is a classifying, a botanizing, a voracity of contemplation. "The actual is a deft beneficence."

These thirty-three poems, composed since the enlarged edition of *Harmonium* appeared, present various conclusions about art as order. They are a series of guarded definitions but also the unembarrassing souvenirs of a man and

> . . . the time when he stood alone,
> When to be and delight to be seemed to be one.

In the untrite transitions, the as if sentimental unsentimentality, the meditativeness not for appraisal, with hints taken from the birds, as in Brahms, they recall Brahms; his dexterousness, but also his self-relish and technique of evasion as in the incident of the lion-huntress who was inquiring for the celebrated Herr Brahms: "You will find him yonder, on the other side of the hill, this is his brother."

Wallace Stevens can be as serious as the starving-times of the first settlers, and he can be Daumier caricaturing the photographer, making a time exposure watch in hand, above the title, *Patience is an Attribute of the Donkey*. The pieces are marvels of finish, and they are a dashing to oblivion of that sort of impropriety wherein "the chronicle of affected homage foxed so many books." They are "moodiest nothings"; "the trees are wooden, the grass is thin"; and they are

> . . . Evening, when the measure skips a beat
> And then another, one by one, and all
> To a seething minor swiftly modulate.

Mr. Stevens alludes to "the eccentric" as "the base of design," "the revealing aberration"; and employs noticeably in such a poem as "Sailing After Lunch," the principle of dispersal common to music; that is to say, a building up of the theme piecemeal in such a way that there is no possibility of disappointment at the end. But ease accompanies the transpositions and pauses; it is indeed a self-weighted momentum as when he says of the eagle,

> Describe with deepened voice
> And noble imagery
> His slowly-falling round
> Down to the fishy sea.

An air of "merely circulating" disguises material of the dizziest: swans, winter stars; that "body wholly body," the sea; "roses, noble in autumn, yet nobler than autumn"; "the mythy goober khan"; "peanut people"; "rouged fruits"; "the vermillion pear"; "a casino in a wood"; "this tufted rock"; "the heroic height"; "tableau tinted and towering"; the fairy-tale we wished might exist; in short, everything ghostly yet undeniable.

Serenity in sophistication is a triumph, like the behaviour of birds. The poet in fact is the migration mechanism of sensibility, and a medicine for the soul. That exact portrayal is intoxicating, that realism need not restrict itself to grossness, that music is "an accord of repetitions" is evident to one who examines *Ideas of Order*; and the altitude of performance make the wild boars of philistinism who rush about interfering with experts, negligible. In America where the dearth of rareness is conspicuous, those who recognize it feel compelled to acknowledgement; yet such a thing as a book notice seems at best an advertisement of one's inability to avoid bluntness.

Turmoil in the Middle Ground
[*Ideas of Order*]
Stanley Burnshaw*

Among the handful of clichés which have crept into left-wing criticism is the notion that contemporary poets—except those on the left and extreme right—have tramped off to some escapist limbo where they are joyously gathering moonshine. That such an idiot's paradise has existed no one can deny; but today the significant middle-ground poets are laboring elsewhere. And the significant trend is being marked by such writers as Wallace Stevens and Haniel Long: poets whose artistic statures have long been recognized, whose latest books (issued in middle age) form a considered record of agitated attitudes toward the present social order. Like all impressive phenomena of the middle ground, *Pittsburgh Memoranda* and *Ideas of Order* show troubled, searching minds. . . .

Confused as it is, *Pittsburgh Memoranda* is a marvel of order alongside Wallace Stevens' volume; and yet to many readers it is something of a miracle that Stevens has at all bothered to give us his *Ideas of Order*. When *Harmonium* appeared a dozen years ago Stevens was at once set down as an incomparable verbal musician. But nobody stopped to ask if he had any ideas. It was tacitly assumed that one read him for pure poetic sensation; if he had "a message" it was carefully buried and would take no end of labor to exhume. Yet he often comes out with flat judgments and certain ideas weave through the book consistently:

> The magnificent cause of being,
> The imagination, the one reality
> In this imagined world

underlies a number of poems. Realists have been bitter at the inanity of Pope's "Whatever is is right," but Stevens plunges ahead to the final insolence: "For realists, what is is what should be." And yet it is hard to

*Reprinted with permission from *New Masses* 17 (1 October 1935):41-42.

know if such a line is not Stevens posing in self-mockery. One can rarely speak surely of Stevens' ideas.

But certain general convictions he admits in such a poem as "To One of Fictive Music." Bound up with the sovereignty of the imagination is his belief in an interfusion of music among the elements and man. And "music is feeling . . . not sound." This trinity of principles makes the business of living to him a matter of searching out the specific harmonies.

Harmonium, then, is mainly sense poetry, but not as Keats's is sense poetry, because this serener poet is not driven to suffuse sensuous imagery with powerful subjective emotions. This is "scientific," objectified sensuousness separated from its kernel of fire and allowed to settle, cool off, and harden in the poet's mind until it emerges a strange amazing crystal. Reading this poetry becomes a venture in crystallography. It is remembered for its curious humor, its brightness, its words and phrases that one rolls on the tongue. It is the kind of verse that people concerned with the murderous world collapse can hardly swallow today except in tiny doses.

And it is verse that Stevens can no longer write. His harmonious cosmos is suddenly screeching with confusion. *Ideas of Order* is the record of a man who, having lost his footing, now scrambles to stand up and keep his balance. The opening poem observes

> . . . This heavy historical sail
> Through the mustiest blue of the lake
> In a wholly vertiginous boat
> Is wholly the vapidest fake. . . .

And the rest follows with all the ironical logic of such a premise. The "sudden mobs of men" may have the answer;

> But what are radiant reason and radiant will
> To warblings early in the hilarious trees. . . .

Sceptical of man's desire in general, there is still much to be said for the ordering power of the imagination. But there remains a yearning—and escape is itself an irony. "Marx has ruined Nature, for the moment," he observes in self-mockery; but he can speculate on the wisdom of turning inward, and a moment later look upon collective mankind as the guilty bungler of harmonious life, in "a peanut parody for a peanut people." What answer is there in the cosmic law—"everything falls back to coldness"? With apparent earnestness he goes a step beyond his former nature-man interfusing harmony:

> Only we two are one, not you and night,
> Nor night and I, but you and I, alone,
> So much alone, so deeply by ourselves,
> So far beyond the casual solitudes,
> That night is only the background of our selves. . . .

And in a long poem he pours out in strange confusion his ideas of order, among them:

> If ever the search for a tranquil belief should end,
> The future might stop emerging out of the past,
> Out of what is full of us; yet the search
> And the future emerging out of us seem to be one.

Paraphrase, always a treacherous tool, is especially dangerous when used on so *raffiné* a poet as Stevens. Does he talk of himself when he explains that "the purple bird must have notes for his comfort that he may repeat through the gross tedium of being rare"? Does he make political reference in declaring "the union of the weakest develops strength, not wisdom"?

Asking questions may not be a reviewer's function, but uncertainties are unavoidable when reading such poets as the two under review; for the texture of their thought is made of speculations, questionings, contradictions. Acutely conscious members of a class menaced by the clashes between capital and labor, these writers are in the throes of struggle for philosophical adjustment. And their words have intense value and meaning to the sectors within the class whose confusions they articulate. Their books have deep importance for us as well.

Of course, objectively, neither poet is weakening the class in power— as yet they are potential allies as well as potential enemies—but one of them looks for a new set of values and the other earnestly propagates (however vaguely) some form of collectivism. Will Long emancipate himself from his paralyzing faith in inner perfection? Will Stevens sweep his contradictory notions into a valid Idea of Order? The answers depend not only on the personal predispositions of these poets but on their full realization of the alternatives facing them as artists.

New Verse
[*The Man with the Blue Guitar*]   Delmore Schwartz*

. . . The poems of Wallace Stevens present an elegant surface. It has been mentioned often, and misunderstood even more frequently, but its affiliations are fairly clear. The same dandyism of speech and the same florid irony is to be found in such writers as James Branch Cabell and Carl Van Vechten, in certain poems of J. C. Ransom and Conrad Aiken, even in the prose style of Santayana, in the poems of the forgotten Donald Evans, and going further back in time, in the moonstruck poems of Dowson,

*"New Verse" by Delmore Schwartz appeared first in the *Partisan Review* 4 (February 1938): 49-52. Reprinted with permission of the *Partisan Review*.

Laforgue, and Verlaine, the Verlaine of "Fêtes Galantes," and the Laforgue who sighs that existence is so quotidian. This is a formidable family, but the resemblances are unmistakeable. They are also superficial; Stevens has made a significant virtue out of the dubious verbal habits involved in the tendency from which he seems, in some way, to have derived his style. He is unquestionably a much better writer than most of the above authors.

Perhaps it is worthwhile attempting to account for the kinship by relating Stevens to the *milieu* which must have surrounded him when he began to write. As a hypothesis, one may suppose that his style crystallized in the days when *The Smart Set* was the leading literary magazine, when one knew French with pride, discussed sophistication, feared to be provincial, and aspired to membership among the élite. The backwash or lag of that day is still apparent in the Greenwich Village tearoom, and one can scarcely doubt that among the admirers of Miss Millay, there are some who still exist in that period of time. To be a poet at that time was to be peculiar; merely to be interested in the arts was to take upon oneself the burden of being superior, and an exile at home. It may be that as a result of some such feeling, Stevens called his wonderful discourse on love *Le Monocle de Mon Oncle*, thus resorting to French, and thus mocking, as so often in his titles, the poem itself, as if the poet were extremely self-conscious about the fact of being a poet. It ought to be added that the title of the poem in question does, nevertheless, have a distinct meaning in the poem.

In the present volume, Stevens provides another example, the best one perhaps, of how much there is in his poetry beneath the baroque decoration. The surface would seem to be a mask, which releases the poet's voice, a guise without which he could not speak. But the sentiments beneath the mask are of a different order. If we rest with our impression of the surface, we get nothing but a sense of play and jocular attitudinizing:

> To strike his living hi and ho,
> To tick it, tock it, turn it true,

If we dig into just such usages and then come back to the poem as a whole, we understand the justice of such verbalism, its necessity, and we are confronted with a mind of the utmost seriousness, aware and involved in the most important things in our lives.

The imagination and actuality, the blue guitar which is poetry and things as they are, constitute the antithesis to which Stevens devotes a varied discourse in the present book. In the title poem or suite of poems, there are thirty-three short lyrics in which the various relationships between art and the actual world are named, examined, turned upside down, and transformed into the terms of Stevens' personal vision. In the opening lyric, we are given the suggestion of some lack in the nature of poetry. The poet is addressed by his audience:

> They said, "You have a blue guitar,
> You do not play things as they are"

The poet replies that the imagination must of necessity alter and distort actuality, and the audience then extends its demand:

> "But play you must
> A tune beyond us, yet ourselves,
>
> A tune upon the blue guitar,
> Of things exactly as they are."

The difficulty is that poetry is somehow insufficient. The incidence of that insufficiency, its present point, is made evident further on in the poem:

> The earth is not earth, but a stone,
> Not the mother that held men as they fell,
>
> But stone, but like a stone, no, not
> The mother but an oppressor

It is because of an enforced awareness that his time is one of immense conflict and derangement that the poet has been compelled to consider the nature of poetry in its travail among things as they are. The basic preoccupation, the apprehension which has produced two volumes in two years, was revealed most explicitly in the previous book, *Ideas of Order*:

> There is order in neither sea nor sun,
> There are these sudden mobs of men,
>
> These sudden clouds of faces and arms,
> An immense suppression, freed,
> These voices crying without knowing for what,
>
> Except to be happy, without knowing how. . . .

This is the way, then, in which Stevens answers these sudden mobs of men, these sudden clouds of faces and arms: he justifies poetry, he defines its place, its rôle, its priceless value. Nothing could be more characteristic of this poet, of his virtues and also of his limitations, and one cannot think of an answer of greater propriety.

The second sequence of poems, "Owl's Clover," consists of five meditations in blank verse, all of them concerned with extending the theme of the fate of art amid terrifying change and destruction, and envisaging the kind of place toward which history is moving:

> Shall you,
> Then, fear a drastic community evolved
> From the whirling, slowly and by trial; or fear
> Men gathering for a final flight of men,
> An abysmal migration into possible blue?

The fear is in the foreground and is complicated by the themes which were Stevens' direct subject in *Harmonium*, the brutality and chaos of Nature, which is here figured forth in a new symbol, Africa; and also the absence of belief, the departure of God, the angels, and heaven. The attitudes toward what is to come are complex and ambiguous, as they ought to be. The poet can only regard the possibilities which he fears and state his hope:

> Basilewsky in the bandstand played
> "Concerto for Airplane and Pianoforte,"
> The newest Soviet reclame. Profound
> Abortion, fit for the enchanting of basilisks. . . .
> What man of folk-lore shall rebuild the world,
> What lesser man shall measure sun and moon,
> What super-animal dictate our fates?
> As the man the state, not as the state the man.

But finally and unequivocally, in the last poem of the volume, the poet salutes the men that are falling, for whom God and the angels have become identical with the cause for which they are falling:

> Taste of the blood upon his martyred lips,
> O pensioners, O demagogues and pay-men!
>
> This death was his belief, though death is a stone
> This man loved earth, not heaven, enough to die.

This is clearly a poetry which flows from a mind in love not only with the beautiful, but also with the just.

There are, however, distinct limitations also. From beginning to end, in *Harmonium* as well as in the present volume, these poems are absorbed in "responses" to various facts. They are absorbed to such an extent that the facts can scarcely get into the poems at all. We may compare Stevens to William Carlos Williams, whom he admires and who may be said to represent the other extreme, a poet whose whole effort is to get facts into his poem with the greatest exactitude and to keep everything else out. One beautiful line in particular in "Owl's Clover" ("The sound of z in the grass all day") emphasizes by contrast how little direct observation there is in Stevens. There is no specific scene, nor time, nor action, but only the mind moving among its meanings and replying to situations which are referred to, but not contained in, the poem itself. "Rocks, moss, stonecrop, iron, merds," another poet writes, "The woman keeps the kitchen, makes tea, Sneezes at evening, poking the peevish gutter." By thus placing the fact within the poem, the response to the fact gains immeasurable strength and relevance. In Stevens, however, the poet "strides" "among the cigar stores, Ryan's lunch, hatters, insurance and medicines" without convincing the reader that he is walking on an actual street. There is always an abstractness present; everything is turned into an object of the imagination. Certain weaknesses result: the word-play does not always escape the adventitious frivolity for which it is always mistaken by the careless reader; the poem is sometimes extended not by a progress of perception, or of meaning, but one word and one phrase multiplies others; and, to sum up these defects, the poet is "too poetic." It may also be that the burden of this style is responsible for the faults which have always been present in Stevens' blank verse, a lack of variety in going from line to line, a difficulty with overflow, and lately, in "Owl's Clover," a tendency to anapestic substitution which unsettles the sonorous Miltonic period.

Virtue and defect, however, seem to be inseparable. The magnificence of the rhetoric necessitates an exclusion of narrative elements, necessitates the whole weight of the verbalism, and, on the other hand, makes possible the extreme range and freedom of the symbols. The blue guitar, the statue, the duck, the greenest continent, and above all the bread and the stone presented here for the first time are figures and metaphors of a richness and meaningfulness which justify the method. The poems taken as a whole constitute a special kind of museum, of a very familiar strangeness, located, because of the extent of the poet's awareness, in the middle of everything which concerns us.

An Abstraction Blooded
[*Notes toward a Supreme Fiction*]   R. P. Blackmur*

In one of Mr. Stevens' early poems he made the simple declaration that "Poetry is the supreme fiction," and in another there was a phrase about "the ultimate Plato, the tranquil jewel in this confusion." Now, in *Notes toward a Supreme Fiction*, he shows us a combination of the two notions with a development into a third thing, which if it is not reached is approached from all round. The poem is like a pie marked for cutting in three pieces, with an imaginary centre which is somehow limited, if you look long enough, only by the whole circumference. A triad makes a trinity, and a trinity, to a certain kind of poetic imagination, is the only tolerable form of unity. I think the deep skills of imagination, by which insights, ideas, and acts get into poetry, thrive best when some single, pressing theme or notion is triplicated. It is not a matter of understanding, but of movement and of identification and of access of being. The doublet is never enough, unless it breeds. War and peace need a third phase, as liquid and ice need vapor to fill out and judge the concept of water, as God the Father and God the Son need the Holy Ghost, or hell and heaven need purgatory, or act and place need time. The doublet *needs* what it makes. This is a habit of creative mind.

Mr. Stevens has acquired that habit. Wanting, as we all do, a supreme fiction, wanting, that is, to conceive, to imagine, to make a supreme being, wanting, in short, to discover and objectify a sense of such a being, he sets up three phases through which it must pass. It must be abstract; it must

*First appeared in the *Partisan Review* 10 (May–June 1943):297-300. Reprinted with permission.

change; it must give pleasure. Each phase is conceived as equal in dimension, each being given in ten sections of seven three-lined stanzas; and each phase is conceived as a version of the other two, that is, with a mutual and inextricable rather than with a successive relationship.

Let us see what the elements of the Fiction look like when taken separately. It must, the poet argues, be abstract, beyond, above, and at the beginning of our experience, and it must be an abstract idea of *being*, which when fleshed or blooded in nature or in thought, will absorb all the meanings we discover. That is to say, it must be arche-typical and a source, an initiator of myth and sense, and also a reference or judgment for myth and sense; it tends to resemble a Platonic idea in character and operation, and its natural prototype, its easiest obvious symbol, will be the sun. But it must change in its abstractness, depending on the experience of it, as a seraph turns satyr "according to his thoughts"; for if it did not change it would tend to disappear or at least to become vestigial. You take character from what is not yourself and participate in what changes you. The process of change in the life of being, like abstraction, requires constant iteration and constant experience. Most of all the Fiction must change because change is the condition of perception, vision, imagination. "A fictive covering/weaves always glistening from the heart and mind." What changes is the general, the instances of the abstract, as they strike a fresh or freshened eye. That is why this fiction which changes, and is abstract, must give pleasure; it must be always open to discovery by a fresh eye, which is the eye of pleasure, the eye of feeling and imagination, envisaging the "irrational distortion."

> That's it: the more than rational distortion,
> The fiction that results from feeling.

In short, an abstract fiction can change and, if the abstraction was soundly conceived, the more it is the same the more it will seem to change, and by the feeling of change in identity, identity in change, give the great pleasure of access of being.

> The man-hero is not the exceptional monster,
> But he that of repetition is most master.

These are the bare bones of doctrine, and in another poet, most likely of another age, might exactly have been in control of the motion of the poem. In Stevens' poem the doctrine is not in control, nor does he pretend that it is; it is not a system, or even an organization, that he provides us with, but a set of notes brought together and graphed by the convention of his triad. If his notes are united, it is partly by the insight that saw the triad outside the poem, and partly by the sensibility—the clusters of perceptions, and the rotation of his rosary of minor symbols—into which he translates it. There is the great unity and the heroic vision in the offing, and they may indeed loom in the night of the poetry, but in the broad day of it there are only fragments, impressions, and merely associated individuations. Their maximum achieved unity is in their formal circumscription: that they are seen together in the same poem.

Whether a poet could in our time go much further—whether the speculative *imagination* is possible in our stage of belief—cannot be argued; there are no examples; yet it seems more a failure of will than of ability. Certainly Stevens has tackled Socrates' job: the definition of general terms. Certainly, too, he has seen one of the ways in which the poet in whom the philosopher has hibernated, muddled in sleep, can go on with the job: he has seen, in the sensibility, the relations between the abstract, the actual, and the imaginative. But he has been contented or been able only to make all his definitions out of fragments of the actual, seeing the fragments as transformations of the abstract: each one as good, as meaningful, as another, but bound not to each other in career but only to the centre (the major idea) which includes them. That is why, I think, so many of the fragments are unavailable except in passing, and the comprehension of what is passing depends too often upon special knowledge of fashion and gibberish in vocabulary and idiom.

Mr. Stevens himself understands the problem, and has expressed it characteristically in one of the segments of the decade requiring that the Fiction change. It is one of the segments, so common in so many poets of all ages, in which the poet assures himself of the nature and virtue of poetry: the protesting ritual of re-dedication.

> The poem goes from the poet's gibberish to
> The gibberish of the vulgate and back again . . .
> Is there a poem that never reaches words
> And one that chaffers the time away? . . .
> It is the gibberish of the vulgate that he seeks.
> He tries by a peculiar speech to speak
>
> The peculiar potency of the general,
> To compound the imagination's Latin with
> The lingua franca et jocundissima.

Granting the poet his own style, it could not be better expressed. Mr. Stevens, like the best of our modern poets, is free master of the fresh and rejoicing tongue of sensibility and fancy and the experience in flush and flux and flower; but he lacks, except for moments, and there, too, resembles his peers, the power of the "received," objective and authoritative imagination, whether of philosophy, religion, myth, or dramatic symbol, which is what he means by the imagination's Latin. The reader should perhaps be reminded that *gibberish* is not a frivolous word in the context; it is a word *manqué* more than a word mocking. One gibbers before a reality too great, when one is appalled with perception, when words fail though meaning persists: which is precisely, as Mr. Eliot suggested in a recent number of the *Partisan Review*, a proper domain of poetry.

One does what one can, and the limits of one's abilities are cut down by the privations of experience and habit, by the absence of what one has not thought of and by the presence of what is thought of too much, by the canalisation and evaporation of the will. What is left is that which one touches again and again, establishing a piety of the imagination with the effrontery of repetition. Mr. Stevens has more left than most, and has handled it with more modulations of touch and more tenacious piety, so that it becomes itself exclusively, inexplicably, fully expressive of its own meaning. Of such things he says:

> These are not things transformed
> Yet we are shaken by them as if they were.
> We reason about them with a later reason.

He knows, too,

> The fluctuations of certainty, the change
> Of degrees of perception in the scholar's dark,

which it is not hard to say that one knows, but which it is astonishing, always, to see exemplified in images of the seasons, of water-lights, the colours of flowers in the colours of air, or birdsong, for they make so "an abstraction blooded, as a man by thought."

It is all in the garden, perhaps, where the poet's gibberish returns to the gibberish of the vulgate, and where the intensity of the revelations of the single notion of redness dispenses, for a very considerable but by no means single occasion, with the imagination's Latin.

> A lasting visage in a lasting bush,
> A face of stone in an unending red,
> Red-emerald, red-slitted-blue, a face of slate,
>
> An ancient forehead hung with heavy hair,
> The channel slots of rain, the red-rose-red
> And weathered and the ruby-water-worn,
>
> The vines around the throat, the shapeless lips,
> The frown like serpents basking on the brow,
> The spent feeling leaving nothing of itself,
>
> Red-in-red repetitions never going
> Away, a little rusty, a little rouged
> A little roughened and ruder, a crown
>
> The eye could not escape, a red renown
> Blowing itself upon the tedious ear.
> An effulgence faded, dull cornelian
>
> Too venerably used.

Recent Poetry
[*Transport to Summer*]

Louis L. Martz*

. . . Finally we come to the unique bird, inimitable. The new volume by Wallace Stevens may well stand as another landmark in American literature, along with his first volume, "Harmonium" (1923). It is true that, unlike this early volume, "Transport to Summer" is marred by a number of labored and muddy pieces. But this is not because Stevens has declined as an artist in his later years (he is now sixty-eight); it is because, having mastered one mode, he has tried to develop in new directions, impelled by a growing vision and by the cataclysmic events of the last twenty years. "Ideas of Order" (1935) marked a turning point; here, along with the "essential gaudiness," the vivid apprehensions of concrete experience, characteristic of "Harmonium," we had a dominant interest in establishing something like a philosophy of the imagination. But theorizing was here still tightly integrated with concrete detail, to produce a distinguished (and neglected) volume. In "The Man with the Blue Guitar" (1937) and "Parts of a World" (1942) it was clear that Stevens was in the throes of working out a considerably different style, dealing explicitly and often abstractly with "the role of the imagination in life, and paticularly in life at present." These volumes were interesting failures: good patches and fine poems were imbedded in an obscure, incoherent, and sometimes prosy mass. Fortunately for Stevens' admirers, 1942 also produced, in a limited edition, the reassuring "Notes toward a Supreme Fiction," while in 1945, in another limited edition, came the impressive "Esthétique du Mal," both of which are now included in "Transport to Summer," along with a large number of other poems which Stevens has evidently written since 1942.

All his essential substance is given at its best in these two long and brilliant sequences, where Stevens has mastered a conversational, meditative style, and also in two shorter sequences, almost as good, entitled "Description without Place" and "Credences of Summer." The vision here expressed is briefly this: in a world of "calculated chaos," the human imagination remains a power for pleasure and victory, since the imagination can create its own intense and ordered world from materials provided by the world of physical objects. The "transport to summer" consists in seizing with the imagination some pleasurable physical object, and then, by metaphor, clarifying it and relating it to other objects, until one has formed an integrated composition of the "ideal" and the "real." By such man-made "credences" we dominate and enjoy our environment, though such domination cannot be sustained for long, and must be vigilantly re-established from moment to moment. This "summer" is no easy flight from ugliness. "Esthétique du Mal" shows clearly that such pleasures are strenuously achieved and depend upon a thorough, unblinking recog-

*Reprinted with permission from the *Yale Review* n.s. 37 (December 1947):339-41.

nition of the existence of pain. That recognition is in itself a work of the imagination:

> Except for us, Vesuvius might consume
> In solid fire the utmost earth and know
> No pain (ignoring the cocks that crow us up
> To die). This is a part of the sublime
> From which we shrink. And yet, except for us,
> The total past felt nothing when destroyed.

These things once understood, it is possible for us to build up imaginative compensations against the fact of pain, through establishing full, acute relationships with other human beings and with the external world. The utter tragedy for man, says Stevens, is to become so "Spent in the false engagements of the mind" that he falls into "the greatest poverty":

> To lose sensibility, to see what one sees,
> As if sight had not its own miraculous thrift,
> To hear only what one hears, one meaning alone. . . .

Certainly we are "Natives of poverty, children of malheur," who must face "the unalterable necessity Of being this unalterable animal." Yet, through the exercise of imaginative sensibility, we may create a metamorphosis such as Stevens describes in the witty, gay mood that marks some of the best parts of his "Notes toward a Supreme Fiction."

When the poems in these four sequences have so eloquently expressed the theme, one finds rather tedious the presence of inferior pieces striving towards the same end. This reader, at least, would wish to keep only about a score of these other poems—among them "Dutch Graves in Bucks County," "Holiday in Reality," "The Red Fern," "Men Made out of Words," "The House was Quiet," and "A Lot of People Bathing in a Stream." Stevens has been in the past sufficiently praised as an "able virtuoso" with a "cunning rhetoric." It has seemed more important to stress here the fact that the superb craft of his best poems grows out of a deep concern for the role of the imagination in a world preoccupied with the tragic plans of the materialist.

[Review of *The Auroras of Autumn*]   William Van O'Connor*

When *Harmonium* was issued in 1923 Wallace Stevens was forty-four years old. In October of 1950, shortly after the publication of *The Auroras of Autumn*, he will be seventy-one. Because he was older than most poets publishing a first book and because he worked inside the same subject matter, enlarging and qualifying it, there is a remarkable consistency

*Reprinted with permission of Mary A. O'Connor from *Poetry* 77 (November 1950):109-12.

among his volumes. But there are differences too. There is a touch of melancholy in *Harmonium*, but it is the melancholy of *Twelfth Night* or *The Merchant of Venice*, the pleasant melancholy, partly satiety, that comes with knowing and enjoying the richness of the world:

> I do not know which to prefer,
> The beauty of inflections
> Or the beauty of innuendos,
> The blackbird whistling
> Or just after.

With *Transport to Summer* (1947) the melancholy is deeper:

> Time is a horse that runs in the heart, a horse
> Without a rider on a road at night.
> The mind sits listening and hears it pass.

In *The Auroras of Autumn*, it is deepest of all. We live as in the earlier volumes in a theatre of trope, of changing appearances:

> It is a theatre floating through the clouds,
> Itself a cloud, although of misted rock
> And mountains running like water, wave on wave,
>
> Through waves of light. It is of cloud transformed
> To cloud transformed again, idly, the way
> A season changes color to no end, . . .

It is the same wondrous world, made out of words, but it is a more frightening world:

> There is nothing until in a single man contained,
> Nothing until this named thing nameless is
> And is destroyed. He opens the door of his house
>
> On flames. The scholar of one candle sees
> An Arctic effulgence flaring on the frame
> Of everything he is. And he feels afraid.

In *Disillusionment of Ten O'Clock*, from *Harmonium*, Stevens was saddened by a world without imagination—the people going to bed in their white nightgowns would not "dream of baboons and periwinkles." He himself dreamed of a world of lutes, wigs, parasols, masques, peristyles, duchesses and barouches, a world of elegant decor. The man with imagination is more completely alive. But, as Conrad knew, and as Stevens of *The Auroras of Autumn* knows, the man with imagination lives not only in a more magnificent but in a more terrifying world:

> Is there an imagination that sits enthroned
> As grim as it is benevolent, the just
> And the unjust, which in the midst of summer stops

To imagine winter? When the leaves are dead
Does it take its place in the north and enfold itself,
Goat-leaper, crystalled and luminous, sitting

In highest night?

The Auroras of Autumn has a more persistently held to and perhaps narrower theme than any of the earlier volumes. It is that we are haunted by the idea of death, when we will cease to create the world in which we live. The theme is fairly explicit in *Puella Parvula*:

Every thread of summer is at last unwoven.
By one caterpillar is great Africa devoured
And Gibraltar is dissolved like spit in the wind.

But over the wind, over the legends of its roaring,
The elephant on the roof and its elephantine blaring,
The bloody lion in the year at night or ready to spring

From the clouds in the midst of trembling trees
Making a great gnashing, over the water wallows
Of a vacant sea declaiming with wide throat,

Over all these the mighty imagination triumphs
Like a trumpet and says, in this season of memory,
When the leaves fall like things mournful of the past,

Keep quiet in the heart, O wild bitch. O mind
Gone wild, be what he tells you to be: *Puella*.
Write *pax* across the window pane. And then

Be still. The *summarium in excelsis* begins . . .
Flame, sound, fury composed . . . Hear what he says,
The dauntless master, as he starts the human tale.

The one stability is the imagination, the agent of change; we live in the world she shows us: "The fire burns as the novel taught it how," or "words of the world are the life of the world," or "what we think is never what we see."

Selden Rodman says that despite the references to the physical world, even the catalogues of insects, birds, trees and fruits, he is not convinced of "Stevens' preoccupation with the physical world." Reading Yeats, on the other hand, he is "convinced of a passionate interest in both the physical world and man." Certainly there is an essential difference between the two poets. Stevens' reality is not Yeats' "blood and mire of human veins" or "this pragmatical, preposterous pig of a world, its farrow that so solid seems." But in the long poem *An Ordinary Evening in New Haven* Stevens has written his own answer to this argument:

> It is not in the premise that reality
> Is a solid. It may be a shade that traverses
> A dust, a force that traverses a shade.

The American world of William James, John Dewey, Theodore Dreiser, Ernest Hemingway, Carl Sandburg, Vernon Parrington, *et al.*, has insisted that this "is a pragmatical, preposterous pig of a world"—and it is. But it is also Mr. Stevens' world—

> The less legible the meaning of sounds, the little reds
> Not often realized, the lighter words
> In the heavy drum of speech.

Yeats too of course was keenly aware of those meanings that seem to be "too subtle for the intellect."

The aesthetic with which Stevens has been allied has never been popular in America, although we are now much more appreciative of it and willing to grant that it too is involved with "reality," probably in crucial ways. In France it was summarized by Anatole France, in England by Pater in the famous "Conclusion" to his *Renaissance*, and in America it had its beginnings with Edgar Saltus, James Huneker, Lafcadio Hearn, Percival Pollard, and Vance Thompson. Later it belonged to the magazine *Others*, to James Branch Cabell, to Elinor Wylie, Carl Van Vechten, to the young F. Scott Fitzgerald—and to Wallace Stevens. It was an aesthetic which did very well in France, rather poorly in England, and for the most part very badly in America. In America it produced mostly wax flowers and undoubtedly destroyed certain careers. But Fitzgerald in fiction and Stevens in poetry were able to modify it, to make it thoroughly their own, to adapt it to American subjects, to their own themes, and to make it live. For the twenty-seven years since the publication of *Harmonium*, which as is generally known sold fewer than a hundred copies before being remaindered, Stevens has continued, usually with no very loud applause in his ears, to perfect his art. The Bollingen Prize for Poetry in 1950 was the first "big prize" he has received. *The Auroras of Autumn* is in the same tradition, of elegance, of unique observations, of wit, of discriminations pushed at least two removes beyond what was expected—an art that still respects the highly individualized imagination:

> Likewise to say of the evening star,
> The most ancient light in the most ancient sky,
> That it is wholly an inner light, that it shines
> From the sleepy bosom of the real, recreates,
> Searches a possible for its possibleness.

The Gaiety of Language
[*The Necessary Angel* and *Opus Posthumous*]

Frank Kermode°

Granted, for an hour, the tongue of a critical angel, one could say of these books° [*The Necessary Angel* and *Opus Posthumous*] nothing that could possibly be more extraordinary than this: they have not been published in this country. If the cause of this inexcusable default is a lack of public demand, how do we explain this lack? It is probably not so much the difficulty as the foreignness of Stevens that has delayed his full acceptance here. He is both familiar and strange. By rethinking the whole modern literary tradition in eccentric semi-solitude he found an odd way back to the Romantic sources; and he owed much to certain French poetry which is a familiar part of the English tradition. Also, one of his two acknowledged masters was Mr. Eliot. But not quite *our* Mr. Eliot; and the other master, whom he does not name, must have been Whitman, whom we hardly recognise by Stevens's description:

> Nothing is final, he chants. No man shall see the end.
> His beard is of fire and his staff is a leaping flame.

Stevens himself remarked, in one of the *Adagia*, that "nothing could be more inappropriate to American literature than its English source, since the Americans are not British in sensibility." And since the poet must use the common language in order to speak a speech which is "only a little of the tongue," Stevens's various compoundings of "the imagination's Latin" with vulgar eloquence are constantly surprising to us. The gaiety of that language is an American gaiety; here imagination and reality have married well "because the marriage place Was what they loved." Stevens often insisted on the relevance of place to the nature of imaginative activity and objects.

This adds to our difficulties in that it adds to that element of the fortuitous which was, for Stevens, essential to poetry. Art is fortuitous because it deals in moments of unpredictable balance, because it works with anomalies and resemblances which can never in themselves be exact, though the product may be; and because the absolute rightness of language (which is its gaiety) bloods the man who feels it with a delight essentially unexpected. Over-reliance on the power of the fortuitous to signify is, in fact, one cause of Stevens's failures (though some poems that seem to me failures are much admired in America). The truth may be that some proportion of Stevens will always remain relatively inaccessible, though this proportion should become very small. The English reader even has the advantage that he can clearly see the greatness of the later poetry without having to get over the dazzle caused by over-long attention to the fireworks

°Reprinted with permission of the author from the *Spectator* 201 (3 October 1958):454-55.
© Frank Kermode.

of *Harmonium*. But it is with much reading that the book of Stevens becomes true, and the English reader needs all the verse and the 300 or so pages of prose in which a great poet speaks greatly of poetry and the *materia poetica*.

The Necessary Angel (1951) consists of essays and lectures mostly of the Forties. It is worth saying, with the help of Mr. S. F. Morse—author of a forthcoming critical biography—how the book came by its title. In 1949 Stevens bought a still-life by Tal Coat; he admired it because "for all its in-door light on in-door objects, the picture refreshes one with an out-door sense of things." (This "out-door sense" is nearly what he elsewhere calls "major weather," a discovery of the real by the "in-door light" of imagination.) Soon he gave the picture the fanciful title of "Angel surrounded by Peasants," the angel being "the Venetian glass bowl on the left" and the peasants the objects surrounding it. Then he described it in language exactly appropriate to his own poems, calling it "an effort to attain a certain reality purely by way of the artist's own vitality." The final poem in *The Auroras of Autumn* (1950) was entitled "Angel surrounded by Paysans." In this masterpiece the angel who grew out of the Venetian glass represents the giant-poet's way of redeeming the earth. He tells the peasants that he has "neither ashen wing nor wear of ore," that he is one of them, yet "the necessary angel of the earth,"

> Since in my sight you see the earth again
> Cleared of its stiff and stubborn man-locked set.

In 1951, persuaded at last to publish his prose, he called the collection *The Necessary Angel: Essays on Reality and the Imagination*.

There are two inferences from this. First, we may suppose that the best of the poetry—that which evades the dangers of mere epistemological doodling on one hand and the fall from ironic exaltation into flatulence on the other—will always derive its strength from hiding-places as deep as this. Second, Stevens came to write his major prose when he was already a doctor incomparably subtle, indeed angelic. When he comes from poetry, which discloses poetry, to prose, which discloses definitions of poetry, he will arrive at these definitions by strange routes. And, indeed, these essays are constructed like meditative poems, circling beautifully round central images, proceeding with a grave gaiety to repetitive but ever-changing statements about the imagination, "the one reality in this imagined world," and about the poet, who must find "what will suffice" to refresh an earth to which the God his predecessors created is no longer relevant. The imagination creates evil as well as good, political value as well as all other value; how important, then, is poetry as the supreme fiction, the sun of the mind, bringer of savour and health, slayer of the dragon of abstract philosophy, destroyer of our poverty?

"The Noble Rider and the Sound of Words" and "Imagination as Value" are the most remarkable of the essays. Within their subtle yet monumental structures there is the quickness of the poet's mind, inventing the dialect of the angel whose joy redeems the world.

> Natives of poverty, children of malheur,
> The gaiety of language is our seigneur.

In the *Adagia*—two or three hundred of them printed in the inaccessible *Opus Posthumous*—we may see, among much else, how this couplet grew from two observations: "Poetry is a purging of the world's poverty and change and evil and death. . . ," "Poetry is the gaiety (joy) of language." Although the posthumous book necessarily contains some inferior material, it has some extremely important prose, notably a late essay called "A Collect of Philosophy," and, above all, the poems of Stevens's last year; one of them, "As You Leave the Room," is fit to stand beside "The Circus Animal's Desertion," its affirmations as emphatic, for all their calm, as the denunciations of Yeats. And this is characteristic, for Stevens's achievement is to have stripped of dead images and assumptions the myth that animates modern art and to have given it new and unforeseen reality. Mr. Morse, to whom we owe this fascinating collection, has also included the two early verse-plays, and some interesting early lyrics and drafts. There is almost nothing in the book that may safely be dispensed with by the reader undertaking the indispensable task of understanding the *mundo*, as he might put it, of Stevens.

Very Graceful Are the Uses of Culture [*Collected Poems*]   Randall Jarrell°

. . . *The Collected Poems of Wallace Stevens* (Knopf, $7.50) contains all the poetry of one of the greatest of living poets. I have before this written about both his best poems and his worst, but on occasion (and a book like this is truly an occasion) a critic can behave like posterity, which memorializes—which memorizes—the good, and which looks by the bad with a sweet uncaring smile. One might as well argue with the Evening Star as find fault with so much wit and grace and intelligence; such knowledge of, feeling for, other times and places, and our own; such an overwhelming and exquisite command both of the words and of the rhythms of our language; such charm and irony, such natural and philosophical breadth of sympathy, such dignity and magnanimity. (Toynbee often has the calm and generosity of a visitor from a better age, and you feel that Stevens would like nothing better than to be such a trav-

°Reprinted with permission of Mrs. Randall Jarrell from *Harper's* 209 (November 1954):100.

eler through time.) Little of Stevens' work has the dramatic immediacy, the mesmeric, involving humanity, of so much of Yeats' and Frost's poetry: his poems, if they were ideally successful, might resemble the paintings of Piero della Francesca. But some of these cool, clear, airy poems, which tower above us in the dazzling elegance, the "minute brilliance" of yachts or clouds, ought to be sailing over other heads many centuries from now.

Another Way of Looking at
the Blackbird [*Opus Posthumous*]   Irving Howe°

Gradually, under the pressure of time, the masks of Wallace Stevens are wearing away, and not because they have become obsolete or been proven deceptive but because they now seem to have figured mainly as preparations for a homelier reality. Gaudy mystifier, Crispin's pilot, flaunter of rare chromatic words, explorer of Yucatan, enemy of the day's routine, afficionado of strange hats, even the gamesman of epistemology— these roles yield to Stevens' "basic slate," an American poet reflecting upon solitary lives in a lonely age and searching for that "inmost allegiance" by which men might live out their years in thousands of Hartfords.

Stevens was the kind of poet who wrote methodically and a good deal, apparently without waiting for, though always delighted to receive, the blessings of inspiration. Writing verse seems to have become for him a means of wresting convictions of selfhood: the visible token of that which he insistently wrote about. His work is therefore very much of a piece, both in its success and failures. In *Opus Posthumous*—a collection of fugitive pieces, poems omitted from the *Collected Poems*, a few verse plays, a group of aphorisms on poetry, some critical essays and 30 late poems devoted to preparation for death—one can trace out something of the scheme and direction of Stevens' work, perhaps even a bit more easily than in the *Collected Poems*. For *Opus Posthumous* is a much less imposing book, and one therefore in which Stevens' intention juts out all the more sharply.

After the publication of *Harmonium* in 1923, the main job of his critics was to become familiar with his decor: the exotic places, the tropical language, the cheerful jibing at bourgeois norms, the apparent *fin-de-siècle* estheticism, the flip nose-thumbing of his titles. So luxuriant did the world of his poems seem, so free of traditional moral demands, that his early admirers could hardly avoid thinking of this world as primarily a sensuous landscape. It was a view that lingered into Marianne Moore's description of Stevens as "a delicate apothecary of savors and precipitates"—though in

°Reprinted with permission from the *New Republic* 137 (4 November 1957):16-19. © 1957, the *New Republic*, Inc.

that last word there is a hint that Miss Moore, as usual, saw more than she said.

While this was a way of reading Stevens that could yield genuine pleasures, it hardly went very far toward penetrating his deeper concerns, and even when confined to *Harmonium* it could be maintained only if one focused on the shorter poems and neglected "Sunday Morning" and "The Comedian as Letter C." In an early study of Stevens, R. P. Blackmur quickly saw that the strange cries, hoots and words that ran through the poems, far from being mere exotica, were oblique and humorous tokens of a profoundly serious effort to grapple with the distinctively "modern" in modern experience.

Later there was a tendency to read Stevens as if he were a versifying philosopher, a misfortune for which he was himself partly to blame, since at his prolific second-best he had a way of sounding like a versifying philosopher. Stevens' poetry, now in the hands of new exegetes, was said to be about the writing of poetry, and was regarded as a series of variations on the philosophical theme of the relation between reality and imagination. Both of these statements, while true and useful, were needlessly limiting as aids toward a fuller apprehension of the poetry: the first was too narrow, the second too academic, and from neither could one gain a sense of what might be urgent or particular in Stevens' work.

Poetry written mainly about the writing of poetry—could that be the ground for any large claim as to the interest Stevens might command from literate readers? Imagination and reality—did that not increase the peril of regarding Stevens as a shuffler of epistemological categories? Neither gambit is enough; another way is needed for looking at the blackbird: not the only or the best, but another.

As the base of Stevens' work, as a force barely acknowledged yet always felt, lies a pressing awareness of human disorder in our time—but an awareness radically different from that of most writers. Only rarely does it emerge in his poems as a dramatized instance or fiction; Stevens seldom tries and almost never manages to evoke the modern disorder through representations of moral conduct or social conflict. When in *Owl's Clover* he did write a poem with a relatively explicit politics, the result, as he later acknowledged, was unfortunate: rhetoric overrunning thought, an assault upon a subject which as a poet Stevens was not prepared to confront.

Lacking that "novelistic" gift for portraiture-in-depth which is so valuable to a good many modern poets, Stevens does not examine society closely or even notice it directly for any length of time; he simply absorbs "the idea" of it. A trained connoisseur in chaos, he sees no need to linger before the evidence; there is enough already. And that is why it seems neither a paradox nor a conceit to say that in Stevens' poetry the social world is but dimly apprehended while a perspective upon history is brilliantly maintained: history as it filters through his consciousness of living and writing at a given time. The disorder that occupies the foreground of so much modern literature is calmly accepted by Stevens, appearing in his work not as a dominant subject but as a pressure upon all subjects.

In a somewhat similar way, Stevens, though sharply responsive to the crisis of belief which has troubled so many sensitive persons in the twentieth century, is not himself directly or deeply involved in it. He knows and feels it, but has begun to move beyond it. When he writes that . . .

> The death of Satan was a tragedy
> For the imagination. A capital
> Negation destroyed him in his tenement
> And, with him, many blue phenomena . . .

the force of these lines is clearly secular, releasing an attitude of comic humaneness. Perhaps they are also a little blasphemous, since it is hard to imagine a religious writer making quite this complaint about the consequences of the death of Satan. Here, as elsewhere in Stevens, a secular imagination measures the loss that it suffers from the exhaustion of religious myths and symbols, and then hopes that emotional equivalents can be found in . . .

> One's self and the mountains of one's land,
>
> Without shadows, without magnificence,
> The flesh, the bones, the dirt, the stone.

At times, it is true, Stevens can resemble the typical intellectual of his day (or the idea of the typical intellectual) and describes himself as "A most inappropriate man / In a most unpropitious place." He can appear to regret that "The epic of disbelief / Blares oftener and soon, will soon be constant." Yet if one compares him to Eliot and the later Auden, it becomes clear that Stevens is relatively free from religious or ideological nostalgia:

> The truth is that there comes a time
> When we can mourn no more over music
> That is so much motionless sound.
>
> There comes a time when the waltz
> Is no longer a mode of desire, a mode
> Of revealing desire and is empty of shadow.

Only occasionally does one find in Stevens that intense yearning for a real or imaginary past which has become so prevalent an attitude in our century. There is instead a recognition, both sensitive and stolid, of where we happen to be. And this, in Stevens' reckoning, imposes a new burden on the poet

> . . . since in the absence of a belief in God, the mind turns to its own
> creations and examines them, not alone from the esthetic point of view,
> but for what they reveal, for what they validate and invalidate, for the
> support they give.

Stevens is not, I think, directly affected by the usual religious or intellectual uncertainties, at least not nearly so much as by the predicament—and possibilities—of the mind experiencing them, the mind that still moves within the orbit of some waning belief yet strives for a direction and momentum of its own. Even in those poems, such as "Sunday Morning" and "The Comedian as Letter C," which do seem to deal explicitly with belief, one finds a recapitulation of a progress Stevens has already taken, not in freeing himself entirely from the crisis of belief or its emotional aftereffects (for to claim that would be impudent), but in learning to write as if in his poetic person he were a forerunner of post-crisis, post-ideological man. In "The Man With the Blue Guitar," where the guitar serves as the instrument of poetry, Stevens relates this role to an estimate, lovely in its comic modesty, of his own work:

> . . . Poetry
> Exceeding music must take the place
> Of empty heaven and its hymns,
> Ourselves in poetry must take their place,
> Even in the chatter of your guitar.

Yet Stevens is too much of a realist, too aware (as in "The Comedian as Letter C") of the sheer inertia of human existence, to suppose that the crisis of belief can be quickly overcome either by private decision or by public commitment.

Accepting the condition of uncertainty and solitariness as unavoidable to man once he has freed himself from the gods, Stevens poses as his ultimate question not, what shall we do about the crisis of belief, but rather, how shall we live with and perhaps beyond it? And one reason for thinking of Stevens as a comic poet is that he makes this choice of questions.

How shall we live with and then perhaps beyond the crisis of belief?—it is to confront this question that Stevens keeps returning to the theme of reality and imagination. Not merely because he is interested in epistemological forays as such—though he is; nor because he is fascinated with the creative process—though that too; but because his main concern is with discovering and, through his poetry, *enacting* the possibilities for human self-renewal in an impersonal and recalcitrant age.

How recalcitrant that age can be, Stevens knew very well. The fragmentation of personality, the loss of the self in its social roles, the problem of discovering one's identity amid a din of public claims—all this, so obsessively rehearsed in modern literature, is the premise from which Stevens moves to poetry. When Stevens does write directly about such topics, it is often with lightness and humor, taking easily on a tangent what other writers can hardly bear to face. An early little poem, "Disillusionment of Ten O'Clock," is about houses that are haunted by "white night-gowns," for Stevens the uniform of ordinariness and sober nights.

> None are green,
> Or purple with green rings,
> Or green with yellow rings,
> None of them are strange,
> With socks of lace
> And beaded ceintures.

In this flat world "People are not going/To dream of baboons and periwinkles." Only here and there an old sailor, one who by age and trade stands outside the perimeter of busy dullness . . .

> Drunk and asleep in his boots,
> Catches tigers
> In red weather.

I hope it will not seem frivolous if I suggest that this drunken sailor embodies a central intention of Stevens' mind, and that when Stevens in his later poems turns to such formidable matters as inquiries into the nature of reality or the relation between the perceiving eye and the perceived object, he still keeps before him the figure of that old sailor dreaming in red weather.

The elaborate conceptual maneuvers of Stevens' longer poems have as their objective not any conclusion in the realm of thought but a revelation in the realm of experience. They are written to rediscover, and help us rediscover, the human gift for self-creation; they try to enlarge our margin of autonomy; they are incitements to intensifying our sense of what remains possible even today. Each nuance of perspective noted in a Stevens poem matters not merely in its own right, but as a comic prod to animation, a nudge to the man whose eye is almost dead. And in Stevens' poetry the eye is the central organ of consciousness.

When Stevens writes about the writing of poetry, he needs to be read not only on the level of explicit statement, but also as if the idea of poetry were a synecdoche for every creative potential of consciousness, as if poetry were that which can help liberate us from the tyranny of mechanical life and slow dying. In that sense, Stevens is a revolutionist of the imagination, neither exhorting nor needing to exhort but demonstrating through poetry the possibilities of consciousness. And he can do this, among other reasons, because in the background of his work loom the defeats and losses of the century.

Time and again Stevens turns to the clause, "It is as if . . . ," for that clause charts a characteristic turning or soaring of his mind, which then is followed by another opening of perception. And these, in turn, are openings to the drama of the mind as it reaches out toward new modes of awareness and thereby "makes" its own life from moment to moment. There may be thirteen or three hundred and thirteen ways of looking at a blackbird, but what matters is that the eye, and the mind behind the eye, should encompass the life of these possible ways and the excitement of their variety. What also matters, as Mr. Richard Ellman has remarked, is that the mind behind the eye should remember that the blackbird, no matter how it may be seen, is always there in its mysterious tangibility.

Putting it this way I may seem to be making Stevens into a moralist of sorts: which readers awed by his urbanity of style might well take to be implausible. But in his relaxed and unhurried way Stevens is, I think, a moralist—a moralist of seeing.

Like any other convention, Stevens' utilization of the theme of reality and imagination as a means of reaching to his deeper concerns, can slide into formula and habit. His extraordinary gifts as a stylist aggravate rather than lessen this danger, since they allow him to keep spinning radiant phrases long after his mind has stopped moving. The reader accustomed to Stevens' habits and devices may even respond *too* well to the poems, for their characteristic inflections and themes have a way of setting off emotions which are proper to Stevens' work as a whole but have not been earned by the particular poem. At other times Stevens' insistence upon human possibility can itself become mechanical, a ruthlessness in the demand for joy. And perhaps the greatest weakness in his poems is a failure to extend the possibilities of self-renewal beyond solitariness or solitary engagements with the natural world and into the life of men living together. (Yet Stevens, humorous with self-knowledge, wrote some of his most poignant lines about this very limitation: "I cannot bring a world quite round,/Although I patch it as I can./I sing a hero's head, large eye/And bearded bronze, but not a man,/Although I patch him as I can/And reach through him almost to man.")

At his best, however, Stevens transforms each variant of perception into a validation of the self. Sometimes the self is to achieve renewal by a sympathetic merger with the outer world:

> One must have a mind of winter
> To regard the frost and the boughs
> Of the pine trees crusted with snow . . .

At other times the self gains a kind of assurance from entire withdrawal, as if to grant the outer world its own being. In "Nuance on a Theme by Williams," Stevens quotes William Carlos Williams' lines, "It's a strange courage/you give me, ancient star" and then proceeds to tell the star:

> Lend no part to any humanity that suffuses
> You in its own light.
> Be no chimera of morning,
> Half-man, half-star.

The act of discovery by which sentience is regained can

> Be the finding of a satisfaction, and may
> Be of a man skating, a woman dancing, a woman
> Combing. The poem of the act of the mind.

It may be a sheer pleasure in the freshness of the physical world:

> How should you walk in that space and know
> Nothing of the madness of space,
>
> Nothing of its jocular procreations?
> Throw the lights away. Nothing must stand
>
> Between you and the shapes you take
> When the crust of shape has been destroyed.

In the "Idea of Order at Key West" the self "takes over" the outer world by endowing it with a perceptual form:

> She was the single artificer of the world
> In which she sang. And when she sang, the sea,
> Whatever self it had, became the self
> That was her song, for she was the maker . . .

In "Three Travellers Watch a Sunrise," a play printed in *Opus Posthumous*, one of the voices says:

> Sunrise is multiplied
> Like the earth on which it shines,
> By the eyes that open on it,
> Even dead eyes,
> As red is multiplied by the leaves of trees.

And finally in Stevens' last poems, which form the glory of *Opus Posthumous*, the cleared mind listens for solitary sounds in winter, waiting patiently for death. These astonishing poems, like Chinese paintings in their profound simplicity and rightness, are Stevens' last probings, the last quiet efforts to realize life through connecting with whatever is not human. The idea of the world, now as lucid as its single sounds, becomes the final objection of contemplation:

> The palm at the end of the mind,
> Beyond the last thought, rises
> In the bronze distance,
> A gold-feathered bird
> Sings in the palm, without any human meaning,
> Without human feeling, a foreign song.

Reading these last poems one encounters again the theme of discovery, the desire to transform and renew, that has given shape to all of Stevens' work. Here, if anywhere, is the answer to Santayana's question, the "ultimate religion" of our secular comedy:

> The honey of heaven may or may not come,
> But that of earth both comes and goes at once.

[Review of *The Necessary Angel* and *Opus Posthumous*]

Henry Reed[*]

These two books, so far as this country is concerned, may perhaps be regarded as books for which we are not yet ready, but which will probably have immense value and charm for us when we are. I would be the last to underestimate their value and charm even now: but over here we are in a peculiar position as regards Stevens. Most of us don't, quite simply, know him well enough. It is not our fault entirely; but it is possible to feel, with some resentment, that when Stevens was finally published in England a few years ago, it was because the event could no longer be decently delayed. For well over thirty years Stevens has been an accepted part of the American scene; even for younger readers there, the mere previous presence of his work in the world will have quickened appreciation and enjoyment. They will know what comes where and when in his work; and this is important for intelligent love of any poet.

Here, alas, there is the dangerous possibility that the 150 pages of verse in *Opus Posthumous* may be used as an introduction, though the real interest of these poems for the habituated reader lies in the fact that Stevens himself rejected them from his *Collected Poems*. They are indeed for the most part specialists' material. It is usually possible to see why Stevens pushed them aside. This is so even in the case of *Owl's Clover*, one of Stevens's longest poems, constantly referred to by American critics. The editor of *Opus Posthumous*, who contributes a valuable introduction, has seen fit to publish a version of this poem that restores 200 or more lines deleted by Stevens in previously published versions (here inaccessible). This is no way to edit anything; or if it is, Stevens's cuts should surely have been indicated by brackets. Much of the poem is powerfully moving in a way rather unusual in Stevens: in it he is often more like "other" poets. He himself considered the poem "rhetorical", and out it went. But it brings us strangely near to him personally—rather as *Stephen Hero* does to Joyce, or *Jean Santeuil* does to Proust.

Most of the other things in *Opus Posthumous*, and the whole of *The Necessary Angel* (assembled by Stevens himself, and published in America in 1951) consist of public statements about poetry and poets. Many of the pieces are lectures, and perhaps suffer a little because of this: a lecture has to be fitted unnaturally to a certain length of time. Stevens writes with alluring grace even when he is appallingly difficult to follow. One is glad to sense a certain reluctance about the performance. Exhibitionism—that most damaging diversion for the creative man—is nowadays much encouraged in poets, both here and in America. Stevens resists this with fair nobility: but certainly the momentous statements we expect on such occasions are there; many of them have passed already into the reserve battery of useful quotes:

[*]Reprinted with permission from the *Listener* 63 (14 April 1960):675-76.

> What is his [the poet's] function? Certainly it is not to lead people out of the confusion in which they find themselves. Nor is it, I think, to comfort them while they follow their leaders to and fro. I think that his function is to make his imagination theirs and that he fulfils himself only as he sees his imagination become the light in the mind of others. His role, in short, is to help people to live their lives. Time and again it has been said that he may not address himself to an élite. I think he may. There is not a poet whom we prize living today that does not address himself to an élite. The poet will continue to do this: to address himself to an élite even in a classless society, unless, perhaps, this exposes him to prison or exile.

This is the poet who has often been called a dandy and a hedonist: the terms have not always been consciously dismissive: but they do in fact belittle him, even if indulgently. For the idiosyncrasies of Stevens's thought and expression are not merely endearing perversities: a man who pleads his agnosticism so earnestly must be taken seriously even if he does so with elegance, humour and calm.

This is a theme of his prose as of his verse. Indeed it may be his passionate delight in what we can do with our own imagination, and in the sense of a happy power over our own lives and the things we are called on to contemplate ("reality"): all this may still disconcert us. We are so doggedly used to the idea that poetry springs from repeated bouts of torment, religious or erotic, or is a repeated conquest of despair, or a repeated act of autotherapy, that it is still strange to find a poet who eschews conflict and seems to believe that the autotherapy must be done before the pen is set to paper. Stevens extends the possible consciousness of future poets by an unexpected valuation of psychic health. It is poignant to think that but for the insularity of English culture we might have been enjoying Stevens's work in the years when he was still alive to be thanked for it.

Essays

The Realistic Oriole:
A Study of Wallace Stevens

Northrop Frye*

Wallace Stevens was a poet for whom the theory and the practice of poetry were inseparable.[1] His poetic vision is informed by a metaphysic; his metaphysic is informed by a theory of knowledge; his theory of knowledge is informed by a poetic vision. He says of one of his long meditative poems that it displays the theory of poetry as the life of poetry (486), and in the introduction to his critical essays that by the theory of poetry he means "poetry itself, the naked poem" (*N.A.* viii). He thus stands in contrast to the dualistic approach of Eliot, who so often speaks of poetry as though it were an emotional and sensational soul looking for a "correlative" skeleton of thought to be provided by a philosopher, a Cartesian ghost trying to find a machine that will fit. No poet of any status—certainly not Eliot himself—has ever "taken over" someone else's structure of thought, and the dualistic fallacy can only beget more fallacies. Stevens is of particular interest and value to the critical theorist because he sees so clearly that the only ideas the poet can deal with are those directly involved with, and implied by, his own writing: that, in short, "Poetry is the subject of the poem" (176).

It has been established in criticism ever since Aristotle that histories are direct verbal imitations of action, and that anything in literature with a story in it is a secondary imitation of an action. This means, not that the story is at two removes from reality, but that its actions are representative and typical rather than specific. For some reason it has not been nearly so well understood that discursive writing is not thinking but a direct verbal imitation of thought; that any poem with an idea in it is a secondary imitation of thought, and hence deals with representative or typical thought: that is, with forms of thought rather than specific propositions. Poetry is concerned with the ambiguities, the unconscious diagrams, the metaphors and the images out of which actual ideas grow. Poet and painter alike operate in "the flux Between the thing as idea and the idea as thing" (295). Stevens is an admirable poet in whom to study the processes of

*Reprinted with permission by the author from Northrop Frye's *Fables of Identity* (New York: Harcourt, Brace & World, 1963).

poetic thought at work, and such processes are part of what he means by the phrase "supreme fiction" which enters the title of his longest poem. The poet, he says, "gives to life the supreme fictions without which we are unable to conceive of it" (*N.A.* 31), and fictions imitate ideas as well as events.

Any discussion of poetry has to begin with the field or area that it works in, the field described by Aristotle as nature. Stevens calls it "reality," by which he means, not simply the external physical world, but "things as they are," the existential process that includes ordinary human life on the level of absorption in routine activity. Human intelligence can resist routine by arresting it in an act of consciousness, but the normal tendency of routine is to work against consciousness. The revolution of consciousness against routine is the starting-point of all mental activity, and the centre of mental activity is imagination, the power of transforming "reality" into awareness of reality. Man can have no freedom except what begins in his own awareness of his condition. Naturally historical periods differ greatly in the amount of pressure put on free consciousness by the compulsions of ordinary life. In our own day this pressure has reached an almost intolerable degree that threatens to destroy freedom altogether and reduce human life to a level of totally preoccupied compulsion, like the life of an animal. One symptom of this is the popular demand that the artist should express in his work a sense of social obligation. The artist's primary obedience however is not to reality but to the "violence from within" (*N.A.* 36) of the imagination that resists and arrests it. The minimum basis of the imagination, so to speak, is ironic realism, the act of simply becoming aware of the surrounding pressures of "things as they are." This develops the sense of alienation which is the immediate result of the imposing of consciousness on reality:

> From this the poem springs: that we live in a place
> That is not our own and, much more, not ourselves. (383)

The "act of the mind" (240) in which imagination begins, then, is an arresting of a flow of perceptions without and of impressions within. In that arrest there is born the principle of form or order: the inner violence of the imagination is a "rage for order" (130). It produces the "jar in Tennessee" (76), the object which not only is form in itself, but creates form out of all its surroundings. Stevens follows Coleridge in distinguishing the transforming of experience by the imagination from the re-arranging of it by the "fancy," and ranks the former higher (ignoring, if he knew it, T. E. Hulme's clever pseudo-critical reversal of the two). The imagination contains reason and emotion, but the imagination keeps form concrete and particular, whereas emotion and reason are more apt to seek the vague and the general respectively.

There are two forms of mental activity that Stevens regards as unpoetic. One is the breaking down of a world of discrete objects into an amorphous and invisible substratum, a search for a "pediment of appearance" (361), a slate-colored world of substance (15, 96) which destroys all form and particularity, symbolized by the bodiless serpent introduced in "The Auroras of Autumn" (411), "form gulping after formlessness." This error is typically an error of reason. The other error is the breaking down of the individual mind in an attempt to make it a medium for some kind of universal or pantheistic mind. This is typically an error of emotion, and one that Stevens in his essay calls "romantic," which is a little confusing when his own poetry is so centrally in the Romantic tradition. What he means by it is the preference of the invisible to the visible which impels a poet to develop a false rhetoric intended to be the voice, not of himself, but of some invisible super-bard within him (N.A. 61). In "Jumbo" (269), Stevens points out that such false rhetoric comes, not from the annihilation of the ego, but from the ego itself, from "Narcissus, prince Of the secondary men." Such an attitude produces the "nigger mystic" (195, 265), a phrase which naturally has nothing to do with Negroes, but refers to the kind of intellectual absolute that has been compared to a night in which all cows are black, a world clearly no improvement on "reality," which is also one color (N.A. 26).

A third mode of mental activity, which is poetic but not Stevens' kind of poetry, is the attempt to suggest or evoke universals of mind or substance, to work at the threshold of consciousness and produce what Stevens calls "marginal" poetry and associates with Valéry (N.A. 115). Whatever its merit, such poetry for him is in contrast with "central" poetry based on the concrete and particular act of mental experience. Stevens speaks of the imagination as moving from the hieratic to the credible (N.A. 58), and marginal poetry, like the structures of reason and the surrenderings of emotion, seeks a "hierophant Omega" (469) or ultimate mystery. There is a strong tendency, a kind of intellectual death-wish, to conceive of order in terms of finality, as something that keeps receding from experience until experience stops, when it becomes the mirage of an "after-life" on which all hierophants, whether poets or priests, depend. But for the imagination "Reality is the beginning not the end" (469), "The imperfect is our paradise" (194), and the only order worth having is the "violent order" produced by the explosion of imaginative energy, which is also a "great disorder" (215).

This central view of poetry is for Stevens based on the straight Aristotelian principle that if art is not quite nature, at least it grows naturally out of nature. He dislikes the term "imitation," but only because he thinks it means the naive copying of an external world: in its proper Aristotelian sense of creating a form of which nature is the content, Stevens' poetry is as imitative as Pope's. Art then is not so much nature methodized as nature realized, a unity of being and knowing, existence and consciousness, achieved out of the flow of time and the fixity of space. In content it is reality and we are "Participants of its being" (463); in form it is an art which "speaks the feeling" for "things as they are" (424). All through Stevens' poetry we find the symbol of the alphabet or syllable, the imaginative key to reality which, by bringing reality into consciousness, heightens the sense of both, "A nature that is created in what it says" (490).

However, the imagination does bring something to reality which is not there in the first place, hence the imagination contains an element of the "unreal" which the imaginative form incorporates. This unreal is connected with the fact that conscious experience is liberated experience. The unreal, "The fabulous and its intrinsic verse" (31), is the sense of exhilaration and splendor in art, the "radiant and productive" atmosphere which it both creates and breathes, the sense of the virile and the heroic implied by the term "creative" itself, "the way of thinking by which we project the idea of God into the idea of man" (*N.A.* 150). All art has this essential elegance or nobility, including ironic realism, but the nobility is an attribute of art, not its goal: one attains it by not trying for it, as though it were definable or extrinsic. Although art is in one sense an escape from reality (i.e., in the sense in which it is an escape *of* reality), and although art is a heightening of consciousness, it is not enough for art simply to give one a vision of a better world. Art is practical, not speculative; imaginative, not fantastic; it transforms experience, and does not merely interrupt it. The unreal in imaginative perception is most simply described as the sense that if something is not there it at least ought to be there. But this feeling in art is anything but wistful: it has created the tone of all the civilizations of history. Thus the "central" poet, by working outwards from a beginning instead of onwards toward an end, helps to achieve the only genuine kind of progress. As Stevens says, in a passage which explains the ambivalence of the term "mystic" in his work: "The adherents of the central are also mystics to begin with. But all their desire and all their ambition is to press away from mysticism toward that ultimate good sense which we term civilization" (*N.A.* 116).

Such ultimate good sense depends on preserving a balance between objective reality and the subjective unreal element in the imagination. Exaggerating the latter gives us the false heroics that produce the aggressive symbols of warfare and the cult of "men suited to public ferns" (276). Exaggerating the former gives us the weariness of mind that bores the "fretful concubine" (211) in her splendid surroundings. Within art itself there has been a corresponding alternation of emphasis. In some ages, or with some poets, the emphasis is on the imaginative heightening of reality by visions of a Yeatsian "noble rider"

> On his gold horse striding, like a conjured beast,
> Miraculous in its panache and swish. (426)

At other times the emphasis is ironic, thrown on the minimum role of the imagination as the simple and subjective observer of reality, not withdrawn from it, but detached enough to feel that the power of transforming it has passed by. These two emphases, the green and the red as Stevens calls them

(340), appear in Stevens' own poetry as the summer vision and the autumn vision respectively.

The summer vision of life is the *gaya scienza* (248), the "Lebensweisheitspielerei" (504), in which things are perceived in their essential radiance, when "the world is larger" (514). This summer vision extends all over the *Harmonium* poems, with their glowing still lifes and gorgeous landscapes of Florida and the Caribbean coasts. Its dominating image is the sun, "that brave man" (138), the hero of nature who lives in heaven but transforms the earth from his mountain-top (65), "the strong man vaguely seen" (204). As "we are men of sun" (137), our creative life is his, hence the feeling of alienation from nature in which consciousness begins is really inspired by exactly the opposite feeling. "I am what is around me" (86), the poet says; the jar in Tennessee expresses the form in Tennessee as well as in itself, and one feels increasingly that "The soul . . . is composed Of the external world" (51) in the sense that in the imagination we have "The inhuman making choice of a human self" (*N.A.* 89), a subhuman world coming to a point of imaginative light in a focus of individuality and consciousness. Such a point of imaginative light is a human counterpart of the sun. The poet absorbs the reality he contemplates "as the Angevine Absorbs Anjou" (224), just as the sun's light, by giving itself and taking nothing, absorbs the world in itself. The echo to the great trumpet-call of "Let there be light" is "All things in the sun are sun" (104).

There are two aspects of the summer vision, which might be called, in Marvellian language, the visions of the golden lamp and of the green night. The latter is the more contemplative vision of the student in the tradition of Milton's penseroso poet, Shelley's Athanase, and Yeats's old man in the tower. In this vision the sun is replaced by the moon (33 ff.), or, more frequently, the evening star (25), the human counterpart of which is the student's candle (51, 523). Its personified form, corresponding to the sun, is often female, an "archaic" (223) or "green queen" (339), the "desired" (505) one who eventually becomes an "interior paramour" (524) or Jungian anima (cf. 321), the motionless spinning Penelope (520) to whom every voyager returns, the eternal Eve (271) or naked bride (395) of the relaxed imagination. Here we are, of course, in danger of the death-wish vision, of reading a blank book. Some of the irony of this is in "Phosphor Reading by his Own Light" (267), as well as in "The Reader" (146). The bride of such a narcist vision is the sinister "Madame La Fleurie" (507). But in its genuine form such contemplation is the source of major imagination (387-8), and hence Stevens, like Yeats, has his tower-mountain of vision or "Palaz of Hoon" (65; cf. 121), where sun and poet come into alignment:

> It is the natural tower of all the world,
> The point of survey, green's green apogee,
> But a tower more precious than the view beyond,
> A point of survey squatting like a throne,
> Axis of everything. (373)

From this point of survey we are lifted above the "cat," symbol of life absorbed in being without consciousness, and the "rabbit" who is "king of the ghosts" and is absorbed in consciousness without being (209, 223).

The autumnal vision begins in the poet's own situation. To perceive "reality" as dingy or unattractive is itself an imaginative act ("The Plain Sense of Things," 502), but an ironic act, an irony deepened by the fact that other modes of perception are equally possible, the oriole being as realistic as the crow (154), and there can be no question of accepting only one as true. It is a curious tendency in human nature to believe in disillusionment: that is, to think we are nearest the truth when we have established as much falsehood as possible. This is the vision of "Mrs. Alfred Uruguay" (248), who approaches her mountain of contemplation the wrong way round, starting at the bottom instead of the top. (Her name is apparently based on an association with "Montevideo.") The root of the reductive tendency, at least in poetry, is perhaps the transience of the emotional mood which is the framework of the lyric. In *Harmonium* the various elaborations of vision are seen as projected from a residual ego, a comedian (27 ff.) or clown (Peter Quince is the leader of a group of clowns), who by himself has only the vision of the "*esprit bâtard*" (102), the juggler in motley who is also a magician and whose efforts are "conjurations." When we add the clown's conjurations to the clown we get "man the abstraction, the comic sun" (156): the term "abstraction" will meet us again.

This *esprit bâtard* or dimmed vision of greater maturity, *un monocle d'un oncle*, so to speak, comes into the foreground after the "Credences of Summer" (372) and the "Things of August" (489) have passed by. In September the web of the imagination's pupa is woven (208); in November the moon lights up only the death of the god (107); at the onset of winter the auroras of a vanished heroism flicker over the sky, while in the foreground stand the scarecrows or hollow men of the present (293, 513).

To this vision belong the bitter "Man on the Dump" (201); the ironic "Esthétique du Mal" (313), with its urbane treatment of the religio-literary clichés, such as "The death of Satan was a tragedy For the imagination," which are the stock in trade of lesser poets, and the difficult and painfully written war poems. It is more typical of Stevens, of course, to emphasize the reality which is present in the imaginative heightening of misery, the drudge's dream of "The Ordinary Women" (10) which none the less reminds us that "Imagination is the will of things" (84). The true form of the autumnal vision is not the irony which robs man of his dignity, but the tragedy which confers it ("In a Bad Time," 426).

At the end of autumn come the terrors of winter, the sense of a world disintegrating into chaos which we feel socially when we see the annihilation wars of our time, and individually when we face the fact of death in others or for ourselves. We have spoken of Stevens' dislike of projecting the religious imagination into a world remote in space and time. The woman in "Sunday Morning" (66) stays home from church and meditates on religion surrounded by the brilliant oranges and greens of the summer vision, and in "A High-Toned Old Christian Woman" (59) it is suggested that the poet, seeking an increase rather than a diminishing of life, gets closer to a genuinely religious sense than morality with its taboos and denials. For Stevens all real religion is concerned with a renewal of earth rather than with a surrender to heaven. He even says "the great poems of heaven and hell have been written and the great poem of the earth remains to be written" (*N.A.* 142). It is part of his own ambition to compose hymns "Happy rather than holy but happy-high" (185) which will "take the place Of empty heavens" (167), and he looks forward to a world in which "all men are priests" (254). As this last phrase shows, he has no interest in turning to some cellophane-wrapped version of neo-paganism. He sees, like Yeats, that the poet is a "Connoisseur of Chaos" (215) aware that "Poetry is a Destructive Force" (192), and Stevens' imagery, for all its luxuriance and good humor, is full of menace. From the "firecat" of the opening page of the *Collected Poems*, through the screaming peacocks of "Domination of Black" (8), the buzzard of "The Jack-Rabbit" (50; cf. 318), the butcher of "A Weak Mind in the Mountains" (212), the bodiless serpent of "The Auroras of Autumn" (411) and the bloody lion of "Puella Parvula" (456), we are aware that a simple song of *carpe diem* is not enough.

In the later poems there is a growing preoccupation with death, as, not the end of life or an introduction to something unconnected with life, but as itself a part of life and giving to life itself an extra dimension. This view is very close to Rilke, especially the Rilke of the Orpheus sonnets, which are, like Stevens' poetry in general, "a constant sacrament of praise" (92). "What a ghastly situation it would be," Stevens remarks, "if the world of the dead was actually different from the world of the living" (*N.A.* 76), and in several poems, especially the remarkable "Owl in the Sarcophagus" (431), there are references to carrying on the memories or "souvenirs" of the past into a world which is not so much future as timeless, a world of recognition or "rendezvous" (524), and which lies in the opposite direction from the world of dreams:

> There is a monotonous babbling in our dreams
> That makes them our dependent heirs, the heirs
> Of dreamers buried in our sleep, and not
> The oncoming fantasies of better birth. (39)

In the poems of the winter vision the solar hero and the green queen become increasingly identified with the father and mother of a Freudian imago (439). The father and mother in turn expand into a continuous life throughout time of which we form our unitary realizations. The father, "the bearded peer" (494), extends back to the primordial sea (501), the mother to the original maternity of nature, the "Lady Lowzen" of "Oak Leaves are Hands" (272). In "The Owl in the Sarcophagus" these figures are personified as sleep and memory. The ambivalence of the female figure is expressed by the contrast between the "regina of the clouds" in "Le Monocle de mon Oncle" (13) and the "Sister and mother and diviner love" of "To the One of Fictive Music" (87). The poet determined to show that "being Includes death and the imagination" (444) must go through the same world as the "nigger mystic," for a "nigger cemetery" (150) lies in front of him too, just as the sunrise of the early play, *Three Travellers Watch a Sunrise*, is heralded by a hanged man. The search for death through life which is a part of such recreation leads to a final confronting of the self and the rock (*N.A.* viii), the identification of consciousness and reality in which the living soul is identified with its tombstone which is equally its body (528). In this final triumph of vision over death the death-symbols are turned into symbols of life. The author of the Apocalypse prophesies to his "back-ache" (which is partly the *Weltschmerz* of the past) that the venom of the bodiless serpent will be one with its wisdom (437). The "black river" of death, Swatara (428), becomes "The River of Rivers in Connecticut" (533), a river *this* side of the Styx which "flows nowhere, like a sea" because it is in a world in which there is no more sea.

If we listen carefully to the voice of "the auroral creature musing in the mind" (263), the auroras of autumn will become, not the after-images of remembrance, but the *Morgenrot* of a new recognition. As the cycle turns through death to a new life, we meet images of spring, the central one being some modification of Venus rising from the sea: the "paltry nude" of the poem of that name (5); "Infanta Marina" (7); Susanna lying in "A wave, interminably flowing" (92); "Celle qui fût Heaulmiette" (438) reborn from the mother and father of the winter vision, the mother having the "vague severed arms" of the maternal Venus of Milo. This reborn girl is the Jungian anima or interior paramour spoken of before, the "Golden Woman in a Silver Mirror" (460). She is also associated with the bird of Venus, "The Dove in the Belly" (366; cf. 357 and "Song of Fixed Accord," 519). It is also a bird's cry, but one outside the poet, which heralds "A new knowledge of reality" in the last line of the *Collected Poems*. The spring vision often has its origin in the commonplace, or in the kind of innocent gaudiness that marks exuberant life. Of the spring images in "Celle qui fût Heaulmiette" the author remarks affectionately, "Another American vulgarity"; the "paltry nude" is a gilded ship's prow, and the "emperor of ice-cream" presides over funeral obsequies in a shabby household (64). "It is the invasion of humanity That counts," remarks a character in *Three Travellers Watch a Sunrise*. "Only the rich remember the past," the poet says (225) and even in "Final Soliloquy of the Interior Paramour" (524) there is still a parenthetical association of new vision with a poverty which has nothing to lose.

In "Peter Quince at the Clavier" beauty is called "The fitful tracing of a portal." Portal to what? The word itself seems to mean something to Stevens (*N.A.* 60, 155), and in the obviously very personal conclusion of "The Rock" it is replaced by "gate" (528). Perhaps Stevens, like Blake, has so far only given us the end of a golden string, and after traversing the circle of natural images we have still to seek the centre.

The normal unit of poetic expression is the metaphor, and Stevens was well aware of the importance of metaphor, as is evident from the many poems which use the word in title or text. His conception of metaphor is regrettably unclear, though clearer in the poetry than in the essays. He speaks of the creative process as beginning in the perception of "resemblance," adding that metamorphosis might be a better word (*N.A.* 72). By resemblance he does not mean naive or associative resemblance, of the type that calls a flower a bleeding heart, but the repetitions of color and pattern in nature which become the element of formal design in art. He goes on to develop this conception of resemblance into a conception of "analogy" which, beginning in straight allegory, ends in the perception that "poetry becomes and is a transcendent analogue composed of the particulars of reality" (*N.A.* 130). But nowhere in his essays does he suggest that metaphor is anything more than likeness or parallelism. "There is always an analogy between nature and the imagination, and possibly poetry is merely the strange rhetoric of that parallel" (*N.A.* 118).

Clearly, if poetry is "merely" this, the use of metaphor could only accentuate what Stevens' poetry tries to annihilate, the sense of a contrast or great gulf fixed between subject and object, consciousness and existence. And in fact we often find metaphor used pejoratively in the poems as a form of avoiding direct contact with reality. The motive for metaphor, we are told, is the shrinking from immediate experience (288). Stevens appears to mean by such metaphor, however, simile or comparison, "the intricate evasions of as" (486; cf. "Add This to Rhetoric," 198). And metaphor is actually nothing of the kind. In its literal grammatical form metaphor is a statement of identity: this is that, A is B. And Stevens has a very strong sense of the crucial importance of poetic identification, "where as and is are one" (476), as it is only there that one finds "The poem of pure reality, untouched By trope or deviation" (471). Occasionally it occurs to him that metaphor might be used in a less pejorative sense. He speaks of "The metaphor that murders metaphor" (*N.A.* 84), implying that a better kind of metaphor can get murdered, and "Metaphor as Degeneration" (444) ends in a query how metaphor can really be degeneration when it is part of the process of seeing death as a part of life.

When metaphor says that one thing "is" another thing, or that a man, a woman and a blackbird are one (93), things are being identified *with* other things. In logical identity there is only identification *as*. If I say that the Queen of England "is" Elizabeth II, I have not identified one person with another, but one person as herself. Poetry also has this type of identification, for in poetic metaphor things are identified with each other, yet each is identified as itself, and retains that identity. When a man, a woman and a blackbird are said to be one, each remains what it is, and the identification heightens the distinctive form of each. Such a metaphor is necessarily illogical (or anti-logical, as in "A violent disorder is an order") and hence poetic metaphors are opposed to likeness or similarity. A perception that a man, a woman and a blackbird were in some respects alike would be logical, but would not make much of a poem. Unfortunately in prose speech we often use the word identical to mean very similar, as in the phrase "identical twins," and this use makes it difficult to express the idea of poetic identity in a prose essay. But if twins were really identical they would be the same person, and hence could be different in form, like a man and the same man as a boy of seven. A world of total simile, where everything was like everything else, would be a world of total monotony; a world of total metaphor, where everything is identified as itself and with everything else, would be a world where subject and object, reality and mental organization of reality, are one. Such a world of total metaphor is the formal cause of poetry. Stevens makes it clear that the poet seeks the particular and discrete image: many of the poems in *Parts of a World*, such as "On the Road Home" (203) express what the title of the book expresses, the uniqueness of every act of vision. Yet it is through the particular and discrete that we reach the unity of the imagination, which respects individuality, in contrast to the logical unity of the generalizing reason, which destroys it. The false unity of the dominating mind is what Stevens condemns in "The Bagatelles the Madrigals" (213), and in the third part of "The Pure Good of Theory" (331-2), where we find again a pejorative use of the term metaphor.

When a thing is identified as itself, it becomes an individual of a class or total form: when we identify a brown and green mass as a tree we provide a class name for it. This is the relating of species to genera which Aristotle spoke of as one of the central aspects of metaphor. The distinctively poetic use of such metaphor is the identifying of an individual with its class, where a tree becomes Wordsworth's "tree of many one," or a man becomes mankind. Poets ordinarily do not, like some philosophers, replace individual objects with their total forms; they do not, like allegorists, represent total forms by individuals. They see individual and class as metaphorically identical: in other words they work with *myths*, many of whom are human figures in whom the individual has been identified with its universal or total form.

Such myths, "archaic forms, giants Of sense, evoking one thing in many men" (494) play a large role in Stevens' imagery. For some reason he speaks of the myth as "abstract." "The Ultimate Poem is Abstract" (429; cf. 270, 223 and elsewhere), and the first requirement of the "supreme fiction" is that it must be abstract (380), though as far as dictionary meanings are concerned one would expect rather to hear that it must be concrete. By abstract Stevens apparently means artificial in its proper sense, something constructed rather than generalized. In such a passage as this we can see the myth forming out of "repetitions" as the individual soldier becomes the unknown soldier, and the unknown soldier the Adonis or continuously martyred god:

> How red the rose that is the soldier's wound,
> The wounds of many soldiers, the wounds of all

> The soldiers that have fallen, red in blood,
> The soldier of time grown deathless in great size. (318)

Just as there is false metaphor, so there is false myth. There is in particular the perverted myth of the average or "root-man" (262), described more expressively as "the total man of glubbal glub" (301). Whenever we have the root-man we have, by compensation, "The superman friseured, possessing and possessed" (262), which is the perversion of the idea of *Übermenschlichkeit* (98) into the Carlylean great man or military hero. Wars are in their imaginative aspect a "gigantomachia" (289) of competing aggressive myths. The war-myth or hero of death is the great enemy of the imagination: he cannot be directly fought except by another war-myth; he can only be contained in a greater and more genuine form of the same myth (280, section xv). The genuine form of the war-hero is the "major man" (334; 387-8) who, in "The Owl in the Sarcophagus," is personified as peace (434), the direct opposite of the war-hero, and the third of the figures in "the mythology of modern death" which, along with sleep and memory, conquer death for life.

We thus arrive at the conception of a universal or "central man" (250), who may be identified with any man, such as a fisherman listening to wood-doves:

> The fisherman might be the single man
> In whose breast, the dove, alighting, would grow still. (357)

This passage, which combines the myth of the central man with the anima myth of the "dove in the belly" (366), is from a poem with the painfully exact title, "Thinking of a Relation between the Images of Metaphors." The central man is often symbolized by glass or transparency, as in "Asides on the Oboe" (250) and in "Prologues to What is Possible" (515). If there is a central man, there is also a central mind (298) of which the poet feels peculiarly a part. Similarly there is a "central poem" (441) identical with the world, and finally a "general being or human universe" (378), of which all imaginative work forms part:

> That's it. The lover writes, the believer hears,
> The poet mumbles and the painter sees,
> Each one, his fated eccentricity,
> As a part, but part, but tenacious particle,
> Of the skeleton of the ether, the total
> Of letters, prophecies, perceptions, clods
> Of color, the giant of nothingness, each one
> And the giant ever changing, living in change. (443)

In "Sketch of the Ultimate Politician" (335) we get a glimpse of this human universe as an infinite City of Man.

To sum up: the imaginative act breaks down the separation between subject and object, the perceiver shut up in "the enclosures of hypothesis" (516) like an embryo in a "naked egg" (173) or glass shell (297), and a perceived world similarly imprisoned in the remoteness of its "irreducible X" (*N.A.* 83), which is also an egg (490). Separation is then replaced by the direct, primitive identification which Stevens ought to have called metaphor and which, not having a word for it, he calls "description" (339) in one of his definitive poems, a term to which he elsewhere adds "apotheosis" (378) and "transformation" (514; cf. *N.A.* 49), which come nearer to what he really means. The maxim that art should conceal art is based on the sense that in the greatest art we have no sense of manipulating, posing or dominating over nature, but rather of emancipating it. "One confides in what has no Concealed creator" (296), the poet says, and again:

> There might be, too, a change immenser than
> A poet's metaphors in which being would
>
> Come true, a point in the fire of music where
> Dazzle yields to a clarity and we observe,
>
> And observing is completing and we are content,
> In a world that shrinks to an immediate whole,
>
> That we do not need to understand, complete
> Without secret arrangements of it in the mind. (341)

The theoretical postulate of Stevens' poetry is a world of total metaphor, where the poet's vision may be identified with anything it visualizes. For such poetry the most accurate word is apocalyptic, a poetry of "revelation" (344) in which all objects and experiences are united with a total mind. Such poetry gives us:

> . . . the book of reconcilation,
> Book of a concept only possible
> In description, canon central in itself,
> The thesis of the plentifullest John. (345)

Apocalypse, however, is one of the two great narrative myths that expand "reality," with its categories of time and space, into an infinite and eternal world. A myth of a total man recovering a total world is hardly possible without a corresponding myth of a Fall, or some account of what is wrong with our present perspective. Stevens' version of the Fall is similar to that of the "Orphic poet" at the end of Emerson's *Nature*:

> Why, then, inquire
> Who has divided the world, what entrepreneur?
> No man. The self, the chrysalis of all men
>
> Became divided in the leisure of blue day
> And more, in branchings after day. One part
> Held fast tenaciously in common earth

And one from central earth to central sky
And in moonlit extensions of them in the mind
Searched out such majesty as it could find. (468-9)

Such poetry sounds religious, and in fact does have the infinite perspective of religion, for the limits of the imagination are the conceivable, not the real, and it extends over death as well as life. In the imagination the categories of "reality," space and time, are reversed into form and creation respectively, for art is "Description without Place" (339) standing at the centre of "ideal time" (N.A. 88), and its poetry is "even older than the ancient world" (N.A. 145). Religion seems to have a monopoly of talking about infinite and eternal worlds, and poetry that uses such conceptions seems to be inspired by a specifically religious interest. But the more we study poetry, the more we realize that the dogmatic limiting of the poet's imagination to human and subhuman nature that we find, for instance, in Hardy and Housman, is not normal to poetry but a technical *tour de force*. It is the normal language of poetic imagination itself that is heard when Yeats says that man has invented death; when Eliot reaches the still point of the turning world; when Rilke speaks of the poet's perspective as that of an angel containing all time and space, blind and looking into himself; when Stevens finds his home in "The place of meta-men and para-things" (448). Such language may or may not go with a religious commitment: in itself it is simply poetry speaking as poetry must when it gets to a certain pitch of metaphorical concentration. Stevens says that his motive is neither "to console Nor sanctify, but plainly to propound" (389).

In *Harmonium*, published in the Scott Fitzgerald decade, Stevens moves in a highly sensuous atmosphere of fine pictures, good food, exquisite taste and luxury cruises. In the later poems, though the writing is as studiously oblique as ever, the sensuousness has largely disappeared, and the reader accustomed only to *Harmonium* may feel that Stevens' inspiration has failed him, or that he is attracted by themes outside his capacity, or that the impact of war and other ironies of the autumnal vision has shut him up in an uncommunicative didacticism. Such a view of Stevens is of course superficial, but the critical issue it raises is a genuine one.

In the criticism of drama there is a phase in which the term "theatrical" becomes pejorative, when one tries to distinguish genuine dramatic imagination from the conventional clichés of dramatic rhetoric. Of course eventually this pejorative use has to disappear, because Shakespeare and Aeschylus are quite as theatrical as Cecil de Mille. Similarly, one also goes through a stage, though a shorter one, in which the term "poetic" may acquire a slightly pejorative cast, as when one may decide, several hundred pages deep in Swinburne, that Swinburne can sometimes be a poetic bore. Eventually one realizes that the "poetic" quality comes from allusiveness, the incorporating into the texture of echoes, cadences, names and thoughts derived from the author's previous literary experience. Swinburne is poetic in a poor sense when he is being a parasite on the literary tradition; Eliot is poetic in a better sense when, in his own phrase, he steals rather than imitates. The "poetic" normally expresses itself as what one might loosely call word-magic or incantation, charm in its original sense of spell, as it reinforces the "act of the mind" in poetry with the dream-like reverberations, echoes and enlarged significances of the memory and the unconscious. We suggested at the beginning that Eliot lacks what Stevens has, the sense of an autonomous poetic theory as an inseparable part of poetic practice. On the other hand Eliot has pre-eminently the sense of a creative tradition, and this sense is partly what makes his poetry so uniquely penetrating, so easy to memorize unconsciously.

In Stevens there is a good deal of incantation and imitative harmony; but the deliberately "magical" poems, such as "The Idea of Order at Key West," "To the One of Fictive Music," and the later "Song of Fixed Accord" have the special function of expressing a stasis or harmony between imagination and reality, and hence have something of a conscious rhetorical exercise about them. In "The Idea of Order at Key West" the sense of carefully controlled artifice enters the theme as well. In other poems where the texture is dryer and harder, the schemata on which "word-magic" depends are reduced to a minimum. The rhymes, for instance, when they occur, are usually sharp barking assonances, parody-rhymes (e.g., "The Swedish cart to be part of the heart," 369), and the metres, like the curious blank *terza rima* used so often, are almost parody-metres. A quality that is not far from being anti-"poetic" seems to emerge.

Just as the "poetic" is derived mainly from the reverberations of tradition, so it is clear that the anti-"poetic" quality in Stevens is the result of his determination to make it new, in Pound's phrase, to achieve in each poem a unique expression and force his reader to make a correspondingly unique act of apprehension. This is a part of what he means by "abstract" as a quality of the "supreme fiction." It was Whitman who urged American writers to lay less emphasis on tradition, thereby starting another tradition of his own, and it is significant that Whitman is one of the very few traditional poets Stevens refers to, though he has little in common with him technically. It is partly his sense of a poem as belonging to experiment rather than tradition, separated from the stream of time with its conventional echoes, that gives Stevens' poetry its marked affinity with pictures, an affinity shown also in the curiously formalized symmetry of the longer poems. "Notes toward a Supreme Fiction," for instance, has three parts of ten sections each, each section with seven tercets, and similarly rectangular distributions of material are found in other poems.

When we meet a poet who has so much rhetorical skill, and yet lays so much emphasis on novelty and freshness of approach, the skill acquires a quality of courage: a courage that is without compromise in a world full of cheap rhetoric, yet uses none of the ready-made mixes of rhetoric in a world full of compromise. Stevens was one of the most courageous poets of our time, and his conception of the poem as "the heroic effort to live expressed As victory" (446) was unyielding from the beginning. Courage implies persistence, and persistence in a distinctive strain often develops its complementary opposite as well, as with Blake's fool who by persisting in his folly became wise. It was persistence that transformed the tropical lushness of *Harmonium* into the austere clairvoyance of *The Rock*, the luxurious demon into the necessary angel, and so rounded out a vision of major scope and intensity. As a result Stevens became, unlike many others who may have started off with equal abilities, not one of our expendable rhetoricians, but one of our small handful of essential poets.

Note

1. All references to Stevens' poetry are accompanied by the page number in *The Collected Poems of Wallace Stevens*, 1954, and all references to his critical essays by the page number in *The Necessary Angel*, 1951, preceded by the letters *N.A.* I am sorry if this procedure makes the article typographically less attractive, but the proper place for such references, the margin, has disappeared from modern layout.

Wallace Stevens   J. Hillis Miller*

We were as Danes in Denmark all day long
And knew each other well, hale-hearted landsmen,
For whom the outlandish was another day

Of the week, queerer than Sunday. We thought alike
And that made brothers of us in a home
In which we fed on being brothers, fed

And fattened as on a decorous honeycomb.

There was once a time when man lived in harmony with his fellows and his surroundings. This harmony was a unified culture, a single view of things. Men thought alike and understood each other perfectly, like the most intimate of brothers. Since they shared an interpretation of the world they did not think of it as one perspective among many possible ones. It was the true picture of reality. Any other interpretation was queer, outlandish, something wild, ignorant, barbarian. Each man felt at home, like a Dane in Denmark, not a Dane in Greece or Patagonia. Just as he possessed his fellows in the brotherhood of a single culture, so he possessed nature through their collective interpretation of it. He was a landsman, an inlander, someone dwelling close to the earth. Since man, society, and environment made one inextricable unity, as of Danes in Denmark, no one

*Reprinted by permission of the publishers from J. Hillis Miller, *The Poets of Reality* (Cambridge, Mass.: Harvard University Press, 1965). © 1965 by the President and Fellows of Harvard College.

was aware of himself as a separate mind. Each was as much at home in the world as the bee in his honeycomb, the dwelling place which he has exuded from his own body and which now forms his food. All self-consciousness was lost in this reflexive feeding and fattening, and man "lay sticky with sleep."

So enduring and beneficent did this order seem that it was impossible to believe that man himself could have made it. Surely, we thought, our happy world must be the gift of some supernatural beings, and these gods must guarantee its rightness and permanence. They seemed outside or beyond our world, "speechless, invisible." They ruled us and sustained us "by / Our merest apprehension of their will." Our culture was revelation of the invisible and speech of the speechless gods.

Suddenly something catastrophic happened, and this happy order was destroyed:

> A tempest cracked on the theatre. Quickly,
> The wind beat in the roof and half the walls.
> The ruin stood still in an external world.
>
> . . . .
>
> It had been real. It was not now. The rip
> Of the wind and the glittering were real now,
> In the spectacle of a new reality.[1]

Once the theater is ruined it can never be rebuilt. The fact that it can be destroyed proves that even when it existed it was not what it seemed. It seemed a divine gift, something as solid as the earth itself. Now man knows that all along it was a painted scene. The true reality has always been the wind and the indifferent glittering of an external world, a world in which no man can ever feel at home.

When the tempest cracks on the theater the whole thing disintegrates: "exit the whole / Shebang" (CP, 37). Men are no longer brothers, but strange to each other. The land withdraws to a distance and comes to be seen as no longer included in man's interpretations of it. Only cold and vacancy remain "When the phantoms are gone and the shaken realist / First sees reality" (CP, 320). As soon as nature becomes outlandish the gods disappear like ghosts dissolving in sunlight. They do not withdraw for a time to an unattainable distance, as they did for De Quincey or Matthew Arnold. They vanish altogether, leaving nothing behind. They reveal themselves to be fictions, aesthetic projections of man's gratuitous values. Having seen the gods of one culture disappear, man can never again believe in any god. "The death of one god is the death of all" (CP, 381; see also OP, 165).

This vanishing of the gods, leaving a barren man in a barren land, is the basis of all Stevens' thought and poetry. His version of the death of the gods coincides with a radical transformation in the way man sees the world. What had been a warm home takes on a look of hardness and emptiness, like the walls, floors, and banisters of a vacant house. Instead of being intimately possessed by man, things appear to close themselves within themselves. They become mute, static presences:

> To see the gods dispelled in mid-air and dissolve like clouds is one of the great human experiences. It is not as if they had gone over the horizon to disappear for a time; nor as if they had been overcome by other gods of greater power and profounder knowledge. It is simply that they came to nothing. Since we have always shared all things with them and have always had a part of their strength and, certainly, all of their knowledge, we shared likewise this experience of annihilation. . . . It left us feeling dispossessed and alone in a solitude, like children without parents, in a home that seemed deserted, in which the amical rooms and halls had taken on a look of hardness and emptiness. What was most extraordinary is that they left no mementos behind, no thrones, no mystic rings, no texts either of the soil or of the soul. It was as if they had never inhabited the earth. There was no crying out for their return. (OP, 206, 207).

There was no crying out for their return because man knew they would never come back. They would never come back because they had never been there at all. In the impoverishing of the world when the gods disappear man discovers himself, orphaned and dispossessed, a solitary consciousness. Then are men truly "natives of poverty, children of malheur" (CP, 322). The moment of self-awareness coincides with the moment of the death of the gods. God is dead, therefore I am. But I am nothing. I am nothing because I have nothing, nothing but awareness of the barrenness within and without. When the gods dissolve like clouds they "come to nothing," and then man is "nothing himself." Since this is so, he "beholds / Nothing that is not there and the nothing that is" (CP, 10).

This nothing is an annihilating force which rejects everything fictitious. It wipes away each incipient reconstruction of the old harmony before it has had time to crystallize, and sees all "the integrations of the past" as a mere "Museo Olimpico" (CP, 342). The "nothing" is the resolute misery of the man who refuses to accept anything unreal as real and holds to the nothing within as that which destroys the blandishments of appearance. This rejection allows man to retain the nothing that *is* there. For this reason "poetry is a destructive force." As the poem of that title says, the positive nothing is as strong and real as would be a live ox breathing in the breast of a lion:

> That's what misery is,
> Nothing to have at heart.
> It is to have or nothing.
>
> It is a thing to have,
> A lion, an ox in his breast,
> To feel it breathing there. (CP, 192)

The destructive force of the nothing can be seen not only in the bewildering metamorphoses of the rest of the poem (from ox to dog to ox again, then to bear, and finally to man as embodiments of the inner nothing), but also in the dislocation of syntax in the sentence: "It is to have or nothing." The nothing is there in the reader's frustrated attempts to make logical sense of these words, and it is there in the absent object of the verb "to have": It is to have   or nothing. The sentence seems to say that misery is to have either nothing or nothing. If to have nothing is not to have something then man has nothing else.

What has caused this collapse of man's happy world, leaving him as in a hall of empty mirrors where nothing multiplies nothing? The answer to this question could be historical, an appeal to the world-destroying events which led to the appearance of a relativistic sense of the past in the eighteenth century, to Nietzsche's "Gott ist tot" in the nineteenth, and to the currents of nihilism in our own day. Stevens sometimes writes this way, as in "The Noble Rider and the Sound of Words" (1942). "[I]n speaking of the pressure of reality," he says, "I am thinking of life in a state of violence, not physically violent, as yet, for us in America, but physically violent for millions of our friends and for still more millions of our enemies and spiritually violent, it may be said, for everyone alive" (NA, 26, 27). But the real answer to the question is simpler than this, and in a way more disquieting. It takes no French or Copernican revolution, no catastrophic world wars, no industrializing of the world to overturn everything. A change of place or change of season is enough. Put a Dane in Patagonia and his sense of being at home will be blotted out, never to be unblotted. The first section of "The Comedian as the Letter C" is the story of this dissolution, a dissolution which happens as naturally and irrevocably as the falling of leaves in autumn.

Crispin has been at home in his New England milieu of "berries of villages," "simple salad-beds," and "honest quilts." He has been the "sovereign ghost" of his place, its "intelligence," "principium," and "lex" (CP, 27). A "simple jaunt" from Bordeaux to Yucatan, and then to Carolina by way of Havana is his undoing. The sea is a great heaving monster speaking its own incomprehensible speech, an inscrutable mystery to a mind accustomed to salad-beds and "mythology of self" is "blotched out beyond unblotching" (CP, 28). At the same time there is an annihilation of the residual sense that there are gods in nature. Triton dissolves to "faint, memorial gesturings, / That were like arms and shoulders in the waves" (CP, 29). The primitive feeling that nature is full of gods is replaced by self-conscious awareness that man has an incorrigible habit of personifying nature. Mythology of self and mythology of the world disappear together. What seemed the work of vast historical changes is accomplished in a moment by the confrontation of a mind equipped with its local mythology and a material reality which that mythology cannot comprehend. The regional fiction reveals itself as hollow, and so dissolves. Now man sees "The World without Imagination" (CP, 27). At the same time the self, deprived of its mythology, shrinks to nothing. The dialogue of the mind with itself commences, and Crispin becomes "an introspective voyager" (CP, 29).

Though this dissolving of the self is in one way the end of everything, in another way it is a happy liberation. There are only two entities left now that the gods are dead: man and nature, subject and object. Nature is the physical world, visible, audible, tangible, present to all the senses, and man is consciousness, the nothing which receives nature and transforms it into something unreal—"description without place" (CP, 339). In conceiving the world in this way Stevens inherits the tradition of dualism coming down from Descartes and the seventeenth century. Like that tradition generally, he is an unfaithful disciple of Descartes. The Cartesian God disappears from his world, and only mind and matter remain, mind confronting a matter which it makes into a mirror of itself. This bifurcation of reality is the universal human condition, from the creation until now:

> Adam
> In Eden was the father of Descartes
> And Eve made air the mirror of herself,
>
> Of her sons and of her daughters. (CP, 383)

If the natural activity of the mind is to make unreal representations, these are still representations of the material world. "The clouds preceded us / There was a muddy centre before we breathed" (CP, 383); matter is prior to mind and in some sense determines it. So, in "Sunday Morning," the lady's experience of the dissolution of the gods leaves her living in a world of exquisite particulars, the physical realities of the new world: "Deer walk upon our mountains, and the quail/Whistle about us their spontaneous cries; / Sweet berries ripen in the wilderness" (CP, 70). This physical world, an endless round of birth, death, and the seasons, is more lasting than any interpretation of it. Religions, myths, philosophies, and cultures are all fictions and pass away, but "April's green endures" (CP, 68).

"Sunday Morning" is Stevens' most eloquent description of the moment when the gods dissolve. Bereft of the supernatural, man does not lie down paralyzed in despair. He sings the creative hymns of a new culture, the culture of those who are "wholly human" and know themselves (CP, 317). This humanism is based on man's knowledge that "the final belief is to believe in a fiction, which you know to be a fiction, there being nothing else. The exquisite truth is to know that it is a fiction and that you believe in it willingly" (OP, 163). There is "nothing else"—the alternatives are to be nothing or to accept a fiction. To discover that there never has been any celestial world is a joyful liberation, and man says of himself: "This happy creature—It is he that invented the Gods. It is he that put into their mouths the only words they have ever spoken!" (OP, 167).

To discover that man has invented the gods is to find out the dependence of the mind on nature. Mental fictions are derived from material things: "All of our ideas come from the natural world: trees=

umbrellas" (OP, 163). Since this is true, the only way to give mental fictions authenticity is to base them on the world of sun and rain and April: "The real is only the base. But it is the base" (OP, 160). When Stevens speaks this way, he is a poet of a happy naturalism. In many eloquent passages he celebrates the joy of "the latest freed man" (CP, 204), the man who has escaped from the gods and is able to step barefoot into reality. This man has shed the old myths as a snake sheds its skin, and can cry in exultation: "the past is dead. / Her mind will never speak to me again. / I am free" (CP, 117). Liberated from the bad faith which attributed to some never-never land the glory of earth, man does not lose the golden glory of heaven. He transfers to what is close and real, the "in-bar," what he had falsely ascribed to transcendent realms, the "ex-bar" (CP, 317). Culture has always been based on the permanences of sun, air, and earth. Now man knows that this is so. He knows that "The greatest poverty is not to live / In a physical world" (CP, 325), and this brings about a sudden miraculous recovery of the vitality of earth.

But umbrellas are not trees. Even the nakedest man is not part of nature in the same way that stones or trees are. Man possesses imagination, and, though "the imagination is one of the forces of nature" (OP, 170), the peculiar potency of this force is to transform nature, to make trees into umbrellas. In changing nature, the imagination irradiates it with its own idiosyncratic hue. The poet must accept this distortion as in the nature of things. The green of reality is altered by the blue of imagination, and there is no helping this fact. The mind turns to reality and is enriched by it, but it also shapes the real into myths, religions, and other forms of poetry. The worst evil is a victory of one power over the other, a romanticism which kicks itself loose of the earth, or a pressure of reality so great that it overwhelms imagination. "Eventually an imaginary world is entirely without interest" (OP, 175), but, on the other hand, man today is confronting events "beyond [his] power to reduce them and meta-morphose them" (NA, 22), and as a result "There are no shadows anywhere. / The earth, for us, is flat and bare" (CP, 167). Fresh fictions must now replace the old. The creation, after the death of the gods, of new fictions, based on fact and not pretending to be more than fictions, is the act of poetry. "After one has abandoned a belief in God, poetry is that essence which takes its place as life's redemption" (OP, 158). In defining poetry as a substitute for religion Stevens is joining himself to a tradition extending from the romantics through Matthew Arnold down to our own day.

The dialogue between subject and object is Stevens' central theme, and it seems that this interchange can become a "mystic marriage," like that of the great captain and the maiden Bawda in "Notes toward a Supreme Fiction" (CP, 401). Imagination and reality can merge to produce a third thing which escapes from the limitations of either, and we can triumphantly "mate [our] life with life" (CP, 222). "If it should be true that reality exists / In the mind . . . it follows that / Real and unreal are two in one" (CP, 485). The red of reality and the blue of imagination join to become the "purple tabulae" on which may be read the poem of life (CP, 424). It is not necessary to choose between Don Quixote and Sancho Panza. Man can have both, and poetry is the search for those fortuitous conjunctions between self and world which show that they are not irreconcilable opposites, but two sides of the same coin, "equal and inseparable" (NA, 24).

The poverty following the death of the gods can apparently be transcended without difficulty. Stevens' real choice is neither for the subjectivism coming down from Descartes nor for the submission to physical nature which he sometimes praises. His tradition is rather perspectivism, historicism, *lebensphilosophie*. He is one of the subtlest expositors of this tradition. His predecessors are Feuerbach, Dilthey, Nietzsche, Ortega y Gasset, Santayana, and Henri Focillon, the Focillon whose *Vie des formes* Stevens calls "one of the really remarkable books of the day" (NA, 46). Like these thinkers, Stevens sees human history as the constant proliferation of forms of art and culture which are valid only for one time and place. These are determined exclusively neither by geography nor by the untrammeled human mind, but everywhere are the offspring of a marriage of man and the place where he lives. The fact that one man's fictions can be accepted by others makes society possible. "An age is a manner collected from a queen./An age is green or red. An age believes/Or it denies," and "Things are as they seemed to Calvin or to Anne/Of England, to Pablo Neruda in Ceylon,/To Nietzsche in Basel, to Lenin by a Lake" (CP, 340, 341, 342).

In human history two things are constantly happening. Men are always being bent to their environment, driven to make their life forms a mirror of the weather of their place, for "the gods grow out of the weather./The people grow out of the weather" (CP, 210), and "the natives of the rain are rainy men" (CP, 37). On the other hand, the mind organizes the land in which it finds itself, as the moon makes concentric circles in the random twigs of a leafless tree, or as the jar in Tennessee orders the wilderness around it and takes dominion everywhere. The jar is a human artifact. Its man-made shape has the power to structure everything radially around it, as the red queen makes a whole age red. The jar is one of the "Imaginary poles whose intelligence/Stream[s] over chaos their civilities" (CP, 479).

Stevens' work can be summed up in two adages: "The soul . . . is composed/Of the external world" (CP, 51); "It is never the thing but the version of the thing" (CP, 332). His poetry is the reconciliation of these two truths, truths which are always simultaneously binding in the endless intercourse of imagination and reality. Words are the best marriage-place of mind and world. In language a people gives speech to its environment, and at the same time it creates itself in that speech. Language is at once the expression of a style of life and the embodiment of a local weather and geography. . . .

Note

1. The following texts of Stevens' work have been used in this chapter. Each is accompanied by the abbreviation which will hereafter be employed in citations. *The Necessary Angel: Essays on Reality and the Imagination* (New York: Alfred A. Knopf, 1951): NA; *The Collected Poems of Wallace Stevens* (New York: Alfred A. Knopf, 1954): CP; *Opus Posthumous* (New York: Alfred A. Knopf, 1957): OP. Quotations in the initial paragraphs of this chapter come, respectively, from CP, 419, 419, 262, 262, 306.

Reduction to the First Idea   Harold Bloom[*]

Early in 1918, Stevens wrote his version of a "war poem," *The Death of a Soldier:*

> Life contracts and death is expected,
> As in a season of autumn.
> The soldier falls.
>
> He does not become a three-days personage,
> Imposing his separation,
> Calling for pomp.
>
> Death is absolute and without memorial,
> As in a season of autumn,
> When the wind stops,
>
> When the wind stops and, over the heavens,
> The clouds go, nevertheless,
> In their direction.

I think that readers deeply versed in Stevens recognize in this poem, as in *The Snow Man*, written three years later, the emergence of the poet's most characteristic voice. *The Death of a Soldier* introduces Stevens the reductionist, though it does not show us the goal of his reductiveness, the First Idea, which enters his poetry with *The Snow Man*. Stevens later found a term in Simone Weil for his process of reduction, the rather inappropriate term "decreation." His own *Mrs. Alfred Uruguay*, of 1940, a far more exuberant being than Simone Weil, splendidly defines reductiveness as having "said no / To everything, in order to get at myself. / I have wiped away moonlight like mud." When Stevens, in a letter, attempted an explanation of the First Idea, in regard to *Notes toward a Supreme Fiction*, he gave a wholly positive tone to his most reductive thinking: "If you take the varnish and dirt of generations off a picture, you see it in its first idea. If

[*]Reprinted with permission from *Diacritics* 6 (Fall 1976):48-57 and Harold Bloom's *Wallace Stevens: The Poems of Our Climate* (Ithaca: Cornell University Press, 1977).

you think about the world without its varnish and dirt, you are a thinker of the first idea" (*L*, 426-27).

The only relevant philosophical notion would seem to be C. S. Peirce's Idea of Firstness. In a letter of 1944, Stevens said he long had been curious about Peirce but implied that other interests had kept him from reading the philosopher. Yet he may have seen some summary of Peirce, or quotation from Peirce, since the First Idea and the Idea of Firstness are so close. Stevens emphasizes a stripped-down idea of the sun, while Peirce cites a heliotrope as one instance of Firstness. Firstness is the chance variation or *clinamen* of any one felt quality in relation to any other, that is, an Idea of Firstness is a mere appearance, an "unanalyzed total impression made by any manifold not thought of as actual fact, but simply as a quality."

Whether or not Peirce contributed to Stevens' notion, the need to get down to a First Idea seems always to have inhered in Stevens' consciousness. He does not name the First Idea as such until he writes *Notes toward a Supreme Fiction* in 1942, but *Harmonium* contains the notion and process without the name. The root meaning of "first" is "forward" or "early," and the root meaning of "idea" is "to see." We might say that a First Idea always involves priority, "to see earliest," which makes it a necessity for a poet like Stevens, who could not tolerate any sensation of belatedness and who refused to acknowledge the influence of any precursors.

But what has the First Idea, or an idea of Firstness, to do with the poem *The Death of a Soldier*? Stevens seeks what is not possible, in a tradition that goes back to Homer yet never has gone beyond Homer. He seeks to see earliest what the death of a soldier is. His reduction is fourfold:

1) The soldier falls expectedly, in and by seasonal contraction; this is the primal *ethos*, the soldier's character as it is autumn's, and so a limitation of meaning.

2) The soldier is not and has no part in Christ; he will not rise, after three days, separated from the common fate and requiring celebration.

3) Any death, by synecdoche, is as final in itself and beyond language as is an autumnal moment of stasis.

4) That is, any death is also without consequence, in the context of natural sublimity; for us, below the heavens, there is stasis, but the movement of a larger intentionality always goes on above the heavens.

As paraphrase, this omits what matters about the poem, which is rhetorical gesture, tonal *askesis*, dignity of a minimal *pathos*, excluding lament. Yet what it most omits is the poem's undersong, which is its *logos* or crossing. Rhetorically, the poem intimates that any such earliest seeing of a soldier's death is dehumanizing, intolerable, not to be sustained. This brief poem is almost all *ethos*, all contraction; the human in us demands more of a poem, for us, and where *pathos* is so excluded a death-in-life comes which is more that of the poem's shaper, speaker, reader than it could have been of the fictive soldier before he fell.

This self-chastisement of the First Idea, by the First Idea itself, is worked out with startling dialectical skill in a triad of poems written in 1921, which seem to me to possess among them all the elements that were to emerge, in triumphant integration, two decades later in *Notes toward a Supreme Fiction*. The reader who masters the interrelationships of these three brief texts, *The Man Whose Pharynx Was Bad*, *The Snow Man*, and *Tea at the Palaz of Hoon*, has reached the center of Stevens' poetic and human anxieties and of his resources for meeting those anxieties. I will read the three poems as though they formed one larger, dialectical lyric when run together, akin to Coleridge's *Dejection: An Ode* and Wordsworth's *Intimations* ode. The *Pharynx* poem states the crisis of poetic vision; *The Snow Man* meets the crisis by a reduction to the First Idea; exuberantly, the great hymn of Hoon, so invariably misread as irony, reimagines the First Idea and restitutes, momentarily yet transumptively, the contraction of meaning provoked by the crisis. We can say, in the terms I have been developing, that the *Pharynx* poem is answered first by a poem of Fate and then by a poem of Power. Freedom lies between, in the *aporia* that separates the Snow Man and Hoon, the grand reductionist and the still grander expansionist. But twenty years will have to pass before Stevens will know how to write his great poem of that Freedom, *Notes toward a Supreme Fiction*.

The poet begins as the man who has more than a psychic sore throat; he has writer's block, *acedia*: "I am too dumbly in my being pent." The malady, as I now unsurprisingly suggest, is a badly repressed case of the anxiety of influence, manifested here as the inability to achieve earliest seeings. In the poem's last line, we are assured that belatedness is the context of the illness: "But time will not relent." A reader needs to beware of the Flaubertian colorings of the poem. "The grand ideas of the villages" and "The malady of the quotidian" unquestionably are indebted to the complex ironies of *Madame Bovary* and the *Sentimental Education*. But French colorings in Stevens, in *Harmonium* and after, invariably are evasions of more embarrassing obligations to Anglo-American literary tradition. The *ennui* of Flaubert or of Baudelaire is invoked to mask the more domestic "diffident" turns of the crisis-precursors: Coleridge, Wordsworth, Shelley, Keats, Tennyson, but more strongly still the masters of the Native Strain: Emerson, Whitman, Dickinson. Summer and winter here, the weather of the mind as of the sky, belong to the seasons of the soul in High Romanticism. The oceans, as elsewhere in Stevens, are from Whitman's *Sea-Drift* Kosmos, and the deprecated function of the poet is the Emersonian and American one, to be a new orator, even if spouting, of the cold. Nature, in Stevens' poem, is Coleridgean and Emersonian nature, rather than the post-Rousseauistic nature of Flaubert and Baudelaire. This nature is *ethos* or Fate, a universe of death whose cyclic repetitions can be broken through only by transgressive acts of origination, an origination that can be performed only as and by the Will, the *pathos* or *potentia* of Power.

Two years before, in 1919, Stevens had written a cruder version of his *Pharynx* poem in *Banal Sojourn*:

Two wooden tubs of blue hydrangeas stand at the foot of the
    stone steps.
The sky is a blue gum streaked with rose. The trees are black.
The grackles crack their throats of bone in the smooth air.
Moisture and heat have swollen the garden into a slum of bloom.
Pardie! Summer is like a fat beast, sleepy in mildew,
Our old bane, green and bloated, serene, who cries,
"That bliss of stars, that princox of evening heaven!" reminding
    of seasons,
When radiance came running down, slim through the bareness.
And so it is one damns that green shade at the bottom of the land.
For who can care at the wigs despoiling the Satan ear?
And who does not seek the sky unfuzzed, soaring to the princox?
One has a malady, here, a malady. One feels a malady.

Stevens, with only rare exceptions, did not comment very usefully upon his own poems. This is not one of the exceptions. Of it, he remarked: "*Banal Sojourn* is a poem of (exhaustion in August!) The mildew of any late season, of any experience that has grown monotonous as, for instance, the experience of life" (*L*, 464). Repeated readings of *Banal Sojourn* may not convince that the malady is monotony or all of life having become a belatedness. The malady appears to be again that "no spring can follow post meridian," or that the poet feels acutely the universal nostalgia that he is now a touch old to be what clearly he never was, a "princox," a roaring boy or saucy fellow. Instead he is rather august, green and bloated like the season, "sleepy in mildew," not in "the immense dew of Florida," and damning with considerable gusto his not-so-Marvellian retirement into that green shade. What the poem shows, more uneasily even than the *Pharynx* poem will show, is Stevens' anxiety that the poetic voice in him may fail, an anxiety rendered more acute by an imaginative maturity so long delayed.

The Man Whose Pharynx Was Bad offers itself two ways out of crisis, the one of Hoon-like expansion and the other a Snow Man's reduction. But the summer possibility was edited out by Stevens when he included the poem in the second edition of *Harmonium*. By mutilating his poem he exposed a fear of his own capacity for solipsistic transport, and we can be grateful that the lines have been restored to us:

> Perhaps, if summer ever came to rest
> And lengthened, deepened, comforted, caressed
> Through days like oceans in obsidian
>
> Horizons full of night's midsummer blaze.

Horizons like volcanic glass would be both black and shiny, and the horizons epitomize the baffling attractions of this passage, with its Edenic days that are gorgeous nights, the oceanic sense all but infinitely extended. From this Sublime of *pathos*, Stevens characteristically recoils, in lines he felt no hazard in retaining:

> Perhaps, if winter once could penetrate
> Through all its purples in the final slate,
> Persisting bleakly in an icy haze;
>
> One might in turn become less diffident.

Certainly he recalls the trope of *ethos* in stanza VI of *Le Monocle*: "The basic slate, the universal hue." As certainly, he thus suggested to himself the very ecstasy of reduction, *The Snow Man*, on which the critics of Stevens too frequently follow Stevens by seeing the poem as a *celebration* of the Freudian reality principle. But here I want to urge a very comprehensive reading indeed.

I've said that there may be a link between Peirce's Idea of Firstness and Stevens' First Idea, but Peirce himself was in one sense in Emerson's tradition, in his view of Fate. More profoundly, Stevens in this notion is the direct heir of several traditions. One passes from Montaigne through Pascal to Descartes and ultimately leads to Valéry in our time. Another embraces Emerson, Pater, and Nietzsche in the nineteenth century, as well as certain related figures, including Whitman and Ruskin. A third, more specifically American, includes William James, Santayana, and such Emersonian poets as E. A. Robinson and Frost. The fourth is not so much a tradition as it is one titan without true precursors, Freud. All these strains have in common the quest for a reality principle, a moral, aesthetic, and psychological reductiveness willing to risk the ruin brought about by the destruction of illusions, in oneself and in others, by knowing the worst truths about our condition. None of these strains falls into the reductive fallacy, which is to assume that the ultimate truth about us is, by definition, the very worst that can be said about us. Stevens frequently was tempted to that fallacy, and he fought against the temptation. To use the Emersonian terms, Fate in Stevens is the First Idea, Freedom is the realization that the First Idea cannot suffice, and Power or Will is a finding of what may suffice, a revision of the First Idea.

That is, of course, rather too much tradition to apply to *The Snow Man*, complex as this brief poem is. I will confine my account of the poem's anteriority to some inescapable precursors: Ruskin on what he called the pathetic fallacy; Emerson in *Nature* experiencing his notorious metamorphosis into a transparent eyeball; Whitman, at the close of *Song of Myself*, diffusing himself in air; Nietzsche, propounding the will; and lastly, but I think most crucially, Shelley, reinventing the Homeric-Miltonic figuration of the leaves in a form that was to haunt Stevens till the very end.

The voice speaking *The Snow Man*, which by the end of the poem has become the voice of the Snow Man, urgently seeks to avoid any indulgence of the pathetic fallacy. There is no evidence that Stevens knew Ruskin well, but he is rather likely to have known the most famous passage in *Modern Painters*. Here is a cento of Ruskin on the pathetic fallacy, from *Modern Painters*, III (1856), where he begins by saying the point in question is the difference between the ordinary, proper, and true appearances of things to us; and the extraordinary, or false appearances, when we are under the influence of emotion, or contemplative fancy; false appearances, I say, as being entirely unconnected with any real power or character in the object, and only imputed to it by us. . . .

When Dante describes the spirits falling from the bank of Acheron "as dead leaves flutter from a bough," he gives the most perfect image possible of their utter lightness, feebleness, passiveness, and scattering agony of despair, without, however, for an instant losing his own clear perception that *these* are souls, and *those* are leaves; he makes no confusion of one with the other. But when Coleridge speaks of

> The one red leaf, the last of its clan,
> That dances as often as dance it can,

he has a morbid, that is to say, a so far false, idea about the leaf; he fancies a life in it, and will, which there are not; confuses its powerlessness with choice, its fading death with merriment, and the wind that shakes it with music.

The temperament which admits the pathetic fallacy, is . . . that of a mind and body in some sort too weak to deal fully with what is before them or upon them; borne away, or over-clouded, or over-dazzled by emotion; and it is a more or less noble state, according to the force of the emotion which has induced it. For it is no credit to a man that he is not morbid or inaccurate in his perceptions, when he has no strength of feeling to warp them; and it is in general a sign of higher capacity and stand in the ranks of being, that the emotions should be strong enough to vanquish, partly, the intellect, and make it believe what they choose. But it is still a grander condition when the intellect also rises, till it is strong enough to assert its rule against, or together with, the utmost efforts of the passions; and the whole man stands in an iron glow, white hot, perhaps, but still strong, and in no wise evaporating; even if he melts, losing none of his weight.

If one were to print just these Ruskinian extracts as a critique of *The Snow Man*, one would be rather closer to the poem than many of its exegetes have been, even though Ruskin's Snow Man is "the whole man" glowing with his own heat. Pragmatically, this difference makes little difference; both fictive "men" will melt, though only one will evaporate. But though the problematic is shared, Ruskin and Stevens do differ, complexly and subtly. Where is the emphasis in Ruskin? Is it on the *pathos*, or the untruth, in Romantic trope?

I recall having written, in another context, that Ruskin's analysis of the pathetic fallacy is an attack against Wordsworthian imagistic homogeneities, an attack implying that such homogeneities were the product of a Romantic further estrangement of the object-world, and so of a dualism more extreme even than the Cartesian vision that Romanticism supposedly wished to overturn. I am more inclined to this judgment than before. When

Wordsworth and Coleridge speak of a joy in seeing the beauty of nature, they rejoice in their own reductions to a First Idea, their own initial substitutions of the tropes and topics of *ethos* for those of *pathos*. When they go on to further substitutions and arrive at figurations of *pathos*, then they arouse in their ephebe, Ruskin, an acutely ambivalent response. He distrusts both their mode of limitation and their mode of representation, yet he knows that such modes are inevitable for "reflective" poetry, his word for a consciously belated poetry, for a heightened rhetoricity.

Though he was to lose this balance later, the Ruskin of *Modern Painters*, III, is persuasively and sanely judicious in his view of the Romantic trope or pathetic fallacy as a necessary lie against nature and so also against time. Whereas the classical and medieval poets and painters, according to Ruskin, expressed the actual qualities of the thing itself, the Renaissance and modern artists first made the thing itself into an imagined thing and then reimagined that already altered object. Stevens, in *The Snow Man*, is less judicious than Ruskin, or perhaps ironically he is willing to *appear* less judicious. He knows, as Ruskin does, that no modern can write a poem without tropes of *pathos* dominating, yet he writes a poem that *seems* to exclude *pathos* or at least announces as its manifesto the intention of such an exclusion:

> One must have a mind of winter
> To regard the frost and the boughs
> Of the pine-trees crusted with snow;
>
> And have been cold a long time
> To behold the junipers shagged with ice,
> The spruces rough in the distant glitter
>
> Of the January sun; and not to think
> Of any misery in the sound of the wind,
> In the sound of a few leaves,
>
> Which is the sound of the land
> Full of the same wind
> That is blowing in the same bare place
>
> For the listener, who listens in the snow,
> And, nothing himself, beholds
> Nothing that is not there and the nothing that is.

Is there a difference, for Stevens, between regarding and beholding, or is this merely an elegant variation? How would the poem change if it ended saying that "the listener . . . nothing himself, regards / Nothing that is not there and the nothing that is"? In the immensely moving *Nomad Exquisite*, my personal favorite in *Harmonium*, the hymn-maker is a beholder beholding rather than a regarder regarding. I think that the difference is very much there, in Stevens, and that, as almost always, he is an orator with accurate speech. To "behold" is to gaze at or look upon, but with a touch of expressed amazement. The beholder *possesses* the object; his scrutiny is active, going back to the root *kel*, meaning to drive or to set in swift motion. To "regard" is a warier and more passive verb. It is to look at something attentively or closely, but with a touch of looking back at, a retrospect, stemming ultimately from the root *wer*, meaning to watch out for something. *The Snow Man* starts with a wary "regard" that is replete with negative intentionality, prophesying such characteristic later Stevensian instances as those in *Dry Loaf*, in *Credences of Summer*, IX, most memorably in the *Auroras* where the father sits in space "of bleak regard," and in *The Rock* where the poet must "regard the freedom of seventy years ago" and finds, "It is no longer air." When *The Snow Man* closes, with the hint of an amazement of possession in "beholds," we encounter one of Stevens' most persistent, even obsessive verbs. From a wealth of instances, we might choose Crispin the Comedian who, when he beheld, "was made new," or the vision of the singing girl at Key West, "as we beheld her striding there alone," or the beholding of the Sublime in *The American Sublime*, or most movingly the grand *pathos* of the final lines of *Extracts from Addresses to the Academy of Fine Ideas*:

> Behold the men in helmets borne on steel,
> Discolored, how they are going to defeat.

I venture the formula that, in Stevens, "regard" tends to introduce a trope of *ethos* or of Fate, or of a reduction to the First Idea, while "behold" tends to commence a trope of *pathos* or of Power, a revision or reimagining of the First Idea. When Stevens "regards," he indeed guards again and guards against, and here at the opening of *The Snow Man* it is against the major Romantic fiction of the leaves, which is not the Coleridgean passage from *Christabel* quoted by Ruskin but is of course this:

> Thou, from whose unseen presence the leaves dead
> Are driven, like ghosts from an enchanter fleeing,
>
> Yellow, and black, and pale, and hectic red,
> Pestilence-stricken multitudes.

Nothing could be more unlike Stevens, in tone, burden, and spirit, and yet no poem haunts his poetry more. I will return to Shelley's poem often again, in discussing the conclusion of *Like Decorations in a Nigger Cemetery*, section XXVIII of *The Man with the Blue Guitar*, *The Motive for Metaphor*, *Notes toward a Supreme Fiction*, *The Auroras of Autumn*, *An Ordinary Evening in New Haven*, *The Rock*, and *The Course of a Particular*—in short, major Stevens. *Sombre Figuration* (*OP*, 66-71), a section of *Owl's Clover*, sums up this central fiction in Stevens, both by its title and by some highly revelatory lines:

> The man below beholds the portent poised,
> An image of his making, beyond the eye,

> Poised, but poised as a mind through which a storm
> Of other images blows, images of time
> Like the time of the portent, images like leaves,
> Except that this is an image of black spring
> And those the leaves of autumn-afterwards,
> Leaves of the autumns in which the man below
> Lived as the man lives now, and hated, loved,
> As the man hates now, loves now, the self-same things.
> The year's dim elongations stretch below
> To rumpled rock, its bright projections lie
> The shallowest iris on the emptiest eye.
> The future must bear within it every past,
> Not least the pasts destroyed, magniloquent
> Syllables.

Certainly *The Snow Man* would destroy all the poet's fictions of the leaves, fictions which culminate in Shelley's *Ode to the West Wind*, and yet Stevens' poem bears within it Shelley's transumption of the past. The fiction of the leaves begins with Homer, in Book Six of the *Iliad*, when Diomedes and Glaukos come together bent on battle in the space between the two armies. Diomedes asks Glaukos his ancestry, lest he make the mistake of fighting a god. Glaukos begins his reply with the magnificent simile that compares the generation of leaves with that of humanity: "The wind scatters the leaves on the ground, but the live timber / burgeons with leaves again in the season of spring returning. / So one generation of men will grow while another / dies." In the *Aeneid*, Virgil recalls this simile, transposing it to the crowds of the newly dead, waiting for Charon to take them across the river. Dante, developing Virgil, relates the image to the Fall of Man. Milton, gathering all these together, and overgoing them, applies the image to the fallen host of Satan, before they are rallied by their leader. All four of these poets are in Ruskin's "creative" grouping, rather than in the post-Wordsworthian "reflective" order (including Shelley) who rely upon the pathetic fallacy or, as I would say now, upon the substitution of a trope of *pathos* for one of *ethos*, so as to internalize the fiction of the leaves. For Shelley, there is an apocalyptic misery in the sound of the wind and in the fall of the leaves, and in his trope life is being imputed to the stricken object-world.

I am ready at last to attempt a close reading of *The Snow Man*, reserving the poem's relation to Emerson, Whitman, and Nietzsche for its closing trope, where that relation is most illuminating. *The Snow Man* begins with the impersonal "one," but before the single sentence that constitutes the poem has finished bending back upon itself that "one" will have become "the listener," who is also the man of the title. I have remarked already on the Stevensian use of "regard," which is the poem's opening mode of perception, where I suggest "regard" can be translated as a retrospective *aftering* or a finding of retroactive meaningfulness, on Freud's model of belatedness in his *Nachträglichkeit*. Protectively impersonal, as though holding oneself at arm's length, one appeals to the *ethos* of Fate, to the necessity of having a mind of winter, in order to avoid indulgence in the fallacy of imputing human "misery" to the wind and the leaves. What does it mean, though, to "have a mind of winter," and how does such a having differ from having "been cold a long time"? The mind of winter *regards* pine-trees *crusted* with snow; one who has been cold a long time *beholds* junipers *shagged* with ice. There is a slight touch of figuration in the crusting, and a rather larger figuration in the shagging. "Crusted" need not refer to bread-making, having a proper meaning as any hard, crisp covering, but "shagged" means to be tangled as with rough hair or perhaps rough cloth. "Regarding" as a retrospective, negating Stevensian term for perception leads to at most an ironic figuration, and so is appropriate for the *mind* of winter rather than the emotions of winter. But "beholding" with its more positive edge of astonishment or discovery leads to an image bordering on a *pathos*, and so is more appropriate for the affective, indeed almost temperamental, condition of having been cold a long time. The trope is faint but there, just as a figuration is hinted again by "the spruces *rough* in the distant glitter / Of the January sun."

It is not simple to locate the rhetorical disjunctions I have been calling "crossings" in a poem that knots itself into one intricate sentence. But I think the crucial crossing in *The Snow Man* comes between lines 9 and 10, where "the sound of a few leaves" acquires the deeper tonality of being identified with "the sound of the land," since each is equal to the same thing, the wind's sound. We are not hearing a Shelleyan or Ruskinian plenitude of music in the wind; more New Englandly, we are hearing a few dead leaves being blown about as we stand in the snow, in a bare place.

I suggest now that we can identify that "bare place" as precisely as we have identified the wind and the leaves. Here is what can be called, without hyperbole, the central passage in American literature, since it is the crucial epiphany of our literature's Central Man, Emerson. The text is the Sublime and grotesque triumph, uneasily melded into one, from *Nature*, I:

> Crossing a bare common, in snow puddles, at twilight, under a clouded sky, without having in my thoughts any occurrence of special good fortune, I have enjoyed a perfect exhilaration. I am glad to the brink of fear. . . . There I feel that nothing can befall me in life,—no disgrace, no calamity (leaving me my eyes), which nature cannot repair. Standing on the bare ground,—my head bathed by the blithe air, and uplifted into infinite space,—all mean egotism vanishes. I become a transparent eyeball; I am nothing; I see all.

Emerson will go on to say that "nature always wears the colors of the spirit," so that for him the pathetic fallacy is no fallacy but is *potentia*, or *pathos* as Power, the Will rampant. Stevens is a very involuntary Emersonian here or later, but the intertextual crossing between his poem and Emerson's rhapsody is unmistakable. Emerson's "bare common, in snow puddles" is Stevens' "bare place." The Snow Man is "nothing himself"; Emerson says, "I am nothing." The Snow Man "beholds / Nothing that is not there and the nothing that is"; Emerson says, "I see all" and earlier had said that nothing could happen to him that nature could not repair, with the single proviso of his eyes. Stevens would have protested that as Snow Man he was stripped of delusions ("nothing that is not there") and of illusions ("the nothing that is") whereas Emerson was obsessed with Transcendental delusions and illusions. To which Emerson might reply by falling back into that Sublime emptiness or great American repression, the "transparent eyeball" which certainly qualifies as a "nothing that is not there and the nothing that is." Nietzsche, in the most celebrated aphorism of *On the Genealogy of Morals*, had judged that man would prefer the void as purpose or "the nothing that is" rather than be void of purpose. His remark is closer to Emerson's supposed idealism than to Stevens' only apparent surrender to the reality principle.

How are we to interpret *The Snow Man?* I want to juxtapose to the poem Whitman, at the close of *Song of Myself*, and Nietzsche in *The Birth of Tragedy*. Whitman, in section 52, the concluding passage in *Song of Myself*, reduces not to a Snow Man but to a man of air and of grass. Effusing his flesh in eddies, drifting it in lacy jags, he bequeaths himself to the dirt. He too could say he is nothing himself, but he prefers to be more enigmatic: "You will hardly know who I am or what I mean." Is he still celebrating himself when he diffuses into the atmosphere and into the earth? "Yes," ought to be our wary response, because his reduction is, as he said in section 51, a concentration: "I concentrate toward them that are nigh, I wait on the door-slab." Whitman may have reduced to a First Idea, but he remains Whitman: "I stop somewhere waiting for you." Is the Snow Man, in any sense, waiting for his reader?

I return to the distinction between "regard" and "behold." As the Snow Man listens to the wind, a wind in which he hears no fictions, of misery or of music, he beholds as a nihilist beholds. Only those who do not know Emerson well, in his last phase, would be surprised at how close this is to the Emerson of 1866: "For every seeing soul there are two absorbing facts, —*I and the Abyss*." What, we can ask about Stevens' seeing soul, can one behold in the "nothing that is"? How can the beholder possess "nothing," in a positive sense of seeing-with-amazement? Or, most simply, how can a "nothing that is" be a trope of *pathos*, a fiction of Power, a variation upon or reimagining, however slight, of the First Idea?

J. Hillis Miller appears to read "nothing that is" more as a trope of *ethos*, by equating this "nothing" with "being," in the sense that "being is a pervasive power, visible nowhere in itself and yet present and visible in all things. It is what things share through the fact that they are. Being is not a thing like other things and therefore can only appear to man as nothing, but it is what all things must participate in if they are to exist at all." This reading seems to me persuasive for elsewhere in Stevens, particularly later Stevens, but not quite so much for *The Snow Man*, where I read the final "nothing" as a passion for transumption, as a trope-undoing trope, rather than as a trope for "being." To behold the "nothing that is" is also "to behold the junipers *shagged* with ice," so that "nothing" is rather a tangled and mangled nothing. "Being" in Stevens can live with the First Idea, but at the price of ceasing to be a "human" being. The listener, reduced to nothing, remains human because he beholds something shagged and rough, barely figurative, yet still a figuration rather than a bareness. This "nothing" is the most minimal or abstracted of fictions, and yet still it is a fiction.

I juxtapose, at the last, Nietzsche, in *The Birth of Tragedy,* saying that the self must be made divine because the human being stands now empty in the wreck of all past times. But, before this god-making takes place in the self, the last mythologies must be stripped from the human. This appears to be the purpose of the reduction in *The Snow Man.* The poem does not go on to intimate the return of the divinity to man; that takes place in its gorgeous counterpoem, *Tea at the Palaz of Hoon.* The Snow Man is not yet Hoon, but he is going to be, and that *potentia* is felt in the *pathos* of his poem's closing trope. The worst reading possible then of this poem, I suggest, is the canonical one we received from Stevens himself, when he said in a letter: "I shall explain *The Snow Man* as an example of the necessity of identifying oneself with reality in order to understand it and enjoy it" (*L,* 464). That takes care of less than half the poem, the part in which "reality" is "regarded," and not the larger part in which "reality" is "beheld" and so begins to become a passion.

Replying to the apt suggestion of Norman Holmes Pearson that Hoon was Hoon, Stevens made one of his most stimulating remarks about a poem of his own: "You are right in saying that Hoon is Hoon although it could be that he is the son of old man Hoon. He sounds like a Dutchman. I think the word is probably an automatic cipher for 'the loneliest air,' that is to say, the expanse of sky and space" (*L,* 871). I think that Hoon is a composite of Stevens and Whitman, with an edge of Pater, all three of them "Dutchmen" in their ancestry and all of them Epicurean-Lucretian in their ultimate metaphysics. The poem should be regarded as the synthesis or third term of the triad, of which *The Man Whose Pharynx Was Bad* and *The Snow Man* are thesis and antithesis. Let us call *Pharynx* a large, composite trope of *ethos, The Snow Man* such a trope of *logos* or "crossing," and *Hoon* the most beautiful, so far, of Stevens' exaltations of the will or of *pathos* conceived as Emersonian Power.

As with the two antecedent poems, *Hoon* is spoken as a little dramatic monologue, or rather as an apostrophe, which is what most dramatic monologues after Browning and Tennyson are anyway. An apostrophe originally was directed to the dead but swerved into an address to the absent. *Tea at the Palaz of Hoon* is directed against what is absent in the reader, which is the imagination or a felt potential of the reader's own power of representation. The reader is all but present, in the crossing between *The Snow Man* and this poem, for in that intervenient space the reader, or the skeptic-in-Stevens, has said something like this to Hoon: "Descending into the ocean, through the loneliest air, as a purple sunset, you have ceased to be yourself."

To this, the expanse of sky and space, the spirit that we seek, grandly replies:

> Not less because in purple I descended
> The western day through what you called
> The loneliest air, not less was I myself.
>
> What was the ointment sprinkled on my beard?
> What were the hymns that buzzed beside my ears?
> What was the sea whose tide swept through me there?
>
> Out of my mind the golden ointment rained,
> And my ears made the blowing hymns they heard.
> I was myself the compass of that sea:
>
> I was the world in which I walked, and what I saw
> Or heard or felt came not but from myself;
> And there I found myself more truly and more strange.

Let us commence with the Sublime title. The palaz of Hoon is sky and space seen as a gaudy and ornate dwelling; to have tea at the palaz is to watch the twilight while conversing with the setting sun, who is hardly lonely since all the air is his and since all directions are at home in him. He is himself when most imperial, in purple and gold, and his setting is a coronation. To the Idiot Questioner who grants the coronation but stints on the ceremonial, he makes a doubly crushing reply. The ointment, hymns, and sea are not external to him; and because he, Hoon, is the center and origin, he is unstinting in his own investiture. The golden ointment rained, not sprinkled, on his beard, as it came out of his mind. The hymns blew like trumpets, not buzzed, for his ears both made and heard such music. If the tide swept through Hoon, it did not encompass him. Seeing, hearing, and feeling find objects only from his own self, and nothing through which he moves is outside him. And yet, as his triumphant final line makes clear, he is *not* a solipsist, because the "there" of his world is an arena in which he is at work finding himself, more truly the more he expands, and more strange, probably because Pater, one of his high priests, had defined the Romantic imagination as adding strangeness to beauty. The formula "I was the world in which I walked" thirteen years later would become the germ of *The Idea of Order at Key West*. But Hoon was to have other progeny, since I would judge that he appears again in 1935 as the Walt Whitman in section I of *Like Decorations*, and in his own name and right again, later in 1935, in *Sad Strains of a Gay Waltz*, and finally as the insouciant *Well Dressed Man with a Beard* in 1941. Why link him to Whitman? Compare to Hoon's appearances, and to Whitman's in Stevens, the start of section 25 in *Song of Myself*. Whitman has challenged nature, it taunts him, and he rises triumphantly to the challenge:

> Dazzling and tremendous how quick the sun-rise would kill me,
> If I could not now and always send sun-rise out of me.

We also ascend dazzling and tremendous as the sun,
We found our own O my soul in the calm and cool of
   the day-break.

My voice goes after what my eyes cannot reach,
With the twirl of my tongue I encompass worlds and volumes
   of worlds.
Speech is the twin of my vision, it is unequal to measure itself,
It provokes me forever, it says sarcastically,
Walt you contain enough, why don't you let it out then?

Come now I will not be tantalized, you conceive too much
   of articulation,
Do you not know O speech how the buds beneath you
   are folded?
Waiting in gloom, protected by frost,
The dirt receding before my prophetical screams,
I underlying causes to balance them at last,
My knowledge my live parts, it keeping tally with the meaning
   of all things.

We can compare Whitman and his vision with Hoon, and speech or the skeptic with Hoon's Idiot Questioner. Whitman, like Hoon, both contains everything else and is an idea of the sun, not as a god but as a god might be. Hoon is himself the compass of the sea whose tides sweep through him; Walt encompasses worlds but himself is not to be encompassed. The line in which the two are closest is "My knowledge my live parts, it keeping tally with the meaning of all things." It ought not to surprise us then that Whitman is both the sun and the world in which he walks, in the sublime opening of *Like Decorations*:

> In the far South the sun of autumn is passing
> Like Walt Whitman walking along a ruddy shore.
> He is singing and chanting the things that are part of him,
> The worlds that were and will be, death and day.
> Nothing is final, he chants. No man shall see the end.
> His beard is of fire and his staff is a leaping flame.

Walt, Hoon, and the girl at Key West stride against a seascape, singing and chanting the things that are part of them, their knowledge their live parts, and what they know keeping tally with the meaning of all things. But this glory, constant in Emerson, wavered in Stevens even as it did in Whitman. After fourteen years, the Hoon of *Sad Strains of a Gay Waltz* was more than a little chastened:

> And then
> There's that mountain-minded Hoon,
> For whom desire was never that of the waltz,
>
> Who found all form and order in solitude,
> For whom the shapes were never the figures of men.
> Now, for him, his forms have vanished.

> There is order in neither sea nor sun.
> The shapes have lost their glistening.

It is Stevens' own illumination of *Tea at the Palaz of Hoon*, reminding us that Hoon's solitude was not solipsism but also that the spirit withers, however gloriously, in the air of solitude. Hoon was too large a reimagining of the First Idea, and Stevens could not sustain, in *Harmonium* or in *Ideas of Order*, so belatedly High Romantic a vision. But it is important to see what criticism has mostly evaded seeing. Of the two contrary answers to *The Man Whose Pharynx Was Bad*, Stevens' later poetry finally relies more upon Hoon's chant than upon the Snow Man's reductive regardings and somewhat less reductive beholdings.

Versions of Existentialism   Frank Lentricchia[*]

It is . . . difficult to overestimate the vogue of Wallace Stevens in the 1960s. No young academic coming out of graduate school in the middle of the decade with an advanced degree in literature could claim critical sophistication unless he could discourse knowingly, off the cuff, on "supreme fictions," the "gaiety of language," and the "dialectic of imagination and reality." No mature literary intellectual could be comfortable unless he could move smoothly into such ponderous conversation. Not long after the poet's death in 1955 the Stevens industry began to prosper such that it eventually swallowed whole all competition in the criticism of modern poetry. Between 1960 and 1969—or beginning roughly with Frank Kermode's little book—we were inundated with a concordance, a bibliography, three collections of scholarly essays, two pamphlets, fifteen critical books (or about twice as many as were published on Robert Frost), about a hundred essays in scholarly journals, over forty doctoral dissertations (not counting those only in part on Stevens), and frequent admonitions from Harold Bloom that Stevens was the great modern poet, the culmination of the romantic spirit, and the true alternative to Pound, Eliot, and Auden, his hated New-Critical writers. All of this in the space of ten years. But the clearest sign of all of Stevens's ascendancy was the publication in 1967 by Frank Kermode of a brilliant new cultural synthesis, *The Sense of an Ending: Studies in the Theory of Fiction*, a book which, as it related traditional apocalyptic thought about beginnings and ends to novelistic plot-making and a general (epistemological) theory of fictions, picked up the story of modern criticism where *Romantic Image* had left off ten years earlier.

[*]Reprinted with permission of Frank Lentricchia and the University of Chicago Press from Frank Lentricchia's *After the New Criticism* (Chicago: University of Chicago Press, 1980). © 1980 by the University of Chicago.

To what extent Kermode's themes and biases are controlled by the poetics of Wallace Stevens is perhaps best attested to by the absence in *The Sense of an Ending* of any substantial, frontal discussion of Stevens himself. The poet is present in one of the epigraphs preceding the first chapter, and he is present in a closing quotation—Kermode gives him the last words of the book. But most tellingly he is present in the book's texture and rhythm, in words and phrases from his poems and essays which Kermode repeatedly and skillfully weaves into his sentences at key points in the argument. Stevens need no longer be confronted directly because, Kermode appears to have assumed, by 1967 his poetic theories and the very tone of his thought are givens within the long tradition of postromantic epistemology which begins with the reorientation of the knowing subject effected by Kant and is later radicalized in directions that Kant would never have approved. Nietzsche, Hans Vaihinger, William James and the American pragmatists, José Ortega y Gasset, and Jean-Paul Sartre (particularly in important early books, *The Psychology of Imagination* and *Being and Nothingness*) are the chief figures in a post-Kantian line which, in its ultimate extension in Sartre, concludes in an odd mixture of Kantian and anti-Kantian themes. But Stevens assumes such proper prominence in *The Sense of an Ending* because he is the culmination and summary representative of what I am going to call the conservative fictionalist tradition in modern poetics and philosophy. It is a tradition which captured the American theoretical imagination because it appeared to offer a clean break both with Northrop Frye's grander aestheticism and with the isolationists of the image represented by the New-Critical tradition. In *Romantic Image* Kermode had shown us that since Kant and Coleridge we were sunk in aesthetic isolationism; Frye's *Anatomy of Criticism* had not rescued us but, rather, had pushed us down deeper. With its unspoken purpose of radically undermining Frye's premises, *The Sense of an Ending* would show us the way out of the closed literary universe.

The epigraph that Kermode chooses from the late long poem "An Ordinary Evening in New Haven" gives us access to several of the postulates of conservative fictionalism:

> a more severe,
> More harassing master would extemporize
> Subtler, more urgent proof that the theory
> Of poetry is the theory of life
>
> As it is, in the intricate evasions of as,
> In things seen and unseen, created from nothingness,
> The heavens, the hells, the worlds, the longed-for lands.
> (CP 486)

The ground of Stevens's lifelong obsessive irony toward his poetic vocation is that he is just such a harassing and severe master who is incapable of extemporizing urgent (or any other kind of) proof "that the theory / Of poetry is the theory of life." Against an irrepressible will to identify the projections of desire, those "longed-for lands," with reality itself, he sets a critical self-consciousness which incessantly subverts and dismantles his fictions and shows them for what they are: "intricate evasions of as." So the agonists of a poetics of supreme fictions are opposed in this way: a fictional thrust generated out of the great voids of desire (a "nothingness") and bodied forth through the metaphoric modes of language (the creative power of "as" and "like") is confronted with the "as it is," and in such confrontation the fictions of desire are unveiled as evasions of a truth which is generally represented in Stevens as everywhere and always hostile to human being. Implicitly identified with the "as it is," or nonlinguistic state of things as they are, "truth" and the classical conception of reality are often called into question by Stevens as fictions. At the close of *Notes toward a Supreme Fiction*, in a moment of apparent ontological breakthrough and contact, he "names" reality "flatly" his "fat girl." But with exquisite self-consciousness of metaphor he tells us that he "finds" her (a realist's favorite verb) only in "difference" (a key post-structuralist term that carries the most devastating criticism yet known of realism, traditional conceptions of representation, and mimetic poetics). The "fat girl" is no more than a "rational distortion." Yet his point (there is no "literal" or "proper" meaning by which to judge metaphoric deviance) may be set aside. The main tradition of Stevens criticism is correct: "truth" and "reality" are terms in Stevens that tend to stand for that objectively knowable lump of thereness—a conception close to what Frye calls our "environment"—which awaits metamorphosis on the blue guitar.

The structure of Stevens's thought and of the entire fictionalist theoretical tradition on its conservative side is radically dualistic and very often paranoid:

> From this the poem springs: that we live in a place
> That is not our own, and much more, not ourselves. . . .
>   (*CP* 383)

Reality, as alien being, is a "violence" which ever pressures us, as he put it in a well-known formulation in *The Necessary Angel,* and the imagination is the response of our subjective violence which presses back against an inhuman chaos. Imagination makes space between us and chaos and thereby grants momentary release from sure engulfment, madness, and death. With reality so horribly privileged, fictions may be understood as heroic evasions, but they may also be seen as pitifully unheroic lies; perhaps the projections of a secular humanism's man-god; or perhaps just the escapist fantasies of those without sufficient courage to face the facts. Stevens had difficulty deciding whether his was a poetics of courage and high risk, or simply a poetics of cowardice; this indecision generates a highly playful, self-conscious, and hypothetical sort of discourse which constantly tests both stances as it oscillates between belief and skepticism, fiction and reality, the longed-for lands and chaos. But Stevens's dominant tendency to align truth and reality with an inhuman chaos "outside" human consciousness and human discourse produces an antipoetics whose constant lament and wearisome message is the futility of all human effort. The young man may dance nakedly in a ring on a Sunday morning, but the older man, increasingly denied delights of the flesh, and increasingly aware of the tragic meaning of the pigeon's flight, "downward to darkness," turns repeatedly to self-ironic celebration of the illusory efficacy of the human imagination. In the wake of a certain reading of Nietzsche, romantic humanism rushes toward its finale of despair.

Stevens is not quite the dramatic alternative to Frye that he appeared to be a decade or so back. Both Stevens and Frye imply systems of last-ditch humanism in which human desire, conscious of itself as "lack," to cite Sartre's term, and conscious of the ontological nothingness of its images, confronts a grim reality which at every point denies us our needs: "not to have is the beginning of desire / To have what is not is its ancient cycle." Our "environment" is alien, but—here is the silver lining in this dark cloud—its very alien quality beckons forth our creative impulses to make substitutive fictive worlds. Yet the difference of Frye and Stevens on the pivotal place of desire is as impressive as their coincidence. In Frye's system desire finally overwhelms ("swallows") all exteriority. Sometime not very long after the primal face-off of consciousness and the inhuman environment, consciousness takes over. Reality in itself, after it receives its initial "formal" humanization, is put forever out of play and—in spite of some inconsistency on the point in his discussion of satire and demonic imagery—comes to occupy the peculiar limbo state of the Kantian *ding an sich*. (Though out of reach, it is yet reality, somehow, which confers the value of freedom upon the constructed worlds of desire.) Hence again the justice of Meyer Abrams's charge of monism: Frye's is a one-term system which permits literary structures to draw upon, imitate, and displace one another, but never to move outside of the literary universe. In Frye there is no exit from what Stevens called the "world of words."

If Frye is the better neo-Kantian, then Stevens is much the truer existentialist. Frye's dominant theme is the celebration of the potentially unqualified freedom of the mind's structuring capacities, as in its anagogic phase the poetic consciousness ingests the natural order of things; Stevens's dominant theme is the stubborn independence, the final freedom of being from mind and the priority of natural existence over consciousness. As he puts it in "The Connoisseur of Chaos": "The squirming facts exceed the squamous mind. . . ." Stevens's poetics is a two-term system where fiction and reality engage in endless and complex play in which one term, while open to qualification by the other, always successfully resists subsumption by its opponent. So that if Frye's mythic structures are perfectly "closed" to existential reality, then Stevens's fictions would appear to be "open"— which is a way of saying that Frye's myths are spatially isolated, while Stevens's fictions participate in and are subject to the flowing of time. (The title of the second section of *Notes toward a Supreme Fiction* is "It Must Change.") What presumably guarantees the openness of fictions to time is the severe and harassing master, self-consciousness, the governing third force in Stevens's system which enables desiring consciousness to step away from itself and watch its fictive projections fail to enclose the real in its transformative vision. Frye lacks this principle of self-consciousness: Kermode charges him with forgetting the "fictiveness of all fictions." With Stevens self-consciousness is a key to his vogue, for in it, or so it seemed, the tenacious hold of aestheticism on the American critical mind was finally broken as fictions were opened to all the contamination of unliterary temporality, to history in an inclusive sense.

Of Parents, Children, and Rabbis: Wallace Stevens and the Question of the Book

Joseph G. Kronick*

It was a rabbi's question, let the rabbis reply.

—(Reb?) Stevens

Onto an answer Elohim grafted a question. Thus the innumerable supplanted the Unique.

—Reb Redel

There is the book of God in which God questions himself, and there is the book of man which is proportionate to that of God.

—Reb Rida

When, as a child, I wrote my name for the first time, I knew I was beginning a book.

—Reb Stein

Mark the first page of the book with a red marker. For, in the beginning, the wound is invisible.

—Reb Alcé

I

Before Stevens had ever eaten the fruit which "might be a cure of the ground,"[1] he first had to read what he was about to consume:

> An apple serves as well as any skull
> To be the book in which to read a round,
> And is as excellent, in that it is composed
> Of what, like skulls, comes rotting back to ground.
> (*CP*, p. 14)

*Reprinted with permission from *Boundary 2: A Journal of Postmodern Literature and Culture* 10 (Spring 1982):125-54.

The fruit that would be "a cure of the ground / Or a cure of ourselves" (*CP*, p. 526), itself rises from the ground; hence the disease produces its own antidote. The devourer of this homeopathic cure, therefore, seeks to restore the ground on which he stands and from which he can begin to write, for the fruit also cures leaves, that is, books.[2] The site where writing begins lies elsewhere; it is not empirical, but calls to us from beyond memory.[3] It is the father before speech and, thus, also a call to the future. Yet these leaves are rotted pages driven to the ground by Shelley's (Ode to the) West Wind. To read the sibylline leaves one must regather them into a book and thus come to repossess the poem. But our voracious reader devours much more than an apple, or a mango's rind, or even a pineapple pieced together—"the irreducible X" (*NA*, p. 83)—he must eat the rotted remains of literature. Both apples and skulls have an attraction to the ground from which they have risen because compost proves the richest of soils for literature. The apple serves Milton as well as the skull served Shakespeare in their respective meditations on death; now Stevens meditates on the book, which must be a regathering of his precursors' remains and thus a meditation on death.

   J. Hillis Miller provides the most thorough examination of Stevens' metaphors of the cure in "Stevens' Rock and Criticism as Cure." In *Poets of Reality*, Miller had already pointed out the importance of the ground as a figure for reality,[4] but now the bottom has dropped out (was it when he left Geneva for Paris?) to reveal the abyss of endless interpretation leading him from Stevens through Whitman, Emerson, and Milton to the *OED* and *The American Heritage Dictionary*. Despite all his appeals to the endless series of interpretations opened by the modern poem, Miller's metaphors, particularly that of the *mise en abyme*, return literature to a genealogical sequence and thus set the text on solid ground. The *mise en abyme* is, shall we say, the mirror image of genealogy; it is a series of reproductions stretching back to a promised but indiscernible origin. Miller's two key examples of this effect are the heraldic shield which implies, according to Miller, "some break in the genetic line of filiation," and what he calls, "the Quaker Oats box effect."[5] While metaphors drawn from feudalism and corporate America are rich in their suggestiveness (both systems depend upon an unquestioned acceptance of hierarchical order), I here wish to emphasize the symmetry of this schema, even if, as Miller astutely points out, "without the production of some schema, some 'icon,' there can be no glimpse of the abyss, no vertigo of the underlying nothingness" (*GR*, p. 12). The abyss, says Miller, is created even as it is covered over. By turning Stevens into the demystified heir of Emerson and Whitman, Miller sets him in a tradition in which the deviation from his literary parents, or what Miller calls Stevens' "deconstruction" of Emerson and Whitman,[6] both keeps him within the genealogical line and, at the same time, reaffirms that this line progresses to a clearer vision of the illusion of onto-theo-logical beliefs. However, before we start "deconstructing the deconstructors," that is, Emerson and Stevens, we would do well to keep in mind Stevens' warning against the "inescapable romance . . . disillusion as the last illusion" (*CP*, p. 468).

As the above suggests, the *mise en abyme* is but a metaphor for intertextuality, a gathering of allusions to forebears that grounds a text in an ascertainable order whereby the descents of tropes are mapped out in genealogical reconstructions. Stevens appeared to be excruciatingly conscious of the nature of influence, and thus of genealogy, and he stubbornly disavowed any suggestion that he was indebted to other poets. In a letter to José Rodriguez Feo, he denies that he reads "a lot of poetry." What makes this claim more interesting than similar remarks is the way Stevens turns the question into one of reading, not originality:

> My state of mind about poetry makes me very susceptible and that is a danger in the sense that it would be so easy for me to pick up something unconsciously. In order not to run that danger I don't read other peoples' poetry at all. There seems to be very few people who read poetry at the finger tips, so to speak. . . . Most people read it listening for echoes because the echoes are familiar to them. They wade through it the way a boy wades through water, feeling with his toes for the bottom: the echoes are the bottom. This is something that I have learned to do from Yeats who was extremely persnickety about being himself. It is not so much that it is a way of being oneself as it is a way of defeating people who look only for echoes and influences.

> (*L*, p. 575)

With his nearly Emersonian capacity for contradiction, Stevens credits Yeats for having taught him how to avoid being indebted to others. Usually, he reserves his rare ackowledgements of debts for letters in which he is not denying them, such as one to Bernard Heringman in which he reverses his normal position and says, "I never plan to do a lot of writing without also planning at the same time to do a lot of reading" (*L*, p. 798). The strength that allows him to reject those who hunt for influences does not, Stevens suggests in his letter to Rodríguez Feo, lie in the self, for it is those who listen for echoes who believe in psyches and selves. Reading, like writing, must be guided by the hand, not by eyes and ears, the portals of the psyche. Reading at one's finger tips requires an openness to the text, thereby allowing the reader to break through the familiar and, without touching some solid, though earthy, foundation, to tread in an unfathomable sea, "a sea of ex" (*CP*, p. 175).[7]

To hear the echoes of, say, Whitman, Emerson, and Shelley, is to touch bottom or, to borrow another of Thoreau's metaphors, to find a *point d'appui*. We might say, in fact, that the water upon which the reader floats is Walden, whose depth Thoreau measured to see how much room it left for writing: "The greatest depth was exactly one hundred and two feet. . . . This is a remarkable depth for so small an area; yet not an inch of it can be spared by the imagination. What if all ponds were shallow? Would it not react on the minds of men? I am thankful that this pond was made deep and pure for a symbol."[8] The pond, we can easily surmise, is a book containing the tradition, and Thoreau is not the first to fathom it: "Successive nations perchance have drank at, admired, and fathomed it, and passed away, and still its water is green and pellucid as ever. . . . Who knows in how many unremembered nations' literature this has been the Castalian Fountain? or what nymphs presided over it in the Golden Age?" (W, p. 124). Unlike Stevens, who chooses to float, however uncomfortably, over measureless depths, Thoreau finds "a solid bottom everywhere" (W, p. 225). What Miller finds in an advertisement and calls the *mise en abyme*, Thoreau finds in nature, albeit a literary one, and calls "kittlybenders," a child's game in which the aim is to skate quickly over thin ice and risk breaking through. The most adept player of this game among Thoreau's readers is Walter Michaels, who writes, "To read *Walden*, then, is precisely to play at kittlybenders, to run the simultaneous risks of touching and not touching bottom."[9]

Thoreau, as I have argued elsewhere, would like to touch solid bottom, but the echoes of the past reverberate with an unending series of puns and allusions that mark him as a belated writer. Thoreau, who so wanted to be the father of an American literature, seems to be the perpetual son unable to assume his independence. Although Joseph Riddel has suggested that Stevens' rock may have its origin in Thoreau's *point d'appui*,[10] Thoreau usually appears as an appendage to Emerson, if he appears at all, in critical evaluations of Stevens' literary genealogy. As Stevens suggests, the hunt for allusions is the reader's way of taming a poet by uncovering the roots that extend from his poems into the ground or, in other words, into the past and into pre-texts. Now that we have Stevens' genealogy charted, we can erase the negative of *umheimlich* (unhomely and uncanny) and make his poetry *heimlich* (homely and canny).[11] Having caught an echo of Emerson or Whitman, we know how, or think we know, where Stevens lives and who he is; we have touched "the visible rock, the audible" (CP, p. 375). We have given ourselves over to an empirical Here that confuses the visible with the audible. The rock, however, is a site that opens history to the adventure of reading. It is from this rock that we gaze down to the sea:

> The exact rock where his inexactnesses
> Would discover, at last, the view toward which they had edged,
> Where he could lie and, gazing down at the sea,
> Recognize his unique and solitary home.
>
> (CP, p. 512)

The poet spies the unique home, not because he rests upon the rock of certainty, but because he himself is the uncertain, the inexact child who must recreate the home. To be at home in Stevens is to hear the echoes of "An ancestral theme" (CP, p. 412) of father, mothers, and children. It is to dwell in the "mythology of modern death": "an alphabet / By which to spell out holy doom and end, / A bee for the remembering of happiness" (CP, p. 434). There is a lapse between parents and child, a gap that cannot be bridged by discourse. It is not, however, a rupture within a genealogical line; it is writing, a fragment that is "neither a determined style nor a failure, but the form of that which is written" (*WD*, p. 17). And between the letters that recall a lost happiness walks Death. The images of sleep, peace, and memory, "the mother of us all," protect us from the encroachments of nothingness. They are the grammar and syntax of being in which we read life as the memorial (a spelling bee?) to death; for in man's faith in the continuity between life and death, there lies a debilitating servitude to the past as the origin of the past. The modern myth of death is the myth of genealogy: "These are death's own supremest images, / The pure perfections of parental space. . . ." (*CP*, p. 436).

In "The Rock," the desire to return home to that most unhomely of places, the "parental space," is dismissed as the myth of origins (a myth of ends requires a myth of beginnings): "It is an illusion that we were ever alive, / Lived in the houses of mothers" (*CP*, p. 525). This is the illusion of genealogy, of a genetic line that takes us back before language to the father:

> Who is my father in this world, in this house,
> At the spirit's base?
>
> My father's father, his father's father, his
> Shadows like winds
>
> Go back to the parent before thought, before speech,
> At the head of the past.
>
> (*CP*, p. 501)

The father is but a shadow, a ghost at the threshold who has no need to write; he is the God who does not question the distance between Himself and language; for His son is the Word made flesh. And it is to God the father (or is it the father of God?) that another son, who is a writer, turns as he seeks to restore the home. But in his turning, he measures the distance between himself and his desire.

In a poem about his grandfather, "The Bed of Old John Zeller," Stevens uncovers the "ghostly sequence" hidden within a belief in the structure of ideas:

> This structure of ideas, these ghostly sequences
> Of the mind, result only in disaster. It follows,
> Casual poet, that to add your own disorder to disaster
>
> Makes more of it. It is easy to wish for another structure
> Of ideas and to say as usual that there must be
> Other ghostly sequences and, it would be, luminous
>
> Sequences, thought of among spheres in the old peak of night:
> This is the habit of wishing, as if one's grandfather lay
> In one's heart and wished as he had always wished, unable

To sleep in that bed for its disorder, talking of ghostly
Sequences that would be sleep and ting-tang tossing, so that
He might slowly forget. It is more difficult to evade

That habit of wishing and to accept the structure
Of things as the structure of ideas. It was the structure
Of things at least that was thought of in the old peak of night.
(CP, pp. 326-27)

Logical thought—that is, thought as it is determined by grammar—harbors an implicit genealogy, a sequence that binds the chaos of things to the order of the sentence. Yet the incompatibility of "the structure of ideas" with "the structure of things" disturbs the grandfather, who is unable to sleep in a disorderly bed, that is, in an open book. The ghostly presence of the grandfather sleeps within the book and dreams the dream of the total book, or the dream of the family—these two are one—and expresses the desire to break through language to a "Pure rhetoric of a language without words" (CP, p. 374) and "step barefoot into reality" (CP, p. 423).

II

This desire to recover the "parent before thought" not only appears as a motivating force in many of Stevens' greatest poems, but it also occupied his personal affairs from 1942 until his death. There exist several hundred letters devoted entirely to his efforts to trace his genealogy. The reasons for this interest are somewhat obscure. Holly Stevens suggests it may have been prompted by her decision to leave school and not pursue the academic career her father had hoped for her. Around this time his sister Elizabeth died, leaving Stevens as the last member of his generation, and perhaps he saw himself as the guardian of the family's history. Finally, he very much desired to be admitted to the Holland Society, which meant he had to show an unbroken line of Dutch ancestry on the male side back to 1674 or earlier. These reasons are hardly satisfactory. And Stevens' infrequent personal remarks in his correspondence concerning this matter are of only limited value. In a letter to Emma Stevens Jobbins, a first cousin he discovered thanks to the research of his genealogists, he says when the genealogy is complete, "we shall really know who we are, without any fiction."[12] Elsewhere, he says he wishes "to ascertain as a matter of fact who I am," and he speaks of this interest at greater length in a letter to Hi Simons:

This was a subject that I scorned when I was a boy. However, there has become a part of it something that was beyond me then and that is the desire to realize the past as it was. . . . It is extraordinary how little seems to have survived when you first begin to study this sort of thing and then later on, when you have learned how to go about it, what an immense amount has survived and how much you can make of it.
(L, p. 457)

It is startling to read Stevens expressing the desire to know "the past as it was." Is this the poet who refuses to play "A tune beyond us, yet ourselves, / A tune upon the blue guitar / Of things exactly as they are" (*CP*, p. 165)? "The Irish Cliffs of Moher" suggests that to uncover things as they are, we must "Go back to the parent before thought." To play a tune— that is, to reduce the world to language—is to open the world to metaphor. Yet Stevens' obsession with genealogy seems to belie his insistence that "It is a world of words to the end ot it, / In which nothing solid is its solid self" (*CP*, p. 345). The world for Stevens, as it is for Edmond Jabès, is in a book, but "the book is not in the world" (*WD*, p. 76). To trace the genealogy is to bind the world in a book: "I don't suppose anyone is in a hurry about genealogy because piecing the past together is very much like binding a book" (*L*, p. 406). The reluctance to conclude the genealogy is a reluctance to close the book, which must remain open to writing, and thus to the son's questioning. And it is through his questions that the reader feels for the earth, but solid ground is a first metaphor, a filling of nothingness with the words of the world.

To inhabit a world of words, we must read, thus the desire to trace the genealogical line back before language, to the fecund minimum out of which writing begins. Reading, for Stevens, as it was for Emerson, is another name for writing:

> It is difficult to read. The page is dark.
> Yet he knows what it is that he expects.
>
> The page is blank or a frame without a glass
> Or a glass that is empty when he looks.
>
> The greenness of night lies on the page and goes
> Down deeply in the empty glass . . .
>
> Look, realist, not knowing what you expect.
> The green falls on you as you look,
>
> Falls on and makes and gives, even a speech.
> And you think that that is what you expect,
>
> That elemental parent, the green night,
> Teaching a fusky alphabet.
>   (*CP*, p. 267; ellipsis in Stevens' text).

The page is the dark receptacle of the reader's expectations, a frame without a mirror in which to see the self. Stevens' tone indicates his annoyance with the reader who is unable to put aside his expectations, which is to recognize his self, when he confronts the book. The green to which Stevens refers is a trope for nature, the "elemental parent" of a "natural" language. Unable to illuminate the writings of "a fusky alphabet," Phosphor listens for echoes, the voice of an author in the poem; he clings to the myths of speech and origin, of a parent who oversees the descent of meaning and language.

III

In order to rethink the meaning of descent, Stevens had to turn to the family, his reality, as the metaphoric substitution for the idea of textuality. Thus he comes to look upon the family as he would a book: "My father came from Bucks County. He was a farmer's son although he himself was a lawyer and lived and practiced in Berks County. My brother came to own the farm and eventually sold it to one of the Cornells who still live there. I look back to that farm and the people who live in it the way American literature used to look back to English literature" (*L*, p. 732). The home of one's parents serves as the trope of desire for a metaphysical origin. Yet Stevens' comparison suggests that he has declared his independence from the ancestral home just as Emerson and, after him, the modern American writer successively made such declaration against the past. Nevertheless, the home remains indissociable from the self, even though Stevens recognizes that to possess the home would be to close the book. In a letter of 1951 to Thomas McGreevy, he writes, "I should like to do as you do: go back to the original chez moi. When I was a boy and used to go home from college, I used to feel as if it was going back to mother earth. . . ." (*L*, p. 728). The return to mother earth would be a return to the mother tongue, the words growing from the ground, and thus a return to the home and nature (a mother language).

From his scattered comments on genealogy and his massive correspondence devoted entirely to tracing his family line, we get a strong sense of his ambivalence toward the past. Although he once instructed someone that "the way to read American history . . . is to interest yourself in your family" (*L*, p. 479), he also knew that family histories are subject to as many interpretations as they have readers: in his "Adagia," he writes, "Genealogy is the science of correcting other genealogists' mistakes" (*OP*, p. 170). But it is in such late poems as "The Auroras of Autumn" that Stevens' massive strength emerges, breaking through the pessimism of a poem such as "The Comedian as the Letter C" and its nostalgia for "Loquacious columns" (*CP*, p. 41) to an uncompromising awareness of the illusion of the parental home that has nothing to do with either pessimism or optimism:

> Farewell to an idea . . . A cabin stands,
> Deserted, on a beach. It is white,
> As by a custom or according to
>
> An ancestral theme or a consequence
> Of an infinite course. The flowers against the wall
> Are white, a little dried, a kind of mark

> Reminding, trying to remind, of a white
> That was different, something else, last year
> Or before, not the white of an aging afternoon,
>
> Whether fresher or duller, whether of winter cloud
> Or of winter sky, from horizon to horizon.
>
> (*CP*, p. 412)

In this, the second canto of the "Auroras," along with the third and fourth cantos, Stevens proceeds to negate the ideas of the home: the mother, and the father. As Joseph Riddel has remarked, "Each beginning again is a turning of an image that repeatedly dismantles the 'ancestral theme' of continuity, of the passage of truth from origin to end or from father to son."[13] The whiteness of the cabin suggests "The dominant blank, the unapproachable" (*CP*, p. 477), a past vacated by the tenants of memory leaving the poet free to imagine the present.

In a rarely discussed late poem, "The Role of the Idea in Poetry," Stevens reexamines the descent of the idea from father to son:

> Ask of the philosopher why he philosophizes,
> Determined thereto, perhaps by his father's ghost,
> Permitting nothing to the evening's edge.
>
> The father does not come to adorn the chant.
> One father proclaims another, the patriarchs
> Of truth.
>
> (*OP*, p. 93)

Meaning inhabits the philosopher's chant, or the poem, as a ghost announcing the presence of other ghosts and other fathers. The idea in poetry is the bloodless abstraction of the patriarchal descent of truth from parent to son, for truth inheres in linear descent. Stevens, however, transforms the diachronic descent of parentage into a synchronic pattern of relation—fathers do not breed sons; they bear the dream of patriarchal order:

> They strike across and are masters of
>
> The chant and discourse there, more than wild weather
> Of clouds that hang lateness on the sea. They become
> A time existing after much time has passed.
>
> (*OP*, p. 93)

Fathers are the masters of language and nature at "the evening's edge," the threshold of the imagination. And their temporal priority is the daily recreation of a myth that places a father at the head of the past and, therefore, at the border of night:

> Therein, day settles and thickens round a form—
> Blue-bold on its pedestal—that seems to say,
> "I am the greatness of the new-found night."
>
> (*OP*, p. 93)

The father is the giant guarding truth and, consequently, blocking access to the book:

> Here, then, is an abstraction given head,
> A giant on the horizon, given arms,
> A massive body and long legs, stretched out,
> A definition with an illustration, not
> Too exactly labelled, a large among the smalls
> Of it, a close, parental magnitude,
> At the centre on the horizon, concentrum, grave
> And prodigious person, patron of origins.
>
> (*CP*, p. 443)

The giant designates the poet as a secondary man condemned to chant "ancestral themes" of a lost home. But in the final stanza of "A Primitive Like an Orb," Stevens discloses that the giant is a figure of language's eccentricity:

> That's it. The lover writes, the believer hears,
> The poet mumbles and the painter sees,
> Each one, his fated eccentricity,
> As a part, but part, but tenacious particle,
> Of the skeleton of the ether, the total
> Of letters, prophecies, perceptions, clods
> Of color, the giant of nothingness, each one
> And the giant ever changing, living in change.
>
> (*CP*, p. 443)

"The centre on the horizon" proves to be eccentric, that is, remote from the center. We know of the poem of the whole only through the lesser poems, the fragments that make of every particle an ever-changing giant on an eccentric center. To remove the giant, who is the father, from his privileged position is to free language from the regulations of a central control. No longer "the centre of the horizon," the father now stands, like Emerson on the "horizon" in "Experience," at the threshold of the book, but not in it. Like the son, he, too, will be a reader seeking to recapture words that he can never possess.[14]

Stevens gives his most programmatic statement on the poet's genealogy in "Recitation after Dinner," a poem published by the Saint Nicholas Society, a group composed of men descended from early Dutch settlers of America. Judging by the first stanza, the poem was apparently read after one of the dinners the society held:

> A poem about tradition could easily be
> A windy thing . . . However, since we are here,
> Cousins of the calendar if not of kin,
> To be a part of tradition, to identify
> Its actual appearance, suppose we begin
> By giving it a form. But the character
> Of tradition does not easily take form.
>
> (*OP*, p. 86)

Ostensibly addressed to his fellow members, the poem of tradition also speaks to other poets, for this family is bound, not by filiation, but by affiliation. The tradition upheld by this society is subjected to numerous questions as Stevens explores the difficulties of giving form to the book of family history. The poem of tradition is written on leaves that the wind drives to the ground. Thus, to give it form one must gather them and bind them together in a book. But tradition is not a book of laws: "There is / No book of the past in which time's senators / Have inscribed life's do and don't. The commanding codes / Are not tradition." Stevens dissolves the bonds that linked tradition to institutionalized codes, a bondage that must be artificial, for it is predicated on a belief in the immutability of writing. Nor is tradition memory:

> It is the memory
> That hears a pin fall in New Amsterdam
> Or sees the new North River heaping up
> Dutch ice on English boats? The memory
> Is part of the classic imagination, posed
> Too often to be more than secondhand.
> Tradition is much more than the memory.
> (*OP*, pp. 86-7)

Stevens bows to the nostalgic desires of his Dutch cousins as he gives priority to the Dutch navigators of the North River, a portion of the Hudson, who preceded the English. But memory belongs to the classical imagination, a stale tradition that perpetuates such beliefs in the priority of Dutch settlers. For Stevens, the ancestral land is situated beyond memory. Tradition is a cry from beyond memory to a site that is always elsewhere, that is, in a book that remains to be written (*WD*, p. 66). Home lies in a memory of the cry of fallen leaves:

> It is the cry of leaves that do not transcend themselves,
> In the absence of fantasia, without meaning more
> Than they are in the final finding of the ear, in the thing
> Itself, until, at last, the cry concerns no one at all.
> (*OP*, pp. 96-7)

These are the leaves that speak to the living of death.[15] They cry for "life as it is," a life abandoned to the uncertainty of Being.

The questioning continues as Stevens asks, "Is it experience(?)" and "is tradition an unfamiliar sum, / A legend scrawled in script we cannot read?" With this final question, tradition is inscribed in an indecipherable hand as the question of the book, and as Stevens begins to define the past, we confront the "original" illegibility, the indeterminable that inhabits every book. This is not a primal and irrational mystery of origins indecipherable by man. Once again, it is Derrida on the illegible in Jabès who offers the best gloss on Stevens' truly indecipherable hand: "Prior to the book (in the nonchronological sense), original illegibility is therefore the very possibility of the book and, within it, of the ulterior and eventual opposition of 'rationalism' and 'irrationalism.' The Being that is announced within the illegible is beyond these categories, beyond, as it writes itself, its own name" (*WD*, p. 77). For Stevens, this Being is the son's promised inheritance as the successor to the father as the gatherer of leaves; yet this will's illegibility, which makes it impossible to probate, allows for the perpetual contestation whereby Being is never named, but always waits a step beyond the threshold of the book. And at this threshold stands tradition, a son who bears the father on his back:

> It has a clear, a single, a solid form,
> That of the son who bears upon his back
> The father that he loves, and bears him from
> The ruins of the past, out of nothing left,
> Made noble by the honor he receives,
> As if in a golden cloud. The son restores
> The father. He hides his ancient blue beneath
>
> His own bright red. But he bears him out of love,
> His life made double by his father's life,
> Ascending the humane. This is the form
> Tradition wears, the clear, the single form
> The solid shape, Aeneas seen, perhaps,
> By Nicholas Poussin, yet nevertheless
> A tall figure upright in a giant's air.
>
> (*OP*, p. 87)

Perhaps the ceremonial occasion of the poem explains why this is Stevens' most generous acceptance of the father's priority. The son serves as an undertaker in a duel with dead fathers. Stevens rests only momentarily in the dream of recuperation as he inscribes the past in a double inscription that folds in upon itself and thus is the reflection of its own beginning as a figure of a figure. The past is Nicholas Poussin's reimagining of Virgil's allegory of genealogical order, and thus the legitimacy of the Caesars, in the tale of Aeneas' bearing his father on his shoulders after the destruction of Troy. This "solid shape" inhabits "a giant's air" which, we know from other Stevens poems, is a trope of origins.

The final stanza leaves little room to doubt the thoroughly fictive grounds of genealogy:

> The father keeps on living in the son, the world
> Of the father keeps on living in the world
> Of the son. These survivals out of time and space
> Come to us every day. And yet they are
> Merely parts of the general fiction of the mind:
> Survivals of a good that we have loved
> Made eminent in a reflected seeming-so.
>
> (*OP*, pp. 87-8)

The continuity of the past lies within the fiction of the mind, the desire to give reality to what remains of faith in orderly descent. But the father is but a reflection of a fiction, a double of trope itself.

IV

One of Stevens' favorite figures of the parent is the giant, for it is he who stands like the sun (son?) "on the horizon": "a close, parental magnitude,/At the centre on the horizon, concentrum grave/And prodigious person, patron of origins" (*CP*, p. 443). The central being of the central poem—in other words, the parent—this is the supreme fiction. (Harold Bloom identifies the "you" to whom Stevens addresses the introductory verse of "Notes toward a Supreme Fiction" as the family.)[16] For to believe in the family is to believe in origins and ends, and thus, in divinity: "We knew one parent must have been divine" (*CP*, p. 331). And like parents, the poem shares in "the first idea":

> It satisfies
> Belief in an immaculate beginning
>
> And sends us, winged by an unconscious will,
> To an immaculate end. We move between these points:
> From that ever-early candor to its late plural. . .
>
> (*CP*, p. 382)

The poem situates man between beginnings and ends, between the pure origin and the innumerable. The "ever-early candor" opens the poem to the "late plural" out of which the first idea is reimagined; the first idea, then, is never original, nor derived, and like Nietzsche's "first metaphor" is always already (in) language.

In canto IV of *"It Must be Abstract,"* Stevens undoes the myth of the first idea:

> The first idea was not our own. Adam
> In Eden was the father of Descartes
> And Eve made air the mirror of herself,
>
> Of her sons and of her daughters. They found themselves
> In heaven as in a glass; a second earth;
> And in the earth itself they found a green—
>
> The inhabitants of a very varnished green.
>
> (*CP*, p. 383)

The fall is Cartesian dualism; thus Adam is neither the author nor issue of the first idea but is the father of self-consciousness, a son who is a father, a doubled father. In a complementary manner, Eve, like Narcissus, finds her image wherever she looks. The "original" parents are writers, makers of metaphors. Heaven is but a "glass," or a mirror of earth, a "varnished green," that is, an artifice or an artificial nature. In "The Pure Good of Theory," these same metaphors are reshaped to form the myth of metaphor:

> Man, that is not born of woman but of air,
> That comes here in the solar chariot,
> Like rhetoric in a narration of the eye—
> (*CP*, p. 331)

The son is an ephebe, a diminutive Phoebus, who is himself a rhetorical figure dragging his father on his back like a double inscription. The eye's (I's) narration tells the story of perception, which Stevens says is always an aftering: "The idea that because perception is sensory we never see reality immediately but always the moment after is a poetic idea. We live in mental representations of the past" (*L*, p. 722). The past, however, is not recuperated by the eye, for when "Man" (the son as Adam) woke, "He woke in a metaphor: this was / A metamorphosis of paradise, / Malformed, the world was paradise malformed. . ." (*CP*, pp. 331-32; ellipsis in Stevens' text). Contrary to Keats, "Man" does not wake to find his dream is reality; he wakens to a dream of a dream, a "mal" form, a metaphor—an aesthetic of "mal." Thus Stevens declines to rest in a metaphor because it is too comfortable a place for so severe a reader:

> Yet to speak of the whole world as metaphor
> Is still to stick to the contents of the mind
>
> And the desire to believe in a metaphor.
> It is to stick to the nicer knowledge of
> Belief, that what is believed in is not true.
> (*CP*, p. 332)

If we speak of the world as metaphor, and thus turn our backs on what Stevens calls "reality," we have merely given ontological priority to mind over nature.

Stevens evades settling for either imagination or reality out of a distrust of metaphor as a bridge between man and nature, or idea and thing. In his "Adagia," he writes, "There is no such thing as a metaphor of a metaphor. One does not progress through metaphors. Thus reality is the indispensable element of each metaphor. When I say that man is a god it is very easy to see that if I also say that a god is something else, god has become reality" (*OP*, p. 179). Stevens implies that reality emerges only in naming; to say man is a god displaces previous notions of god, who must be named anew. Reality is therefore indistinguishable from unreality: "Metaphor creates a new reality from which the original appears to be unreal" (*OP*, p. 169). Reality is neither some prior absolute, a rock upon which man and language rests, nor a supreme fiction. Once we appeal to reality and metaphor we enter into a search for the present, the governing idea that will root metaphor in a stable edifice.

Stevens dramatizes the search as the descent from the first idea:

> But the first idea was not to shape the clouds
> In imitation. The clouds preceded us
>
> There was a muddy centre before we breathed.
> There was a myth before the myth began,
> Venerable and articulate and complete.
>   (*CP*, p. 383)

Stevens exposes mimesis as a genealogical descent from the first idea to nature. The copy exists as the variation of an original untouched by time; this is as true for nature as it is for poetry. Nor will he rest in some belief in the priority of nature; the muddy center is that ground which is neither solid nor water, neither an earthy foundation nor an abyss. It is the myth before myth, for, as Stevens writes in another poem, "The origin could have its origin" (*OP*, p. 85). While myths preceding myths and origins before origins appear to throw Stevens into an infinite regress whereby illusion succeeds illusion, the "venerable and articulate" myth shatters the specular descent into infinity and displaces the central poem of being. The frame bordering the *mise en abyme* is broken open to the uncertainty of writing, a process that refuses to settle on either solid ground or in a specular descent that controls the indeterminable by framing it within a recognizable image. For in the muddy center, the irreducible myth, the poem has its beginning:

> From this the poem springs: that we live in a place
> That is not our own and, much more, not ourselves
> And hard it is in spite of blazoned days.
>   (*CP*, p. 383)

Homelessness, or "the celestial ennui of apartments," is what "sends us back to the first idea" (*CP*, p. 381). The world consists of rooms for rent and the manager is nowhere to be found. And to be without a home is to be without what Stevens variously calls the "first idea," "the myth before myth began," or the muddy center—all of which are tropes of generation or, more particularly, of the single parent who determines the descent of language. Yet, for Stevens, the first idea functions not as a source but as a bareness, an elemental blank, situated in language. Therefore, when he speaks of the disappearance of the gods in "Two or Three Ideas," he interprets it as a displacement of beliefs embodied in language, since the gods are a matter of style. The starting point of his discussion is Baudelaire's "La Vie Antérieure" and the line "J'ai longtemps habité sous de vastes portiques." When we read this, Stevens says, "It is as if we had stepped into a ruin and were startled by a flight of birds that rose as we entered. The familiar experience is made familiar. . . . We stand looking at a remembered habitation. All old dwelling-places are subject to these transmogrifications and the experience of all of us includes a succession of old dwelling-places: abodes of the imagination, ancestral or memories of places that never existed" (*OP*, p. 204). The ancestral home exists only as a belated fiction of the familiar or what Freud calls *das heimlich* (*OC*, pp. 122-61). But the repressed in Freud is never a lost presence; it is known only in its double, that is, as a belated reimagining of a first desire.[17] Similarly, for Stevens, the home is the most unhomely (*unheimlich*) of places, as it is the reminder of the gods' and the parents' absence.

In the same essay, Stevens refers to the disappearance of the gods not only as their own annihilation but also as man's:

> It was their annihilation, not ours, and yet it left us feeling that in a measure, we, too, had been annihilated. It left us feeling dispossessed and alone in a solitude, *like children without parents, in a home that seemed deserted*, in which the amical rooms and halls had taken on a look of hardness and emptiness. *What was most extraordinary is that they left no mementos behind, no thrones, no mystic rings, no texts either of the soil or of the soul*. It was as if they had never inhabited the earth.
>
> (*OP*, p. 207; my emphasis)

Stevens' poetry will serve as the mementoes, the archival remains, of these absent gods. The reimagining of the first idea discloses metaphor as a perpetual naming that at once points to the gods and annihilates them, along with man, with the same stroke of the pen.

Stevens' most dramatic treatment of the reimagining of the gods, which is also their annihilation, comes in the first canto of "*It Must Be Abstract*":

> Begin, ephebe, by perceiving the idea
> Of this invention, this invented world,
> The inconceivable idea of the sun.
>
> You must become an ignorant man again
> And see the sun again with an ignorant eye
> And see it clearly in the idea of it.
>
> Never suppose an inventing mind as source
> Of this idea nor for that mind compose
> A voluminous master folded in his fire.
> (*CP*, pp. 380-81)

Asked to perceive the idea of the sun, the ephebe, a youth just entering manhood, must strip away all the metaphors that this metaphor, the sun, has accrued. Yet the sun is present to neither the mind nor the senses; man only perceives the world in and as a metaphor, thus the need to be ignorant again, for it is only the ignorant man, one free from the accretions of language, who has access to the first idea:[18] "The poem reveals itself only to the ignorant man" (*OP*, p. 160). The first idea, however, is a fiction, a belated reimagining of origins in which the lateness of the son is inscribed in the father's instructions for him to forget the old names. As Riddel has argued, the ephebe "can only recapitulate the fiction of Adamic naming by using an old memory system (language) to forget or overwrite that system, so as to overcome, if only in a fiction, the belatedness signified by all naming" (*WS*, p. 317). And as the third stanza instructs us, the first idea is also a fiction; there is no "inventing mind as source," no "voluminous master"—that is, no transcendent author situated within either nature or the book.

When the ephebe has proceeded by an act of willful forgetting to pass through memory to a "first idea," he can then see the sun:

> How clean the sun when seen in its idea,
> Washed in the remotest cleanliness of a heaven
> That has expelled us and our images . . .
>
> The death of one god is the death of all.

Heaven is the other of man; it can only be seen when it is stripped of human trappings. But to do so would be to hide it. This other is not the dialectical opposite, and thus partner, of man; it is a metaphor for what cannot be named:

> Phoebus is dead, ephebe. But Phoebus was
> A name for something that never could be named.
> There was a project for the sun and is.
>
> There is a project for the sun. The sun
> Must bear no name, gold flourisher, but be
> In the difficulty of what it is to be.
>
> (*CP*, p. 381)

In the absence of the gods, man must face the simultaneous project of naming and being, for naming is being, even if the sun is to "bear no name." Escape from language is impossible, as Stevens lapses into words to speak of the sun's (son's?) project, which bears the father (Phoebus) inscribed within itself. The sun is already language, and "gold flourisher" is a rather hackneyed metaphor.

V

Stevens will return again and again to the myth of proper naming, and thus to tales of absent gods, deserted homes, and nascent poets. These metaphors, of course, are part of Stevens' inheritance from Romantic poetry. He seemed to require the polar terms of reality and imagination as the instruments of thought.[19] In adopting these terms from Romantic philosophy and aesthetics, he declares his literary genealogy. Yet, to do so was to confess to a secondary stature that he simply could not accept. Thus we find him undercutting these tropes in his early works as well as in the late poems of his greatest phase when age begins to impress upon him the essential poverty from which poetry emerges. In "Extracts from Addresses to the Academy of Fine Ideas," he writes of the poet's need to live "naked of any illusion, in poverty,/In the exactest poverty" (*CP*, p. 258). Stevens is at his most eloquent in his elegy for the dying Santayana when the poem is transformed into a meditation on his own impending death and the "grandeur" that is found

> Only in misery, the afflatus of ruin,
> Profound poetry of the poor and of the dead,
> As in the last drop of the deepest blood,
> As it falls from the heart and lies there to be seen,
>
> Even as the blood of an empire, it might be,
> For a citizen of heaven though still of Rome.
> It is poverty's speech that seeks us out the most.
> It is older than the oldest speech of Rome.
> This is the tragic accent of the scene.
>
> (*CP*, pp. 509-10)

"Poverty's speech" has existed before the tradition, before Rome. It is "the irreducible X" (*NA*, p. 83) that Santayana discloses "On the threshold of heaven" (*CP*, p. 508):

> It is kind of total grandeur at the end,
> With every visible thing enlarged and yet
> No more than a bed, a chair and moving nuns,
> The immensest theatre, the pillared porch,
> The book and candle in your ambered room,
>
> Total grandeur of a total edifice,
> Chosen by an inquisitor of structures
> For himself. He stops upon this threshold,
> As if the design of all his words takes form
> And frame from thinking and is realized.
>
> (*CP*, pp. 510-11)

The "total edifice" is realized in, what is for Stevens, an uncharacteristic affirmation of closure of the total book. Perhaps, as Harold Bloom suggests, "Freed by an identification with Santayana as a liminal figure, Stevens for once allowed himself to repress his strong awareness that the mind could never be satisfied lest it fall into the error of ceasing to remember that ceaselessly it was an activity" (*PC*, p. 363). While Stevens' elegy is free from irony, its celebration of Santayana's devotion to thought gently acknowledges that the vision of heaven is the last illusion afforded by a belief in the "total book"; it is a lapse into the evasions of metaphor. Santayana is like the "harassing master" of another poem, who, dissatisfied with "the theory of poetry,/As the life of poetry," extemporizes

> Subtler, more urgent proof that the theory
> Of poetry is the theory of life,

> As it is, in the intricate evasions of as,
> In things seen and unseen, created from nothingness,
> The heavens, the hells, the worlds, the longed-for lands.
>
> (*CP*, p. 486)

Stevens refuses to console himself in the "evasions of as," that is, in tropes. For Santayana's vision is realized in a trope, in the "As if" of the final stanza. The threshold Santayana stands on leads from "The Pure Good of Theory" to a final belief that Stevens could never allow for himself.

In an earlier poem, "Crude Foyer," Stevens bitterly denies that thresholds lead to vision upon death:

> Thought is false happiness: the idea
> That merely by thinking one can,
> Or may, penetrate, not may,
> But can, that one is sure to be able—
>
> That there lies at the end of thought
> A foyer of the spirit in landscape
> Of the mind, in which we sit
> And wear humanity's bleak crown;
>
> In which we read the critique of paradise
> And say it is the work
> Of a comedian, this critique;
> In which we sit and breathe
>
> An innocence of an absolute,
> False happiness, since we know that we use
> Only the eye as faculty, that the mind
> Is the eye and that this landscape of the mind
>
> Is a landscape only of the eye; and that
> We are ignorant men incapable
> Of the least, minor, vital metaphor, content,
> At last, there, when it turns out to be here.
>
> (*CP*, p. 305)

This is perhaps as vehement a rejection of a belief in thought free from reality as one may find in Stevens. The foyer points to the threshold of "To an Old Philosopher in Rome"—it is the vestibule situated between life and death. But this vestibule is, according to the *OED*, "The principle seat (in the body)" of a disease. This is a dis-ease of false beliefs in mind and in ends. But the foyer lying at the "end of thought" is, after all, only a waiting room, a threshold opening onto an end that does not exist. We are incapable of the "vital metaphor" that will transform the landscape of the mind into paradise. Stevens relentlessly disabuses his readers of whatever faith they may have in transcendence as he reduces man's yearnings for the divine to a satisfaction with the illusion that "there," or heaven, may be found here on earth. In this poem ignorance means a belief in paradise, unlike the use of the word in "Notes toward a Supreme Fiction," where it means precisely the opposite, a stripping away of all false beliefs reified in language.

VI

As is well known, Stevens knew Santayana at Harvard, where the young teacher invited the future poet to his rooms occasionally. Holly Stevens has said, "It is obvious that Santayana had a lifelong influence on my father. . . ." (*SP*, p. 69). Frank Doggett has made a rather thorough study of Santayana's influence on Stevens' poetry.[20] Santayana provided Stevens with a necessary model for his belief in the unity of poetry and philosophy. But it was as a man of reason, a scholar, that Santayana seems to have impressed Stevens the most. The frequent appearance of the word "scholar" in Stevens' poetry indicates its importance to him, for the scholar occupies a unique position as a reader in Stevens' canon. "An Ordinary Evening in New Haven" contains one of the most striking passages on the scholar:

> A scholar, in his Segmenta, left a note,
> As follows, "The Ruler of Reality,
> If more unreal than New Haven, is not
>
> A real ruler, but rules what is unreal."
> In addition, there were draftings of him, thus:
> "He is the consort of the Queen of Fact.
>
> Sunrise is his garment's hem, sunset is hers.
> He is the theorist of life, not death,
> The total excellence of its total book."
> (*CP*, p. 485)

The scholar, Professor Eucalyptus, conceives this god, the ruler of reality, as a scholar or a seeker of "the extremest book" (*CP*, p. 380). Married to Fact, the ruler of reality is thus wedded to a belief that life is a unity reducible to the book; hence, he seeks reality "In the metaphysical streets of the physical town. . ." (*CP*, p. 472). Belief in reality requires the same leap of faith as does belief in God:

> Professor Eucalyptus said, "The search
> For reality is as momentous as
> The search for god." It is the philosopher's search
>
> For an interior made exterior
> And the poet's search for the same exterior made
> Interior: breathless things broodingly abreath
>
> With the inhalations of original cold
> And of original earliness. Yet the sense
> Of cold and earliness is a daily sense,

Not the predicate of bright origin.
Creation is not renewed by images
Of lone wanderers. To re-create, to use

The cold and earliness and bright origin
Is to search.
                                        (*CP*, p. 481)

Harold Bloom has called these lines "Stevens' conscious palinode in the matter of the First Idea. . . . The First Idea is no longer seen as a reduction, 'the predicate of bright origin,' but simply as the eye's plain version, the daily sense of cold and earliness" (*PC*, p. 328). The search for an "original cold," which, as Bloom says, is a search to make the Not-Me of nature into the Me, does not, however, lead to contact with the world the immediacy of perception. To use origins is to dissociate the "bright origin" from its generative capacity and to displace it from the head of the past. The origin is to be used, not found, in the daily search in which "The point of vision and desire are the same" (*CP*, p. 466). This search, then, is an evening's gathering of "days' separate several selves . . . together as one." In this identity of day and night, self and other, the scholar uncovers the absence that perpetuates the search:

In this identity, disembodiments

Still keep occurring. What is, uncertainly,
Desire prolongs its adventure to create
Forms of farewell, furtive among green ferns.
                                        (*CP*, p. 482)

The scholar creates by night the fragments, the "segmenta," that remind him by day of the "total book." Between the issue and the absence of these writings lies the perpetual, and thus unfulfilled, devotion to reality, a reality known only in and as the book.

The scholar's search for the total book is a substitute for faith in god. And perhaps it was Stevens' professed agnosticism that restrained him from endorsing Santayana for Henry Church's projected Poetry Chair: "The holder of the Chair would necessarily have to be a man of dynamic mind and, in this field, something of a scholar and very much of an original force. A man like Dr. Santayana illustrates the character, although in him the religious and the philosophic are too dominant" (*L*, p. 378). The scholar's religious fetish of the book is, nevertheless, attractive to Stevens, for he recognized the close ties between reading and faith: "I believe in pure explication de texte. This may in fact be my principal form of piety" (*L*, p. 793).

Despite his attraction to the book, Stevens withheld his endorsement of the scholar as priest. The poet must himself be free from the pieties of his readers. And to be a strong poet, one must deny himself the scholar's hunger

            for that book,
    The very book, or less, a page
    Or, at least, a phrase, that phrase
    A hawk of life, that latined phrase:

    To know; a missal for brooding-sight.
                    (*CP*, p. 178)

The scholar seeks the poem that would be a new testament "like a missal found / In the mud. . ." (*CP*, p. 177). This is the dream of the total book. In the final canto of "The Man with the Blue Guitar," Stevens refers to this desire as "That generation's dream, aviled / In the mud, in Monday's dirty light. . ." (*CP*, p. 183). The book, or its dream, has been lost in the mud; it has been degraded by life in the world, "Monday's dirty light."

    The scholar's dream recuperates God in what Stevens calls "The extremest book of the wisest man" (*CP*, p. 380). But turning the poem into scripture, the scholar is tempted to substitute the illusion of God for the abyss opening up between the poet and his subject, or, as Stevens puts it, "Theology after breakfast sticks to the eye" (*CP*, p. 245). The scholar would be content with a poetry that affirms the One in face of the chaos of experience. This is what Stevens cannot accept:

    After all the pretty contrast of life and death
    Proves that these opposite things partake of one,
    At least that was the theory, when bishops' books
    Resolved the world. We cannot go back to that.
                    (*CP*, p. 215)

Yet Stevens will not turn around and accept disorder, for it is only "a violent order." Unwilling to resurrect theology through its negation, Stevens entertains the possibility of order in disorder:

    But suppose the disorder of truths should ever come
    To an order, most Plantagenet, most fixed . . .
    A great disorder is an order. Now, A
    And B are not like statuary, posed
    For a vista in the Louvre. They are things chalked
    On the sidewalk so that the pensive man may see.
          (*CP*, p. 216; ellipses in Stevens' text)

The model for order comes from royal succession; order is guaranteed by genealogy (though we might think of it as an imposed order, rather than natural, because the Plantagenets were Normans living in and ruling a foreign land). Stevens, however, reimagines this order so that it resembles no other. In his world, writing, or scrawl upon a sidewalk, is the poem waiting for the pensive man; there is no "missal" to be found in "the mud" (*CP*, p. 177).

    Stevens' world is not a world for scholars, who are, after all, only students, too old to be ephebes and too young to be poets. The priestly robes of these youths must be cast off for the somber garb of the rabbi, who is no student but a teacher. And in Stevens' world "the poet would be the Metropolitan Rabbi, so to speak" (L, pp. 292-93). Late in life, Stevens wrote of the significance of rabbis in a letter to Bernard Heringman:

> In the view of Mr. Wagner's very philosophic papers on my things, I am beginning to feel like a rabbi myself. I have never referred to rabbis as religious figures but always as scholars. When I was a boy I was brought up to think that rabbis were men who spent their time getting wisdom. And I rather think that that is true. One doesn't feel the same way, for instance, about priests or about a Protestant pastor, who are almost exclusively religious figures.
>
> (L, p. 571)

Here Stevens uses the word "scholar" in what the OED calls the "vulgar" sense as a man of learning, rather than simply as a discipline or a university student. Nevertheless, this letter is much more helpful than his gloss of "The Sun This March" in a letter to Renato Poggioli: "The rabbi is a rhetorical rabbi. Frankly, the figure of the rabbi has always been an exceedingly attractive one to me because it is the figure of a man devoted in the extreme to scholarship and at the same time to making some use of it for human purposes" (L, p. 786). Stevens' prose commentaries are reassuring—no one can offer a weaker reading of his poems than he does. What, I ask, is a "rhetorical rabbi"?

"The Sun This March" is a particularly important poem because it broke six years of silence. The poem concerns the loss of poetic spirit:

> The exceeding brightness of this early sun
> Makes me conceive how dark I have become,
>
> And re-illumines things that used to turn
> To gold in broadest blue, and be a part
>
> Of a turning spirit in an earlier self.
>
> (CP, pp. 133-34)

While the poem begins as a reawakening of the self, it quickly turns into an acknowledgment of a loss of self that has fundamentally altered the poet. Hence, the solemnity and the pathos of these lines bespeak a reimagining of the poet rather than an awakening of a lost self. Instead of the opulent poetry of *Harmonium*, the poems of "gold in broadest blue," he will need to write poems of "winter's air." Yet there seems to be a hesitancy before the cold, and Stevens cries, "Oh / Rabbi, rabbi, fend my soul for me / And true savant of this dark nature be" (CP, p. 134). Bloom has commented that "the rabbi, like the poet, is always in the sun, and his function is both to defend and to shift Stevens, to reilluminate the poet's dark nature so that he can write poems again" (PC, p. 89). While it wasn't till twelve years later that Stevens denied the existence of "A voluminous master folded" in the sun's fire, the sun has always been foreign to the poet. If the rabbi is the reader of Stevens' soul, and thus his defender, it is because he lives with him in the darkness of a winter's night.

The "dark rabbi" himself had previously appeared in the final canto of "Le Monocle de Mon Oncle":

> Like a dark rabbi, I
> Observed, when young, the nature of mankind,
> In lordly study. Every day, I found
> Man proved a gobbet in my mincing world.
> Like a rose rabbi, later, I pursued,
> And still pursue, the origin and course
> Of love, but until now I never knew
> That fluttering things have so distinct a shade.
>
> (*CP*, pp. 17-18)

The rabbi, like the scholar, is a figure for the reader. In this rejection of "The honey of heaven," the rabbi passes from a devourer of man to a reader of the fluctuations and shades of difference in human love. Stevens' rabbi strikes a more optimistic note than does his "dull scholar," who beholds in love the new mind (an ephebe?) that "bears its fruits and dies" and thus he laments, "Our bloom is gone. We are the fruit thereof" (*CP*, p. 16).

Unlike the priest, or the priestly scholar, the rabbi is the secular reader of man and his texts; thus, in "Notes toward a Supreme Fiction," he is told to observe the poet as tramp, as "The man / In that old coat, those sagging pantaloons," and "to confect / The final elegance, not to console / Nor sanctify, but plainly to propound" (*CP*, p. 389). But it is in the final canto of "The Auroras of Autumn" that the rabbi appears most forcefully:

> An unhappy people in a happy world—
> Read, rabbi, the phases of this difference.
> An unhappy people in an unhappy world—
>
> Here are too many mirrors for misery.
> A happy people in an unhappy world.
> Now, solemnize the secretive syllables.
>
> Read to the congregation, for today
> And for tomorrow, this extremity,
> This contrivance of the spectre of the spheres,
>
> Contriving balance to contrive a whole,
> The vital, the never-failing genius,
> Fulfilling his meditations, great and small.
>
> In these unhappy he meditates a whole,
> The full of fortune and the full of fate,
> As if he lived all lives, that he might know,

>In hall harridan, not hushful paradise,
>To a haggling of wind and weather, by these lights
>Like a blaze of summer straw, in winter's nick.
>   (*CP*, pp. 420-21)

The rabbi is the reader situated not only between man and world, but also between language—in a play of prefixes, negatives, and adjectives that multiply reproductions, and thus interpretations, of the text. The rabbi must therefore be a reader of difference, which is the linguistic play in which man and nature are situated without ever coming into contact. To keep with the initial text, "unhappy people in a happy world," the rabbi must seek to balance the difference and thereby "contrive a whole." It is the rabbi's "never-failing genius" to meditate a whole in the unhappy people as if he had lived their lives, had lived in the harridan halls, in the haggling and shrewish weather of winter, and still be able to "know . . . by these lights/Like a blaze of summer straw, in winter's nick." To know is to lighten the dark soul; it is not a contrivance of the whole, but a moment's interpretation, a lighting of a text "at the finger tips" and not a resting in a final object, as the absence of an object for the verb "to know" suggests.

There is a far reaching significance in Stevens' desire that the rabbi interpret the differences in the words "An unhappy people in a happy world." Hegel defined the unhappy consciousness as the "dualizing of self-consciousness within itself," whereupon self-consciousness is perceived as divided and double. Thus we have "the *Unhappy Consciousness*, the Alienated Soul which is the consciousness of self as a divided nature, a doubled and merely contradictory being. This unhappy consciousness, divided and at variance within itself, must, because this contradiction of its essential nature is felt to be a single consciousness, always have in the one consciousness the other also; and thus must be straightway driven out of each in turn, when it thinks it has therein attained to the victory and rest of unity."[21] In the dialectic of master and slave, dualism was embodied in two individuals; now it is concentrated into one, which subsequently perceives the consciousness that exists for itself and the consciousness that exists for others as the divided consciousness of a single, but contradictory, being. It gazes at itself as a double-consciousness and thus its unity is not a true unity of both.

In Stevens, the unhappy people perceive the other, the world, as happy; in other words, the world is a reality foreign to the individual's consciousness. Aware of this difference, it seeks to overcome the contradiction of the self, but for an unhappy consciousness to rest in an unhappy world is to remain in the duality of a contradictory being. But when Stevens turns to "A happy people in an unhappy world," he rejects it as an impoverished language. The contradiction of being and the world inheres in language, in the words of the world. Thus, the reconciliation of "A happy people in a happy world" is a comedy, a joke, while the belief that man can be happy in a foreign world is a tragedy. Consequently, in the return to the original proposition, he dismisses the possibility of sublation for the unchangeable existence of the unhappy consciousness.

The unhappy consciousness is what Alexandre Kojève called the "Judaic attitude,"[22] which Hegel, without actually using this term, describes as the process whereby consciousness assumes the simple as the essential and the manifold as unessential, or as two foreign realities, whereupon it identifies its own contradictory consciousness with the unessential and is thus unable to free itself from the unessential that inhabits it as the definition, the essence, of its own consciousness.

Derrida, following Kojève and Hegel, has remarked on Jabès' convergence with Hegel, "The Jewish consciousness is indeed the unhappy consciousness. . . ." (*WD*, p. 68). For Stevens, as for Jabès, the unhappy consciousness finds itself "inscribed just beyond the phenomenology of the mind" in a book in which the absence of nature and God is announced "and is lost in being pronounced." Absence "knows itself as disappearing and lost, and to this extent it remains inaccessible and impenetrable. To gain access to it is to lose it; to show it is to hide it; to acknowledge it is to lie (*WD*, pp. 68-9). Derrida here follows both Hegel and Heidegger in describing God, nature, and consciousness as an other that "cannot be found where it is sought; for it is meant to be just a 'beyond,' that which cannot be found" (*PM*, p. 258). "This is where the serpent lives, the bodiless" (*CP*, p. 411), on an horizon where the flash of an unnatural light, a light without origins, illuminates an empty home: "Upstairs/The windows will be lighted, not the rooms" (*CP*, p. 413). The auroras are a figure for the impossibility of language to trace back to an origin a governing power that can control the force of writing.[23] We know the home, the "original chez moi," only by a foreign light, not by an eternal source, and thus we know it only as the impenetrable, as the grave of the unhappy consciousness. And as Hegel says, "Consciousness . . . can only come upon the *grave* of its life. But since this is itself an actuality to afford a lasting possession, the presence even of that tomb is merely the source of trouble, toil, and struggle, a fight which must be lost" (*PM*, p. 258). For Hegel, the unhappy consciousness will eventually abandon the concrete and seek particularity in a force that is universal (*PM*, p. 259), but for Stevens' rabbi, as for Jabès, the unhappy consciousness finds the tomb in the book, a book that can never be possessed but only traced in the path of writing: "Thus the theory of description matters most./It is the theory of the word for those/For whom the word is the making of the world,/The buzzing world and lisping firmament" (*CP*, p. 345). God's "I Am" is a splintered speech, a "latent double" that separates God from his creation and thus usurps speech from man, who must always write and can never speak. The original voice has been shattered with the Tables of the Law and now only rabbis can read the broken words which are our freedom. To be secondary, displaced from God's original speech, is to be free, for freedom exists only in the indeterminability of writing, a negation of the "patron of origins," of God the Father, and a relocation of the site of Being in the book:

> The house was quiet and the world was calm.
> The reader became the book; and summer night
>
> Was like the conscious being of the book.
>
> (*CP*, p. 358)

The rabbi is the only reader free from the bondage of genealogy. He alone stands outside the linear descent of father to son, teacher to student, or from priest to congregation.

Notes

1. "The Rock," *The Collected Poems of Wallace Stevens* (New York: Alfred A. Knopf, 1954), p. 526. Hereafter cited as *CP*. The following abbreviations will be used for Stevens' texts, all published in New York by Alfred A. Knopf: *L—Letters of Wallace Stevens*, ed. Holly Stevens (1966); *NA—The Necessary Angel: Essays on Reality and the Imagination* (1951); *OP—Opus Posthumous*, ed. Samuel French Morse (1957); *SP—Holly Stevens, Souvenirs and Prophecies: The Young Wallace Stevens* (1977).

2. For an analysis of the homeopathic cure in Plato, see Jacques Derrida, "La pharmacie de Platon," *La dissémination* (Paris: Éditions du Seuil, 1972), pp. 69-197.

3. My discussion of the site of writing is indebted to Jacques Derrida's "Edmond Jabès and the Question of the Book," *Writing and Difference*, trans. Alan Bass (Chicago: University of Chicago Press, 1978), pp. 64-78. Cf.: "The site is not the empirical and national Here of a territory. It is immemorial, and thus also a future. Better: it is tradition as adventure" (p. 66). Hereafter cited as *WD*.

4. J. Hillis Miller, *Poets of Reality: Six Twentieth-Century Writers* (Cambridge: Belknap Press of Harvard Univ. Press, 1966).

5. J. Hillis Miller, "Stevens' Rock and Criticism as Cure," *Georgia Review*, 30 (1976), 12. Hereafter cited as *GR*.

6. See Miller, "Stevens' Rock," p. 23: "Stevens' 'The Rock' . . . in spite of its discovery of a cure of the ground in the equivalence of self, leaves, ground, and rock, is a thorough deconstruction of the Emersonian bedrock self."

7. Cf. Stevens' explications of the "sea of ex" in letters of 1940 and 1953. To Hi Simons, Stevens wrote, "The imagination takes us out of (Ex) reality into a pure irreality. One has this sense of irreality often in the presence of morning light on cliffs which then rise from a sea that has ceased to be real and is therefore a sea of Ex. So long as this sort of thing clearly expresses an idea or impression it is intelligible language" (*L*, p. 30). To Renato Poggioli, Stevens wrote, "A sea of ex means a purely negative sea. The realm of has-been without interest or provocativeness" (*L*, p. 783). Two more divergent interpretations can hardly be imagined.

8. Henry David Thoreau, *Walden and Civil Disobedience*, ed. Sherman Paul (Boston: Houghton Mifflin, 1960), p. 195. Hereafter cited as *W*.

9. Walter Benn Michaels, "*Walden*'s False Bottoms," *Glyph 1* (Baltimore: The Johns Hopkins Univ. Press, 1977), p. 148.

10. Joseph N. Riddel, *The Clairvoyant Eye: The Poetry and Poetics of Wallace Stevens* (Baton Rouge: Louisiana State Univ. Press, 1965), p. 244.

11. Sigmund Freud, "The 'Uncanny,'" trans. Alix Strachey, *On Creativity and the Unconscious: Papers on the Psychology of Art, Literature, Love, Religion*, ed. Benjamin Nelson (New York: Harper & Row, 1958), pp. 122-61. Hereafter cited as *OC*.

12. This quotation and the one following it are from unpublished letters in the Stevens

Collection at the Huntington Library, San Marino, California. The first letter is dated December 27, 1944. The second letter is to Charles R. Baker and is dated March 17, 1944.

13. Joseph N. Riddel, "Metaphoric Staging: Stevens' Beginning Again of the 'End of the Book,'" *Wallace Stevens: A Celebration*, ed. Frank Doggett and Robert Buttel (Princeton: Princeton Univ. Press, 1980), p. 334. Hereafter cited as *WS*.

14. Cf. the following dialogue from Edmond Jabès, *The Question of the Book*, trans. Rosemarie Waldrop (Middletown, Conn.: Wesleyan Univ. Press, 1976), p. 17:

> "'What is your lot?'
> "'To open the book.'
> "'My place is at the threshold.'
> "'What have you tried to learn?'
> "'I sometimes stop on the road to the sources and question the signs, the world of my ancestors.'
> "'You examine recaptured words.'"

15. For Helen Vendler, the cry of the leaves signifies Stevens' gathering together "in a single speaking voice the whole psychology, the self. . . ." See *On Extended Wings: Wallace Stevens' Longer Poems* (Cambridge: Harvard Univ. Press, 1969), p. 277. Also see Joseph N. Riddel's review of Vendler: "Interpreting Stevens: An Essay on Poetry and Thinking," *Boundary* 2, 1, No. 1 (Fall 1972), 79-97.

16. Harold Bloom, *Wallace Stevens: The Poems of Our Climate* (Ithaca: Cornell Univ. Press, 1977), p. 167. Hereafter cited as *PC*.

17. For an analysis of the doubled nature of repression in Freud's texts, see Jacques Derrida, "Freud and the Scene of Writing," *Writing and Difference*, pp. 196-231.

18. The definitive examination of the metaphoricity of the sun is in Jacques Derrida, "White Mythology: Metaphor in the Text of Philosophy," trans. F. C. T. Moore, *New Literary History*, 6 (1974), 5-74.

19. In a letter to Richard Wilbur, Stevens explains the polar and the anti-polar: "The greater part of the imaginative life of people is both created and enjoyed in polar circumstances. However, I suppose that without being contrary, one can say that the right spot is in the middle spot between the polar and the anti-polar. It is the true center always that is unapproachable or rather, extremely difficult to approach" (*L*, p. 470). This can be taken as a rejection of dialectics (the polar) and both monism and anarchy (the anti-polar), thus the impossibility of locating a center.

20. Frank Doggett, *Stevens' Poetry of Thought* (Baltimore: The Johns Hopkins Univ. Press, 1966).

21. G. W. F. Hegel, *The Phenomenology of Mind*, trans. J. B. Baillie, 2nd ed. (1931; rpt. New York: Harper Colophon Books, 1967), p. 251. Hereafter cited as *PM*.

22. Alexandre Kojève, *Introduction à la lecture de Hegel*, réunies et publiées par Raymond Queneau (1947; réimpression Paris: Gallimard, 1968), p. 68.

23. Cf. Riddel, "Metaphoric Staging," pp. 332-33: "The auroras, like a 'serpent body flashing without the skin' (*CP*, 411), are 'light' without a proper origin, a natural aberration, flashings not of the sun but of the clashing play of unequal forces, a light of morning as cold as the end of an autumn's day. The 'auroras' have no origin, and even their northern place is inconceivable outside of some eschatological fiction."

Wallace Stevens' Revisions of Crispin's Journal: A Reaction Against the "Local"

Martha Strom[*]

Shortly before he died in 1955, Wallace Stevens wrote an essay on Connecticut which sums up his lifelong concern with the relationship between human beings and the place they inhabit. In this essay, perhaps the last prose he wrote, Stevens speaks of the "American self" as a product of the environment; human activity is the agent that produces "something deeper that nothing can ever change or remove" which is really "the feel of Connecticut." "Going back to Connecticut is a return to an origin," and that regained origin is felt in human activities: "hardihood, good faith and good will." It is "the joy of having ourselves been created" that forms the "feel of Connecticut":[1] "Now, when all the primitive difficulties of getting started have been overcome, we live in the tradition which is the true mythology of the region and we breathe in with every breath the joy of having ourselves been created by what has been endured and mastered in the past."[2]

By 1955, Wallace Stevens "felt like" a native of Connecticut, which, as he says in this essay, was good enough for him. But thirty-five years earlier Stevens felt out of place among reigning literary notions, and in his poems he was searching for his own way of rendering the American landscape. If we return to Stevens' poetic origins, long before "all the primitive difficulties of getting started [had] been overcome," we will see how he was "formed" as he wrestled with his surroundings.

"The Comedian as the Letter C" tells the story of Stevens' "primitive difficulties of getting started." At first glance, the poem appears to be the tale of a man in search of a felicitous relation to his environment, but a closer look proves that its real subject is Stevens' own specifically literary project. By writing this poem, Wallace Stevens defined his place in the American literary milieu of the early twenties. The uncertain poems which followed the publication of *Harmonium* where "The Comedian" first appeared in 1923 show that Stevens' effort had taken its toll. Stevens found the course he had embarked upon difficult because in leaving behind his involvement with what current discussion called the "local" he was letting go of a shared inquiry into the relationship of "place" to poetry. He would never abandon his interest in place, but now he began a solitary quest, and it took some years before he had a clear sense of how to proceed. "The Comedian as the Letter C" records Stevens' ambivalence as he faced a crossroads where he would choose his route through contemporary currents in American literature.

The recent publication of Stevens' poeticized "journal" in *Wallace Stevens: A Celebration* helps us see more clearly than ever before how he

[*]Reprinted with permission from *American Literature* 54, no. 2 (May 1982):258-76.
Copyright © 1982 Duke University.

used Crispin, his comic persona, to move beyond his youthful experiments, including his temporary flirtation with the "local" mode so popular among his contemporaries.[3] The poem is at some remove from a real journal or diary, but "From the Journal of Crispin" does give us insight into Stevens' personal reaction to the contemporary scene. As Crispin's journal blends into "The Comedian"; as the diary is honed into the published poem; as Stevens and Crispin merge and then separate; as the person is shaped into a stylized persona, Stevens inverts the Pygmalion myth. Then, by sculpting his human experience into solid form, he objectifies and orders his relation to his contemporaries. The parts excised from the original version of "The Comedian as the Letter C" force us to read the poem as a reaction against the "localists," rather than as evidence of the "alliance" which Louis Martz perceives between Stevens and the "local" movement.[4] When Martz refers to this "alliance" he quotes these lines, but breaks off after "To make a new intelligence prevail," before the excisions which I include here:

> What was the purpose of his pilgrimage,
> Whatever shape it took in Crispin's mind,
> If not, when all is said, to drive away
> The shadow of his fellows from the skies,
> And, from their stale intelligence released,
> To make a new intelligence prevail.
> [Hence his despite of Mexican sonneteers,
> Evoking lauras in the thunderstorms.]
> Hence the reverberations in the words
> Of his first central hymns. [Hence his intent
> Analysis of barber-poles and shops,] the celebrants
> Of rankest (was "Invaluable") trivia, tests of the strength,
> Of his aesthetic, his philosophy,
> The more invidious, the more desired.
> ("From the Journal of Crispin," p. 41, deleted portion in brackets)

Martz annotates the change to "his first central hymns . . . Of rankest trivia" as proof of Stevens' attempt to distinguish his "hymns" from the experiments with mere "trivia." He points to an intriguing revision, but he does not take fully into account both versions of the poem.[5] By reading both versions of the poem as parts of a whole that together tell the story of Stevens' break with the localists, the meanings of each part emerge as complementary rather than contradictory. The final version of the last lines of this passage reads, "Hence the reverberations in the words / Of his first central hymns, the celebrants / Of rankest trivia, tests of the strength, / Of his aesthetic, his philosophy, / The more invidious, the more desired." Whether those first central hymns were "rankest trivia" or "invaluable trivia," Stevens' poetic excursions into the territory glorified by the localists, into shops and past barber poles, were "invaluable" precisely because they tested his "strength," "his aesthetic, his philosophy": the more rank, the better, or as Stevens writes in both versions, the "more invidious, the more desired." "From the Journal of Crispin" and "The Comedian as the Letter C" document Stevens' grappling with the "stale intelligence" of his fellow artists; and "when all is said," he has driven away their "shadow," and his own "new intelligence" prevails. The "reverberations in the words / Of his first central hymns" reveal the "purpose of his pilgrimage / Whatever shape it took."

When Wallace Stevens was president of *The Harvard Advocate*, he wrote an editorial for the 10 May 1900, issue which prefigures his later irritations with "local-color" writing:

Local Color
So many of the stories submitted to us of late have had their scenes laid in and about the College . . . that a word in regard to local color may not be out of place. It is of course possible for an amusing event to take place in the Yard . . . But because an event does take place in the Yard does not make it amusing . . . Nevertheless it seems to be a popular fallacy with a great many contributors that it is only necessary to stay within the shadow of the dormitories to write an entertaining story or poem.

Here Stevens interpolates an example of Harvard local-color, and comments, "The anonymous poet probably meant well by the Yard, but he can hardly be said to have expressed himself."[6] The anonymous poet has failed to perform what young Stevens considers his primary task; he has not expressed *himself*. Here we find the seeds of Stevens' essay on Connecticut, in its emphasis on human beings rather than the place they inhabit. Between the time of Stevens' early editorial and his essay on Connecticut, he struggled to define his own relationship to "place." In his *Adagia*, Stevens laments, "Life is an affair of people not of places. But for me life is an affair of places and that is the trouble."[7] The tone of this entry in the *Adagia* suggests that it was written in a moment of depression, and the fact that he ascribes "trouble" to the foregrounding of place in his life shows where his real feelings lay. Happily, by 1955 Stevens had come to feel that for him places were identical with the people who live in them and so managed to close the gap that saddened him when he wrote the *Adagia* entry. In Stevens' poetry, "place" is always a human habitation; concomitantly, Wallace Stevens inhabits his poetry, haunts it; his distinct presence is felt in the poems, more profoundly, I think, than in any poet since Wordsworth, so that even in the poems which purport to be about place, we have a sense of some "trouble," some human feeling. In 1921-1922, Stevens' special vision of place in poetry necessitated a definite break with the localist view of how a work of art ought to convey the American place. "From the Journal of Crispin" and the revised "Comedian" dramatize that moment in Stevens' career.

I

"The Comic Mask" and "Carnival," by George Santayana, whom Stevens had long revered, appeared in *The Dial* in June and July of 1921, just months before Stevens hastened to write "From the Journal of Crispin" in time to submit it before 1 January 1922, for the Blindman prize offered by the Poetry Society of South Carolina. Louis Martz provides compelling evidence that Stevens had a December 1921 *Dial* essay by Paul Rosenfeld on "American Painting" in mind when he wrote the poem. He was, as Martz says, "a steady reader of *The Dial*."[8] The two *Dial* essays by Santayana must have been even more interesting to Stevens than "American Painting," since they were written by the philosopher whom Stevens admired all his life, beginning with his student days at Harvard (1897-1900) when he showed Santayana a sonnet and Santayana slipped a sonnet under his door in response. Years later, in 1952, just before Santayana's death, Stevens wrote "To an Old Philosopher in Rome," which expresses his feelings for his "master." Daniel Fuchs and David P. Young have discussed Stevens' philosophic and aesthetic affinities with Santayana, but no one has paid serious attention to their similar comic sense or, what is specifically pertinent here, linked these two essays with Stevens' major comic poem.[9]

These sequential essays argue the value of comic expression such as we find in "The Comedian," and Stevens echoes these essays not only in general attitude and approach to his subject but in particular rhetorical borrowings as well. "The Comic Mask" and "Carnival" guide us toward the mood we ought to bring with us when we read the poem. Stevens' "new intelligence" prevails over his fellows largely because of his profoundly comic spirit as it is embodied in his delightfully lively verse spectacle:

> The clown is the primitive comedian. Sometimes in the exuberance of animal life, a spirit of riot and frolic comes over a man; he leaps, he dances, he tumbles head over heels, he grins, shouts, or leers, possibly he pretends to go to pieces suddenly, and blubbers like a child. . . . Such mimicry is virtual mockery, because the actor is able to revert from those assumed attitudes to his natural self; whilst his models, as he thinks, have no natural self save that imitable attitude, and can never disown it; so that the clown feels himself immensely superior, in his *rôle* of universal satirist, to all actual men, and belabours and rails at them unmercifully. He sees everything in caricature. . . .[10]

So begins "The Comic Mask," and here we have not only the beginnings of a sturdy defense of Stevens' comic extravagance but an explanation of his clowning posture as the "primitive comedian" in "The Comedian as the Letter C." Santayana's opening remarks urge us to read Crispin's experiments in "local color" as "mimicry" that is "virtual mockery," involving "assumed attitudes" from which Stevens can readily "revert . . . to his natural self." In "The Comedian," Stevens presents the views of his contemporaries "in caricature."

"The Comic Mask" prompts Stevens to play a comic role, and in an uncanny defense of expressive form as we have it in "The Comedian," Santayana encourages the sort of rhetorical flamboyance that this poem enacts to the hilt: "Objections to the comic mask—to the irresponsible, complete, extreme expression of each moment—cut at the roots of all expression. Pursue this path, and at once you do away with gesture; we must not point, we must not pout, we must not cry, we must not laugh aloud; . . . Presently words, too, will be reduced to a telegraphic code."[11]

Stevens obviously heeded this advice in the "complete, extreme expression" that the style of "The Comedian" consciously indulges. Santayana also encouraged the poem's rebellious intention. Santayana stresses that pagan comedy "saw nothing impious in inventing or recasting a myth about no matter how sacred a subject."[12] When Stevens describes "The Comedian" as an "anti-mythological poem," one of the myths he refers to is surely the sacrosanct Americanism which surrounded him on all sides and from which he wrested himself, partly through his clowning in this poem. As Santayana observes, "the clown feels himself immensely superior, in his *rôle* of universal satirist." Herbert Stern's publication of the deletions in the manuscript letter suggests that the myth the poem opposes is excessive Americanism but that Stevens was wary of being misunderstood and so omitted the word "American" from his letter about "The Comedian" written to his translator, Renato Poggioli: ". . . it is what may be called an anti-mythological poem. The central figure is an every-day man who lives a life without the slightest adventure except he lives in a [corrected from "the"] poetic ["American" deleted] atmosphere as we all do."[13] Santayana's sanction of the power of the irreverence of comedy to dislodge myth might well have led Stevens to use his comic style as a weapon against the popular aesthetic creed that in the 1910s and 1920s fostered the literary appropriation of American as myth.

In his essay "American Painting," Paul Rosenfeld describes the epoch that produced Wallace Stevens as "the moment of the root-taking of an American culture."[14] Stevens came to artistic maturity when Alfred Stieglitz, William Carlos Williams, Robert McAlmon, and Robert Coady, among others, were proclaiming the need for a true American art that would portray the changes that had occurred since the "root-taking" a generation before. Rooting one's "intelligence" in the "soil," to use the language of Crispin, was in their view the only way to achieve the American art they envisioned. In relation to the dominance of these localists in America, Stevens was like the little magazine *Secession* in its opposition to *The Dial, The Little Review,* and *Broom. Secession* boldly announced its dream of avoiding immersion in popular literary trends and declared a determination to publish "the unknown pathbreaking artist" and to support stylistic experiment.[15] Just as *Secession*'s main driving force was a sure sense of what it did not want to be, Stevens' secession from current fads pushed him beyond the localism of "From the Journal of Crispin" and toward "The Comedian" and a life as a "pathbreaking artist." A quick survey of the heyday of localism will explain the need for dramatic "secession."

Almost always, those who advocated the "local" also evangelized for a metonymic representation of experience in art. As Bram Dijkstra has documented persuasively, Stieglitz's influence was felt far beyond the sphere of photography, and his preference for a non-metaphoric technique dominated painting, poetry, and criticism.[16] The Stieglitz group believed that anyone who wanted to produce real American art would have to forge "contact" with the environment, which could be done only through the discipline of a technique that directed attention to surrounding objects, away from the human subject. The metonymic technique in photography came to imply the American locale it depicted. Theoretical discussions might concentrate on either the importance of a sense of the American place or the objective technique, but one emphasis inevitably implied the other. Just as a lamppost might convey in a Stieglitz photograph the loneliness of each resident of New York City, the single word "local" rang with many associations, both concrete and theoretical, and we must read the literature of that era with an awareness of the network of related concepts buried in the simple words and slogans that constituted the language of these impassioned artists and thinkers.

Stieglitz's influence is abundantly apparent in the publications which Stevens was likely to have read while he was writing his comedy of letters. The Rosenfeld essay on American painting, for example, decries in Ryder's painting the omission of a "report of New York, with its frantic life," and bewails this painter's "strange and fantastic conceptions."[17] He sees in "the limited convexity" of Ryder's work a "defective contact with life."[18] Rosenfeld's preference for metonymic expression prevents him from appreciating Ryder's attempt to transfigure the object, so much like what Stevens inevitably does as his Imagination hovers over Reality. Since Rosenfeld rejects Ryder's metaphoric premise, he sees physical timidity where an unbiased eye might perceive an active spirit.

Besides the Rosenfeld essay, Stevens probably read James Oppenheim's "Poetry—Our First National Art," which argues that America will produce "a truer and more American art" if only the poets will allow "the direct impact of environment and the direct response."[19] Oppenheim's essay would have spoken to William Carlos Williams, but Stevens must have felt the command to respond "directly" as a vague, rather false constraint. Williams was less dogmatic in tone and gave a more concrete sense of what constituted creative source in "contact" with the local, and Stevens would have responded positively to Williams' essay "Yours, O Youth" (*Contact*, Spring 1921). Williams was Stevens' point of "contact," so to speak, with the localists. A passage representative of Williams helps us understand Stevens' attraction to certain elements of localism: ". . . contact with experience is essential to good writing or, let us say, literature . . . contact always implies a local definition of effort with a consequent taking on of certain colors or sensual values. . . . We have not stated that an American in order to be an American must shut his mind in a corncrib and let the rest of the world go hang."[20] Even Williams would have disapproved of Crispin's extreme localism when he "shut[s] his mind in a corncrib and let[s] the rest of the world go hang."

In *Our America*, Waldo Frank makes pronouncements upon the aims of American art that foreshadow in tone and substance Crispin's projected colony, where

> Sepulchral señors, bibbing pale mescal,
> Oblivious to the Aztec almanacs,
> Shall make the intricate Sierra scan
> [In polysyllabled vernacular.]
>   (p. 43, "Journal")

In order for America to know itself, writes Frank, we must "go to the basic materials of life, not to conceive overwhelming panoramas . . . but to identify with one's native ground, to try to attune oneself to a place rather than to the expanse of a nation. The lowly Mexican is articulate, the lordly American is not. For the Mexican has really dwelt with his soil, cultivated his spirit in it, not alone his maize."[21]

While Frank suggests the general "premises Crispin propounds / and propagates" (p. 43, "Journal"), Marsden Hartley's volume of essays, *Adventures in the Arts*, a book saturated with the influence of Stieglitz, documents a specific instance of Stevens' resistance to contemporary pressures. Hartley's essay "Vaudeville" prefigures the language Stevens uses to describe Crispin in the famous letter to Poggioli, who must, Stevens advises, "try to reproduce the every-day plainness of the central figure and the plush, so to speak, of his stage."[22] A. Walton Litz has compiled a suggestive list of Crispin's predecessors in the "stock figures of the *commedia dell' arte*"; and Hartley's essay on "Vaudeville" reminds us that the burlesque figure of the seventeenth centuries had modern descendants in Vaudeville.[23] Stevens' poetic antics and contortions of language (including his comical C sounds, which recall alliterative titles of Vaudeville acts, such as "Burlington Bertie from Bow") can be seen as verbal equivalents of vaudevillian acrobatics.[24] Crispin is a burlesque figure who performs his routines in language before an audience of readers, and it is easy to envision the title of "The Comedian as the Letter C" on a billboard announcing Crispin as the main attraction.

Stevens echoes the language of Hartley's essay, but he inverts Hartley's recommendations for a new, improved vaudeville. Whereas Hartley advocates a plain backdrop to offset the elaborate performance of the artist, Stevens emphasizes the "every-day plainness of the central figure" in contrast to the "plush . . . of his stage." Just as Stevens harks back stylistically to the time before Stieglitz's influence, to the "fantastic" conceptions of Ryder, when he imitates Vaudeville, it is the conventional burlesque that he recalls. In each case, he ignores or consciously dismisses the ideas of his contemporaries. Stevens' description of Crispin and his stage sounds so much like Hartley's essay turned inside out that it is hard to think he did not read and react against this passage from "Vaudeville": "I would begin first of all by severing them from the frayed traditions of worn plush and sequin, rid them of the so inadequate back drop such as is given them, the scene of Vesuvius in eruption, or the walk in the park at Versailles. They need first of all large plain spaces upon which to perform, and enjoy their own remarkably devised patterns of body."[25] In contrast to Hartley's demand for "large plain spaces upon which to perform," Stevens' "every-day plain figure" is almost entirely upstaged by the "plush and sequin . . . eruption" of the "remarkably devised patterns" of language in "The Comedian as the Letter C." In opposition to the "large plain spaces" in the poetry of Williams, Stevens turns Hartley's injunctions upside down, in another refusal to accept the naive epistemology or limited method of the localists.

Many of the localists' concerns were also Stevens', but his divergence in matters of style removed him from the rest of the group. The issue of the local American place was as important to him as it was to William Carlos Williams, but the irrepressible "spirit of riot and frolic" that Santayana appreciated prevented Stevens from bowing stylistically to Williams' notions of what kind of art is truly American or what style best evokes the "American atmosphere." Stevens could see no reason to forsake his innate love of gesture for the rather narrow popular conception of an American style.

The final sentences of "The Comic Mask" articulate the sportive mood everywhere at play in "The Comedian," and if we allow their spirit to inform our reading of the poem we will avoid taking Stevens' lighthearted experiments in style and tone more seriously than they ask to be taken. Santayana helps us see the futility of trying to lay bare or simplify, for once and for all, Stevens' most irreducible poem. And when we attempt to sort out Stevens' (or Crispin's) relation to his "fellows" we will surely not expect to find the simple "alliance" that Martz perceives, but rather a more likely dalliance, embroidered, as Santayana urges, with "what prodigious allegories it will for the mere sport and glory of it." His conclusion to "The Comic Mask" suggests that he would be the ideal reader of Stevens' comedy:

> . . . the mind is not a slave nor a photograph: it has a right to enact a pose, to assume a *panache*, and to create what prodigious allegories it will for the mere sport and glory of it.... Fancy is playful and may be misleading to those who try to take it for literal fact; but literalness is impossible in any utterance of spirit, and if it were possible it would be deadly.... The foolishness of the simple is delightful; only the foolishness of the wise is exasperating.[26]

The Santayanan comic spirit in the poem discourages harsh judgement of Crispin's misadventures, and for a time he represents what Santayana calls the "delightful . . . foolishness of the simple." At the end of the poem, we are warned against the "exasperating . . . foolishness of the wise" to which Crispin succumbs when he creates his localist prolegomena. The localists might have condemned the absence of "literal fact" in Stevens' "utterance of spirit" that employs "what prodigious allegories it will for the

mere sport and glory of it." But the poem's playful style in either version is a
form of resistance, consciously achieved, to the popular conception of the
mind as a "photograph," a "slave" to "literal fact."

II

The most important revisions of the poem are in Part Three of "From
the Journal of Crispin," and they provide the fullest account of Stevens'
slow inclining toward his own form as they reveal the nature of his
preoccupation with popular modes. A brief scrutiny of key passages
excised from the early draft of "The Comedian as the Letter C" will equip
us to read the whole poem more intelligently.

Whereas the first two sections of the poem depict a "festival" of
"jostling" antinomies (p. 35, "Journal"), the predominate mood of
"Approaching Carolina" (Part III) is that of the oxymoron, evoking
"morose chiaroscuro" produced by "green palmettoes in crepusclar ice."

> The spring came there in clinking pannicles
> Of half-dissolving frost, the summer came,
> If ever, whisked and wet, not ripening
> Before the winter's vacancy returned.
> The myrtle, if the myrtle ever bloomed,
> Was like a glacial pink upon the air,
> The green palmettoes in crepuscular ice
> Clipped frigidly blue-black meridians,
> Morose chiaroscuro, gauntly drawn.
> (p. 37, "Journal")

The mood here, epitomizing Helen Vendler's description of "Stevens' best
verse [which] trembles always at halfway points, at the point of
metamorphosis, when day is becoming darkness,"[27] felt in the cold fire of
the moon and its "boreal mistiness," is that of twilight, between
"wakefulness" and "meditating sleep"; of frost "half-dissolving," of
summer "not ripening," a state where fire and ice merge into "clinking
pannicles." This "fluctuating between sun and moon," "an up and down
between two elements," foreshadows in imagery the ambivalence toward
the "local" which the rest of this section plays out on a large scale.

After this crepuscular moment, Crispin sinks more and more deeply
into the quagmire of a localism so extreme that it consumes all his emotion
and leaves him nothing but the power to reproduce physically. But this is a
gradual sinking, and "Approaching Carolina," of all the poem, imitates
most accurately Stevens' own hesitations and ambivalences toward
localism. This part of the "Journal" shows more than any other section the
depth of Stevens' hope of finding a spiritual axis in "place"; while he mocks
the theories of his peers, we still feel his fundamental sympathy with their
intentions.

As a general rule, the deletions necessitate minimal adjustment in the
surrounding passages which stay in the poem. We can assume that Stevens

made changes when he was uncomfortable with the drift of thought in certain passages because little else changes except that the tone becomes inevitably more ironic as Stevens seeks to distance himself from Crispin's plight. The first deletion in Part III contains a clear example of the conflation of poet and persona that Stevens wants to avoid:

> [. . . The poet, seeking the true poem, seeks,
> As Crispin seeks, the simplifying fact,
> The common truth. Crispin, however, sees]
> (p. 37, "Journal")

The parallel between Crispin, who seeks "the simplifying fact," and the nameless, generalized "poet" who seeks "the true poem" suggests too facile an identification between Stevens and Crispin; and the ponderous tone here is out of keeping with the irony which increasingly cushions our view of Crispin in surrounding passages. Stevens' own "seeking" for "true poetry" was after all something like Crispin's quest, so that Stevens would have identified with Crispin's "researches." When Crispin tries to grapple with Stevens' real concerns, the poet becomes involved with the activities of his persona. The revisions restore Stevens' integrity, as they render Crispin's character more distinct.

Consider this major excision, which resonates with the poetics of Williams:

> Moonlight is an evasion, or, if not,
> A minor meeting, facile, delicate,
> [Chanson evoking vague, inaudible words.
> Crispin is avid for the strenuous strokes
> That clang from a directer touch, the clear
> Vibration rising from a daylight bell,
> Minutely traceable to the latest reach.
> Imagination soon exhausts itself
> In artifice too tenuous to sustain
> The vaporous moth upon its fickle wings.]
> (p. 38, "Journal")

From our present perspective, Crispin's preference for "strenuous strokes / That clang from a directer touch"—the sort of direct "strokes" that Williams or James Oppenheim advocated—and his lack of faith in the imagination clearly distinguish him from Stevens. In 1921-1922, however, Stevens could not expect his readers to be familiar with his ideas or count on them to separate the poet from the speaker of these lines. Stevens could well have feared that the last three lines would be read as his own statement of despair, especially since they sound much softer than the preceding lines, so that they seem voiced by someone other than Crispin. And if they are an outpouring of the poet's own feeling, the fact that he removed them from the poem corroborates the impression of Stevens' insistent departure from intimate identification with Crispin.

By suppressing this explicit reference to a localist idea of "strenuous strokes," connecting the less transparent lines that surround it and stretching a fabric of dense ambiguity over the gap, Stevens withdrew from the current aesthetic controversy. Compare the final version; here Crispin's aesthetics remain a mystery:

> Moonlight was an evasion, or, if not,
> A minor meeting, facile, delicate.
>
> Thus he conceived his voyaging to be
> An up and down between two elements . . .

In the revisions, we witness Stevens' growing sense of the privacy possible for him as he acquires skill in manipulating his comic mask, and we perceive his strengthening refusal of social pressures.

The longest excision, predictably, occurs in the stanza which bears the strongest resemblance to a piece of local color writing. This long deletion in Part III is preceded by a passage which Martz likens to Williams' poem "Smell!" (*Al Que Quiere!*). This comparison is illuminating, but Stevens' ironic "Crispin tilts his nose" mocks the sincere Whitmanesque celebration that is felt beneath the scolding that cloaks Williams' rapture in "Smell!" By reading in one sweep the comparable passages, the disparity in their poets' attitudes toward the same subject is heard at once in their contrasting tones.

> Smell!
> Oh strong-ridged and deeply hollowed
> nose of mine! What will you not be smelling?
> what tactless asses we are, you and I boney nose,
> always indiscriminate, always unashamed,
> and now it is the souring flowers of the bedraggled
> poplars: a festering pulp on the wet earth
> beneath them. With what deep thirst
> we quicken our desires
> to that rank odor of a passing springtime!

The lines which lead into the long excision in Part III are a parody of Williams' olfactory approach to spring:

> A river bears
> The vessel inward. Crispin tilts his nose
> To inhale the rancid rosin, burly smells
> Of dampened lumber, emanations blown
> From warehouse doors, the gustiness of ropes,
> Decay of sacks, and all the arrant stinks
> That help him round his rude aesthetic out.
> He savors rankness like a sensualist.
>
> (p. 39, "Journal")

The first part of the long excision is cluttered with an assortment of ingredients typical of the poetry of Williams. A random sampling from, for example, *Al Que Quiere!* yields a list of things remarkably similar to the components of Crispin's "metropole." In *Al Que Quiere!* we find "lawns of the rich," yards filled with chicken wire, "furniture gone wrong," "fences and outhouses built of barrel staves," "great docks," "ships moored in the river," "hawsers that drop and groan," "the old man . . . gathering doglime," and a cityscape similar in structure to Crispin's river city:

> Who knows the Palisades as I do
> knows the river breaks east from them
> above the city—but they continue south
> —under the sky—to bear a crest of
> little peering houses that brighten
> with dawn from behind the moody
> water-loving giants of Manhattan
> ("January Morning," stanza XI)[28]

The first half of the excision clearly imitates Williams' localist mode:

> He notes the marshy ground around the dock,
> The crawling railroad spur, the rotten fence,
> [That makes enclosure, a periphery
> Of bales, machines and tools and tanks and men,
> Directing whistles, puffing engines, cranes,
> Provocative paraphernalia to his mind.
> A short way off the city starts to climb,
> At first in alleys which the lilacs line.
> Abruptly, then, to the cobbled merchant streets,
> The shops of chandlers, tailors, bakers, cooks,
> The Coca Cola-bars, the barber-poles,
> The Strand and Harold Lloyd, the lawyers' row,
> The Citizens' Bank, two tea rooms, and a church.
> Crispin is happy in this metropole.
> (p. 39, "Journal")

   In the lines that follow, however, we find the mind of Stevens involved in the world presented in the preceding passage, processing the opaque landscape through the questions he had about current notions, transforming the solid scene into a shimmering mirage.

> If the lilacs give the alleys a young air
> Of sentiment, the alleys in exchange
> Make gifts of no less worthy ironies.
> If poems are transmutations of plain shops,
> By aid of starlight, distance, wind, war, death,
> Are not these doldrums poems in themselves,
> (the carbon shows Stevens first wrote
> "Are not these spoils of starlight poems in themselves")
> These trophies of wind and war? At just what point
> Do barber-poles become burlesque or cease
> To be? Are bakers what the poets will,
> Supernal artisans or muffin men,
> Or do they have, on poets' minds, more influence
> Than poets know? Are they one moment flour,

> Another pearl? The Citizens' Bank becomes
> Palladian and then the Citizens' Bank
> Again. The flimsiest tea room fluctuates
> Through crystal changes. Even Harold Lloyd
> Proposes antic Harlequin. The bars infect
> The sensitive. Crispin revitalized
> Makes these researches faithfully, a wide]
> Curriculum for the marvelous sophomore.
>
> (p. 40, "Journal")

Stevens' interest in imaginative activity prevents him from resting easy with the localists' reluctance to consider the role of the subject in their object-ridden poetry.

The essay by Santayana called "Carnival" appears to have fed Stevens' misgivings about the simple pleasure the localists took in presenting a poetry of surfaces. The second half of this excision, in fact, can be envisioned as a recast version of the first half, modified by Santayana's ideas, which alter the effect of the localist material. Filtered through the attitudes expressed in the article, the pure local detail is diffused by concerns closer to Stevens' deeper interests. Santayana's essay opposes the reigning localist ideas, articulating in essay form the limitations of those ideas that Stevens quarrels with in the last half of the excision.

In "Carnival" Santayana writes, "Life is free play fundamentally and would like to be free play altogether."[29] The extremely playful attitude in the rhetoric—which falls just short of "free play altogether"—in Stevens' poem is certainly attuned to Santayana's observation. In this passage in particular Stevens argues against the localist tendency to grasp for "contact" with "reality" with such ardor that the "free play" of "life" is falsified. Just as Crispin discovers through "these researches" that "much / Of what he sees he never sees at all," so the localist, bent on snapshot vision, does not really see the "crystal changes" that even "the flimsiest tea room fluctuates / Through." The endless vicissitudes Stevens depicts here illustrate Santayana's remark that "this world is contingency and absurdity incarnate, the oddest of possibilities masquerading momentarily as fact."[30]

As Stevens reworks the "local" components in Crispin's "metropole" he pictures Santayana's feeling that grasping for "contact" with an everchanging environment is not at all desirable: "Thus the universe changes its hues like the chameleon, . . . as it appears in one perspective or another: for everything in nature is lyrical in its ideal essence, tragic in its fate, and comic in its existence."[31] As Stevens puts it, "If the lilacs give the alleys a young air / Of sentiment, the alleys in exchange / Make gifts of no less worthy ironies." The lilacs appear to provide an air of sentiment in the alleys; from another perspective, the alleys comment ironically on the lilacs' "young air / Of sentiment." Their coexistence creates a comedy of relativity, mutually conferred by their "exchange" of "gifts."

The most clearcut Santayanan rendition of local particulars is found in the lines which assert outright the evanescence of the poetic object. Santayana writes, "Existence involves changes and happenings and is comic inherently, like a pun that begins with one meaning and ends with another."[32] In the following passage, Stevens reverses Santayana's comparison and shows that "[poetry] involves changes and happenings and is comic inherently, like [life, which] begins with one meaning and ends with another."

> At just what point
> Do barber-poles become burlesque or cease
> To be? Are bakers what the poets will,
> Supernal artisans or muffin men,
> Or do they have, on poets' minds, more influence
> Than poets know? Are they one moment flour,
> Another pearl? The Citizens' Bank becomes
> Palladian and then the Citizens' Bank
> Again. The flimsiest tea room fluctuates
> Through crystal changes. Even Harold Lloyd
> Proposes antic Harlequin.
>
> (p. 40, "Journal")

Stevens' anti-localist repairs inevitably create a more humanized poetry. He could not be a localist, gravely intent on imitating objects, because he refused to quell his comic vision or deny his belief that the exchange between the environment and the human mind is a more central subject for poetry than an unpopulated scene.

The manuscript version of "To the One of Fictive Music," recovered from the trash along with "From the Journal of Crispin," stresses the primary role of the human imagination as animator of the environment, as Stevens declares outright in the final lines the principle that operates in the revisions of the "Journal."

> Unreal, give back to us what once [we] gave:
> The imagination that we spurned and crave.[33]

Stevens' appeal to the "Unreal" adds to our store of evidence against his "alliance" with the localists. As it deifies the "Unreal," the urgent cry emphasizes the importance of the human subject, whether presented as the deleted "we" or as the projection of the human imagination dubbed "you" in the final version. In this poem, Stevens enacts his divergence from the localists, who often dissolved the subject into the scene and erased apparent exchange between the human subject and the object in the environment. When Crispin is cut off from the possibility of *exchange* with his surroundings; when he is absorbed into the "soil"; when the first line of Part IV announces "His soil is man's intelligence," the separation of Crispin and Stevens is complete, and Crispin sinks further and further into the "soil," away from the potentialities in the "intelligence."

The last excision forces us to see that Stevens intended from the earliest version of the poem that became "The Comedian as the Letter C" to create a "book" that would "contain" Crispin. After shaping a poetic container for the Crispin part of himself, Stevens was free to "stalk in other spheres." As the last lines of the "Journal" tell it,

> [As Crispin in his attic shapes the book
> That will contain him, he requires this end:
> The book shall discourse of himself alone,
> Of what he was, and why, and of his place,
> And of its fitful pomp and parentage.
> Thereafter he may stalk in other spheres.]
>
> (p. 45, "Journal")

Notes

1. *Opus Posthumous* (New York: Knopf, 1957), pp. 295-96.

2. *OP*, p. 295.

3. See Louis Martz, "Manuscripts of Wallace Stevens," *Yale University Library Gazette*, 54, no. 2 (1979), 51-67; and Martz, "From the Journal of Crispin," in *Wallace Stevens: A Celebration*, ed. Frank Doggett and Robert Buttel (Princeton: Princeton Univ. Press, 1980), pp. 3-45. Page numbers in parentheses in the text refer to this edition.

4. Martz, "From the Journal of Crispin," p. 10.

5. Martz's note is at the bottom of p. 41, "Journal."

6. *Harvard Advocate*, 69, no. 5, rpt. in *Souvenirs and Prophecies*, ed. Holly Stevens (New York: Knopf, 1977), pp. 65-66.

7. *Adagia, OP*, p. 158.

8. Martz, "Journal," p. 10.

9. For a history of Stevens' relationship with Santayana, see A. Walton Litz, *Introspective Voyager* (New York: Oxford Univ. Press, 1972), pp. 275-80; see also David Young, "A Skeptical Music," *Criticism*, 7 (1965), 263-83; Daniel Fuchs, "Wallace Stevens and Santayana," *Patterns of Commitment in American Literature*, ed. Marston LaFrance (Toronto: Univ. of Toronto Press, 1967), pp. 135-64; Jerome Griswold, "Santayana on Memory and 'The World as Meditation,'" *Wallace Stevens Journal*, 3, nos. 3-4 (1979), 113-16.

10. Santayana, "The Comic Mask," *Dial*, 70 (1921), 629.

11. Santayana, p. 631.

12. Santayana, p. 630.

13. *Wallace Stevens: Art of Uncertainty* (Ann Arbor: Univ. of Michigan Press, 1966), p. 141. The manuscript letter, dated 3 June 1953, to Renato Poggioli, is in the Wallace Stevens Manuscripts, Houghton Library, Harvard.

14. *Dial*, 71 (1921), 651.

15. G. B. M., "Interstice Between Scylla and Charybdis," *Secession*, no. 2 (1922), 32.

16. *Cubism, Stieglitz, and the Early Poetry of William Carlos Williams* (Princeton: Princeton Univ. Press, 1969), p. 160; pp. 168-69.

17. Rosenfeld, p. 653.

18. Rosenfeld, p. 651.

19. *Dial*, 68 (1920), 242.

20. "Yours, O Youth," in *Selected Essays* (New York: Random House, 1954), p. 32.

21. (New York: Boni and Liveright, 1919), p. 96.

22. This is letter number 862, dated 3 June 1953, *Letters of Wallace Stevens* (New York: Knopf, 1977), p. 778.

23. Litz, pp. 122-23.
24. Marsden Hartley, *Adventures in the Arts* (New York: Boni and Liveright, 1921), p. 167.
25. Hartley, pp. 162-63.
26. Santayana, p. 632.
27. Helen Vendler, *On Extended Wings* (Cambridge: Harvard Univ. Press, 1969), p. 46.
28. Williams, *Collected Earlier Poems* (New York: New Directions, 1966), pp. 115-74.
29. *Dial*, 71 (1921), 44.
30. "Carnival," p. 45.
31. "Carnival," p. 45.
32. "Carnival," p. 44.
33. See Martz, "Manuscripts of Wallace Stevens," pp. 52-54.

The Climate of Our Poems   Joseph N. Riddel*

It is never the thing but the version of the thing

. . . .
The day in its color not perpending time,
Time in its weather, our most sovereign lord,
The weather in words and words in sounds of sound
                                        ("The Pure Good of Theory")
                        — — — — — —
Progress in any aspect is a movement through changes in terminology.
                                        ("Adagia")
                        — — — — — —
Weather is a sense of nature. Poetry is a sense.

                                        ("Adagia")

There seems to be an increasing anxiety of late that the "poems of our climate" have been used and abused by a conspiracy of mis-readers more intent on producing a "climate" of criticism than in honoring the poetic "thing itself." After all, wasn't it Harold Bloom who wrote *The Poems of Our Climate*—the book of criticism that re-writes, as it were, the poem, itself a re-writing of Emerson—Bloom who in one elaborate gesture canonized Stevens as the primary voice in that garden of dissent we call the "new rhetoric." I still hear some complaints that our poems just don't mean what they used to—that criticism has dishonored their privilege by turning them into its own metaphysical grist. It is a common lament, and it occurs every time the critical scene changes. There is always the plea to get back to the poem itself, and to a criticism which in its echo of the poem will efface itself in order to let "The the" stand forth. The "climate" of criticism has always been wintry—recall even Heidegger's metaphors, in his remarks on

*Reprinted with permission from the *Wallace Stevens Journal* 7 (Fall 1983):59-75.

a Holderlin poem, that commentary should be like the fall of snowflakes upon a bell, a self-effacing utterance that allows the poem finally to speak its own silences. Criticism should be language unlanguaging itself in the scene of poetic revelation, that spring-time of a primordial language-ing.

Perhaps more than any other modernist American poet, Stevens has been a "central man" in the history of a critical clamor, including Heidegger and Heideggerianism, that not only refuses silence but which threatens to appropriate to criticism itself the privileged status of the poetic. If Stevens never seemed to belong in the "enclosed garden" of the New Criticism, however, many will hasten to remark that he does not deserve to be identified with the nihilistic blight of the yet newer criticism, that discouraging word with which some of us here in the West are even associated: "Deconstruction." Now I've said or, at least, written it. Why is Stevens today affiliated with the avantest garde-in, with a nihilism or "mortal no" that he explicitly renounced in a "passion for yes"? Bloom, indeed, not only asked the question but insisted that the "poems of our climate" were an answer to it, that Stevens was the eternally American answer to European negative theology, and hence to "deconstruction." And Bloom's project, however much rumor has associated him with the moroseness of evenings in New Haven, has been to reject the very thing this symposium of essays is apparently organized to do: to read Stevens deconstructively, to appropriate Stevens to the latest graft (all puns intended) of criticism. "Shall I uncrumple," to quote a passage some of you will recognize, "this much crumpled thing?" At least I will try to be the avuncular critic.

I wish it were a question of saying that Stevens, or any other modern poet for that matter, was the appropriate poet for a certain kind of criticism; for it would argue not only that poets produce or motivate the criticism adequate to their innovations (and thus that such notions as literary periods, like Romanticism, were historically rooted in poems or were scientific categories), but that certain kinds of poetry were more amenable to certain kinds of criticism: for example, that existentialism is the critical philosophy of the post-WW II novel, or, more precisely for our purposes, that phenomenology, as Hillis Miller and others used it in the sixties, is or is not more appropriate to Stevens' poetry than is the New Criticism, or neo-Romantic epistemology, or, above all, deconstruction. I would like to take up the larger theoretical issue of this confused argument that holds, on the one hand, that external methodologies (drawn from various philosophies or ideologies, say, Freud, Marx, or Heidegger) are not appropriate to the privileged self-referential language of poetry, and, on the other, that certain kinds of criticism (say, Romantic epistemology, or neo-Aristotelian formalism, contextualism or structuralism) are more useful than others for approaching different kinds of styles: for example, that a criticism of consciousness can help us with Stevens' "acts of the mind" but not with the "impersonal" or objectivist poetry of Pound or Williams. But time and the restrictions of this forum do not permit such speculations. What I want to do, then, is to trace out the variety of climatic vortices into which Stevens' poetry has been swept, and to suggest why, more than any other modernist poet, he has been made to stand at the crossroads of contemporary criticism and thus, in a certain sense, become the displaced source of it.

Except for that feat of canonical exorcism called *The Pound Era* (which not so incidentally led to Bloom's counter-canon, the "Stevens era"), the various critical schools and modes which make up that din of dissent by which we recognize the modern critical dialogue have been consistently accommodating of Stevens. And even while Kenner relegates him, in *A Homemade World*, to a footnote of American parochialism, an "American Edward Lear," it was not until Frank Lentricchia's *After the New Criticism* that there has been any serious attempt to dislodge Stevens from the eccentric center of what some call post-modernism—and in Lentricchia's case, as we will see, it is not so much a question of Stevens' centrality as it is the dangerous supplement his writing represents.[1] Kenner's era-gazing and Lentricchia's moralizing aside, for the moment, we might recall that the beginning of Stevens' elevation into the critical canon was coincidental with the rise of the academic New Criticism, an aesthetic of formal closure that seemed at odds with his subjectivist, Romantic, open-ended, meditative kind of verse. The New Criticism was resilient enough, of course, to expand its spatial and hermetic preconceptions in order to account for a poetry of undeniable force and, if you will, originality; but as one can discover in such late masterpieces of formalist or aestheticist reading as Helen Vendler's *On Extended Wings*, the mixture of romantic self-consciousness, rhetorical extravagance, and quasi-philosphical reflection produced several reservations about a poetry that not only offended the Pound / Williams validation of objectivity and precision but playfully violated the decorums of the New Critics' intellectual lyric with its own irresponsible flaunting of a romantic epistemology.

But as Lentricchia puts it, the impact of Stevens' poetry from the beginning was to point a way "beyond" the New Criticism; and in his "fable for critics," he makes Stevens both the stimulus and the symptom of that "change of paradigm," to use Thomas Kuhn's phrase, that has led to post-modernist pluralism, the self-conscious retreat from the world into fiction, and has led to a nihilistic crisis in recent criticism that was the logical conclusion of Mallarmé's "crisis in poetry" nearly a century earlier. Lentricchia points specifically to the figure provided by Stevens' modernism in Frank Kermode's attack upon "spirits grown Eliotic" (the line is Allen Tate's) in his *Romantic Image*; and sets Kermode's text at once beside and in opposition to Northrop Frye's hypostatizing of Romance as the first major breach of New Critical formalism. Curiously enough, Lentricchia forgets that Stevens became for Frye a kind of modern avatar of Blake, and therefore, in a sense quite different from Kermode's, a modernist example of the mythopoeic poet; nor does he recognize yet another version of Romanticism, M. H. Abrams' *Natural Supernaturalism*, which makes Stevens a culminating figure in an unbroken history of

Western literature. But whatever the Romanticism, it has ultimately culminated for Lentricchia in the curse of the modern narcissism and despair which also afflicted the New Criticism in the form of a post-Cartesian dualism and post-Kantian aesthetics, a retreat into the poem itself if not simply into the self and that ultimate dilemma of nihilism Lentricchia sees lurking at the end of any retreat from the "world" or "reality." (For Lentricchia reality would appear to be anything other than "text" taken in the literal sense. Lentricchia presumes to be making a political point about the dangers of Romanticism, but it is really the moralistic indictment of Yvor Winters returned to combat the latest form of irrationalism, deconstruction or the "new rhetoric." And ironically, though they came to different conclusions, both Lentricchia and Abrams ascribe to the same history that sees modern poetry and recent criticism as the inevitable continuity of a poetics that stresses the privilege of the imagination to the world which it struggles, successfully or not, to transform.)

The question about the climate of nihilism in contemporary theory, rejected alike by Lentricchia and Abrams, each for the wrong reason, I must postpone for the moment, but there is surely one inescapable truism in Lentricchia's "descanted" (or de:Kant-ed) history of criticism, to use the phrase of a young friend. Wallace Stevens, or a certain version of several Wallace Stevenses, has unquestionably become the "central man" of the most radical (in a non-political sense) of recent American criticisms. One must discount, then, a history like Lentricchia's which indicts Stevens for his aestheticism and metaphysical pathos, his elitist and private language, and offers in opposition the idiom of Frost as an index of the poet speaking to and for the community of man—a history which, however, stumbles upon the crucial issue of modernist and post-modernist—again, a word I am becoming uneasy with—criticism.[2] One has only to point to the central figure of Stevens in both the practical and theoretical criticism of Bloom, and his epigrammatic place in the very different but complementary Romanticism of Geoffrey Hartman, to see the schematic accuracy of Lentricchia's centralizing of Stevens in a modernist "history," if not the moralistic, or better, dogmatic conclusion he draws from it. And to reinforce the evidence, recall the appropriateness, not to say adaptability, of that Stevens who would tie together the developments of Hillis Miller's career, from the phenomenology of *Poets of Reality* to the post-structuralist tenor of his latest essays. This is to say, Stevens seems to have provided the "ordinary" literary reference point for the so-called newest "Yale School," which, partly through advertisements for itself, has now become identified as a "deconstruction company." This necessarily discounts Paul de Man, whose literary models remain largely European and modern only in the sense that they are in his very special sense Romantic; and Jacques Derrida, who if he has heard of Stevens at all may think of him only as an American Mallarmé. And since Derrida and de Man are the theoretical core of the school, and only Miller among the doctrinaire "deconstructionists" employ Stevens as a central metaphorician, as it were, such histories of "schools" not yet accredited are at best useful for polemics.

In other words, the Stevens on whom Lentricchia centers the entire modern history of an abysmal nihilism, Stevens the aesthete, is hardly the one who turns up as a paradigm for the two major proponents of deconstructive criticism, and as for the other three, Stevens would seem to be at least four different poets: 1. the Gnostic poet of Bloom, who passes through the negative or skeptical abyss—which Bloom misconstrues as the deconstructive moment—in order to signify the "transumption" or overcoming that is America's and Emerson's answer to Europe and Nietzsche; 2. Hartman's provider of metaphors for the ultimate privilege of poetic warmth over philosophical coldness; 3. Miller's "sure questioner" suspended over the abyss of language who nevertheless offers us a "cure" for criticism's appetite to retrieve truth or knowledge from poetry, thereby making poetry a certain kind of undeceived discourse; 4. that Stevens who for all three signifies the privilege of poetry to philosophy and who can thus provide the critique for all extant literary theories while offering a medium out of which to fashion a new one. Only for Miller would Stevens become the paradigm for the modernist as deconstructor, and Miller's Stevens is the one described by Lentricchia only if one accepts the latter's gross misreading of deconstruction as a purely textual practice which repeatedly arrives at the same conclusion, exposing everything beneath words as empty, a nothingness, and thereby leaving us to cling to fictions we know not to be true in order to avoid the void. Lentricchia finds deconstruction, or at least its twilight—since he gives it a history within a history—as a negative aestheticism and thus as the entropic culmination of the New Criticism. Deconstruction is for him—as it is, incidentally, for Bloom—only a reversal of the aestheticism (and thus the materialist textualism) of the New Criticism, and hence a reversal that repeats the very structure it negates or empties out. But, ironically, Lentricchia's admonition for a return to history and ordinary language, or a return to history through ordinary language, arrives at a similarly frosty impasse, and blindness. The hermeneutical circle of our climate is truly enough impoverished, a "merely going round," without the "pleasures" of circulating that Stevens projected.

The critical weather which today buffets our poems seems to fall into two distinct seasons. In effect, the difference is as moot as the auroras of autumn in California, or, to abuse a Stevens line, as the "tropics of resemblance." The argument divides, quite simply, into whether one views literature primarily in an aesthetic or in an ideological mode—that is, whether the poem is the "cry" of its own occasion, a thing or poem itself, or a cultural object, at once the issue and representation of a history which shaped it. (Neither definition, by the way, is sufficient, for as the best of our theoretical critics, Paul de Man, has argued, the aesthetic and the ideological can never be ultimately separated—as in Kant's third Critique, for example.) If the latter, as Lentricchia tends to argue, it would be at once the issue of its circumstances or determinations and a confirmation that modernism and the bourgeois worship of art had arrived at the end of (its) history: thus Stevens as bourgeois solipsist, an exemplary modern. But only because the exemplary modern holds the first position, that a poem is, in John Crowe Ransom's terms, a "precious object" or thing itself, or in Stevens', "part of the res itself and not about it." Critics like Lentricchia seem to accept this definition of Stevens' rhetorical poetry—that it is a self-referential or self-reflective linguistic object—all the while condemning those, from the New Criticism to the Newer Rhetoric, who in his view hold this solipsistic and immoral position. In the aesthetic view, the poem will, by a self-reflective or reflexive play, bear its own critical language within itself; in the ideological view, it demands an extra-poetic mode or discipline (philosophy, history, psychoanalysis, Marxism, and so on) which will provide an adequate language to explicate the poem. In either case, whether the language of criticism comes from inside or outside the poem (and the question here of inside/outside is the crucial one) the two positions remain the same: criticism is the provision of an adequate external language (discursive, or descriptive) that opens up or frees the creative or internal language of the poem even as it effaces itself. Criticism in this view must be at once a metalanguage and a parasite that exhausts the poem and yet provides it with its nature as the true "site" of meaning, the "host" or proper word. And one other thing is thereby assumed: if poetic language has its own priority and privilege, is autotelic and/or self-reflexive, then the masterful and mastering language of criticism can only be a provisional translation into an underprivileged language. In the case of Stevens, Lentricchia assumes that the epistemological relation of imagination and reality (or subject and object), which demonstrates Stevens' adherence to the Kantian aesthetic tradition, is at once an accurate description of his poetry and a symptom of the metaphysical pathos distinguishing that tradition which has uncritically assumed the mimetic play between poetry and philosophy, as Abrams insists. Thus Stevens, for Lentricchia, is both motive and model for all aesthetic criticism, which is to say, all recent philosophical criticism that engages philosophical and ideological "canniness" with its "irrational reasoning."

Like Kermode, Abrams, and even Bloom, however, Lentricchia does not deviate from the position that allows the poet to legislate his own critical terms. All the different ideological criticisms, whether Abrams' or Kermode's history of (Romanticist) ideas or Bloom's rhetoric—even Lentricchia's curiously literal Marxism—allow Stevens to provide the critical terminology for his own poems; though each judges its consequences differently, each takes Stevens as the modernist representative of what Derrida called "white mythology" or a poetry that confirms the uneasy relation between poetry and philosophy in Western metaphysics. However different the ideologies, they each maintain the distinction between a poetic and a critical language, and the subordination of the latter to the former, a mimesis of the former by the latter. In this regard, there is no double bind, but only the issue of ideological judgment—of which critical language is better; or whether the creative language being judged belongs to some historical anachronism. (There is, however, a contradiction always at play here, as signified by Lentricchia's identification of a responsible poetic language with idiomatic or ordinary language. It would seem that the poet, in speaking directly to his fellow man—a Romantic dream, by the way—and not for him, is responsible for maintaining the same commonality as the critic whose clarifications are necessarily self-effacing and non-elitist, while at the same time not celebrating the poem either as "object" or as complex and cryptic discourse.) One may argue, for example, whether Miller's phenomenological dialectic of consciousness in *Poets of Reality*, or Bloom's neo-rhetorical dialectic of tropes in *The Poems of Our Climate*, or even Abrams' historical dialectic in *Natural Supernaturalism*, which takes Stevens as at once example and culmination of the Western tradition, is more or less adequate to the poem(s); or with Lentricchia agree that it is and then condemn one dialectic as morally reprehensible while another is true. But the issue is the same—the search for a critical discourse adequate to the creative.

Now, the arrival of yet another new form of "aestheticism," called deconstruction or textualism, would seem in no way to advance the question, especially since each of the previously named critics, excepting Miller, has already rushed to judge it as just another version of the old structure, unfortunately gone awry: thus Lentricchia's story of Stevens' appropriation by this strange discourse of continental nihilism, or Bloom's view of "deconstruction" as a negative theology which Stevens, in a distinctly American way, answers with a "passion for yes," and Abrams' regret that this dangerous anti-humanism has been imported to destabilize the foundations of the "central" self upon which all poems turn and to which they owe their determinate and determining meanings. All, however, admit reluctantly that "deconstruction," whatever it is, has become the tornado—the twister or trope—of our critical climate, and that those who have come to treat Stevens as if he were Nietzsche and not Emerson, are right if for the wrong reasons. For the humanist critics, essays like Miller's (and even mine) in the Centenary volume (Princeton U.P., 1980) highlight the aberration of any poet who reflects upon the motives of metaphor, as if Eliot's prophecy in "From Poe to Valéry," that madness awaits anyone who reflects so much upon language as did Poe, had been realized in both the poet and his post-modern ventriloquists. Lentricchia merely assumes that we were correct in describing the inevitable submission of the poet to the pleasures of the text, and that the critics are merely following the lure of the poet which makes us all "Connoisseurs of Chaos." The debates of modern criticism have regrettably become melodramatic and banal, and the Stevens we have gathered here to (mis-)read has, probably to his grave surprise, been thrust into its dialogical heat. The issue, simply stated, is whether deconstruction is the appropriate method for reading Stevens or any poet—a method intrinsic to poetic or literary texts in general, but especially post-Romantic or modernist literature, even when it seems to disturb everything held meaningful by literary humanism. Or whether it is only the latest ideological lie against reason, as Bloom claims poems are "lies against time." But this is to presume, quite wrongly, that deconstruction is a method, one among others, or even a reading program or strategy adapted to certain kinds of texts. Despite their very different conclusions about its pertinence to literature in general and Stevens in particular, Bloom and Lentricchia agree on one thing—deconstruction is a negative theology or skeptical method, and while for Bloom Stevens has borne us beyond this impasse while leaving us with its memory, for Lentricchia he is the sign of our continuing self-indulgence.

The critical debate, then, might best be described as turning upon the calculated misreading of deconstruction—whatever "it" is?—rather than of Stevens. We are involved in a misconstruction that demands its own clearing; so that we can understand why a critic like Miller can claim that we cannot deconstruct Stevens because his texts are already self-deconstructions, yet must insist that his own reading of deconstructive moments in Stevens is intended to challenge the claims of other methods to read him properly. It might be prudent, then, to discount the word, if not the notion, "deconstruction," and substitute instead the notion of "strong reading," were it not for the perils of misunderstanding that attend such a notion of "mis-reading" as Bloom advocates. In any event, it would be impossible to describe in brief or in a descriptive mode just what deconstruction is, if it is, as Derrida points out, at once a methodical strategy for opening a reading and an interference with or disruption of method, a *pas de method* to underscore his phrase, in which the *pas*, meaning at the same time "step" and "not," or being at the same time a nominative and a negative, indicates the disturbance in every reading which begins to attend to the way language breaks its own laws. In this sense, that enfolds a nonsense, deconstruction has already begun in every text, and not just in literature, because whatever the text there is already at work at least two texts or two languages—that is, an intertextual exchange that Derrida explores on the model of translation and transformation, and de Man on the model of a rhetorical *aporia* that opens up in every attempt to define the function of trope or figural language, to generate a metalanguage or metacriticism.

Stevens, then, is not a poet unique in his fixation upon language or the "motive for metaphor," not simply a post-modern or avant-garde performer in the "Theatre of Trope," but only one of the more extravagant recent instances where the "turn toward language" has surfaced to reveal and renew once again a crisis in criticism. Without asking whether such and such an interpretation or "reading" of a poem is "deconstructive" or otherwise, we might ask, though in its asking the question is not innocent and is already a quotation, just where the deconstructive linguistic "moment" may reside in a Stevens text or con-texts. We already know some of the questions deconstruction posits, or better, de-positions: first, the

question of the subject, and in regard to Stevens, the very notion of a
creative or genetic imagination; second, the determinacy of the other, or in
Stevens' terms, the ontological status or "ground" of any "reality" outside
consciousness, and of any consciousness outside language, and so on; third,
any binary relation, whether it suggests the stability of oppositions, as in
structuralism, or is revolved into a hierarchy which privileges one term
over the other, as occurs with dizzying effect in Stevens' play between
tropes of imagination and tropes of reality; and fourth, the impossibility of
arriving at any metalanguage that might stabilize or master the play or
performance of the text, and by extension, the impossibility of ever
determining within any text the absolute demarcation between a critical
and a creative language, or what de Man calls the irreducible difference
between the cognitive and the performative. In other words, deconstruction posits by depositioning the impossibility of any text (or texts)
achieving that self-reflexivity which is fundamental to our defining and
privileging the notion of literature or poetry as a unique, closed discourse.

As we have seen, Stevens criticism, of whatever ideology, never really
deviates from the assumption that the problematic of his poems rests on his
(as well as criticism's) incapacity to decode or resolve the epistemological
relativism of subject and object. While a deconstructive reading, so-called,
might begin by reminding itself that this harassed epistemology is already
inscribed in Stevens as a linguistic and textual tangle, not as a psychology,
and hence that the polarities he engages have never been stabilized, or
better, that they exist only in the structures of language. It might begin by
arguing that what Stevens does is appropriate these concepts from
philosophy and revolve them into tropes: that is, trope them, at once
undermining their conceptual power and revealing that in belonging to
language they are a part of our power to signify or to produce multiple
significations, the "merely going round" that undoes as surely as it "cures"
the "ground" (see Miller's recent essays). Deconstruction, then, does not
empty out language but disturbs the illusion of language's ontological
status—not however as a nihilism in the vulgar sense of meaninglessness but
as a prelude to "dissemination." Deconstruction has as its fundamental
project not the denial of meaning but the disruption of closure, in whatever
text, and thus it challenges the totalitarianism of reading. Or to put it all too
simply, deconstruction keeps pointing up those moments when the illusion
of self-reflexivity in a text breaks down, whether upon an undecidable sign
or a rhetorical crux, and where in this catachresis a play takes over that we
may call spermatic, dis-semic, or even poetic, if we do not forget that the
poetic, from Plato's time at least, was associated with the lawlessness of
language, with *paidia*.

Deconstruction can remind us that the essential concept for reading as
well as describing literature is its self-referential or self-reflexive nature,
and this is as true of a notion of realistic or representational fiction, which
accentuates the reciprocity between the figural and the literal, as it is of the
New Critics' autotelic poem. Self-reflexivity permits what Kant called the

freeplay of poetic language, while at the same time protecting the world of reality from the dangers of such frivolousness. The question of reading Stevens for most of his critics has been a question of finding the adequate method to define the play between a language of sounds without meaning, or what he called "life's nonsense" which "pierces us with strange relation," and those aphoristic and quasi-philosophical metaphors about metaphor, language, poetry, and the like. That is, we have been forced to pursue logically through his most alogical (and for some hedonistic) twirling of words a dialectical line that will make the poem comment coherently upon itself: "poetry is the subject of the poem"; and this assertion, you will remember, suggests that whatever the itinerary of sounds and nuances the poem makes, it must eventually return to the solidity of the statement. Whether one calls his poems meditations or philosophical lyrics, variations on a theme or visionary rhetoric, the principle that underlies such descriptions points us toward the dialectical moment of sublation, where the negated meaning is restored and the poem closed: for Bloom the movement from *tropos* to *topos*; for the formalist or thematic critic, a resolution of those variations on a theme, a reduction of the poem to its logical assertion of the illogical. Deconstruction can only remind us that such closures belong not to the poems, which are readings themselves, but to the readings of the poems which have grown tired of Stevens' challenge to, if not lack of, seriousness. Stevens' poems should be allowed to weather such calm, and to pass beyond it, but that would require another kind of reading, perhaps a "theory of reading," or as Stevens would put it—"pages of illustrations."

"Pages of illustrations"—I want to offer now, in conclusion, a textual case in point, though not necessarily as a deconstructive reading, or in any case, not as anything like an exhaustive reading of a poem. And I take my example—all the while reminding you that deconstruction perforce recognizes that the exemplary can never prove the case—from a poem which appears to many critics to be the most affirmative or triumphant of the late Stevens pieces, at least as regards the poet's desire to escape narcissism or solipsism and once again, whatever that could mean, "walk naked in reality." That poem, you might have guessed, is "Credences of Summer," a moment of apogee and not apology in the poet's emotional weather; a poem which seems to say, in a calm that leaves the indulgences of *Harmonium* far behind, that one can pass beyond spring's "infuriations" and pause before the absences or "exhalations" of autumn, and see, even if the mediations or fictions of poetry leave their trace, the world again as if for the first time, directly or without "evasion" by language.

In "Credences" one arrives at a rhetorical moment which claims that what you see is what you get, where what is sensed makes sense, beyond enigma. This desire to become "an ignorant man again," as in "Notes toward a Supreme Fiction," to achieve "poet's metaphors in which being would/Come true," as in "Description without Place," to become the "latest freed man" and realize the "figure" that is "not/An evading metaphor"—such metaphors proliferate in Stevens' canon—is to arrive at the ultimate moment of "repose" that Bloom celebrates as transumption and Lentricchia condemns as a narcissistic retreat into fictions. Thus "Credences":

> Postpone the anatomy of summer, as
> The physical pine, the metaphysical pine.
> Let's see the very thing and nothing else.
> Let's see it with the hottest fire of sight.
> Burn everything not part of it to ash.
>
> Trace the gold sun about the whitened sky
> Without evasion by a single metaphor.
> Look at it in its essential barrenness
> And say this, this is the centre that I seek.

The Stevens problematic is joined in these metaphors which would (almost) murder metaphor. His characteristic style, especially in the later poetry, is evident here in the rhetorical play between what appears as at once a statement of desire and a statement of fact, but which, even in isolation, undermines or tropes its own rhetoric into the indeterminate status of an aphorism, in which "saying" is at the same time "seeing" and "seeking." Even if one were to pass over the vocabulary of "trace" and "sun" in the most remarkable of these metaphors—figures which have, some will recognize, a crucial place in deconstructive readings of theories of metaphor—there is no ignoring the irony of a statement protesting the negative or mediating force of metaphor that can only be made in the most vivid of metaphors. To trace the gold sun is to trace a trace, a sun not seen except in the colorations of language. To "see the very thing" is to pass through the fiction of perception, to achieve an "ignorance" or "innocence" by a process of Nietzschean forgetting.[3] Thus the "hottest fire of sight" (a mixed metaphor at best) is a figure of cancellation or blindness, not that caused by looking directly at the sun but that caused by averting our self-consciousness. In other words, the poem states by metaphorical in-direction that the ideal of pure or unmediated perception is a philosophical construction and would be realized in a poem only if the poem purified its own means or burned away its own representational language.

One never encounters the "sun" in Stevens without confronting this complication. Recall the familiar critical distribution of sun and moon as figures respectively of reality and imagination in Stevens' symbology—a polarity imposed upon us by his poetry as well as his criticism, but a polarity which is as systematically undone as it is systematically inscribed. As we have seen, Stevens criticism has reified these poles as more or less things in themselves, denoted by proper names, and then read their exchanges or interrelationships in terms of a shifting priority of the one to the other, as Stevens' skeptical encounter at once with traditional epistemology and with experience: thus Lentricchia's solipsistic and Bloom's pragmatic Stevens; thus the phenomenological readings of Stevens as a "realist of the imagination." But it is just the question of deciding which term is primary and which secondary that produces the contention in any reading of Stevens, since to read him properly means to decide on one or the other as the "centre that I seek." In "Credences of Summer," apparently, the mind or self foregoes its claims for the origin and center, effaces itself and reappears as a reflection: "as / The physical pine, the metaphysical pine." In what sense is the sun physical, or even the origin of the physical; or to put it another way, in what sense is sense primary? In the sense, perhaps, that the "primary noon" of "The Motive for Metaphor" is an "X," that is, already a trope, a chiasmus, an originally doubled or extended figure.[4] The sun is never properly seen; yet the act of seeing (and tracing) is said to reduce everything to ashes or to burn away the exterior in a way that will unveil the "very thing," the "essential barrenness." The "sun," indeed, is a figure for the act of seeing, of burning away, and seeing is a trope, a trope of troping. If we are to trace the "gold sun" about the "whitened sky," then, we are to trace and efface a figure. The poet is in search of a metaphor that will be adequate to, or not evade, a "primary" metaphor.

But note, either the "gold sun" or "physical pine," the origin and issue of summer, can only be traced by a metaphor that effaces, burns away our consciousness of figurality. To arrive at "summer," the "centre that I seek," is to achieve an unmediated vision by forgetting; since summer, which follows spring's "infuriations" and precedes fall's "exhalations," is like a moment in a breath—or quite simply, it is a trope that falls in a tropological sequence, a trope that suddenly appears as a thing, visible and physical. The primary, then, is secondary; and the secondary (trope) primary—just as in the relation of sun and moon. The "centre" at which one arrives is a "credence," and is produced in one's "saying," a perception that is only a "trace" or which exists only in the structure of language: "Look at it in its essential barrenness / And say this, this is the centre that I seek."[5]

Summer, that is, is a most arresting season; and if one wants to chart the dialectics of this poem he will have to recognize that it cannot close because it has no opening. The plenitude of summer does not precede and lead to fall, nor does it bring the passions of spring to a moment when word and thing, seer and seen, self and world, are one. The physical pine is not some thing itself that is a simple reversal of a paradigmatic or "Platonic perhaps" tree, as Ransom's line puts it. The "physical" too is at once literal and figural, or irreducibly a trope. To burn away every exterior or every representation in order "to see the very thing and nothing else," to reduce everything to the "centre" of one's desire, is still to arrive at what the poem calls an "eternal foliage," or to the metaphysical folded in the physical, to poetic "leaves" (cf. Whitman's leaves of grass) or metaphors whose "meaning" is in their sensory or irrational folds. Despite the poem's admonition, Stevens cannot postpone what in another title he calls the "anatomy of figuration." The "eternal foliage" is a figure for the poem. The poet's desire for a "barrenness" fixed in this "eternal foliage" or figuration exposes the nature of nature, as relentlessly as Nietzsche exposes the metaphoricity of any "thing-in-itself." To burn everything away to one's pure sense of it is still to remain within the realm of "sense," and as Nietzsche has revealed, the realm of the sensory is always already metaphorical. A sense is a stimulus, he argues in that metaphysical fable, "Truth and Falsity in the Non-Moral Sense," and hence a "First metaphor": "a nerve stimulus first transformed into a percept," and each subsequent substitution, of a sound which we make stand for the percept and the word/concept which we make stand for the sound, is a figure of a figure. Nor can we, in the same sense, trace back through the traces to some "essential" which is itself not already a trace or a representation. Nietzsche again: man "forgets that the original metaphors of perception *are* metaphors, and takes them for things themselves," and this is what allows him to situate a cause before an effect, an imagination at the origin of reality, or a reality at the center of appearance; and at the same time allows him to proceed from the notion of self to the "centre" by an act of forgetting himself as an "artistically creating subject." We forget, Nietzsche says, "that the insect and the bird perceive a world different from our own" and that the question of which perception is right or adequate is a "senseless one." Rather than truth, the center that we seek is aesthetic, but not in the sense that Lentricchia sees it, as a world of fiction that lies in contrast to a more substantial world of reality. We live in constructions that are "credences" and hard it is "in spite of blazoned days."

This is a scene which Stevens' poems endlessly revolve: thus the "sun" of canto three is conceived in the figure of a man reading a text which is at the same time illuminated by him, and the reality of the physical perceived in canto four is presented not to the "clairvoyant eye" but to the "secondary senses of the ear," the "Pure rhetoric of a language without words." The "senses" still belong to language, to rhetoric, even if that rhetoric of the senses (or of sensation) precedes words.

The move from metaphor to metaphor, or this displacement of one figure by another, which Stevens celebrates as the inherently poetic nature of nature, or reveals to be a nature that is structured like a language, at once opens up the abyss beneath what one wants to know as the substance of things (the metaphysical that undergirds the physical), and carries us beyond (meta) the physical. Thus a poem can become a ground or "rock of summer," but a ground that is always already figural. That is why Stevens' late poetry only feigns a dialectical movement, and does not, as Lentricchia suggests, wallow in the "mortal no," or as Bloom insists, entertain the negative only as a strategic moment in the agon of transumption, the "passion for yes." The play of imagination and reality in the poetic scene has long since begun, just as the relation of visible and invisible rock already exists in the presuppositions of Western metaphysics, that "white mythology," as Derrida calls it, which works to make us forget that its concepts are, in truth, tropes, and thus not *in* Truth, not "The the." The invisible has been spun out of the vortex or saturnalia of the visible, that is, out of the play of tropes.

Thus in canto seven of "Credences," the turning of the "thrice concentered self," which itself is neither origin nor issue of the "object" it tropes or "averts," is itself no more and no less than a trope. Thus the "stratagems" of canto eight, which allow us to discover the self or "man's mind" as the unreal behind the "real." Thus the drama of canto nine, where the human self senses that the bird's perception of things is "another complex of emotions" than man's, and hence another language. But he can only think of it, as Nietzsche said of the perception of birds, as a language different from our own. We cannot help but think of nature as anthropomorphic, or, as Paul de Man has shown us, as tropological. Language, then, is not a fragile bridge over an abyss nor an empty fiction without ground, but the "real" in every sense, the "sense" of every real. Reality belongs to the realm of judgment, and not truth; the aesthetic and not the cognitive. The cognitive is inscribed in the aesthetic, the critical in the creative, to the point that they can never be absolutely distinguished nor reduced to one univocal "word." Poetry postpones the "anatomy" of summer, or any effort to describe the real in an adequate language, to represent the metaphysical in the physical, and it leaves us with a climate of "characters," or an anatomy of figuration. The final canto of "Credences" brings us to a physical world that, far from being burned away to ashes, can be called nothing other than a plenitude of trope, a world (or better, scene) in which the "personae of summer play the characters / Of an inhuman author, who meditates / With the gold bugs, in blue meadows, late at night." In this "Theatre of Trope," this spectrum of colored masks, the allusion to Poe and to cryptology is only slightly masked. The inhuman author—that anthropomorphized nature—"does not hear his characters talk. / He sees them mottled in the moodiest costumes." This scene, this spectrum of tropes, is the poem—words which do not talk or mean, in one sense, so that they appear only as pure sense, in both senses (aesthetic / cognitive) of that word. But their sense lies in their relation one to the other. Like tropes, they signify only in a play of relations with other tropes, and mean only in the space of this tropological play—"Complete in a completed scene, speaking / Their parts as in a youthful happiness."

What is at stake here, in a poem that asserts the desire to "trace" the "gold sun" in its orbit, "without evasion by a single metaphor," when as Aristotle first taught us, or made us self-conscious, it is precisely the sun that cannot be traced, let alone directly sensed, especially in its eclipse? The sun cannot be sensed or seen directly, and appears most real when it is beyond sense, eclipsed and thus yclept or named in its absence, beneath or beyond the horizon, or when it appears in its reflection, as "mental moonlight," to use another Stevens figure. It is precisely the "sun" that is the name for metaphor, the metaphor of metaphor, a misnomer for that which, as the poet/father says to the ephebe in "Notes," will "bear no name"—will not be what it bears, will not bare what it is, will not be a "bearer-being" in the phrase from yet another poem. For every poem in Stevens which offers us the escape from intelligence, "almost successfully," there is another that marks this "innocence" or "ignorance" as always already figural, a "world of words to the end of it" ("Description without Place"):

> Yet to speak of the whole world as metaphor
> Is still to stick to the contents of the mind
>
> And the desire to believe in a metaphor.
> It is to stick to the nicer knowledge of
> Belief, that what it believes in is not true.
> ("The Pure Good of Theory")

Of course, this is what rationalist critics, wearing "square hats," condemn as the immoralism or the nihilism of the indulgent aesthete—from the cold of Yvor Winters to the francophobia of Lentricchia.

What is implied in this "desire," to use a similar figure from "An Ordinary Evening in New Haven," that wants to achieve the still-point where "vision and desire are the same," where "Reality is a thing seen by the mind" (and thus where to *see* or perception is already a metaphor, "truth" as "apprehended" and hence also a captive), and where "We seek / The poem of pure reality, untouched / By trope or deviation, straight to the word"? In every instance, "reality" is never other than the otherness of the "word" that stands in its stead, a "res itself" that is a "transfixing object" or a figure which, as Nietzsche has told us, is a "forgotten" displacement—a view, in Stevensian words, of "New Haven, say, through a certain eye," an I which has a stance or (in)stead only in "simple seeing, without reflection." But "without reflection" does not mean "before" and only in a "certain" sense can it mean "beyond." Innocence in Stevens is not something that has preceded a fall into experience, but is the metaleptic issue of the "deviations" of metaphor, what "We seek" through and beyond "trope."

"Credences of Summer" appears as one of three major "long" poems in the volume with which its title shares a figure, *Transport to Summer*, the book in its turn sharing a seasonal relation to *The Auroras of Autumn*. The titular metaphors should not, especially since they come so close together and contain poems that are only slightly modified in style and tone, be considered expressions of the poet's own seasons. A decade does not a generation make. It is the "transport" of the title, therefore, which should hold us, or better turn our attention, more so than the season, transport being itself another figure of figure, indeed a trope of turning as well as of transcendence. (Or as Heidegger might have noted, a trope of ecstasy or the ek-stase, a certain going beyond or out of its [one]self.) Transport to summer clearly posits no such thing as an arrival, either at a place or at a point (summit or apogee of some cycle), and far from naming summer as a conclusive or pure moment, the title names the season as itself transporting, thus a trope which would have its independent character and identity only if we forgot that it was a part of an ever metamorphosing series, that which is at once a moment and a place (an apogee and crossing), a time of presence that is never present to itself or "complete" unless we name it as part of a "completed scene." The seasonal cycle is thus only a totalized tropic sequence, without beginning or end.

"Summer," that is, is a "name" in a generalized code that includes "spring's infuriations" and autumn's "exhalations," or a phase within the cycle of a breath or an articulation. It is the "time" that Stevens calls, in "Someone Puts a Pineapple Together," the "tropic of resemblance," and therefore *resembles*, to mark the moment, the "place" of "primary noon" in another of his favorite cycles (almost a cliché): the moment of the "X" or crossing/gathering, of the chiasmus, that he features in a poem like "The Motive for Metaphor." "Summer," like "primary noon," is not an unmediated or transcendental moment, not the moment in which every substitution is effaced or effaces itself in "face of the object." It is instead a doubled moment in a tropic sequence, the moment of the most intense re:semblance; it is the fictive moment of "green's green apogee," or of the word transformed into the thing itself, into "nature." Summer is at once the most intense moment of forgetting—hence another name for the poem, a meta- and a metonym, or misnomer—and the most stylized fiction (a "nicer knowledge") of innocence. Summer is at once the culmination of spring and the beginning of fall, between in- and ex-halation. "Credences," as that titular figure indicates, ritualizes this moment of crossing and turning of subjugation and capture (as in canto vii), or that moment when poetic language appears also as natural language, the fictive as the real. It is a season of "substitutes" and "stratagems" (not only of strategic maneuvers but of the relating of strata of figurations), and thus offers us as "sight" that which is also (and perhaps only) "memory," not the thing itself but only displacements and replacements of "what is not" (canto viii).

The trope that displaces displaces nothing, but is originally in-stead. It is genetic, then, only in the sense that the genesis is a law that exceeds or breaks the law, that generation is an always already dis-re-placement. The "trumpet" or announcement of beginnings "supposes that / A mind exists"; the "cry" is "clarion," both announcement of that which will appear and, as "diction's way," the appearance that precedes what it stands for. Mind, that is, does not announce itself and then appear, divided, in language. But mind is (if is can have any bear-ing here) language, or better, language is the sign of mind, itself originary when it is "aware of division." Summer is the predominant, but not singular, trope of this primary mind / language that is what Stevens calls elsewhere the "fecund minimum" ("The Comedian as the Letter C"), or what in "Credences" he names "green's green apogee," and irreducible multiplicity, a Derridean *différence*.

One could pursue this interrogation, but it would lead not beyond or behind the "cry" that is so fundamental a figure in Stevens. We might, for example, pursue the figure of the "rock," here the "rock of summer" that at first appears so much more concrete or physical than the titular figure of that later poem, "The Rock," in which, as Hillis Miller has shown, it serves as a figure of the metaphysical which is always folded in some physical name and thus can only appear as the ungrounding moment or "Abgrund" which poetry effects within language, which poetry offers us as a "cure" of our illusions that there is an absolute bottom or metaphysical end-point to our "desire" for such. Even here, in his most physical "metaphysical" poem, Stevens can offer the "rock of summer" or the "visible" as no more than "characters" or "personae," a plural rock(s) in a scene (that is not, as it were, seen, except as a fiction). The "rock of summer" is the poem as "illustrous scene," the "vital son." The poem entertains this rock, or as it were names itself, as a reality, just as in "An Ordinary Evening in New Haven" the poem discourses on itself as a "res" itself. In "Credences," to note only the transitional sixth canto, it names itself as the "extreme" moment of "repose" or displacement/repossession in which, to recall "Notes," we forget that the "first idea" resides only in a "hermit's metaphors" and come to believe that the poem is something like a "hermit's truth," which is to say, a "symbol in hermitage." A symbol is "hermitage," both literally and figuratively, if one can use the name literally for the figurative. Home is another metaphor for metaphor. But in this case, Stevens is precise. Tropes are metaphors. Are all metaphors tropes? Not necessarily. At least in one sense a trope, as part of a sequence or series, is "real"; and thus Stevens' turning of the notions of "real" and "unreal," like those of "bearer" and "being," indicate that in the "Theatre of Trope," or in poetry, this undecidable yet decisive moment is "supreme." Summer is not a summation or proper name, but only the illusion and the "illustrous" moment of what an unmediated moment might be, as in a poem that seems like something "Complete in a completed scene." Yet it is also no more than another dawn, whether a spring or the "auroras" of autumn. The summer poem is never beyond "trope or deviation" nor purified of the "intricate evasions of as" ("New Haven") even when it "seems" so. Especially when it seems so—like summer seeming to be eternal; like autumn seeming to be the philosopher's, and the critics', season of genuine reflection; like winter which is the "accent of deviation in the living thing" ("A Discovery of Thought"). And so on.

Notes

1. I will not offer here a detailed bibliography of the critical texts discussed or referred to in these pages. The books and essays should be generally familiar to those aware of the contemporary critical dialogues, and to those concerned more particularly, if more narrowly, with "Stevens criticism."

2. In a recent series of public lectures on the socio-textuality of modernism, Fredric Jameson has attempted to give the modernist movement of the last half-century a "history," which also includes a history of the criticism it has inspired. He identifies the canonical elevation of Stevens in the late sixties and early seventies with what he calls "high modernism," and, somewhat in the temper of Lentricchia, though with more subtlety, links Stevens'

influence on a certain development of American criticism with the textual fetishism characteristic with modernism's attempted withdrawal from history.

3. Cf. the following "Adagia," which at once play with the dream of unmediated perception and dispatch any such illusion: "Perhaps there is a degree of perception at which what is real and what is imagined are one: a state of clairvoyant observation, accessible or possibly accessible to the poet or, say, the acutest poet"; "The tongue is an eye"; "The eye sees less than the tongue says. The tongue says less than the mind thinks." Even in the first, the "perhaps" and the "possible" deter the illusion of an "immediate" perception and mark it as a fiction. In Stevens every immediacy is already displaced: "Metaphor creates a new reality from which the original appears to be unreal." (*Opus Posthumous*, 166, 167, 170, 169)

4. Jacques Derrida, in his "Hors Livre" (or as it is translated, "Outwork"), the preface on prefaces to the three other essays which with "Hors Livre" make up the quadrangular text *Dissemination*, notes parenthetically that the chiasmus "can be considered a quick thematic diagram of dissemination or of those excessive and unregulative effects of language (of which literature is our most notable resource). Derrida offers instead of the monolinear and univocal idea of "work" and "book," that dream of Western man to arrive at the moment Stevens calls "clairvoyant observation." Derrida, taking the lower case Greek sign of the chiasmus or "x" as his emblem (though he always resists the notion of an example adequate to its idea), notes that the chiasmus is not only foursided and therefore a breaking open of the dream of triangulation (the diagram of dialectic), but that the fourth "foot" is somewhat oedipal, swollen, extended, excessive—and thus that a preface, which might be thought to organize a work, which itself has been written after the text and yet is placed before it, which announces at the start what is to be arrived at but announces it belatedly because a preface must have been written after what it introduces, a "preface" therefore is chiasmatic in that it is at once crossing and disorganization, reminder and remainder.

5. In "saying" his desire, the Stevensian poet marks its fictionality, and in the irony of one of his "Adagia": "The final belief is to believe in a fiction, which you know to be a fiction, there being nothing else. The exquisite truth is to know that it is a fiction and that you believe in it willingly" (*Opus Posthumous*, 163). This is, of course, virtually repeated at the end of the second section of his poem "The Pure Good of Theory," in a passage quoted a few pages further on in this essay.

Riddles, Charms, and Fictions in Wallace Stevens
Eleanor Cook°

> No man though never so willing or so well enabl'd to instruct, but if he discerne his willingnesse and candor made use of to intrapp him, will suddainly draw in himselfe, and laying aside the facile vein of perspicuity, will know his time to utter clouds and riddles.
>
> —Milton, *Tetrachordon*

> But not yet have we solved the incantation of this whiteness, and learned why it appeals with such power to the soul.
>
> —Melville, *Moby-Dick*, XLII

°Reprinted from *Centre and Labyrinth* by permission of Toronto Press. © University of Toronto Press, 1983.

Among the many riddling poems Wallace Stevens has given us are
some that are riddles structurally. That is, they cannot be read with much
beyond pleasurable puzzlement until we have found the questions for
which the poem provides answers. One example, published in the last year
of Stevens' life, is *Solitaire under the Oaks* (1955):[1]

> In the oblivion of cards
> One exists among pure principles.
>
> Neither the cards nor the trees nor the air
> Persist as facts. This is an escape
>
> To principium, to meditation.
> One knows at last what to think about
>
> And thinks about it, without consciousness,
> Under the oak trees, completely released.

The key to this compact little poem is Descartes: René Descartes and
des cartes, the cards with which we play card games. The wit lies in the
questions and answers implicit in the poem. What card game would a
Cartesian, would M. Cards himself play? Why, solitaire, of course. We all
know that our problems as *solitaires*—isolating self-consciousness, separation of nature into thinking self and outer object—stem from Descartes'
principle, *cogito ergo sum*. Solitaire is the quintessential Cartesian card
game. But what has M. Descartes forgotten? (He has forgotten something:
"In the oblivion of cards . . .") Answer: trees and air and indeed the cards
themselves (which is to say, himself) as facts rather than as principles. Yet
the card-game of solitaire does offer compensating escape to principium,
to meditation, as in Descartes' *Principia philosophiae* and *Les Méditations*.
One escapes the burden of consciousness as long as one exists within this
card game, thinking according to its rules.

I am not interested here in Stevens' view of Descartes. (It has more to
do with the Descartes of Coleridge and Valéry, I think, than with the
seventeenth-century Descartes.) I am interested in the function of the
riddle-poem. Itself a game, this little riddle simultaneously enacts a game
and comments on other games, both small and large—solitaire and
Cartesian philosophy and poetry too. In its play with paradoxes of outside
and inside, it suggests that there are multiple ways to think of a player and a
game, or of a reader and a text. Poetry comes closest to game in riddle-
poems, those "generic seeds and kernels, possibilities of expression
sprouting and exfoliating into new literary phenomena," as Northrop Frye
says of both riddles and charm poems.[2] And "those who want to study the
relation between form and function in a contemporary setting" may well
"turn . . . to the rigid context of games."[3] The topography of riddles and
charms has been finely mapped by Frye in his 1976 essay, "Charms and
Riddles"; my exploration here proposes to extend that map only a little
farther.

Games in riddle-poems may be multiple in less logical ways, as my
second example is meant to demonstrate. What question do we ask to
bridge the gap between title and couplets[4] in the opaque poem of 1950, *The
Desire To Make Love in a Pagoda (OP* 91)?

> Among the second selves, sailor, observe
> The rioter that appears when things are changed,
>
> Asserting itself in an element that is free,
> In the alien freedom that such selves degustate:
>
> In the first inch of night, the stellar summering
> At three-quarters gone, the morning's prescience,
>
> As if, alone on a mountain, it saw far-off
> An innocence approaching toward its peak.

We begin by noting the double sense of the title: the desire (felt by a
human) to make love in a pagoda, and the desire felt by a pagoda to make
love. We note also the different senses of "peak," and reflect that the act of
making love has a peak physiologically and emotionally, and that pagodas
are "strange buildings which come to a point at the end," as Ruskin says. We
recall the old trope of the body as the temple of the Lord, and remember
that a pagoda is for most of Stevens' readers a foreign or "alien" temple.
Finally, we read the second line as if the noun clause were written by Lewis
Carroll. "Rioter," "when things are changed," is anagrammatically a near-
complete "erotic," which we might expect in a poem about a desire to make
love. These preparations are sufficient for a reading of the poem as the
gently witty, erotic, multi-layered verse that it is: on desires of the body and
of feelings; on primal desires for morning, which a temple might desire, as
in love; on the desire to make riots or anagrams of letters, and to trope. The
riddle takes the following form. Query: Is the body a temple? A temple of
the Lord? Answer: Sometimes it is a pagoda. We begin with a sailor and a
rioter and an anagram, but by the time the word-play culminates in "peak,"
only six lines later, Stevens has left behind the mode of Lewis Carroll. This
is a riddle-poem whose games can touch as well as amuse the reader.

These two examples are built as riddle-poems. More often, Stevens
will include a riddle as part of the larger argument of a poem. For example,
why does Jerome beget the tubas in *Notes toward a Supreme Fiction* (III.i)?

> To sing jubilas at exact, accustomed times,
> To be crested and wear the mane of a multitude
> And so, as part, to exult with its great throat.
>
> To speak of joy and to sing of it, borne on
> The shoulders of joyous men, to feel the heart
> That is the common, the bravest fundament,

> This is a facile exercise. Jerome
> Begat the tubas and the fire-wind strings,
> The golden fingers picking dark-blue air . . .

In his letters, Stevens' answer to my question is carefully and courteously straightforward and also carefully limited: "Jerome is St. Jerome who 'begat the tubas' by translating the Bible. I suppose this would have been clearer if I had spoken of harps" (*L* 435, 12 Jan. 1943). But why tubas and not simply harps? It is true that through his translation of the Bible into Latin Jerome begat sundry *tubae*; that he begat the "jubilas" of line 1 as in the best-known plural "jubilas," *Jubilate Deo*; that he begat the association of "exult" and "jubilas" through his several pairings of forms of *exultare* and *jubilare*. It is also true that he gave us the sound-association of *tuba-jubilate* in the Vulgate, to say nothing of Jubal and Tubalcain, which we also know from the English Bible.[5] (Joyce exploited the sound-association three years before Stevens: "jubalent tubalence," "tubular jurbulence.")[6] But there is another reason. Stevens owned a Lewis and Short Latin dictionary, whose use gave him "delight," as he testified to Robert Frost when making Frost a present of one.[7] There he would have found two meanings for the word *juba*: "the flowing hair on the neck of an animal, the mane," and "crest." These are precisely the tropes of Stevens' second line, in a happy mingling of nonsense-echo and metaphor, the metaphor being, "A multitude is a lion." Stevens' huge Christian lion—not so much the Church triumphant as the Church rampant—is related to an earlier lion in *Notes* (i.v) and also to the lion that iconography commonly places beside Saint Jerome. After all this, how could Jerome beget only harps? He begat the tubas not only through orthodox biblical association, but also for the good poetic reason that they rhyme with *jubas* (in a proper Latin feminine accusative plural ending too), and together the two words offer heterodox associations for the word "jubilas," whose power we might otherwise reverence unduly.

I offer these examples partly as cautionary tales, for I think that sometimes Stevens' seeming obscurity and nonsense are in fact examples of wit we have not yet come to appreciate, riddles whose sibylline ideas of order we have not yet pieced together. To christen a questing, mountain-climbing lady Mrs Uruguay has a good deal more point when we recall that the capital of Uruguay is Montevideo, as Frye once noted. To marry her to a Mr Alfred Uruguay also has a certain point when we recall that the most famed Alfred in modern poetry has as a surname Prufrock, and begins his poem thus:

> Let us go then, you and I,
> When the evening is spread out against the sky
> Like a patient etherised upon a table . . .

To which famous simile, Stevens' opening line to *Mrs. Alfred Uruguay* mischievously replies in an Eliot ragtime rhythm:

> So what said the others and the sun went down . . .

It does not do to underestimate the capacities for riddling and general word-play of a poet who can pun on the words "artichoke" and "inarticulate": . . . "a dream they never had, / Like a word in the mind that sticks at artichoke / And remains inarticulate" (*OP* 47)—"rather an heroic pun," as its inventor endearingly remarked (*L* 366, 27 Aug. 1940).

If all Stevens' riddles worked as these and many others do, we would be dealing with a fine, formidable wit.

> Logos and logic, crystal hypothesis,
> Incipit and a form to speak the word
> And every latent double in the word,
>
> Beau linguist.
>
> (*Notes* i.viii)

Our problems as readers come when Stevens' hypotheses are clouded, when the latent doubles in the word refuse to become patent and remain half-shadowed, figurae without fulfilment. I have offered readings of some of Stevens' riddles using as means of interpretation puns, logic, well-known tropes, Latin equivalents, nonsense-rhymes, iconography, literary antecedents. Though these riddles stand in varying relations to the arguments of their poems, and though their effects differ, they may all be read coherently. The interpretive devices I have mentioned satisfy our desire as readers that consistent if multiple answers be possible for riddles in texts.

But Stevens sometimes moves toward more problematic kinds of riddle. I am not thinking so much of impenetrable lines, which await a wise reader, as of lines where the riddles appear only partly soluble, and the problem becomes not only how to answer the riddle but also how to read the answer. Such lines include sinister-metamorphosis or horrid-metamorphosis poems like *Oak Leaves Are Hands*; "metamorphorid" is Stevens' fine portmanteau word for the process. They also include lines in which Stevens engages in intertextual word-play. For example, in *Esthétique du Mal*, part v, what are the "obscurer selvages"? "For this . . . we forego / Lament, willingly forfeit the ai-ai / Of parades in the obscurer selvages." We can answer this question only so far. Selvages are edges, of course, and so belong in this canto of limits and bars. They may be more precisely placed, however, by reading them against the first five lines of the opening canto of Dante's *Inferno*. There Dante finds himself in a dark wood, *una selva oscura*, and the noun *selva* is repeated in line 5, where its sounds at once expand into *selvaggia—esta selva selvaggia: selva oscura . . . selvo selvaggia, oscura . . . selvaggia*, obscure selvage. *Selvaggia*, however, is cognate with our word savage and not with the word selvage. Eliot makes use of correct etymology in *The Dry Salvages*, third of the *Four Quartets*, published three years before Stevens' poem. The Dry Salvages are a small group of rocks off Cape Ann, Massachusetts, as Eliot tells us; the name, he says, was originally *les trois sauvages*. By anglicizing this name, New Englanders have brought it somewhat closer to its Latin root (*silvaticus*, from *silva*) and much closer to its Italian cognate, *selvaggia*. In Eliot's poem, there is an implicit play on salvages (the rocks), savage, salvage (flotsam and jetsam), and I think salvation (which has the same Latin root as salvage)—play that includes the metaphor of the rock of salvation and allegories of travelling. I read Eliot's title as interwoven in this word-play, and as echoing the *selva . . . selva selvaggia* of the beginning of Dante's journey.

Stevens echoes sound but dislocates denotative meaning, as he summons the ghost of a Dantean *topos* only to de-centre it. For Dante's *selva oscura* is not in the middle of life's way for Stevens—neither as doctrinal allegory nor as personal allegory nor as a place for poetry. As allegory, it is on the edge of things, peripheral to Stevens' earthly vision. Even more on the edge—and thus the "obscur*er* selvage*s*"—is Eliot's poem, *The Dry Salvages*. Yet, having answered this riddle, we find problems in reading the answer. Is this simply ironic distancing? If so, what is the angle of difference between Stevens' troping and Dante's, Stevens' troping and Eliot's? Or is this perhaps what John Hollander calls metaleptic echoing?[8]

Another example of a problematic riddle is the passage about the Arabian in *Notes toward a Supreme Fiction* i.iii. Here the relation of the reader to the text, even of the interior "we" to his own text, shifts as we read and reread the canto. I should like to pause over these lines and to look at the different relations of reader and text, for I think they may tell us something about the functions of riddles, and of charms as well. Here is the entire canto:

> The poem refreshes life so that we share,
> For a moment, the first idea . . . . It satisfies
> Belief in an immaculate beginning
>
> And sends us, winged by an unconscious will,
> To an immaculate end. We move between these points:
> From that ever-early candor to its late plural
>
> And the candor of them is the strong exhilaration
> Of what we feel from what we think, of thought
> Beating in the heart, as if blood newly came,
>
> An elixir, an excitation, a pure power.
> The poem, through candor, brings back a power again
> That gives a candid kind to everything.
>
> We say: At night an Arabian in my room,
> With his damned hoobla-hoobla-hoobla-how,
> Inscribes a primitive astronomy,
>
> Across the unscrawled fores the future casts
> And throws his stars around the floor. By day
> The wood-dove used to chant his hoobla-hoo

> And still the grossest iridescence of ocean
> Howls hoo and rises and howls hoo and falls.
> Life's nonsense pierces us with strange relation.

We are not surprised to find a "Coleridgean idealization of poetry"[9] (lines 1-12) in a meditation upon a supreme fiction, but the presence of what appears to be nonsense-verse in such a meditation is startling, and its relation to lines 1 to 12 a problem for commentators. If lines 13 to 20 are pure nonsense[10] with no affective function,[11] why does Stevens say in line 21 that life's nonsense pierces us? We can hardly exclude nonsense-verse from life's nonsense when we have just been given several lines of it. And whether lines 13 to 20 are read affectively or not,[12] what connection is there with the canto's first part? And what does the movement from the Coleridgean lines into the "hoobla" lines have to do with a supreme fiction?

At least two different types of word-play run through this canto. The first is word-play which makes sense; the second is closer to the uses of nonsense-verse. One proliferates from the English word "candid" and the Latin word *candidus* and dominates the first part. The other plays with Coleridgean echoes, which are submerged in the first part and surface in the second. *Candidus* in Latin, like "candid" in English, means white, but a dazzling white as against a lustreless white (*albus*). It has been used in Latin of the moon, the stars, day; of swans and snow; of Dido's beauty; of gods and persons transformed to gods. It also means "spotless" and is thus synonymous with "immaculate" in Stevens' canto. Figuratively, of discourse, it means clear, open, perspicuous, and therefore the opposite to riddle or *aenigma*, which is in rhetorical tradition an "obscure allegory"[13] and into which Stevens moves in line 13. Until then, he weaves an entrancing web out of multiple meanings and associations of "candid" and *candidus*.[14]

Simultaneously, we may hear an uncanny echoing of Coleridge when we read this canto as a type of riddle poem. Thus: Stevens has transposed the dove's conventional English-language sound of "coo" to "hoo." If we similarly transpose the Arabian's sounds, we hear "coobla-coobla-coobla-cow." Then we don't. We hear "coobla-can," and we begin to hear a nonsense refrain, much like something out of James Joyce: Kubla Khan but hoobla how? This refrain suggests that lines 13 to 20 function at least in part as a riddle whose answer is Coleridge's *Kubla Khan*. Once we have begun to hear this echo, other Coleridgean echoes proliferate. We ask ourselves if it is nonsense to hear subliminal assertions of power in the homonyms for "do" and "can" in the opening line of *Kubla Khan*: "In Xanadu did Kubla Khan." And to read in Stevens' canto that the poem brings back a power again that gives a can-did kind to everything. Of course it is. But in the realm of nonsense riddle, this is how we read.

Outside this realm, back in the realm of rational discourse, we recall that *Kubla Khan* came to Coleridge "without any sensation or consciousness of effort," to quote his phrase, and comes as close as any poem to showing the "pure power" of the imagination. We recall also that the Khan could simply decree a stately pleasure-dome, while Stevens must work toward a supreme fiction which "must give pleasure." *Kubla Khan* in this reading is at least one of the poems, and I think the prototypical poem, which refreshes life in the ways suggested in lines 1 to 12 of Stevens' canto.

Lest this riddle-reading appear too arbitrary, I should observe that Stevens engaged in word-play with *Kubla Khan* elsewhere. In 1923, in *Academic Discourse at Havana*, he invented a "mythy goober khan," which is a peanut stand. ("Khan" as "building" we are most likely to know from *The Arabian Nights*.) But the phrase "goober khan" functions chiefly as a parody—"a peanut parody/For peanut people"—through its unmistakable echo of "Kubla Khan." (I read the entire poem as a forerunner of *Notes* i.iii, for it ends with sleepers awakening and watching moonlight on their floors, and comments of itself that it "may . . . be/An incantation that the moon defines.") In 1942, the year of *Notes*, Stevens opened his weird and haunting *Oak Leaves Are Hands* with a parody of the opening lines of *Kubla Khan*, as Helen Vendler has noted:[15] "In Hydaspia, by Howzen,/Lived a lady, Lady Lowzen . . . ." Coleridge is present in other ways in the work of Stevens at this time. Among Stevens' essays, he appears only in a quotation in a 1942 essay, and in the 1943 essay, *The Figure of the Youth as Virile Poet*, where Stevens calls Coleridge "one of the great figures."[16] In a letter of 1942, Stevens makes use of Coleridge's phrase, "willing suspension of disbelief," along with William James's "will to believe," in a discussion crucial to an understanding of *Notes* (*L* 430, 8 Dec. 1942). In *Notes* itself, he echoes part of Coleridge's definition of the primary imagination (iii.viii).[17] Coleridge is pretty clearly one of the ancestral voices with whom Stevens does battle, or records past battles, in *Notes toward a Supreme Fiction*. A *Kubla Khan* riddle, given other parodies of the great Khan's name and poem, and given Coleridge's place in *Notes*, does not seem to me an overly arbitrary reading.

How do lines 13 to 20 function in Stevens' debate with Coleridge? They work, I think, as a reversal of lines 1 to 12, and their first function is to demonstrate how disabling such a reversal may be. "Hoobla how?" sings or plays or challenges the Arabian, and the phrase is "damned" because one answer is: Kubla Khan but you cannot. The voice of this canto's first part talks about a power in which the reader feels invited to share as part of a communal "we." To give a "kind to everything" is to bring about unity and kinship, a process quite unlike "strange relation." Power in the second part is exercised by the Arabian certainly, but it is a power that excludes the reader in the sense that we cannot agree on even an approximate common stance for reading lines 13 to 20. If the first part shows us the power of the human imagination, just as *Kubla Khan* does, the second part shows us the helplessness of that same imagination, just as the longer *Kubla Khan* we do not have also and most painfully does. (Coleridge's preface to *Kubla Khan* makes a useful gloss on this canto: the return to "his room" and to a dissipated, fragmented vision is, I think, one source for Stevens' Arabian lines. Yet one hardly likes to bring a hoobla-how-Kubla-Khan riddle too close to the memory of Coleridge, even in fancy.)

We can work out the reversal: suggestions of white magic to suggestions of black; radiance to night, with eerie moonlight and broken constellations; openness to riddle; the future as immaculate end to the future as something cast—a context of fate rather than destiny. The visual becomes vague or erratic; the oral reduces itself to the same limited series of sounds as if the Arabian made the memory of the wood-dove chant to his own tune and allied himself with the ancient continuing hooing of the ocean. Language, once glowing with power and moving outward in its ex-prefixes, becomes fitful and nothing to read by or into. The Arabian splits fores and casts, and into the split he throws the future. By line 20, the salt ocean has prevailed over the freshening of line 1. Incantatory multilingual echoes cry through this line, with its monosyllabic equivalent of a Latinate ululate-undulate word-play, and an implicit French-English pun on *houle* (sea-swell) and "howl."[18] "Oh! Blessed rage for order . . . The maker's rage to order words of the sea." But the Arabian with his damned words is master now, the moon at its most unpropitious (the connection is presumably through the figure of the crescent).[19] Against the human "will" and "can" of lines 1 to 12, another voice says "how?" The puns move away from vanished chant and down toward incantation:[20] adnominatio to parnomasia to monotonous echo. How, hoo, who, indeed.

The movement to wood-dove and then to ocean is toward losses other than the loss of poetic power, one of love and the other (I think) in death. A sequence of "gross, grosser, grossest" is implied in the superlative form of the adjective at the end; iridescences may also be of the moon and of doves,[21] and if we use the word "gross" in the sense of "material," we may see here a logical sequence of downward imagery (moonlight, bird, ocean) and of loss (of poetic power as the least fleshly, then of love, finally of the body itself). I think also that the memory of the erotic dove merges with some memory of the poetic dove who broods creatively over the abyss—descendant of the biblical and Miltonic bird of the Holy Ghost through Wordsworth's "brooding mind" to Joyce's "Coo" and Stevens' chanter of hoobla-hoo. The poetic voice has now lost the voice of the dove; the operative forces are the Arabian and the howling, hooing sea. The three realms here (moon, woods, ocean) are those of the triform goddess (Luna, Diana, Hecate) if we accept the ocean as Stevens' form of the underworld. The chanting of hooblas and how and hoos, a circle woven thrice as in the charm-poems of Theocritus and Virgil, resounds like some mage's spell to undo the white and shining enchantment of the first part.

Stevens' riddling here verges on the type of poetry Frye calls charms, poetry whose rhetoric "is dissociative and incantatory," uses repetitive devices ("refrain, rhyme, alliteration, assonance, pun, antithesis"), and seeks to "break down and confuse the conscious will."[22] Charms and riddles are two different kinds of play with language; "Magic would disrupt Nonsense," Elizabeth Sewell argues. But the two may converge:

"the game or the dream, logic or irrationality, may lead us to the same point in the end."[23] For "charms and riddles . . . are psychologically very close together, as the unguessed or unguessable riddle is or may be a charm."[24] That is what I think we have here: a riddle-and-charm poem with two contrasting parts. "Like primitive astronomers, we are free to note recurrences, cherish symmetries, and seek if we can means of placating the hidden power: more for our comfort than for theirs."[25] But there is minimal comfort, if any, in the dwindling symmetries which the reader can ascertain in Stevens' nonsense-lines. The moon has come down from heaven and brought a most uncandid charm, one potentially damning and disabling.

What Stevens accomplishes here is a systematic undoing of his first world, and with it all such "immaculate," idealized first worlds—childhood or erotic or religious paradises—and perforce all idealized theories of poetry. The strategies of undoing dominate the first cantos of *Notes*, and *Kubla Khan*, with its magical transformations of biblical and Miltonic paradises[26] and with its yearning poet, serves Stevens' purposes wonderfully well. Such an undoing may be disabling, as it is, for example, in a lunar sequence in *The Man with the Blue Guitar* which moves from "immaculate" (vii) through "unspotted" (xiii) to "the spot on the floor" (xv). But for Stevens such an undoing may also be a defence. I have read "we say" as "we find ourselves saying" and so have followed the voice of the poem into the power of the fiction of the Arabian. But Stevens' cryptic "we say" also bears the sense of "it is we who say." As soon as we read not "an Arabian . . . with his damned hoobla-hoobla-hoobla-how," but "it is we who say an Arabian . . . with his damned hoobla-hoobla-hoobla-how," another response to his riddle becomes possible: not the accuser saying Kubla Khan but you cannot, but rather the self saying Kubla Khan and I cannot. This is to acknowledge poverty but not helplessness. It is a defensive strategy against the authority of words, including the words of supreme fictions, say "candid" or *candidus*. Riddles and charms do not merely assert that we are makers of our own words, but demonstrate this by showing how words may be reversed and fictions undone. Stevens' nonsense-lines read to me like an archetypal riddle-and-charm poem, the precise opposite of the archetypal "original spell to keep chaos away,"[27] the Word of God or Logos.

"To indulge the power of fictions and send imagination out upon the wing is often the sport of those who delight too much in silent speculation," Imlac says in *Rasselas* (XLIV). "Then fictions begin to operate as realities . . . ." He is speaking of an astronomer, who is persuaded he has the power to control the weather, the sun and even the planets, and so could if he wished do just what Stevens' astronomer does. The astronomer is for Imlac an admonitory example of the hazards of taking fictions for realities. Imlac's idea of what constitutes a fiction differs from Stevens', of course; his religious beliefs are not to him fictions. For Stevens, they are, and Stevens was sensitive to the hazards as well as the benefits of all belief, including poetic belief: "Suppose the poet discovered and had the power thereafter at will and by intelligence to reconstruct us by his transformations. He would also have the power to destroy us" (*NA* 45, 1943). This would be to make art, including sacred art, into magic, and the poet, including the writer of scripture, into an arch-magician and arch-riddler. For Stevens, it is a necessary knowledge that we say and therefore can unsay all our fictions, including our most august stories. Riddles and charms, which by definition are distanced from referential discourse, can make this point very clearly. We not only can unsay all our fictions, but must, for this is how one part of the imagination works, as Stevens says in 1947 in what I read as comment on canto i.iii of *Notes*:

> It must change from destiny to slight caprice . . .
> . . . move to find
> What must unmake it and, at last, what can,
> Say, a flippant communication under the moon.
> (*CP* 417-18)

We are by now so familiar with the ways of deconstruction that my argument thus far appears to claim simply that Stevens is a modern poet. For example, my first reading of *Notes* i.iii. 13-20 would be seen by Derrida as an example of non-radical "illegibility," that "non-sense" (*le nonsens*)which is still "interior to the book, to reason or to logos." My second reading would open the possibility of "radical illegibility" (*l'illisibilité radicale*) or the deconstruction of the traditional doctrine of logos, reason, and the book.[28] Yet the implications of these readings may be disquieting for the reader and lover of fictions. If we deconstruct the old, unifying Coleridgean theories of the imagination, as it seems we must, do we lose the power of illusions, the ability to suspend disbelief? Do all our fictions become Arabian fictions of nonsense, powerful within themselves but without much power over us? Or mirrors of another imagination, Coleridge's perhaps, as the sea mirrors the moon and the moon mirrors a greater light? We seem to be caught. When we are knowledgeable enough and defensive enough about the ways language works, how far can it then affect us? This is a question that John Bayley raises in another context,[29] and it lies behind speculation about the end of narrative. For Stevens, there is the further question: how can we then create or hear a supreme fiction?

Riddles and charms can show us in a nutshell three relations of reader to text. The reader may enter and share the assumed power of the text, answering riddles and feeling exquisite enchantments (in other terms, playing the game or dreaming happily). He may enter the assumed power of the text, unable to answer riddles and feeling sinister enchantments (in other terms, becoming the played-with or experiencing nightmare). Or, he may step outside the blessing and damning power of words, observing that we make the rules of the games and (as we now say) "privilege" the text. But in so far as we still use words, or they us, what power do they then retain?

It takes the whole of *Notes toward a Supreme Fiction* to answer that question fully. Two parts of the answer are pertinent here. The first is suggested in Stevens' final line to *Notes* i.iii: "Life's nonsense pierces us with strange relation." Not "relations," as we might expect, but "relation," which includes more pointedly than the plural noun a relation that is a fiction. The word "pierce" is unexpected too. It is a powerful word in Stevens:[30] one use makes it a function of speech ("the acutest end/Of speech: to pierce the heart's residuum" [*CP* 259]); another use makes it an effect of illusion, and here we need to remember that there is benign as well as harmful illusion for Stevens:[31] ". . . the laborious human [of *Notes* ii.v] who lives in illusions and who, after all the great illusions have left him, still clings to one that pierces him" [*L* 435, 12 Jan. 1943]). In *Notes* i.iii, for all the possible defence in the clause "we say," Stevens does not end defensively. He ends with a piercing or wounding, even by nonsense-language, even by the "hoo" we hear the ocean saying, even in the full knowledge that we say these things ourselves. If we read the poem's last line as in part Stevens' gloss on his own nonsense lines, then he is putting before us the possibility of words as not only a power to bless and damn, a power against which we must defend ourselves, but also a power to pierce and to which we cling because (not although) it pierces us. In *Notes* iii.viii, Stevens asks: "Am I that imagine this angel less satisfied?" Are we who say the riddle and charm of the Arabian less pierced? Only if we defend ourselves completely against the power of all fictions. And a self that cannot be pierced by words cannot be healed or refreshed by them either.

How words "wound" has been explored by Jacques Derrida and more recently by Geoffrey Hartman.[32] This canto suggests another pattern for such speculation through its echoing of religious diction, including the language of grace in line 1 and the language of sacrifice in line 21. Stevens may be said to prefigure here the only version of the incarnate Word which he could accept: the human imagination re-entering and being wounded by a world of language that it has itself created. This is, in effect, what happens in Poe's story, *The Power of Words*, a story which Stevens admired.

A further answer to my question is suggested by *Notes* iii.viii, a companion-piece to canto i.iii and part of the beautiful climactic development of the whole poem. Here the assertive statement that the poem "satisfies/Belief" becomes interrogative: "What am I to believe?" Satisfaction is implied but limited: "Am I that imagine this angel less satisfied?" "Is it I then that . . . am satisfied." All the sentences are interrogative, though one modulates through its clauses into a sufficiently assertive mood to drop the question-mark. This canto does not send us "winged by an unconscious will." "I" both sees as spectator and experiences as angel, and sees his experience, of a movement downward "on his spredden wings," a movement protracted and without landing, a suspension. The time of fulfilment is not in terms of undefined beginning and end, but is specifically limited: an hour, a day, a month, a year, a time. Ex- words here (expressible, external) are limited in comparison with the outward movement—the ex-ness, so to speak—of such words in ɪ.iii (exhilaration, excitation). We might suppose that a movement from first-person plural to first-person singular, from assertive to interrogative mood, from winging our way from immaculate beginnings to immaculate ends to seeing and being a falling angel, from extended to modified adjectives, from excited participation in power to a multiple stance where power is questioned—that all these limitations would make for a lesser canto. But this is not what happens. Stevens' enchanting first world is presented anew here in strength. His canto both enacts and comments on "that willing suspension of disbelief for the moment, which constitutes poetic faith." Coleridge's definition and Stevens' canto are powerful and live for us not in spite of their careful limiting but because of it. Stevens' "I am" claims no more than he can sustain: "I have not but I am and as I am, I am."

At the end of this canto, the Cinderella story reverses the angelic moment, as the Arabian's story reverses the world of "candid" and *candidus*, the two reversals being very different. It also reverses the Miltonic and biblical world of the aspiring Canon Aspirin in the three preceding cantos (v-vii). "Candid" is used only once elsewhere in Stevens' poetry ("candor" never again) in a way that associates it with "canon" and "canonical."[33] When we note that a candidate may also be an Aspirant (*OED*, "candidate," 2.a), the candid-Canon-canonical association appears firm. In 1909, age twenty-nine, Stevens noted the Cinderella story in his journal in a one-word entry: "pumpkin-coach."[34] The entry follows immediately on these lines:

> What I aspired to be,
> And was not, comforts me—

The lines, unidentified, are from Browning's *Rabbi Ben Ezra*, so that Browning's rabbi must take his place as another of the aspirers who make up that compound ghost, Canon Aspirin. For all Stevens' love for the white worlds and aspiring figures of a biblical, Miltonic, Coleridgean, and Browning heritage—rather, because of his love—their power has to be undone, whether by riddle or by charm or by fairy tale. Only then can Stevens lead us toward the exquisite fiction of his fat girl in the final canto of *Notes*. Only then can he write at all, can he "patch together" (Stevens' revisionary version of the word "compose"). For *Notes* ends with a Stevensian poet who

> Patches the moon together in his room
> To his Virgilian cadences, up down,
> Up down. It is a war that never ends.

Notes

1. *Opus Posthumous: Poems, Plays, Prose by Wallace Stevens*, ed. Samuel French Morse (New York, 1957), 111, hereafter cited as *OP*. Other abbreviations in the text are: *CP*, *The Collected Poems of Wallace Stevens* (New York, 1954); *L*, *Letters of Wallace Stevens*, ed.

Holly Stevens (New York, 1972); *NA*, *The Necessary Angel: Essays on Reality and the Imagination* (New York, 1951).

2. "Charms and Riddles," in *Spiritus Mundi: Essays on Literature, Myth, and Society* (Bloomington, 1976), 123.

3. E. H. Gombrich, *Art and Illusion: A Study in the Psychology of Pictorial Representation*, 2nd ed. (Princeton, 1969; pbk.), 119-20.

4. Cf. John Hollander: "Wallace Stevens . . . has frequently been cited as a writer whose titles function with indirection, apparent perversity, or some symbol-making quality that is characteristic of the fundamental methods of his poetry. If they direct a particular kind of attention to the poems that they head, it is much more an analytic or interpretive role that they play than more properly a genre- or type-defining one" (*Vision and Resonance* [New York, 1975], 218).

5. *Biblia Sacra Latina*, Psalmus c:1 (*Jubilate Deo*); Psalmus LXXXI:1 (*Exultate—jubilate*), Psalmus XCVIII:4 (*Jubilate . . . cantate, et exultate, et psallit*), Zacharia IX:9 (*exulta . . . jubila*), Psalmus XCVIII:6 (*In tubis . . . et voce tubae . . . Jubilate*) and Genesis 4:21, 22. This numbering varies slightly from the Vulgate.

6. *Finnegans Wake* (New York, 1958), 338, 84.

7. Letter of 16 July 1935, Dartmouth College Library; quoted by permission of Holly Stevens and Dartmouth College Library. Cf. *L*.275, 4 March 1935.

8. "Echo Metaleptic," in *The Figure of Echo: A Mode of Allusion in Milton and After* (Berkeley, 1981), 113-32. *The Figure of Echo* is essential reading for anyone who talks about echoing, as I do in this essay. It came into my hands after this essay had gone out of them.

9. Harold Bloom, *Wallace Stevens: The Poems of Our Climate* (Ithaca, 1976), 182.

10. I use the term "pure nonsense," that is, self-contained nonsense with no apparent affective function, where others use simply "nonsense." Cf. John M. Munro, "Nonsense Verse," in *The Princeton Encyclopedia of Poetry and Poetics*, ed. Alex Preminger (Princeton, 1974); Elizabeth Sewell, *The Field of Nonsense* (London, 1952); and Michael Holquist, "What Is a Boojum? Nonsense and Modernism," *Yale French Studies*, 43 (1969), 145-64.

11. Cf. Hugh Kenner, "Seraphic Glitter: Stevens' Nonsense," *Parnassus: Poetry in Review*, 5 (1976), 153-9, and Irvin Ehrenpreis, "Strange Relation: Stevens' Nonsense," in *Wallace Stevens: A Celebration*, ed. Frank Doggett and Robert Buttel (Princeton, 1980), 233-4.

12. For an affective reading, see Bloom, *Wallace Stevens*, 181-3.

13. Cicero, *De Or*, III.xlii; Quintilian, *Inst. Or*. VIII.vi.52. On *aenigma* in relation to the structure of allegory, see Angus Fletcher, *Allegory: The Theory of a Symbolic Mode* (Ithaca and London, 1964), under *aenigma*, passim.

14. Cf. William Empson on the word "candid," in *The Structure of Complex Words*, 3rd ed. (London, 1977), 307-10.

15. Helen Vendler, *On Extended Wings: Wallace Stevens' Longer Poems* (Cambridge, Mass., 1969), 151.

16. After quoting at length an anecdote from *Biographia Literaria*, Stevens goes on: "As poetry goes, as the imagination goes, as the approach to truth, or, say, to being by way of the imagination goes, Coleridge is one of the great figures." Coleridge's definitions of poetry are for Stevens "valid enough," though these definitions "no longer impress us primarily by their validity" (*NA*, 40, 41).

17. Cf. Bloom, *Wallace Stevens*, 169.

18. Exploited by Eliot in *Dans le Restaurant* ("Oubliait les cris des mouettes et la houle de Cornouaille"), but lost, or much submerged, in the revised English version (*Waste Land* IV), where Eliot alters the acoustical effect to a whisper. For nightmare associations of "hoo," cf. Eliot, *Sweeney Agonistes*: "You've had a cream of a nightmare dream and you've got the hoo-ha's coming to you. / Hoo hoo hoo." Stevens's associations with the word "hoo-ing" in *The Man with the Blue Guitar* are pejorative (*L* 789, 12 July 1953).

19. "There are several things in the NOTES that would stand a little annotating. For instance, the fact that the Arabian is the moon is something that the reader could not possibly know. However, I did not think that it was necessary for him to know" (*L* 434, 12 Jan. 1943).

20. Cf. Frye: "There is a perilous balance in paronomasia between verbal wit and hypnotic incantation" (*Anatomy of Criticism* [Princeton, 1957], 276).

21. Cf. "the moon . . . with its dove-winged blending" (*CP* 119), and "she . . . bathed the dove in iridescence" (Ruskin, *Love's Meinie* ii).

22. "Charms and Riddles," 126.

23. Sewell, *Field of Nonsense*, 40, 43.

24. "Charms and Riddles," 137-8.

25. Hugh Kenner, not of Stevens but of Samuel Beckett, in *Samuel Beckett: A Critical Study* (New York, 1961), 10.

26. Cf. Thomas McFarland, in *New Perspectives on Coleridge and Wordsworth*, ed. Geoffrey Hartman (New York, 1972), 203. On *Kubla Khan* as a model for other nonsense-verse, see Kenner, "Seraphic Glitter," and James Rother, "Wallace Stevens as a Nonsense Poet," *Tennessee Studies in Literature*, 21 (1976), 86-7.

27. "Charms and Riddles," 129.

28. Jacques Derrida, *Writing and Difference*, trans. Alan Bass (Chicago, 1978), 77.

29. John Bayley, "Tropes and Blocks," *Modern Language Review*, 73 (1978), 748-54.

30. Cf. Bloom, *Wallace Stevens*, 194.

31. "Poetry as a narcotic is escapism in the pejorative sense. But there is a benign escapism in every illusion . . . . Of course, I believe in benign illusion. To my way of thinking, the idea of God is an instance of benign illusion" (*L* 402, 18 Feb. 1942).

32. Jacques Derrida, "Edmund Jabès and the Question of the Book," in *Writing and Difference*, 64-78, and Geoffrey H. Hartman, "Words and Wounds," in *Saving the Text: Literature/Derrida/Philosophy* (Baltimore and London, 1981), 118-57.

33. *From the Journal of Crispin*, in *Wallace Stevens: A Celebration*, 43: "His town exhales its mother breath for him / And this he breathes, a candid bellows-boy. / According to canon."

34. *Souvenirs and Prophecies: The Young Wallace Stevens*, ed. Holly Stevens (New York, 1977), 220.

Wallace Stevens   Fredric Jameson*

There may be some initial perplexity at the inclusion, in a work on the 60s, of some consideration of the work of a poet who died in 1956.[1] Stevens' work, one would have thought, could be analyzed as a characteristic symptom and monument of the poetic ideologies of the 20s and 30s, or even of the immediate post-war era, but is surely at best that with which the 60s sought to break, in terms of cultural values. It would therefore minimally be appropriate to talk about Stevens as somehow symptomatic of the condition of language, aesthetics and culture as the 60s found them in place, but not, as we will do here, as a revealing model of that first moment of the

*© 1985 by Loyola University, New Orleans. Reprinted by permission of the *New Orleans Review* 11 (Spring 1984):10-19.

60s proper, a moment that will gradually be dialectically transformed into something more recognizable as post-modernism.

This is, however, to reduce Stevens' poetry in a doubly restrictive way: on the one hand, to construe the historical reality of Stevens' poetry in so narrow a way as to deprive it of that later historical effectivity and resonance which expresses its formal and structural possibilities fully as objectively as the Stevens people thought they read and understood in the 30s and 40s; and second, to return Stevens' texts to a category of lyric poetry which in many ways they not merely transcend but repudiate:

> This endlessly elaborating poem
> Displays the theory of poetry,
> As the life of poetry. A more severe,
>
> More harassing master would extemporize
> Subtler, more urgent proof that the theory
> Of poetry is the theory of life. . . .
> "An Ordinary Evening in New Haven," (p. 486)[2]

It would be anachronistic to claim for Stevens' use of the term "theory" that later charged meaning with which the development of the 60s will invest it, and which will be one of the stories we have to tell in the present work. "Theory" will then, as we shall see, come to designate a new form of discourse that transcends the older separations of disciplinary categories of philosophy, criticism, belles-lettres, creative writing, and the like; still, Stevens' anticipation of this term may be taken as a warning that the Stevens phenomenon may well involve some initial lifting of the old barriers between "poetry" and "theory" and may involve the emergence of some new and as yet unclassifiable form of discourse.

Indeed, Frank Lentricchia has pointed out that the canonization of Wallace Stevens is not merely a kind of ultimate conclusion and ending for the modernist aesthetic generally: although it is that too, and Stevens' belated triumph over all his modernist rivals (Pound, Eliot, etc.) is consecrated by his institutionalization in the University as the supreme manifestation of New Critical poetic and aesthetic values, not unlike the analogous revival and canonization of Henry James during the same period as the supreme exemplar of modernizing ironic narrative. But if that were all that was involved, the aforecited objections would have much merit, that Stevens' monumental work is at best to be taken as the canonical and hegemonic values of the ending 1950s, as that with which the poetry and the cultural thought of the 60s must desperately break if it is to breathe and to "make something new." Yet this is to reckon without the theoretical component of Stevens' verse: Lentricchia goes on to underscore the hegemony of Stevens as a theoretician during this period, his immense influence as a strange new type of literary "critic" which is in many ways greater than that of his own prose commentators or of the founders of the New Criticism. *This* Stevens—the theoretician of poetry, rather than the poet, insofar as that distinction can be retained—will come to dominate the whole first moment of the emergent 1960s as well; and if in that case one wishes to say that what concerns us here is less the "historical" Wallace Stevens of the poetry than the "idea" of Wallace Stevens who came to be a critical fetish in this period, then the formulation may be pragmatically acceptable, even though it neglects the diachronic transformations of Stevens' own poetry (the emergence of a seemingly distinct and more philosophical-existential "late" Stevens) as well as the whole nature of the dialectic itself, for which there must necessarily be a constant interaction between subject and object, between the "idea" of a thing and the historical "thing itself."

Any evaluation of Stevens' work must start from an initial axiological paradox, which is surely more intense with Stevens than with any other major modernist figure. It must somehow be able to accommodate the seeming irreconcilable impressions of an astonishing linguistic richness on the one hand and an impoverishment or hollowness of content on the other, each of these in constant tension with one another and on various readings each seeming to draw the other into its force field and transfigure it. On the one hand, a familiar modernist practice of the unique personal or private style in these poems opens up into a wealth of vocabulary and syntactical fluidity that seems both absolute (no stammering, the voice never ends, is never reduced to silence or to awkwardness) and somehow impersonal again, as though this style were in reality something like an older rhetoric, with its collective, prepersonal capacities, its preexisting of the individual speaker who only needs to move in it as in an element. Therewith, however, one of the key features of the modernist will to style is lost: the necessity for its violent birth, for a painful conquest of the private voice over against the universal alienation of public speech: that "initial ugliness," as Gertrude Stein liked to say, "which it is our business as critics to recapture [even when standing in front of the insipid canonical loveliness of the Sistine Madonna] and which is that new style's struggle to be born." Nothing of a kind in Stevens: which is to say that in him, or for his discourse, it is for whatever reason no longer necessary to posit a whole universe of degraded speech, a whole world of prose, of the world of alienation and work, of universal instrumentalization and commodification, out of which and against which a specifically disalienating poetic language will emerge.

This extraordinarily supple and resourceful speech will then often seem to express its objects in some remarkably apt and unmediated way: more often, however, what I have called the inner hollowness of this verse will tend to return upon its language to cast some doubt upon the latter's density and authenticity. This steals upon one in those moments in which it becomes (momentarily) clear that Stevens' *only* content, from the earliest masterpieces of *Harmonium* all the way to the posthumous *Rock*, is landscape: and that not even in the visionary sense of many of the great nature poets, for whom the momentary epiphanies of place and object world are rare events, to be preserved over against the encroaching destruction of Nature as well as the alienating features of city or man-made environment. In Stevens, nature is, however, nothing but a given, a ready-made occasion for speech—birds, wind, mountains, the sun, always ready to hand whenever poetic speech needs some kind of objective content for its own production.

This is not to say that such content in Stevens is not also historically specific, as it necessarily always must be: there must be a historical precondition even for this seemingly ahistorical availability of abstract landscape for whatever poetic ends. In fact, landscape in Stevens has a two-fold historical specificity, as a certain type of culturally marked geography, as well as a certain "vocabulary field" of specific and culturally marked placenames. But I will argue in this first moment that Stevens must repress this specificity, whose recognition would at once deflect his work into directions like those of Williams and Olson and raise social and historical issues that would at once undermine his remarkably self-contained or autonomous aesthetic vision.

The repression of the social origins of this neutralized landscape, henceforth given as a kind of abstract "vocabulary," a set of neutral counters for the exercise of poetic speech (not unlike those formal, geometrical vocabulary units of the great architectural modernists such as Le Corbusier), is determined by the subject-object framework of Stevens' poetic practice which we will characterize as rigorously epistemological in all the worst senses of this word. In Stevens we never have anything but an abstract subject contemplating an object world which is thereby construed as being equally abstract. As with the great "illustrations" of classical epistemology (in professional philosophy), where impoverished tokens from the external world (a desk, say) are drawn in as sheer indifferent "examples," the items of the external world must in Stevens equally be laundered of their cultural and social semantics, just as the social world and the existence of other people must equally be bracketed. But this observation is not a solution but a problem in its own right: it should logically lead to the attempt to establish the historical preconditions of even this peculiarly abstract possibility.

Indeed, the preliminary remarks on Stevens should not overhastily, in our present *historicist* and historicizing context, be taken as criticisms, not even yet as an ideological critique, of Stevens' work (we do not even yet, for one thing, know exactly what it is or does). At best, these must be seen as contradictions that will set ultimate limits for Stevens' "achievement," and these will be indicated in time: what is historically significant, however, is the work that is done within those limits. That it is avant-garde or elitist poetry goes without saying: but such extreme language experiments have themselves much to tell us about historical possibilities that one would not have been able to read off of other kinds of texts (the latter may well be revealing in quite different ways, for which Stevens or vanguard modernism would be quite useless). In particular, however, as damaging as the restriction to an epistemological framework may be, we must here too immediately add the qualification that somehow, again in ways that remain to be determined, Stevens' poetry manages to transcend the limits of traditional epistemology: here, as in the gradual foregrounding of the theme of language in his work, he may best be read as registering a process analogous to that we will observe in French "structuralism," namely a dissolution of the older epistemological subject-object framework, which is bought at the cost of a certain reification of "Language."

The well-known problem of beginnings or of the starting point: we will begin with the phenomenon of the ease of speech that has already been mentioned. It is not a particularly unusual starting point: Wordsworth critics, for example, find their privileged points of departure in the distinction of moments in which poetic speech can flow from others which somehow block the latter and cause poetic language to return upon itself and interrogate its own conditions of productivity. Meanwhile, in other kinds of poets, the arbitrariness of certain poetic stances (the personal voice, say, or the prophetic mode, or the dramatic monologue) at once by their very artificiality designate the central problem of a more general blockage of other forms of poetic language. What we have to do with Stevens is artificially to reconstruct a certain stance or mental element that, once determined, accounts for this seemingly effortless coming of sentences and of their content.

This may perhaps best be evoked by a contrast with the (con- temporaneous) speech source of surrealist poetry, which laid claim to an equally effortless flow, although one of a clearly very different type. The problem is essentially one of distracting oneself from everything which intimidates or blocks speech: the surrealists found such an ideal locus of spontaneity through the systematic blocking off of conscious, rational, calculating mental and institutionalized thinking—in other words, by systematically suspending the "reality and performance principle" on the order of free association in Freudian analysis. But this very complex mental operation required them in effect, by their very effort and attention to that reality principle that has to be repressed, to preserve what they cancelled: so that the latter (or better still the inaugural opposition between common sense prose reality and poetic language) returns on the poetic language, which, effortless in principle at least for the poetic producer, is then wildly dissonant for the reader and bears all the marks of the bracketing of reality that instituted it.

Nothing of the sort, as we have said, for Stevens' form of what may still in some way be characterized as free association. If so, then we would have to speak of something like a free association of *preconscious* material in Stevens, to distinguish him sharply and radically from the surrealists. The more appropriate point of reference, as we shall see, and one that anchors Stevens more firmly in our period than has hitherto been done, is with Lévi-Strauss' "discovery" of *pensée sauvage*, of the operation of great preconscious grids and associative systems, which, like a language or like several linguistic systems, subtend the thoughts of "primitive" peoples, that is, of tribal people who have not yet known abstraction in the modern or "scientific" sense (who precede the emergence of "philosophy" in ancient Greece). The ambiguity in Levi-Strauss, marked by our designation of such systems as being "like" languages, is not merely present in Stevens also: it marks out an ambiguous space that is the precondition of the "ease" of his discourse: namely a kind of no-man's-land in which words and images are not yet radically distinguished from one another. In any case, as has been widely observed, this ambiguity is at the very heart of the pseudo-concept of the "image" as well, about which it is never clear whether this word designates the thing of which the image is a representation, or the representation itself. The moment of "structuralist" reflexivity, in which language itself as a separate system is disengaged from *all* of its contents— whether images or things, signifieds or referents—is a later moment, which will in fact cancel this initial moment of possibility.

The latter is thus available only on condition the systemic levels and their dynamics are not yet differentiated: a sense of the systemic relationship of words, which is not yet distinguished from a system of images, itself still naively able to be assumed to be a system of the objects themselves, the subsystems of the natural world, or what we have called Stevens' landscapes:

> Morning and afternoon are clasped together
>
> And North and South are an intrinsic couple
> And sun and rain a plural, like two lovers
> That walk away as one in the greenest body.
> "Notes Toward a Supreme Fiction," (p. 392)

These differential relationships have not yet been dogmatically codified in terms of the binary opposition of structural linguistics: if "North" and "South" offer such a binary opposition in its pure state, the same cannot be said for "morning" and "afternoon"—the elements of a larger system ultimately organized around "morning" and "evening" but eccentric to that opposition—and even more so for "sun" and "rain," in which these secondary or marginal or asymmetrical oppositions have been widened to include quite different semes, before being returned to the more conventional sexual opposition ("the lovers") and revealed to be the unity of growth by means of the adjective "greenest." No yoking of widely disparate contents in a jarring surrealist image here: there seems to be little enough resistance to the play of the mind across these signifying fields, and their reunification is a victory that is not bought at any particularly exorbitant or even visible cost.

The "still point" from which this kind of systemic exploration, this free association of the preconscious, is possible will then be initially one of cultural systems and collective associations (socially institutionalized in the collective *pensée sauvage*) as in Lévi-Strauss. It may be useful to mark the cross-reference to another significant "modernist" literary discovery, namely Flaubert's sudden awareness of the operation of bits of material language in consciousness, the not yet completely determinant yet ominous organization of the "mind" by clichés, commonplaces, forms of "*bêtise*" which are active in crystallized or reified phrases and bits of material speech. Only where in Flaubert these foreign bodies are immediately felt to be degraded speech (and through *bovarysme* already prophetically linked to the nascent media, the vehicles of propagation of these "pseudo-thoughts"), in Stevens there is no particular sense that these associative paths are in any way inauthentic (the same is true for Lévi-Strauss, but for a different reason, namely the restriction of his work to tribal peoples "before the fall," objects, in his Rousseau revival, of the celebration of something like "natural man"). Yet this is what accounts for the peculiar impersonality of Stevens' poetry and imagination: no sense of the urgent need to forge a private and uniquely personal style, to wrest one's individual *pensée sauvage* as an act of revolt from the standardized culture surrounding those last places of the authentic. Stevens' imagination situates itself at once in the universal, thereby forfeiting the peculiar glamour of the modernist poet as *poète maudit*, genius and unique stylist: *style* being above all the ambiguous and historical category in which, in high modernism, the specificity of the individual subject is expressed, manifested and preserved. This peculiarly unmodern commitment to collective association, to an already systemic cultural storehouse—a commitment that does not in Stevens involve the renunciation of the personal and the private, either, since in a sense it precedes the very emergence of the individual subject and of the latter's oppositions—accounts in another way for what we have called the hollowness or impoverishment of his content: Utopian in that it implicitly insists on the undegradedness of the cultural stereotypes, on their freshness and perhaps indeed their immediate or unmediated relationship to Nature itself, the reliance on collective automatisms, in a fallen society, cannot but be somehow, at some ultimate level, the zero degree or average common denominator of a fragmented and atomized *Gesellschaft*; hence the strategic limitation of this material to landscape, where those features may be expected to be least obvious and intrusive.

Still, there is much properly cultural material in Stevens, material that dates him oddly far more than the other great modernists of his generation, and read in a certain fashion obsessively evokes the glossy ads, the art deco, the fashions and interior design of the 20s or the more elegant productions of the silent movie era:

> When the elephant's-ear in the park
> Shrivelled in frost,
> And the leaves on the paths
> Ran like rats,
> Your lamp-light fell
> On shining pillows,
> Of sea-shades and sky-shades
> Like umbrellas in Java.
>   "Tea," (p. 112)

Yet the high luxury of these characteristic interiors is a significant mechanism in the dynamics of Stevens' associative systems: these materials are allowed entrance to the verse, not because Stevens is particularly aware of their social and class character, as rather because—for obvious class reasons—they are felt in their elegance to be something like a subset of the natural. As in contemporary photorealism, the people (debutantes, jazz-age rakes, Newport aristocracy, and the like) are excluded, and only the Utopian *locus* of a peculiarly refined space for life remains behind (as also in some advertising). In fact, of course, such images are not natural, but form a specific "signifying field" among others in Stevens' imagination (others, related in different ways, would include the "popular American" field of associations, Whitman, "the emperor of ice cream," American birds, Indian imagery, a whole marked "American" vocabulary that intersects with various other specific vocabulary fields such as the "French," and so forth).

But what is important to us at present is the return of this seemingly alien content to the base-line natural system: this is achieved by means of a slippage from image to language. The glossy ad for an elegant boudoir, the luxurious empty place of reclining bodies, negligees, intimate receptions, now without any apparent discontinuity or shifting of gears now finds fulfillment in an unexpected way, by the emergence of a place-name: Java. Indeed, place-names in Stevens (he who travelled so little in his life, and was proud of the fact) play a key role in the articulation of systems of natural or landscape *images* to the operation of more properly linguistic systems: the mystery of place-names, like those of proper names generally, lies in their coordination of a general cultural system (see Lévi-Strauss on the naming system for dogs, cats, birds and horses in our culture) with the unique deictic of the here-and-now, the named individual who is incomparable and presumably not systematizable. In Stevens, the place-name will be at one and the same time the very locus and occasion for a production of images: quasi-Flaubertian *bovarysme*, the daydream about the exotic place, the free association on Java, Tehentepec, Key West, Oklahoma, Tennessee, Yucatan, Carolina, and so forth—and the emergence of another level of systematicity in language itself (the generation of place-names out of each other, their association now as a proper vocabulary field), behind which yet a deeper system is concealed and active.

That deeper system, as the majority of place-names in Stevens can testify, centers on the exoticism of the South and most notably of the whole Caribbean area (Stevens was also proud, in particular, of never having been to Europe, a set of place-names that would have been peculiarly intrusive here as we shall see in a moment). We may thus generally characterize this new and very instinct "signifying field" as corresponding generally to what would today be called the material of the Third World (yet another reason why there is some deeper logic in including Stevens in the movement of the early 60's: only Crane of the great American modernists was also sensitive to the specificity of this material—Royal Palm or the seascapes—but Crane's aesthetics are very different from this and the resonance of his Caribbean has nothing in common with Stevens' assimilation of Third World realities to a place-name system and an occasion for infinite imagining reverie).

Yet it is clearly a peculiar view of the Third World, which one might seek to concretize by the experience of the world tour, the liner cruise through the islands, a peculiarly disengaged luxury tourist's contemplative contact with ports and maps (a specific moment, one would think, of aristocratic or moneyed tourism in the 1920s, which has little socially in common with the more universal tourism of the present day). This impoverished experience reconfirms our notion of the underlying purely epistemological stance of Stevens' work—a detached subject contemplating a static object in a suspension of praxis or even rootedness—and is documented in Stevens' one autobiographical "novel" or narrative, "The Comedian as the Letter C." Yet if this is the phenomenological experience, the "social equivalent" of Stevens' fascination with place-names, it also betrays a far deeper social and economic source which is that of the consumption of luxury products and objects at a particular moment in the development of modern capitalism, and reflects, one might say, a kind of luxury-mercantilist *Weltanschauung*, a view of the "world system" as so many sources for expensive imported goods. There is, in other words, a subterranean relationship between the "umbrella in Java"—the fantasy of the exotic holiday—and the "umbrella *from* Java," the luxury item whose own capacity to generate images, daydreams and semic associations lies in its origins in a distant place and culture, and in the momentary function of a Third World handicraft industry to produce just such objects of consumption for the First World.

What we have called the Third World material in Stevens is thus not some mere private aberration in his work, not some mere adjunct due to the accidents of his personal history, his means, travel, and the culture of the age; but is rather a fundamental piece in the overall system, the way by which the latter comes to know a global closure and thus a universality (both Hartford *and* Yucatan, both First and Third Worlds) on which its other procedures depend. At the same time, by means of this crucial mediation of Third World material, a bridge is made between image and word (by means of place-names), and a transformation of purely social and cultural objects (the interiors, the furnishings, the jazz-age luxury items) back into Nature and virtual landscape, since they all come to be associated with exotic *places*.

With the completion of his "world" by such Third World material, then, it would seem that an autonomous or semi-autonomous space has been achieved that can now be felt to "represent" the real world in its fundamental oppositions (nature versus culture, or in other words, landscape versus luxury consumption objects; and First World versus Third World). The next step in our inquiry is to investigate the process of autonomization by which this new "ideal" world of "representation" is felt to separate itself from the empirical one.

But we must first dispel the impression that this ideal sphere of images and words is some Parmenidean place of changelessness or of static being: our characterization of the content of Stevens' world as hollow or impoverished designated the nature of the link between the "ideal" and the "empirical" in Stevens. On the other hand, once we enter completely the realm of the "poem," it is clear that there is a great fluidity, a wealth of movement and micro-event that must now be accounted for in some more adequate fashion. We have suggested that the space of possibility onto which Stevens' imagination for whatever accidents of personal history or inclination happened—that space which unexpectedly opens up a seemingly limitless movement of poetic discourse, without barriers, in all directions—this space is essentially that designated by "structuralism" or by Theory as the Symbolic Order, or in a different way by Hegel as "objective spirit," or by Durkheim as "collective consciousness": that is, the ensemble of representations, representational systems, and their various levels (concepts, images, words), in which the individual consciousness or subject must dwell, and about which the thinkers of this period increasingly suspect that, more than a mere element for thought, or even constellations floating in the mind, this whole system may in fact determine and program individual consciousness to a far greater degree than had hitherto been imagined. This "discovery," if it can really be called that, is significantly contemporaneous with the emergence of media society (or of the *société de consommation*), and may thus be expected at least in part to register this tremendous quantitative increase in material images and representations of all kinds in the new cultural space in question. Always accepting the conception of a Symbolic Order as a kind of space and dynamic beyond the individual subject, we do not, however, necessarily need to endorse the various models and hypotheses devised by high structuralism to describe this new space, and essentially extrapolated from linguistic systems (binary oppositions, the Greimas semantic rectangle, even the more multi-dimensional projections of a Lévi-Strauss or a Foucault of immense systemic relations in constant transformation).

Stevens' freedom to move within the Symbolic Order is at least in part ensured by the absence of such codified models, which often restrict inquiry or exploration in advance. Now that Stevens' work is over and "complete," it would certainly seem possible to imagine an enlarged and complex structural analysis capable of mapping it out after the fact: here we will essentially be content to stress the multiplicity of sub-systems in this ideal space, which is closed, if at all, only in the sense that the Einsteinian universe is closed, by folding back on itself, such that one never meets anything but contents of the same order, rather than, as in traditional closure, by the arrival at limits beyond which some radical otherness or difference from the system is felt to exist.

These "sub-systems," or "fields" as I prefer to call them, are thus in themselves capable of infinite expansion and combination: the dominant one, what in another kind of writer one would have been tempted to call that of the pastiche of Elizabethan language (what I have earlier characterized as the rediscovery, in a modernizing world of *styles*, of an essentially rhetorical practice in Stevens)—this field is capable of as much formal variety, of as unlimited a mutability, as clouds themselves (to use a characteristic Stevens image), and one could, in a pinch, dwell in it forever, were it not for the perpetually nagging sense that it is not itself really a world but merely a specific language. Each of these fields is thus essentially complete, with its own oppositions and its own rich possibilities of dissonance and contradiction: in such a field, for example, "grammarians" can be "gloomy" and still wear "golden gowns" (p. 55). Such eventful tensions are felt to be an interesting heterogeneity only *within* the limits of the field itself: when, as we are admonished to do by the letter "G," we step outside that particular stylistic field, such variety once again falls back into a kind of homogeneity.

What has to be added, however, is the observation that there is also a play of eventfulness, of dissonance, of contradiction and variety or heterogeneity at the *intersections* between the various fields: as when a pseudo-Elizabethan vocabulary, for instance, like two galaxies colliding and interpenetrating on their distinct paths through space, momentarily knows interference with a pseudo-American, Whitmanesque, folkloric vocabulary field, all shot through with hoots and "barbaric" sounds and yawps. . . . These intersystemic combinations ought clearly to produce an even richer sense of eventfulness than those that take place within any given system (all the more so since, as I have suggested, the systems involved are themselves disparate—some being systems of images, some of concepts, and some, simply, of vocabularies and "style").

Yet this is not necessarily the case either: in fact, what tends to happen when a single sub-system or field intersects with another is rather a bracketing or a distantiation in which each is precisely grasped as a "field," seen now for what is an ideal system of representations rather than a "world." Here, too, a certain movement of structuralism, or rather its immediate prehistory, coming upon an analogous phenomenon, has proposed a concept for this process which is relevant: this is Barthes' early notion of "connotation," derived from Hjemslev and later repudiated in Barthes' middle or "mature" structuralist period. Connotation designated a set of messages given off, not by the "things themselves" but by the modes of representation of those things; a moment, in other words, in which (to use another characteristic formulation of the period) the medium turns into its own message, or rather begins to emit its own messages; in which the former "message" or denotation is henceforth only the occasion or pretext for new second-degree messages couched in the language of signs or styles or representational systems themselves. But Barthes' account, at least in relation to Stevens' poetry, needs to be elaborated and refined: for here it is clear that we have to do, not merely with isolated connotations, but with a play between whole "systems" of connotation among each other, systems in which the reference withdraws in order the more surely to foreground style or representation as its new object (in that sense, the concept of connotation would offer yet an alternate model for theorizing the gradual autonomization of Stevens' systems, their reorganization into some ideal sphere beyond the empirical world itself). Thus, even this form of intersystemic play (as open-ended, clearly, as is each of the systems itself) ultimately undergoes an autoreferential momentum in which its very content, at the latter's strongest, ends up rather designating a play of forms.

With this, we may begin to observe the dynamics of autonomization proper as they can be viewed within the small-scale model or experimental laboratory situation of this poetic language:

> Just as my fingers on these keys
> Make music, so the selfsame sounds
> On my spirit make a music, too.
> "Peter Quince at the Clavier," (p. 89)

It is the quintessential Kantian moment in which, as contemporary middle-class subjectivity is forced back inside its own head, the idea of the thing peels off the "thing itself," now forever out of reach—less, to be sure, as a Kantian noumenon than as an infinitely receding "referent," image separating from the thing, idea from image, word from idea, so that as the poem systematically drives itself deeper and deeper into the Symbolic Order, the "absent cause" of its content appears at ever greater distance in the imagined cosmos, its final symbolic form that "absolute referent," as Derrida has called it, the sun, in which, in some ultimate quintessence, all reference becomes itself concentrated and reduced to a point, a pure locus without dimension:

> The sun no longer shares our works . . .
> Not to be part of the sun? To stand
>
> Remote and call it merciful?
> The strings are cold on the blue guitar.
> "The Man with the Blue Guitar," (p. 168)

But this absolute referent was already present in various guises in the earlier poems, most strikingly perhaps in that remarkable exercise "Thirteen Ways of Looking at a Blackbird," in a form Stevens virtually invented for modern poetry, the theme and variations, where the referent is first the intense black point of the "eye of the blackbird," only to return in various forms of punctuation and interference within consciousness as the shadow cast by the real.

This is the most crucial moment in Stevens' poetic operation, the unresolvable contradiction on which the whole system turns and depends absolutely: reference must be preserved at the same time that it is bracketed, and that it is affirmed of it that it can never be known, that it stands outside the system. The system autonomizes itself as a microcosm, a self-contained faithful Utopian reflexion and representation of "things as they are": but in order to assure its continuing autonomy it must retain the link with the real of which it is the Hegelian "inverted world" or the complete mirror reflexion. This link with the real—what we will shortly characterize as the link between the autonomized *sign* (signifier/signified) and the referent—cannot within this system be theorized. We are therefore given two absolute and incommensurable, self-contradictory formulations: on the one hand, "nothing changed by the blue guitar" (p. 167). Since the space of the Symbolic Order is the space of the images, ideas and names of "things as they are," the latter persevere serenely in their being, unmodified by their symbolic representation,

> nothing changed, except the place
>
> Of things as they are and only the place
> As you play them, on the blue guitar,
>
> Placed so, beyond the compass of change;
> Perceived in a final atmosphere. . . .

Yet the opposite is also true, and its affirmation is equally necessary to the poetic system—namely, that in some Utopian sense, everything is changed by the "supreme fiction" of the Symbolic Order. Here is then once again the great paradox of the Symbolic Order thus conceived: it is both ideological and Utopian, both a simple reflexion or projection of the real with all its contradictions, and a small-scale model or Utopian microcosm of the real in which the latter can be changed or modified—one is reminded of Burke's characterization of the ambiguity of the "symbolic act" and the cultural generally, on the one hand, a merely *symbolic* act which is not praxis and which changes nothing, yet on the other a genuine symbolic *act* which has at least the symbolic value of genuine praxis.

My point is that both of these contradictory formulations serve a non-theoretical function, namely to preserve the parallelism between a semi-autonomous symbolic space and the space of reality: this is a functional necessity for Stevens' system, since, as we shall see shortly, when in post-modernism the referent vanishes altogether, with it go the properly symbolic possibilities of Stevens' own specific subject-object relationship. Yet from this necessity (which Stevens must hold in being, which he must not allow to proceed further along the momentum of a properly post-modernist disintegration) a certain number of consequences flow—some of them ideologies, or strategies of ideological containment (in order to keep this contradictory system control) in and some of them inevitable structural results and limits of the system itself, among these that very quality of Stevens' poetry which we posed as an initial problem, namely the ambiguous sense of richness and impoverishment. We will formulate these structural consequences under three headings, with the preliminary reminder that the dialectic outlined up to this point is not ideological and does not yet imply the ideological critique of Stevens' work about to be summarized. Up till now, what we have described is an objective experience of a certain capacity of language or the Symbolic, which for whatever personal accidents Stevens felt himself impelled to explore, of which he made himself the objective vehicle or recording apparatus. The symbolic space opened up by Stevens' work, the autonomization of image from thing, idea from image, name from idea, is in itself neither true nor false, neither scientific nor ideological: it is an experience, and a historical experience, and not a theory about language or a choice susceptible of ethical or political judgement. But given the instability of this experience, which needs to be safeguarded and perpetuated by various strategies, the ideological now makes its appearance as what the Formalists would have called "the motivation of the device."

The strong form of ideology taken in Stevens' work is what we have since come to identify in the most general sense as existentialism (including within it that "fiction-making" thematics of Nietzsche's work which is its initial moment). Here the familiar and banal motifs of *Geworfenheit* and absurdity make their predictable appearance: the death of God, the disappearance of religion, now determine a radically meaningless world in which alone poetry or fiction can restore at least an appearance of meaning, assuming for the moderns the function that religion used to secure in more traditional social systems: .

> The earth, for us, is flat and bare.
> There are no shadows. Poetry
>
> Exceeding music must take the place
> Of empty heaven and its hymns,
>
> Ourselves in poetry must take their place,
> Even in the chattering of your guitar.
>   (p. 167)

This ideology is then systematically elaborated and produced in the poems on death and the religion of art, from the early *Sunday Morning* on, in what are surely for us today the least interesting parts of the Stevens canon.

Yet what must be insisted on is the innate instability of existentialism (understood here as an ideology rather than as a technical and rigorous form of philosphical discourse). For as soon as we come to be convinced of the fictionality of meaning, the whole operation loses its interest: philosophies of "as if" are notoriously unsatisfying and self-unravelling. Yet when such an ideology unravels, then the very conception of fiction disappears along with it. In order to prevent this dissolution of the poetic system, something like an Absolute Fiction must be desperately maintained:

> But to impose is not
> To discover. To discover an order as of
> A season, to discover summer and know it,
>
> To discover winter and know it well, to find,
> Not to impose, not to have reasoned at all,
> Out of nothing to have come on major weather,
>
> It is possible, possible, possible. It must
> Be possible. It must be that in time
> The real will from its crude compoundings come,
>
> Seeming at first a beast disgorged, unlike,
> Warmed by a desperate milk. To find the real,
> To be stripped of every fiction except one,
>
> The fiction of an absolute—Angel,
> Be silent in your luminous cloud and hear
> The luminous melody of proper sound.
>   "Notes Toward a Supreme Fiction," (pp. 403-4)

Here then the ultimate "referent" is affirmed by the very movement that denies it, and what is less an ideology than a desperate conceptual prestidigitation reaffirms the impossible, the Angel, the absent cause, the Absolute or necessary fiction.

Yet in a final moment this desperate systemic readjustment has practical consequences which are like the price to be paid for its continuing existence. This is the great lateral movement of autoreferentiality referred to in the beginning, in which the act of designating the absent referent (blackbird's eye or the sun itself, the impossible Angel) turns out at one and the same time to be a process of designating the Symbolic or poetic space in question as symbolic or poetic, as fictional, such that the poetry will now come to turn on itself and in all of its rotations continue to designate nothing but itself. Hence the richness and impoverishment we spoke of: infinitely rich as the projection of a whole world, a whole geography, this language at once empties itself by calling attention to its own hollowness as that which is merely the image of the thing, and not the thing itself. Yet at this point, at which Stevens would be indistinguishable from the autoreferentiality of high modernism generally, an unusual permutation takes place, and a new thing—theory itself—emerges. What before was merely "poetic" discourse, with its traditional and banal problems of the nature of specifically poetic discourse and of the aesthetic as non-practical and non-cognitive, suddenly opens up into a new form of discourse which is theoretical and poetic all at once, in which "the theory of poetry" becomes at one with "the life of poetry." We do not yet know how to characterize the new structure of this newly emergent discourse called theory: to do so will be the task of a later chapter, in which we will show that theory is itself a new discursive and conceptual space as distinct from traditional criticism or philosophy as the Utopian space of the foco was distinct from traditional politics.[3] Yet this emergence marks the originality of Stevens, now considered as a moment of the 60s, a moment in which "poetry" also, in its traditional sense, dies and is transformed into something historically new. The end of art, perhaps, in the Hegelian sense, but also its realization, and its transformation into the sphere of culture generally or of the Symbolic Order.

Notes

1. The present text, unaltered, is a draft chapter of a book-length study of the 1960s, a shorter piece of which will appear in the special issue of *Social Text* devoted to that subject (pp. 9-10, Spring 1984). The present chapter, on Wallace Stevens, offers an analysis of the transformation of the "sphere of culture" and its "autonomy" (or relative or semi-autonomy) in the contemporary world—a theme obviously inspired by Herbert Marcuse's great essay on the "affirmative character of culture" in *Negations*, as well as by more recent German theory (Habermas, Negt, and Kluge). What is outrageous about it is the comparison between the sphere of high culture in question here and the "Utopian" enclave space of guerrilla warfare as Régis Debray theorized it in *The Revolution in the Revolution*, a book based on the Cuban revolutionary experience and which I analyze in a previous chapter of my as yet unfinished text. As for the theory of modernism presented here, which turns on the relationship between modernist language and forms and the emergence of the imperialist world system in the "monopoly stage" of capitalism, the interested reader may also consult a related study of the poetry of Arthur Rimbaud in the second volume of the proceedings of the 1982 University of Hong Kong Conference on Literary Theory.

2. Parenthetical page numbers refer to *The Collected Poems of Wallace Stevens* (New York: Alfred A. Knopf, 1969).

3. "Foco" is the Spanish term for the French "foyer," the "home base" or center of guerrilla activities, and is used by Debray specifically to refer to Guevarist revolutionary strategy.

"That Which Is Always Beginning": Stevens' Poetry of Affirmation   Steven Shaviro[*]

   Wallace Stevens is commonly read either as an ironic modernist or as a Romantic idealist in the tradition of Emerson. His poetry is generally situated epistemologically within the humanist problematic of subjectivity and self-consciousness and aesthetically within the formalist tradition of poetic self-reflexivity.[1] It seems to me beside the point, however, to ask whether Stevens is a solipsist or a realist or whether his poems reflect the play of language or of a creative mind. I would like, not to provide new answers to these dilemmas, but to suggest that most previous readers of Stevens have been asking the wrong questions.

[*]Reprinted by permission of the Modern Language Association of America from *PMLA* 100 (March 1985):220-33.

Stevens's earlier poetry indeed bears the traces both of Romantic idealism and of modernist experimentation with language, but such points of reference become less and less important in the more mature work. Stevens's later poetry, beginning at least with the "Notes toward a Supreme Fiction" of 1942, is no longer concerned with formal and linguistic innovation or with the familiar dualisms of subject and object and of mind and external world. This radical and disquieting abandonment of traditional poetic concerns accounts for the dryness and austerity that so many readers have found in these poems. Stevens's later poetry is forbidding because it moves in a different space from that of our usual critical paradigms. My aim here is to trace the outlines of this new space, to follow what I call the *affirmative* movement of Stevens's later poetry. My discussion itself may seem forbidding because I reject thematic and phenomenological modes of description, but it is in this way that I can best do justice to the strange, fierce joy that radiates from these poems.[2]

The space of Stevens's later poetry is that of a dazzling clarity in ceaseless agitation. "In an air of freshness, clearness, greenness, blueness," we explore the transformations of "that which is always beginning because it is part / Of that which is always beginning, over and over" (*CP* 530).[3] But the vision of "transparent man in a translated world" (*PM* 394) is "not an empty clearness, a bottomless sight" (*PM* 350-51). Transparency does not signify mere absence. Consider the open space of a poem such as "A Clear Day and No Memories" (*PM* 397):

> No soldiers in the scenery,
> No thoughts of people now dead,
> As they were fifty years ago,
> Young and living in a live air,
> Young and walking in the sunshine,
> Bending in blue dresses to touch something,
> Today the mind is not part of the weather.
>
> Today the air is clear of everything.
> It has no knowledge except of nothingness
> And it flows over us without meanings,
> As if none of us had ever been here before
> And are not now: in this shallow spectacle,
> This invisible activity, this sense.

This clarity is an immanence not susceptible to mediation but also not classifiable as simple immediacy. No objects are present, nor is there a subject of consciousness; yet there seems to be a materiality of thought, a flow, a spectacle, an activity, a sense. It is a nothingness because nothing comes forth, because there is no appearance. But this nothingness is strangely active. A "knowledge . . . of nothingness" is not the same as a simple absence of knowledge. The poem's vacancy marks the insistence of a spectacle that, though nowhere hidden, is never shown. Transparency is a positive and material movement, the clarity of the weather, the motion of the air. It precedes appearance and produces a phantasmic "scenery" irreducible to either memory or simple presence. A Hegelian might be tempted to read this nothingness as the power of negativity that founds the exercise of the imagination, and a Freudian might suspect that the clarity results from some enormous triumph of repression, a purposive forgetting of "people now dead." But the poem evinces no density of resistance, no symptomatology, no priority that had to be negated. The profundity of the labor of the negative and of the task of repression is the one thing absent from this "shallow spectacle." Instead, "no soldiers" and "no thoughts of people now dead" are positive constituents of the "scenery." The clarity of "fifty years ago" and the clarity of the present moment are simultaneously produced in the poem's, or the air's, "invisible activity."

The past is affirmed without being rendered present, just as the presence of the present moment is elided. The appositional chain of the first stanza moves without transition from the positive nonpresence of the past to that of "today." Grammatically, lines 3-6 are subordinated to the "people now dead" of line 2, governed by this initial "No." But the paratactic syntax works against this "No" and foregrounds the positivity of the descriptions. The poem shuttles between past and present, so that neither moment is fully realized but neither can be negated: what Stevens elsewhere describes as "the mobile and immobile flickering/In the area between is and was" (*PM* 338). The thoughts, or nonmemories, of "A Clear Day and No Memories" vibrate endlessly in the virtual space between pure negation and simple presence, between "no" and "now."

In many of his later poems, Stevens explores the ramifications of this "always incipient cosmos" (*OP* 115), this virtual space that precedes all appearance and all meaning. Indeed, "life's nonsense pierces us with strange relation" (*PM* 209). The clarity of the day—invisible activity and visible transparence—produces difference without separation and similitude without correspondence. Difference occurs without separation because disjunct events and images are affirmed without contradiction or mutual exclusion. "He had to choose. But it was not a choice/Between excluding things. It was not a choice/Between, but of" (*PM* 229). Incompatible possibilities subsist together in the poem without undergoing any process of unification or dialectical interaction. Similitude is produced without correspondence because resemblance is always projected "beyond resemblance" (*PM* 378). Thus the very movement of comparison presupposes distance and precludes identity, implying the noncoincidence of the instances being compared. "The object with which he was compared/Was beyond his recognizing. By this he knew that likeness of him extended/Only a little way" (*PM* 378). Resemblance does not refer to an original model. It does not radiate outward from the mind to encompass external objects. Similitude without correspondence is, rather, an ungovernable and never-completed movement that always exceeds the mind's power of recognition and identification.

This production of differences not susceptible to mediation and of

similitudes irreducible to identification is what I call *disjunctive affirma-*
tion. It defines for Stevens a new kind of unity, the unity of a world in
fragments, a whole composed of multiplicities without totalization or
unification.[4] In the words of "July Mountain" (*OP* 114-15), "we live in a
constellation / Of patches and of pitches, / Not in a single world." The unity
of this "constellation" consists, not in any adequation of the disparate parts
to a whole or to one another, but in their anarchic juxtaposition, in "the
way, when we climb a mountain, / Vermont throws itself together." The
parts do not cohere but are thrown together to make up a whole. Stevens
proposes a radical perspectivism in which the unity of the mind or of the
world, the mountain height from which all possible perspectives may be
viewed simultaneously, is only another perspective. "The Rock," in the
poem of that title, is similarly the locus of a unity without finality, "the
habitation of the whole" defined from the vantage of "point A / In a
perspective that begins again / At B" (*PM* 365). In "An Ordinary Evening in
New Haven," this unity of perspectival differences is described as "a
visibility of thought, / In which hundreds of eyes, in one mind, see at once"
(*PM* 351). What is given "at once" is the incessant divergence of multiple
perspectives. The "one mind" is, like the rock, "the starting point of the
human and the end" (*PM* 365): the point of perpetual incipience, "the
imagination's new beginning" (*PM* 257) and its end, which is not a
completion but yet another re-beginning.

This unity of divergent viewpoints is also a unity of different and
irreconcilable beginnings. Beginnings cannot be traced to an origin for the
same reason that they cannot be pressed forward to a fully manifested
finality. Everything remains posed at the point of its first emergence, in the
form of "—escent—issant pre-personae. . . . You were not born yet when
the trees were crystal / Nor are you now, in this wakefulness inside a sleep"
(*PM* 370). A beginning is an event that is still insubstantial, a divergence or
incipient movement of difference, "the accent of deviation in the living
thing / That is its life preserved, the effort to be born / Surviving being
born, the event of life" (*PM* 366). The force or effort of this "Discovery of
Thought," its coming to birth, is preserved against the reification of its
already having been born. The "event of life" is always earlier than the
origin: "the sense / Of cold and earliness is a daily sense, / Not the predicate
of bright origin" (*PM* 345). Thus, it is a liminal movement, never completed
and only thinkable in the mode of "as if." The poet or philosopher "stops
upon this threshold," and then it is "as if the design of all his words takes
form / And frame from thinking and is realized" (*PM* 373). Stevens's
characteristic "as if" is not a negation or a qualification but a perpetual
"accent of deviation" that, continually approaching an unsurpassable
threshold, invigorates and renews.[5]

This force of renewal does not derive from the poetic imagination as
traditionally conceived, for it is not a power of the mind or a term in a
dialectic or a subject-object dualism. In contrast to the Coleridgean
primary and secondary imaginations, metamorphosis for Stevens is

nonoriginary and asubjective, and it "fills the being before the mind can think" (*PM* 328). It is a relational and differential event of transformation, not an ability inhering in a substance or subject. The transparency of the air is the scene of an "invisible activity," of the production of "so many selves, so many sensuous worlds, / As if the air, the mid-day air, was swarming, / With the metaphysical changes that occur, / Merely in living as and where we live" (*PM* 263). This swarming is the motion of an unceasing "will to change" that affirms "a kind / of volatile world, too constant to be denied" (*PM* 224), constant and affirmable precisely in its volatility. As universal "will to change," as multiple productivity, and as incessant rebeginning, the process of imagination in Stevens's poetry does not so much imitatively recreate as actively desire.

Desire for Stevens is at once a want, or a lack, that is never satisfied and an incessant and mobile process of production.[6] Desire may be located "always in emptiness that would be filled, / In denial that cannot contain its blood, / A porcelain, as yet in the bats thereof" (*PM* 333). But this emptiness is a positive latency, that of the unshaped lump of clay not yet formed into the finished porcelain. As the never-completed movement toward completion, desire is that "which nothing can frustrate," precisely because in its restless motion it "cannot / Possess" (*PM* 332). The process can never be finished and, for that reason, can never be contained by the formulas of negation and denial. Any projection of desire is already (even though it can be nothing more than) the imminence of its own goal. Desire does not seek final satisfaction; it continually multiplies and reproduces itself. It cannot be circumscribed by the lack of the object to which it is supposedly directed. The insistent particularity of desire in its movement toward closure keeps it perpetually open. "The desire to be at the end of distances" is the force that opens up new vistas of distance, "new senses in the engenderings of sense" (*PM* 364).

Stevens explores this nondialectical play of desire at the threshold of realization in section 23 of "An Ordinary Evening in New Haven" (*PM* 345-46). Each fresh divergence promises the "single future" of its own realization, the nocturnal repose of a "being part of everything come together as one." But, as Stevens puts it in a later poem, "being part is an exertion that declines" (*PM* 367). The projection of identity never surpasses the threshold of its first postulation, and it cannot for long divorce itself from the multiplicity of "day's separate, several selves." Hence, "in this identity, disembodiments / Still keep occurring." The expression of desire is only a pseudoidentity, a similitude ("as one") in which there is no true correspondence. In continuing to propose possible identities, the force of desire precludes any firm achievement of identity: "what is, uncertainly, / Desire prolongs its adventure to create / Forms of farewell, furtive among green ferns." The movement of desire is a disjunctive event, an incessantly recurring disembodiment. Forever separating and never coming to a final separation, it prolongs itself in the liminal space of its begetting (creation) and departure (farewell). Desire is the imminence of an "adventure"—

etymologically, a coming toward—a projection that never reposes in an attained goal.

Adventure is one of a series of words used to indicate the continually productive structure of desire. The similar terms in "Notes toward a Supreme Fiction" are *invention* (*PM* 207-08) and *to discover* (*PM* 230). An *invention* is both a creation or fabrication and, etymologically, a finding or coming on. The poet proposes "the idea / Of this invention, this invented world" but also warns us "never [to] suppose an inventing mind as source / Of this idea." The invention has no inventor and no origin; its "project" is only to subsist "in the difficulty of what it is to be." Similarly, "to discover" is "to find, / Not to have reasoned at all." The movement of discovery consists not in imposing order on a chaotic object world but in articulating already latent possibilities: "out of nothing to have come on major weather, / It is possible, possible, possible." "To discover" is then "to find the real, / To be stripped of every fiction except one"—a line suggesting that "the real" is already a fiction, "the fiction of an absolute," both the fiction of a pure emergence out of nothingness and without origination and the actual nonoriginary status of such a fiction. "The real" is something "invented," in Stevens's peculiar double use of the term. Discovery, invention, and adventure are projective movements that do not create what they find, yet find that which cannot exist apart from the movement of their projection. Desire at once actively produces and passively encounters the real. Reality is a fiction, but so is the author of the fiction. The real, or the object of desire, is not created by the desiring subject, nor is it something "out there" to which the subject must conform. Rather, the adventure of invention and discovery precedes and places both desiring subject and desired object. "It could be that the sun shines / Because I desire it to shine or else / That I desire it to shine because it shines" (*OP* 85): this paradox is not so much undecidable as not needing to be decided.[7]

In the intimacy of this process, "the poem is the cry of its occasion, / Part of the res itself and not about it" (*PM* 338). The poem participates in the real not as a unit belonging to a totality but as a movement of difference without separation. It is a perpetually incomplete part of a metamorphosing process that is itself always incomplete and partial: "a moving part of a motion, a discovery / Part of a discovery, a change part of a change" (*PM* 380). It is a part constantly in motion, not part of a fixed substance, but "part of the reverberation / Of a windy night as it is" (*PM* 338). It is a cry of desire, the part that always moves apart or elsewhere as "disembodiments / Still keep occurring." The action of the poem is that of an unrealized incipience and an infinitesimal increment: the deficient "not yet" of an incipience that precludes closure and the excessive "already accomplished" of an increment always preceding the substance to which it adds itself. The "cry" is the force of the "occasion" by which the thing is determined, "the accent of deviation . . . that is its life preserved." Poetry is "Description without Place" (*PM* 270-77), "an alteration / Of words that was a change of nature" exceeding nature's own capacity for change (*PM* 350). "An access of color, a new and unobserved, slight dithering," barely perceptible, not quite realized, nevertheless "creates a fresh universe out of nothingness by adding itself,/The way a look or a touch reveals its unexpected magnitudes" (*PM* 378). Poetry is an invisible activity without stability or presence, the expression of difference rather than substance. The poem is "part of the res," part of the world, but "the world is a force, not a presence" (*OP* 172).[8]

This play of excess and defect at once produces and disqualifies the structure of binary opposition running throughout Stevens's work: oppositions of subject and object, imagination and reality, alpha and omega (*PM* 334-35), "the self and the earth" (*PM* 382). "Real and unreal are two in one" (*PM* 349), opposites that coexist without coinciding and without interacting dialectically, that are disjunctively juxtaposed, each lying before and beyond the other. Nature is both an excess transcending mind, "beyond the last thought" (*PM* 398), and the deficient incipience of mind, "so much less than feeling, so much less than speech" (*OP* 115). Similarly, mind is both the transcendence of reality, "fulfilled" only in the creation of "another world" (*PM* 361-62), and the imminence of an uncompleted "search for reality" (*PM* 345). There can be no dialectical interplay of imagination and reality, no joining and no separation, insofar as there is no common measure between them, no correspondence, each remaining irredeemably excessive and deficient with regard to the other, the two united only in the event of their disjunctive affirmation.

The lyric and expressive "cry" evoked so frequently in Stevens's late poetry traverses the space of these binary oppositions, disjunctively affirming and thus destructuring them. At once human and inhuman, solipsistic and universal, the cry is excessive, transcendent, and uncanny; yet it is always rediscovered as something natural and entirely immanent. "The cry that contains its converse in itself" (where "converse" is both an opposite and a conversation or ever-ramifying dialogue) is not quite realized, "not wholly spoken in a conversation between/Two bodies disembodied in their talk," indeed "too fragile" to sustain realization but already surpassing the need for realization, "too immediate for any speech" (*PM* 336).

The "reality" of the cry encompasses "the philosopher's search/For an interior made exterior/And the poet's search for the same exterior made/Interior" (*PM* 345). In this oscillation, the cry of the poet's desire in "An Ordinary Evening in New Haven" is transformed into the distant and alien cries of the final lyrics. In "Not Ideas about the Thing but the Thing Itself" (*PM* 387-88), the cry enacts the "search" in the "as if" mode of the opening and closing similes: the "scrawny cry from outside/Seemed like a sound in his mind," even as the subjective awareness of the cry "was like/A new knowledge of reality." There is no actual accession either of knowledge or of contact with reality; but the production of similitude without correspondence—forever renewed, indefinitely repeatable—takes the place of any epistemological conclusions. The poem enacts a relation with an outside, neither from the point of view of a central and self-enclosed subject nor as the bridging or closing of a subject-object gap, but as the denial of any possibility of closure. The wholly private movement of desire, the interior, is already latent in the natural world, the exterior. The poet is surprised, uncertain where or how to place the cry, because something so intimate has approached him from without, in the barrenness of "the earliest ending of winter," and in the incipience of "a chorister whose c preceded the choir." The cry is immanent in the real world when it is imminent in the mind, and it has already approached when it is "still far away." In the words of another late poem, the cry (here a "howling") is at once "too far / For daylight and too near for sleep" (*PM* 385), too distant to be external and too close to be internal, an intimacy that is yet not personal.

The cry is an excess, something that should not be there, and indeed cannot be there, but nevertheless is there. Forever preceding itself, it is not an externality that breaks in on the poet's solitude but the very population of that solitude: "It was not from the vast ventriloquism / Of sleep's faded papier-mache . . . / The sun was coming from outside." But this outside is an incipience, "at daylight or before," less an interruption of sleep than what Stevens elsewhere calls "this wakefulness inside a sleep" (*PM* 370). The poet does not so much make contact with the outside as he discovers that the outside is already inside. In a movement that exceeds will and awareness, the latency of difference precedes any separation of inside and outside. Solipsism is always already impossible.

The strange logic of the cry is yet more apparent in "The Course of a Particular." Harold Bloom points to the paradox inherent in "the cry of leaves that do not transcend themselves" (*PM* 367): "leaves that do not transcend themselves are not leaves that utter a cry, and such a cry testifies to the presence of fantasia" (*Wallace Stevens* 357-58). But Bloom abruptly resolves this dilemma in favor of a human transcendence, identifying the imaginary with the human and reading Stevens's explicit denial of transcendence as evidence of a repression. Bloom ignores, first of all, other instances of clearly inhuman and non-fantastic cries in Stevens's poetry, extending at least as far back as the "constant cry" of the ocean in "The Idea of Order at Key West" (*PM* 97). For Stevens transcendence, as the noncorrespondent movement of excess and defect, is not exclusively human and not a power of the mind. To the poet the leaves are transcendent precisely in their defect, to the extent that they do not transcend themselves.

In addition, the tone of the poem does not suggest the repression that Bloom's reading requires. The poet who "holds off and merely hears the cry" is tentative and baffled, not anxious or defensive, and the reiteration of the cry comes because of, and not in spite of, the assertion of its immanence. Deeply puzzled by "the absence of fantasia," the poet searches for some transcendental and creative presence to explain and justify the anomalous "cry." But no such manifestation exists. The cry is entirely immanent to the leaves, and one cannot interpret it or give it meaning. The divine, the heroic, and the merely human in turn fail to contextualize it; they are all swept away and, in a subliminal pun, the leaves are all that is left. "It is a busy cry, concerning someone else," but this "someone else" is nowhere to be found. The "conflict" and "resistance" in the poem are not in the poet's psyche but in "the thing/Itself" in its particularity. As wholly immanent, the cry is wholly private, "until, at last, the cry concerns no one at all" (*PM* 367).

Just as "Not Ideas about the Thing but the Thing Itself" reveals the universal prepresence of that which is most interior and private, so "The Course of a Particular" reveals the inaccessible particularity of that which is most pervasive and universal. The poet cannot divorce himself from the cry of the leaves and from the wintry scene, but neither can he claim or recognize that cry as his own. Insofar as "the thing/Itself" is *not* transcendent, it takes on itself the expression of the cry of desire. "Though one says that one is part of everything," and ultimately because one says that one is part of everything, one discovers that "being part is an exertion that declines" (*PM* 367). In this decline, one affirms the "final finding" of one's subjectivity as a nonconcerning and nonrelating. Yet this nonparticipation remains incomplete, so long as the cry continues to insist. The poet, then, neither asserts the universality of his subjective "fantasia" nor, conversely, apprehends the reality of an object world apart from the self. Rather, he discovers a continuing otherness as the very principle of his own self-enclosed subjectivity. If "Not Ideas about the Thing but the Thing Itself" affirms an outside that is already inside, then "The Course of a Particular" affirms the inside as already a difference, already outside.[9]

The binary opposition of inside and outside, self and world, subject and object, imagination and reality, is only an effect produced within a larger economy of excess and defect. This economy is founded on the dissymmetrical (nonbinary) conflict of "course" and "particular," the noncoincident relation between the incessant and universal process of metamorphosis and the particularity of each instance of difference. The particular cannot be separated from the cry of desire, from the universal relation in which it is latently generated; but to the extent that it participates in that relation, its identity is threatened by the continuing play of metamorphosis. Insofar as the particular still insists as a difference, it has not achieved definitive separation from the unity without totality in which it is produced: its "incessant being alive" is always that of "a particular of being, that gross universe" (*PM* 363). "The accent of deviation in the living thing/That is its life preserved" is also the possibility of yet further deviation, as "disembodiments/Still keep occurring." The thing's production and preservation are also the continuing possibility of its destruction and alteration. The particular cannot subsist apart from its inevitably declining course. The part is constituted only in a "conflict" and by virtue of its "resistance" to the process of "being part" that nevertheless produces and encompasses it. "Being part is an exertion that declines," but it is only within this declining exertion that one *is* a part, a determinate particular, a point of conflict and resistance. The relation of part to whole remains always in process: the part continually "holds off" from its whole, and the whole is not the combination of the parts but their breaking apart.

The speaking and perceiving subject is evoked in the poem only in the passage from the impersonal "one," through the hypothetical "someone else," to the definitive "no one." As the exertion of being part declines, the subject is increasingly divorced from the movement within which it is first of all defined. It holds back from the "busy" insistence of the cry and from the transformative phantasmagoria of "icy shades and shapen snow"; but this separation is also its approach to death, its reduction to the bare minimum of recognition, "in the final finding of the ear, in the thing/Itself." The individual realizes its individuality, acquires a subjective identity, feels its own selfhood as "the life of that which gives life as it is," only within such a separation, only to the extent that it is already in decline. The always partial integrity of the subject is the partial integrity only of its death.

The crying of the leaves is an excess in this domain of "life as it is," an uncanny surplus that can be, but need not be, made into signification. The leaves survive the dying of their own impulse, "without meaning more/Than they are," but continuing to cry even at the moment when "at last, the cry concerns no one at all." The cry is an "invisible activity," a play of excess and defect, producing but preceding subjectivity and meaning. The force of the cry passes through and delineates the space of the poem; it is accumulated and released, so that its intensity at once builds up a subject and dissipates it. In "The Auroras of Autumn" the poet calls this movement the "infinite course" of an unending experience of dying (*PM* 308). The subject continually dies, or is impelled toward birth without achieving it, so long as the process (the cry) continues. But if this process were arrested, the subject would already be dead, since the movement of its production would be halted.[10]

Stevens is a poet less of meanings and presences, and their concomitant dearths and absences, than of desire as metamorphosis, the asubjective "will to change" and its noncoincident productions-alterations. The transformative force of desire can be described as a repetition without identity and as a flowing that has no goal. "It is of cloud transformed/To cloud transformed again, idly, the way/A season changes color to no end,/Except the lavishing of itself in change" (*PM* 312).

The movement of repetition without identity is elucidated most fully in "Notes toward a Supreme Fiction." Stevens first dismisses a bad kind of repetition, the exact recurrence of a finite cycle, in which all things return "as if they had never gone." In this kind of repetition, everything is regulated and adjusted "to a metaphysical t," and novelty and divergence are excluded. "The distaste we feel for this withered scene/Is that it has not changed enough. It remains,/It is a repetition" (*PM* 216-17). This repetition, grounded in sameness, can neither generate change nor account for it. But such an assertion of identity is itself subject to destructive alteration. The unbearably repetitive birds' song, rejecting change, is finally "a sound like any other. It will end" (*PM* 221).

In rejecting this monotonous repetition, the poem discovers and affirms a new kind of repetition, one founded not on identity but on the reiterated renewal of the experience of change. Now the birds' song can be welcomed in the perpetual incipience of its arrested development: "Cock bugler, whistle and bugle and stop just short, / Red robin, stop in your preludes, practicing / Mere repetitions" (*PM* 231). Repetition without identity is the movement that stops at the point of its preludes, a movement whose interminable latency is also its finality and its openness to continued alteration:

> A thing final in itself and, therefore, good:
> One of the vast repetitions final in
> Themselves and, therefore, good, the going round
>
> And round and round, the merely going round,
> Until merely going round is a final good,
> The way wine comes at a table in a wood.
>
> (*PM* 232)

The movement of circulation, the "merely going round," takes precedence over any circulated or repeated content. The phrase "one of the vast repetitions" suggests not only the amplitude of each repetition, the multiplicities that it may include, but also the indefinite vastness of the disjunctive series of repetitions. There are many repetitions, rather than an identity successively repeated. Each repetition is "final in itself," a "final good," without ulterior teleology and without reference to any totality or identity of which it would be the expression or to any ideal form or original of which it would be the repetition. Only the act of repetition is repeated, so that "merely going round" is an entirely positive activity, never completed but also permitting no essence beyond itself (the word *mere* generally implies for Stevens such an affirmative nonmanifestation and non-reference; see, for example, the late poem "Of Mere Being," *PM* 398). This circulation is neither original itself nor the repetition of some prior original; rather, it is an inexhaustibly repeatable movement of pure divergence without origination.

Stevens provisionally concludes that "the man-hero is not the exceptional monster, / But he that of repetition is most master" (*PM* 232). In subordinating all fixed identities to the continuing play of metamorphosis, he also proposes a new definition of subjectivity. The repetitions of section 10 of "An Ordinary Evening in New Haven" (*PM* 337) affirm a subject that is not implicated in traditional dualisms. The subject of traditional metaphysics is like the man in the moon, a solipsist "whose mind was made up and who, therefore, died" and who is "imprisoned in constant change," confined to the cyclical lunar repetitions of an empty identity. In contrast, the spirit that has mastered repetition (rather than been imprisoned within it) welcomes and participates in change (instead of helplessly being identified as a content to be repeated). Such a spirit "resides / In a permanence composed of impermanence," in repetition as a "feast" and "festival" of continual renewal. The solipsism of the man in the moon is impossible, for he is dead once his identity has been fixed. "It is fatal in the moon and empty there." But the permanent impermanence of the hero of repetition, his incessant experience of changing and dying, is the "faithfulness of reality" that preserves him from ever actually being dead.

The subject as master of repetition is not a substratum to which varying predicates are super-added but a repeated projection of nonidentity. "This faithfulness of reality," "so that morning and evening are like promises kept," in contrast to time as a closed cycle (like that of the "lunar light") refers to the incessant renewal of metamorphosis. In time conceived as an open sequence, the subject is repeatedly affirmed as that which differs from itself. Such a subject is not opposed to the object, to the outside, or to reality, any more than it simply corresponds to an outside reality. Rather, it is a divergence that inheres within reality, the nontotalizable sum, over time, of varying accents of deviation, the point at which "we do not know what is real and what is not."

The subject thus described is the local effect of a general economy characterized by the incessant circulation of a flowing that has no goal. "The River of Rivers in Connecticut" (PM 386-87) is Stevens's most extended presentation of this invisible activity. The river is pure and unceasing motion, a "mere flowing," a "flashing and flashing in the sun." While its "propelling force" is excessive, it lacks direction and "flows nowhere, like a sea." It is entirely latent, "not to be seen beneath the appearances / That tell of it," so that it neither appears nor subsists as an underlying essence. It is "the third commonness with light and air," not the substance of all things but that which forever permeates them. "An unnamed flowing," it cannot be manifested in language; yet we are "again and again" and ever "once more" impelled to "call it" a river, in repetition of its reiterated difference. It is the world, including the mind, as force rather than presence, "a curriculum, a vigor, a local abstraction," where "vigor" is literally the force of being alive and "curriculum" implies both a course, a specific direction or set of directions, and, etymologically, a running, a movement considered apart from its direction.

A "curriculum" and a "local abstraction," this asubjective flowing necessitates divergent subjects and significations as its final effects. The flowing is at once universal, a movement without direction, and specific and heterogeneous, an infinite series of irreconcilable courses or directions. Similarly, the river is both an "abstraction," an omnipresent "commonness" within which all things are transformed, and "local," found "in Connecticut," anchored in particulars rather than transcending them. The river of rivers is both the ultimate (final or quintessential) river and a flowing composed of the real rivers of which it is the excessive metaphorical transformation. All things are swept away by the excess of its force, and nothing can ever resist its inclusions. Yet its transformations never go beyond the things being transformed and are never separate from them: "the steeple at Farmington/Stands glistening, and Haddam shines and sways." These localities at once stand still and vibrate at the threshold of metamorphosis. The river's immanent activity takes place "far this side of Stygia," preceding and precluding the definitiveness of death and the power of negativity. "On its banks,/No shadow walks"; instead, its constituent local objects are altogether illuminated.

The subject may be defined within this economy of transformation as the locality of a flowing, not as a subsisting essence. The universal action of the river is always local and particular: as Stevens says in a yet later poem, "a mythology reflects its region" (*PM* 398). The river of rivers reflects not one region but all the seasons; it is at least "the folklore/Of each of the senses," if not their mythology. Again, the word *each* implies a universality composed of multiple specifications, of differing sensations or perceptions that may, but need not, overlap. Such a series of local illuminations determines the perpetual restlessness of the whole. The river does not contradict or limit its particulars; it fulfills and expresses them even to excess. It does not transcend its particulars, and it is not transcended by them. Yet this immanence consists not in the unification and effacement of the particulars but in their simultaneous and disjunctive affirmation.

In this affirmation, the river of rivers is opposed to death as a figure of what Stevens frequently calls "fate." "The river is fateful,/Like the last one," like the river of death. "But there is no ferryman" for this river, which does not lead to or promise a beyond. Its fatefulness inheres not in finality or transcendence but in the impossibility of any conclusion. The river of rivers is not a boundary to be crossed once and for all but the perpetual incipience of such a crossing, the fatality of never getting to the other side. It is fateful to such an extent that even the ultimate fatality of death cannot "bend against its propelling force." Entirely immanent, a shallow spectacle, not to be separated from or seen beneath the phenomena that it produces, it is the "propelling force" or fatality of everything, even and especially of that which opposes and resists it. Indeed, it is nothing more than the infinite series of such local resistances. The river of rivers is never "the last one" but always the new one, a repeated beginning without origination, the force of "again and again" (*PM* 386-87). It is fateful in the literal sense of being full of fate, excessively full, impossibly inclusive, in contrast to the definitively exclusive fate that is death. In this excess, it cannot ever be halted, cannot be contradicted even by death, cannot even be fixed by being named.

"Fate" affirms and positively differentiates the particular without imposing a negative limitation on it. The rabbi in the final section of "The Auroras of Autumn" "meditates a whole, / The full of fortune and the full of fate," by conjugating the possible disjunctions of "people" and "world," "the phases of this difference." We "turn back to where we were when we began," repeating the nonfulfillment of "an unhappy people in a happy world." The resulting "contrivance of the spectre of the spheres,/Contriving balance to contrive a whole," involves including and affirming the differences, not canceling them out (*PM* 316). There is no point of final repose. "Balance" remains precarious, contrived out of the very "extremity" described earlier in the poem as the obsessive "accomplishment/Of an extremist in an exercise" (*PM* 308). Unhappiness is not redeemed in the whole but reiterated by it; and this repetition is itself the (only) final good. "In these unhappy he meditates a whole, /The full of fortune and the full of fate, /As if he lived all lives," so that fate is affirmed in the "as if" of living so many incomplete lives. Fate is a whole in that it includes, affirms, and produces all possible outcomes in all localities. The poem concludes in a vision of unlimited metamorphosis: "in hall harridan, not hushful paradise, /To a haggling of wind and weather, by these lights/Like a blaze of summer straw, in winter's nick" (*PM* 316). Even death is thereby affirmed, not as a limitation on being or a power of negation, but as a positive beginning, the "imminence" of an almost wished-for "disaster," so that "it may come tomorrow in the simplest word,/Almost as part of innocence, almost, /Almost as the tenderest and the truest part" (*PM* 315). The reiterated "almost" marks the perpetual incipience both of death's arrival and of its becoming a part of the "innocence" that it threatens to disrupt.

Fate, an excessive movement of metamorphosis, cannot be separated from the localities of subjectivity and signification, which it precedes, determines, and invests. Since fate is the disjunctive affirmation of irreconcilable particulars, that which it determines must necessarily resist its overall determining force, and that which it propels can move only against it. Specific subjects and significations insist in opposition to the metamorphosing flow of difference, endeavoring to arrest it. But such resistance is not negative and dialectical, in that it cannot be sublated, cannot be canceled and preserved, in the fateful flowing that encompasses it. Rather, the point of resistance subsists (instead of being canceled) within the very movement by which it is altered (instead of being preserved and lifted up). The particular remains as an effect, as a positive spatial and temporal determination, the residue of the excess that overwhelms it. It is "a shivering residue, chilled and foregone" (*PM* 313), since the flow has no concern for it, does not correspond to it, and always leaves it behind. But at the same time, and by the same logic, the particular is also the actuality of alteration, "a flick . . . added to what was real and its vocabulary" (*PM* 378), and hence "the difference we make in what we see," the difference that makes reality always "a little different from reality" (*PM* 275).

The particular is always determined as a "poverty" by the fate that produces it, since it is wholly deficient in relation to the flow's infinite excess. "There lies the misery, the coldest coil/That grips the centre, the actual bite, that life/Itself is like a poverty in the space of life" (*PM* 243). "Life" is never equal to itself, and in this "misery" the realization of fate is also an unfulfillable projection of desire. Yet such poverty is not an absolute lack or an impelling negativity but the mode of a still positive subsistence: "He has his poverty and nothing more. / His poverty becomes his heart's strong core" (*PM* 323). The poet can proclaim this residual endurance "in the stale grandeur of annihilation" (*PM* 384) as an innocence of existence: "it is like a thing of ether that exists / Almost as predicate. / But it exists, / It exists, it is visible, it is, it is" (*PM* 314). In the excessive movement of fate, "the trouble of the mind / Is a residue" in which multiple determinations "live / And take from this restlessly unhappy happiness / Their stunted looks" (*OP* 97).

The "stunted looks" of poverty, residues pervading every absence, are aptly determined in an oxymoronic "restlessly unhappy happiness." This paradox precludes resolution. The movement of production of subjects and significations, itself asubjective and nonsignifying, is at once excess and defect, construction and destruction, investment and disinvestment. The determining movement of fate is restlessly oxymoronic, which is why Stevens's language is so frequently happy and unhappy, assertive and dejected, triumphant and defeated all in the same moment. These opposed attitudes are not positive-negative pairs; both are positive qualities, relating to each other by differences in intensity. The poet's happiness and unhappiness, satisfaction and dissatisfaction, simultaneously affirm a movement that is ultimately "without human meaning, / Without human feeling" (*PM* 398). It is beside the point to ask which tone is primary, whether Stevens is a Romantic transcendentalist or a reductive ironist, a poet of "qualified assertion" or of "asserted qualification."[11] Nor is it possible to relate these disjunctively affirmed modes to a dialectical, and therefore resolvable, conflict or to see one of them as an unconscious response to, or defense against, the other. Stevens's poetry of unlimited affirmation does not assert anything, and its irreconcilable statements do not qualify one another. No decision is possible, not even the decision that would relegate the text to undecidability. For excess and defect are not opposed phases or aspects but a single differential movement. The flow of difference is at once accumulated and discharged in the inclusive activity of fate.[12]

Thus when "majesty is a mirror of the self," a line constituting one of the most discussed cruxes in Stevens's poetry, there are also "external regions" filled with "the escapades of death" (*PM* 231) and vice versa.[13] The opposed moments of triumphant immediacy and mediated unfulfillment can neither exclude each other nor unite by canceling, or compensating for, each other, since they are disjunctively affirmed qualities of the same event. In its excess, the flowing that has no goal surpasses all possibilities; yet it is also nothing more than the movement that positively invests every particular possibility. And it is in these investments that the universal is limited and becomes a particular and that affirmation is limited and becomes assertion and signification. Subjectivity and signification are necessary to the flowing insofar as it is entirely positive and entirely heterogeneous, but they are only its final and most transient effects. Fate positively invests a given subject only to the extent that it also exceeds and transforms that subject.

"Poverty" is not a negative term but the point of an affirmation. It is the deficient residue of a passing excess, that which subsists even in absence. It barely exists, and yet it does indeed exist, for each subject, as the minimum of "what he is and as he is" (*PM* 384). This bare minimum does not quite stand forth on its own; it "exists/Almost as predicate," as the unfulfilled latency of a modification, rather than as a stability or a substance. Thus the residual subject of repetition that lacks identity is like an adjective, or a series of adjectives, without a noun to qualify. The subject is an inconstant locus of change, the movement of "the adjectives, an alteration/Of words that was a change of nature, more/Than the difference that clouds make over a town," so that "each constant thing," each substantive, is changed beyond identity and recognized only in its difference from itself (*PM* 350). The altering adjective, instead of being subordinated to the substantive, marks its dissociation and loss of solidity. "It is not in the premise that reality/Is a solid. It may be a shade that traverses/A dust, a force that traverses a shade" (*PM* 351). Reality is nothing more than or apart from its disparate parts; and subjectivity, as a residue, is (like any other part of reality) a matter not of essences but of intensities, of forces, of resistances.

Fate cannot be defined as an overriding impulsion that determines or compels particulars external to it and only negatively related to it. The movement that alters a particular, that deprives it of any coherence or self-identity, is the one thing that remains, as it were, intrinsic to it. Limitation is a positive movement defining an accent of deviation, not a boundary imposed from without. The particular that resists fate experiences fate intimately as its very internality, as the force of its resistance and the latent principle of its individuation. Each particular is also the locus of a change, "true—unreal,/The centre of transformations that/Transform for transformation's self," so that, in this "Human Arrangement," it defines what is alternatively and interchangeably "a being, a will, a fate" (*CP* 363). Universal fate is also that which particularizes and localizes. Any particular is also the self of transformation, since the subject's will is both the apparent internality of its being and the apparent externality of its fate. The particular as a unit of fate is "the centre of transformations," while fate as a whole is only realized in the decenteredness or "fated eccentricity" of its particulars (*PM* 320). Stevens defines repetition without identity as the "constant spin" or incessant deviation of the leaf "spinning its eccentric measure" (*PM* 232); and in such a movement, "the whole race is a poet that writes down/The eccentric propositions of its fate" (*PM* 282). The meditated whole, "the full of fortune and the full of fate," which in poetry is "directly and indirectly [got] at" (*PM* 351), is the sum of a series of fated eccentricities, each of which subsists and insists "as a part, but part, but tenacious particle" of an indeterminate but entirely positive "giant of nothingness, each one/And the giant ever changing, living in change" (*PM* 320).

In this positive nothingness, this invisible activity of the fated eccentricities, the two poles of Harold Bloom's dialectical mapping of Stevens's poetry (and of all American poetry since Emerson)—ethos, or fate, and pathos, or power—contaminate each other before they can be distinguished. Their mutual implication leaves no room for any dialectical interplay through the mediation of the releasing, negative term of logos or freedom.[14] Fate is the actual desire and power of each particular, not an ethos in opposition to particulars. It is not only a particular's overriding destiny or character but, more crucially, its individual will as accent of deviation or eccentricity. Even the most isolated and independent subjectivity "may not evade his [own] will,/Nor the wills of other men; and he cannot evade/The will of necessity, the will of wills" (*PM* 344). Individual wills operate parallel to and in conflict with one another; and necessity, as their summation, is yet again a will. This nondialectical interplay of will and necessity in Stevens closely approaches the great affirmations of Nietzsche:

> The fatality of [man's] essence is not to be disentangled from the fatality of all that has been and will be. . . . One is necessary, one is a piece of fatefulness, one is in the whole. . . . But there is nothing besides the whole. . . . That the world does not form a unity either as sensorium or as "spirit"—that alone is the great liberation; with this alone is the innocence of becoming restored.
>
> (*Twilight* 500-01)

> *This world is the will to power—and nothing besides!* And you yourselves are also this will to power—and nothing besides!
>
> (*Will to Power* 550, sec. 1067)

The world so described is what Stevens calls "my green, my fluent mundo" (*PM* 233) but also "the poem of pure reality, untouched/By trope or deviation," untouched or unmoved by them because there is "nothing beyond reality," because all tropes and deviations are not divergences from it but divergences already "included" within it (*PM* 336). This world is inescapably linguistic, but it cannot be reduced to the effects of language as an instrument of knowledge or assertion. It inescapably implicates subjectivity, but it cannot be reduced to effects generated by a subject or in the course of a subject's grappling with external objects. Stevens's poetry, in its unlimited affirmation of this universe of difference, leaves room for no fixed identities and no cognitive or epistemological moments. The "invisible activity" of fate, the movement of repetition without identity, evinces no labor of the negative and no power of negativity. In the world of Stevens's poetry, "the cancellings,/The negations are never final" (*PM* 310), and the negative is the only thing lacking.[15]

Stevens's poetry ceaselessly deconstructs the integral subject and determinate meaning; but in the same movement, it secondarily produces multiple subjects and significations. Thus the poetry is a concrete and positive occurrence, not a frustration but a deployment of desire.[16] "Yet the absence of the imagination had / Itself to be imagined . . . all this / Had to be imagined as an inevitable knowledge, / Required, as a necessity requires" (*PM* 382-83). This affirmation, in "The Plain Sense of Things," exceeds both voluntarism, which would concentrate, like Bloom's reading, on figures of will and necessity, and intellectualism, which would stress the poem's unavoidable blindness to its own significations. The "inevitable knowledge" is a knowledge only of the bafflement of knowledge, of an uncaused and unmodifiable emptiness and blankness. Yet this impasse is also an imagined necessity, necessity (ethos) as required by and through imagination (pathos), and hence a positive projection of the will to power as well. Conversely, the will seems to predominate here only to the extent that it turns against itself to identify with the necessity that constrains and eventually destroys it. But this destruction is the accomplishment, and not the defeat, of the process of willing, "an end of the imagination" in the sense of a positive fulfillment. The radical indeterminacy of knowledge is positively determined, and the determinateness (in the sense of a limit) of the system of will and necessity is a local abstraction from a field of positive indeterminacies. The "plain sense" (in which *sense* at once indicates a meaning, an affect or feeling, and a simple perception) of decay, emptiness, and failed repetition resides in the necessary fulfillment, as it were, of the very incompletion of the subject and its significations. Imagination affirms the impermanence and instability of the momentary alignment of forces concretized in the "act" of willing. Knowledge and will are both positively implicated as local possibilities within a larger economy of repetition without identity, so that the limitation of each is exceeded without being transcended or dialectically subsumed.

The logic of Stevens's poetry is repetitive and accretive, not dialectical or progressive. It moves toward no transcendence and proclaims no truth. It neither conveys metaphysical reassurances nor heralds the triumph of the narcissistic ego: it functions "not to console / Nor sanctify, but plainly to propound" (*PM* 215). But in so propounding, "the poem refreshes life" (*PM* 209), by returning to and repeating differently "the freshness of transformation [that] is / The freshness of a world" (*PM* 224). Its project is what Nietzsche describes as the highest aim of art: "to be *oneself* the eternal joy of becoming, beyond all terror and pity—that joy which include[s] even joy in destroying" (*Twilight* 563). It is not through any mode of negation but through an unlimited power of affirmation that "Poetry is a Destructive Force" (*PM* 157). The moments of destruction that are repeated throughout Stevens's poetry can indeed be read affectively, as evasions or defensive qualifications of the moments of alleged narcissistic exultation that they accompany, even as they can be read cognitively, as the rhetorical limits of the poems' alleged assertions of presence, authority, closure. But such readings are finally too limiting, too humanistic, remaining within the horizon of the power of the negative, within the totalizing limitations of Western culture that it was Stevens's fortune and fate to transgress and to exceed. A more thoroughly nonidealistic mode of criticism, such as the one adumbrated in this essay, will find Stevens's poetry "more truly and more strange" (*PM* 55), will find it, in the words of Stevens's last poem, "without human meaning, / Without human feeling, a foreign song" ("Of Mere Being," *PM* 398). The bird in the palm is not ours, it does not call us, but it remains, it affects us, in its ungraspable and irreducible insistence. Its "mere being" is all that can be affirmed of it. But such an affirmation also marks a death: the death of identity, the death of truth, the death of religious and humanistic values. Are we to see, in this death, in these lines, in such a song, the horror of the void, the nothingness that threatens to submerge the human, or are we to confront, rather, the possibility of a new and inhuman affirmation, the promise of transformation without end, the positivity of this void and this destruction? This new affirmation, which transgresses the limits of our humanism, is obviously not to be attained by mere force of will. But this affirmation already exists, a threat and promise of metamorphosis, an alterity insinuating itself within the very space of our selfhood and privacy, the positivity of "mere being," the song of the bird "on the edge of space," the incessant movement of the "river of rivers" in which "the mere flowing of the water is a gayety."

Notes

1. The critical literature on Stevens is too extensive to be summarized here. I will mention only the works that have most influenced me or stimulated me to the most fruitful disagreement. The most powerful overall reading of Stevens (and one that energetically argues for seeing him as an Emersonian Romantic) remains Harold Bloom's (*Wallace Stevens*). The most rigorous and convincing "ironic" reading is Helen Vendler's. I have also found extremely useful Hugh Kenner's placing of Stevens within the modernist tradition (50-85).

2. A few further methodological remarks may be in order. Because I am trying to trace the immanent logic of an evanescent and ever-changing movement, my approach to Stevens's texts involves neither a prior and external theoretical grounding nor a seemingly pre-suppositionless "close reading" but something in between. If Stevens's "endlessly elaborating poem / Displays the theory of poetry, / As the life of poetry" (*Palm* 349), then I feel justified in offering a theory of Stevens's poetry that remains within the descriptive field, and even within the very language, of that poetry. Instead of offering an overarching description of *all* Stevens's later poetry or merely explicating a few particular poems, I attempt to trace a path *through* the body of the later poetry. At times I pause to consider individual short poems or sections of longer poems, but most of the time I move freely back and forth from poem to poem. I am not claiming that every line that Stevens wrote fits perfectly into the categories I am proposing here. But I am claiming that the movements of transformation that I trace provide a background or context from which it is perilous to isolate individual poems. It is in this contextual sense that I endeavor to map out the "outlines" and "expressings" (*Palm* 321) of Stevens's later poetry.

3. Hereafter all quotations from Wallace Stevens are identified by abbreviations for the sources—*CP* (*Collected Poems*), *OP* (*Opus Posthumous*), and *PM* (*The Palm at the End of the Mind*)—followed by page numbers. Adopting Harold Bloom's suggestion, I have used the more accurate *PM* as my primary source for any text printed both there and in an earlier volume.

4. My conception of a multiple, untotalizable "unity" in Stevens has been decisively influenced by Gilles Deleuze's simular formulations about Proust. See especially "Antilogos, or the Literary Machine," in *Proust and Signs* (93-157).

5. Thus it is impossible to accept Harold Bloom's claim that the "realization" is achieved "despite the 'as if'" (*Wallace Stevens* 363). I discuss Bloom's reading of Stevens in terms of a dialectic of assertion and negation, ethos and pathos, and so on, at greater length below.

6. Gilles Deleuze and Felix Gauttari oppose "an idealistic (dialectical, nihilistic) conception [of desire] which causes us to look upon it as primarily a lack" and a process of acquisition (25) to a positive materialist conception of desire as a "process of production" (26) that is always already part of the real and that precedes any constitution of a desiring subject. The former conception receives its most powerful expression in the Hegelian notion of negativity as the motor of change. The latter conceives desire as the immanent "will to change" and disjunctive affirmation.

7. This distinction helps to explain how my reading of Stevens relates to, and yet differs radically from, contemporary strategies of "deconstruction." J. Hillis Miller, in "Stevens' Rock and Criticism as Cure," expounds the point that "the vocabulary of a poet is not a gathering or a closed system, but a dispersal, a scattering" (499). The key words of Stevens's poetry have "multiple meanings" that are "incompatible, irreconcilable"; we strive to select a single, determinate meaning, but "it is impossible to decide which one it is" (502). I am disagreeing not with Miller's demonstrations of multiplicity and indeterminability but with his assumption that a choice between, rather than of, the conflicting terms needs to be made. For Stevens, such incompatibilities are points of affirmation, not merely instances of cognitive or hermeneutical bafflement. Miller finally reads Stevens in a key of irony and frustration: "The desire to be at the end of distances can never be satisfied" (516). But as far back as "Sunday Morning," and even more in the later poetry, Stevens regards such nonfinality and nonsatisfaction as a cause for celebration, for it is the force of metamorphosis, that which permits desire to be endlessly renewed.

8. M. Bernetta Quinn carefully traces the event of metamorphosis in its ramifications throughout Stevens's poetry. Her analysis is valuable on a purely descriptive level; but the contexts of her discussion, and the conclusions she draws, are radically different from mine. Instead of working through the logic of difference and metamorphosis as I do here, she starts from the assumption that "Stevens belongs to the idealist tradition" (49). She argues, consequently, that "metamorphosis links the objective and the subjective worlds" and "connects the realm of reality with the realm of imagination" (61), whereas I claim that metamorphosis works in an entirely different dimension, dissolving and displacing, rather than reconciling, the opposed terms.

9. Stevens's surprising treatment of the pathetic fallacy in "The Course of a Particular" is a fine instance of the way in which he dislocates, rather than either perpetuates or negates, traditional Romantic and modernist paradigms. This poem neither imputes inner life to an object world nor denies such an imputation. It alludes to the pathetic fallacy only to undermine the subject-object dualism that determines both its employment and the recognition that it is, after all, false. Stevens is not puzzling over epistemological dilemmas but radically questioning the very terms in which those dilemmas are stated. Thus, I can no more agree with Hugh Kenner's claim that Stevens's poetry "revolves around nothing more profound than bafflement with a speechless externality which poets can no longer pretend is animate" (81) than with Bloom's counterclaim that such an externality does in fact speak. The value of Kenner's discussion lies, rather, in his intuition that such arguments, on either side, have little to do with the way Stevens's poetry *works*.

10. Although I am concentrating here on the production of the subject, I could make similar observations about the production of signification. Linguistic play is an important element of Stevens's poetry, but language is no more his ultimate horizon than consciousness is. Stevens delights in linguistic *effects*: the signifier, like the subject, is the effect of an asignifying, as well as an asubjective, process of metamorphosis. "A poem need not have a meaning and like most things in nature often does not have" (*OP* 177). Thus, instead of

speaking, like Miller, of the undecidability of Stevens's language, I prefer to adopt Kenner's suggestion that Stevens is writing "nonsense poetry"—although I use this term in a less ironic sense than Kenner apparently intends (81-82).

11. "Qualified assertion" is Helen Vendler's phrase; see "The Qualified Assertions of Wallace Stevens." The opposition of "qualified assertion" to "asserted qualification" is Bloom's suggestion (*Ringers* 228).

12. The reading of Stevens that comes closest to sharing my emphasis on inclusion and disjunctive affirmation is J. Hillis Miller's study in *Poets of Reality* (217-84). Miller carefully works through the wildly contradictory epistemological stances evoked in Stevens's poetry and concludes that "his poetry is not dialectical. . . . There is no progress, only an alternation between contradictory possibilities" (259). Miller proposes that Stevens resolves this impasse by "mov[ing] so rapidly from one season to another that all the postures of the spirit are present in a single moment" (267) and by writing "a poetry of fleeting movement, a poetry in which each phrase has beginning and ending at once" (270). Finally, Miller suggests that "the later Stevens is beyond metaphysical dualism, and beyond representational thinking " (274), and that his last poetry instead performs a Heideggerian uncovering of Being. Miller's highly persuasive accounts have strongly influenced my own understanding of Stevens; but I find his insights limited by his phenomenological presuppositions. Despite his disclaimers, he cannot avoid presenting his reading in the form of a dialectic of consciousness. It is by painstakingly exhausting the possibilities of subject-object dualism that Miller's Stevens finally arrives at the immanent unities of imagination and reality and of being and nothingness. The discovery that "there is only one mode of existence: consciousness of some reality" (274) resolves an initial opposition between consciousness and reality. My approach, in contrast, seeks to avoid both the posing of an epistemological problem and the subsequent ontological or phenomeno-logical resolution. I neither start by positing a conscious, perceiving subject nor conclude with a disclosure of the pregiven grounds of perception and consciousness. What I am calling the affirmation of difference is a Nietzschean movement of "going under" and becoming other, not a Heideggerian "event of appropriation" (*Ereignis*). This affirmation is multiple and metamorphic; it can no more be reduced to the unity of a common participation in being than to the dualistic opposition, and dialectical reconciliation, of subject and object.

13. Helen Vendler says that this section (sec. 8 of "It Must Give Pleasure," in "Notes toward a Supreme Fiction"), "after a heroic expansion, turns despairingly on the mind's ramifying extrapolations and evasions, and ends in disgust" (*On Extended Wings* 198). For Harold Bloom, on the contrary, the emphasis falls on the poet's "triumphant solitude," and the concluding reference to "external regions" and "escapades of death" is a dismissive afterthought (*Wallace Stevens* 215). From the position that I am arguing here, the terms of the debate are false. Both critics treat one attitude as a response to or a compensation for the other, and both accord primacy to the self-consciousness of the poet.

14. For Bloom's mapping, see his *Wallace Stevens* (passim, esp. 1-26 and 375-406). Bloom sees Romantic poetry as fluctuating between submission to the action of external necessity (ethos, character, fate) and assertion of the passion of the individual will (pathos, personality, power). The liberating movement (logos, dialectic, freedom) from fate to power involves an influx of inspiration, or "the conversion of mere signification into meaning" (3). Logos for Bloom is thus a rhetorical disjunction and a negative moment. On the one hand, he associates it with Paul de Man's notion of the aporia: "an epistemological moment, with the authority to deconstruct its own text, that is, to indicate the text's cognitive awareness of its own limit as text, its own status as rhetoricity, its own demystification of the fiction of closure" (392). On the other hand, this negative moment makes possible a transition or "poetic crossing" from one sysem of poetic figuration (an ethos) to another (a pathos), and Bloom insists against de Man that a trope thus generated is "a figure of will rather than a figure of knowledge" (393). Bloom thus reinstates a Romantic notion of the will as a capacity for infinite negation, in opposition to the deconstructionists' ironic suspension of the movement of negativity. I am arguing, instead, for a view more like that of Nietzsche's will to power, which mimes both voluntarism (pathos) and fatalism (ethos), while in fact being reducible to neither,

and which excludes the negative moment altogether, rather than sublating it or ironically suspending it (see below). In my reading, Stevens's affirmation is compatible neither with Bloom's subjectivism nor with de Man's (and the later Miller's) linguistic and cognitive skepticism.

15. Gilles Deleuze describes Nietzsche's "eternal return" as a mode of nonidentical repetition that excludes negativity and affirms difference and metamorphosis (*Nietzsche and Philosophy*, passim). Deleuze's reading has been important both for my invocation of Nietzsche in relation to Stevens and for my understanding of difference, repetition, and affirmation in Stevens's poetry.

16. The philosophy of deconstruction is correct in pointing to a movement that at once necessitates and disqualifies the positing of determinate subjects and significations. Yet it insists on viewing this tension only in cognitive or epistemological terms. As a result, it cannot affirm nonidentity and difference (as Stevens's poetry so powerfully does); instead, it falls back into the familiar paradoxes of skeptical idealism. Deconstructionist criticism thus typically presents difference only as the frustration of a (negative) desire for mastery and self-identity. I am arguing instead for difference and disjunction as immanent principles of (nonnegative) desire. (See also nn. 6 and 7.)

Works Cited

Bloom, Harold. *The Ringers in the Tower: Studies in Romantic Tradition.* Chicago: U. of Chicago P, 1971.

———. *Wallace Stevens: The Poems of Our Climate.* Ithaca: Cornell UP, 1977.

Deleuze, Gilles. *Nietzsche and Philosophy.* Trans. Hugh Tomlinson. London: Athlone, 1983.

———. *Proust and Signs.* Trans. Richard Howard. New York: Braziller, 1972.

Deleuze, Gilles, and Felix Guattari. *Anti-Oedipus: Capitalism and Schizophrenia.* Trans. Robert Hurley, Mark Seem, and Helen R. Lane. Minneapolis: U of Minnesota P, 1983.

Kenner, Hugh. *A Homemade World: The American Modernist Writers.* New York: Knopf, 1975.

Miller, J. Hillis. *Poets of Reality: Six Twentieth-Century Writers.* Cambridge: Harvard UP, 1966.

———. "Stevens' Rock and Criticism as Cure." *Aesthetics Today.* Ed. Morris Philipson and Paul J. Gudel. Rev. ed. New York: NAL, 1980. 497-536.

Nietzsche, Friedrich. *Twilight of the Idols. The Portable Nietzsche.* Trans. and ed. Walter Kaufmann. New York: Viking, 1954.

———. *The Will to Power.* Trans. Walter Kaufmann and R. J. Hollingdale. New York: Vintage, 1968.

Pearce, Roy Harvey, and J. Hillis Miller, eds. *The Act of the Mind: Essays on the Poetry of Wallace Stevens.* Baltimore: Johns Hopkins P, 1965.

Quinn, M. Bernetta. "Wallace Stevens' 'Fluent Mundo.'" *The Metamorphic Tradition in Modern Poetry.* New York: Gordian, 1972. 49-88.

Stevens, Wallace. *The Collected Poems of Wallace Stevens.* New York: Knopf, 1954.

———. *Opus Posthumous.* Ed. Samuel French Morse. New York: Knopf, 1957.

———. *The Palm at the End of the Mind: Selected Poems and a Play.* Ed. Holly Stevens. New York: Vintage, 1972.

Vendler, Helen. *On Extended Wings: Wallace Stevens' Longer Poems*. Cambridge: Harvard UP, 1969.

———. "The Qualified Assertions of Wallace Stevens." Pearce and Miller, 163-78.

"A Completely New Set of Objects": The Spirit of Place in Wallace Stevens and Charles Ives   Lawrence Kramer°

> The katy-dids at Ephrata return
> But this time at another place.
> It is the same sound, the same season,
> But it is not Ephrata.
> (Stevens, "Memorandum")

Wallace Stevens and Charles Ives, born just five years apart, came of age in the great era of American expatriate artists. In the late nineteenth and early twentieth centuries, American musicians traveled to Germany, painters to France, and writers to England and the Continent at large. Many chose not to come back in a hurry, if they came back at all. Not only cosmopolitan vagabonds like Henry James, but also figures closely associated with American scenes and themes—Mark Twain, Thomas Eakins, Edward Macdowell—learned or practiced their vocations abroad. But Stevens and Ives stayed home, and more, they made a point of staying home. Each was a strenuously American artist, not least in his determined embrace of that quintessentially American art, making a living in business.[1] Each was profoundly attached to a sense of American place, as Stevens, reflecting on being a "countryman," affirmed:

> He is there because he wants to be
> And because being there in the heavy hills
> And along the moving of the water—
>
> Being there is being in a place,
> As of a character everywhere.
> ("The Countryman")[2]

Impelled by their sense of home, the sphere of what Stevens called "local objects," both Stevens and Ives consciously sought to satisfy the famous

°Revised and abridged by Lawrence Kramer from chapter 6 of his book, *Music and Poetry: The Nineteenth Century and After* (Berkeley and Los Angeles: University of California Press). © 1984 the Regents of the University of California. A portion of this essay appeared earlier in the *Wallace Stevens Journal* 2 (Fall 1978):3-15. Reprinted with permission of the University of California Press and the *Wallace Stevens Journal*.

demand that Emerson had imposed on the American artist in his essay "The Poet" (1841):

> We have yet had no genius in America, with tyrannous eye, which knew the value of our incomparable materials, and saw, in the barbarism and materialism of the times, another carnival of the same gods he so much admires in Homer . . . . Our log-rolling, our stumps and their politics, our fisheries, our Negroes and Indians, our boats and our repudiations, the wrath of rogues and the pusillanimity of honest men, the northern trade, the southern planting, the western clearing, Oregon and Texas, are yet unsung.[3]

Emerson's deliberately ill-assorted catalogue of Americana implies that the concrete particulars of America have not yet been linked to the living metaphysical absolutes of traditional European art. America is over-burdened with locality; it is a vast sprawl of places and local objects that are still radically material, all of them cut off from the privileged sites of the old and ancient worlds where truth enters history and stands unveiled. The task of the authentic American artist is to bring the absolute down home.

Both Stevens and Ives tried to do that, and to do it in much the same ways. The convergence between them is more important than the fact that Stevens had Walt Whitman and Emily Dickinson as predecessors, whereas Ives was essentially unprecedented—though far from naive, persistent misconceptions to the contrary. What Stevens and Ives share is a recognition that constructing an American absolute is above all a problematic enterprise, a dilemma as well as an ideal. Unlike Emerson, Whitman, or Dickinson—the first two figures of a heroic age already remote by 1915, the third still a marginal presence—Stevens and Ives always find that the transfiguration of place is never enduring. They find, too, that the transfigured places themselves, for all that one is a countryman of them, are strangely elusive and imponderable. The katy-dids at Ephrata do return. But it is not Ephrata.

The great task envisioned by Emerson can be described as the creation of what Stevens calls "a completely new set of objects": works of art in which the local and the absolute, the contingent and the transcendent, fuse into a single form. Both Stevens and Ives feel emphatically that this cannot be accomplished simply by giving poetry or music a local character. The problem cannot be solved for poetry as William Carlos Williams tried to solve it, with an infusion of gritty regional imagery and idiomatic speech "in the American grain." Nor can it be solved for music as Ives is often misunderstood to have solved it, by incorporating folk and popular elements into sophisticated compositions; Daniel Gregory Mason could do that. As Ives put it with a case in point: "Someone is quoted as saying that 'ragtime is the true American music.' Anyone will admit that it is one of the many true, natural, and, nowadays, conventional means of expression. . . . But it does not 'represent the American nation' any more than some fine old senators represent it."[4]

For Stevens and Ives, the problem of making a completely new set of objects is defined by the fact that the local and the absolute are fundamentally incompatible with each other. These terms form part of a rigorous dialectic, drawn by Ives directly from the Concord Transcendentalists, and familiar in Stevens as the quarrel between reality and the imagination. For both men, art is the expression of a transcendental force, a faculty of mind or spirit which is the source of all value and the interpreter of all desire. Stevens, of course, calls that faculty the imagination, and it is worth noting the persistence of the definite article; there is only one imagination, though its embodiments are infinitely various. For both Stevens and Ives, the imagination is transcendent of all local facts, all the contingent realities of historical place and time—everything that makes up the landscape of individual life, and in so doing inevitably defines the limits of individual life. Both men also maintain, however, that the imagination can only act, only speak, through the local things to which it does not belong. "It is one of the peculiarities of the imagination," writes Stevens, "that it is always at the end of an era. What happens is that it is always attaching itself to a new reality and adhering to it. It is not that there is a new imagination but that there is a new reality."[5]

The process of this "attachment" is neither smooth nor simple. The imagination and reality are not passive opposites; they resist and belittle each other, and they cannot be made to go hand in hand without a strain. In order to attach itself to a reality, the imagination must at the very least create a momentary disordering or distortion; a violent disruption is equally possible and perhaps more tempting.[6] To use the imagination, according to Stevens, is to generate "those violences which are the maturity of [our] desire" (NA 63-64). Prior to Notes Toward a Supreme Fiction (1942), such violences in Stevens's work usually take the form of thrusts or displacements; that is, the imagination makes room for itself in reality by shoving reality out of the way. In "The Idea of Order at Key West," the song of "the maker," the girl on the beach, displaces "the dark voice of the sea":

> It may be that in all her phrases stirred
> The grinding water and the gasping wind;
> But it was she and not the sea we heard.
> (12-14)

The same thing happens more rudely in "The Man With the Blue Guitar," where the world is reduced to the ball on the nose of a clown by the guitar player's "fat thumb":

> He held the world upon his nose
> And this-a-way he gave a fling.
> His robes and symbols, ai-yi-yi—
> And that-a-way he twirled the thing.
> (XXV)

Between Notes and "Description Without Place" (1945), the thrust at reality tends to become a cut, a tearing—the parting of one thing from another by abstraction, which, according to Stevens, is the imagination's essential activity. In "Description," for example, the workings of the imagination appear in the gap between the way a place looks—its description—and the place itself. The description comes to us as "a sight indifferent to the eye," "a little different from reality." Yet the result of this abstraction, "an artificial thing that exists," is not entirely satisfactory. Even though it shapes a place on which the dove of creation alights, the description without place is incomplete: "a knowledge incognito," a "column in the desert," "an expectation, a desire" (V).

In the work of Stevens's last decade (1946-55)—the portion of his poetry that most converges with Ives—the thrust or cut of earlier imaginative acts is replaced by a fusion in which the imagination coincides with the reality that it transcends. Stevens compares the imagination in this aspect with light (NA 60): like light, it adds nothing to reality except its own presence. The poetic form taken by this strange addition—an "addition" of sheer transparency—is the pivotal use of minimal descriptions: local place-names. Named in the presence of the imagination, the local becomes an abstraction, an imagined thing; while the imagination "localizes" itself in the act of naming. In "Reality Is an Activity of the Most August Imagination" (OP), for example, Stevens places himself on a drive between Cornwall and Hartford on a given Friday night. The placement is emphatic: the night, we read, was "not a night blown at a glassworks in Vienna/or Venice"; it is pure Connecticut, pure Americana. Stevens's drive becomes an act of the imagination as the movement of the car creates "the visible transformations of summer night"; and the presence of the imagination constitutes Cornwall and Hartford as the borders of an absolute space. The poem calls that space "night's moonlight lake," an area defined by what it is not—"neither water nor air"—and where it is not, just as a moonlight lake is neither moonlight nor a lake. Night's moonlight lake is a composite form—a space, a duration, a perception—in which the local and the absolute overlap: a visionary locality that blends into one thing both the night's "visible transformations" and its fixed identity as the darkness between Cornwall and Hartford.

Ives fully shares Stevens's sense that the maturity of desire involves the "violence" of transformation. For Ives, there is a radical duality to be found between "substance" and "manner," terms that he applies freely to action, to the self, and to art.[7] Ives's "substance" corresponds roughly with Stevens's "imagination," though Ives literally thinks of it as absolute in the sense of being noumenal, unlike the skeptical Stevens, for whom the absoluteness of the imagination is itself finally an imagined thing. "Manner," in turn, aligns itself with Stevens's "reality": the local, the contingent, the historical. For Ives, the aim of art is to consume manner by substance. "We are going to be arbitrary enough to claim," he writes,

> with no definite qualification, that substance can be expressed in music, and that it is the only valuable thing about it; and, moreover, that in two

separate pieces of music in which the notes are almost identical, one can be of substance with little manner, and the other can be of manner with little substance.

(*EBS* 77)

Obviously, the way to write unauthentic music is to let manner predominate over substance; and for Ives, this means in particular to be hemmed in by the musical equivalent of locale, whether it belongs to the Boston Symphony—a *bête noire*—or to ragtime. His remarks on the subject ought to dispel forever the notion that he is a straightforward nationalist or local colorist; in fact, Ives insists that if local color is a part of manner, then "either the color part is bound eventually to drive out the local part, or the local drive out all color" (*EBS* 78). Indigenous material belongs in music only as an echo, a precious trace, of substance, a musical memory linked to a transfiguration of locality that forms part of the composer's "spiritual consciousness." (What this often means for Ives is an idealized boyhood on a Wordsworthian model.[8]) It does not matter how such material sounds as long as it carries the music into "the showers of the absolute" (*EBS* 92). A self-conscious folk-tune is no more than a song about "the cherry on the cocktail."

Ives's most characteristic way of subsuming American material into the substance of an absolute is a form of allusion that is often misunderstood as quotation. Stevens offers a close parallel in his use of American place-names. To take Stevens first, it is generally true that when he wants to symbolize the imagination in radical opposition to reality, he uses exotic imagery in order to do it. This is most characteristic of his early poetry, where the imagination appears in the shapes of savage and tropical lushness, as in "Floral Decorations For Bananas," where leaves "plucked from Carib trees" go "Darting out of their purple craws / Their musky and tingling tongues." When, however, Stevens wants to represent reality yielding to the pressure of the imagination, he commonly represents it by the locale of his native regions, Pennsylvania and Connecticut. For Stevens, when an ordinary evening becomes the scene of an "inescapable romance," it is an ordinary evening in New Haven. An important poem in this mode, though a little-noticed one, is the lyric that gives this chapter its title:

From a Schuylkill in mid-earth there came emerging
Flotillas, willed and wanted, bearing in them

Shadows of friends, of those he knew, each bringing
From the water in which he believed and out of desire

Things made by mid-terrestrial, mid-human
Makers without knowing, or intending, uses.

These figures verdant with time's buried treasure
Came paddling their canoes, a thousand thousand,

Carrying such shapes, of such alleviation,
That the beholder knew their subtle purpose,

Knew well the shapes were the exactest shaping
Of a vast people old in meditation . . .

Under Tinicum or small Cohansey,
The fathers of the makers may lie and weather.

In this poem, the imagination is the force that brings "alleviation" to human desire by shaping new objects through meditation; reality is the local, pure and simple; and the two become one. This fusion has its source in a quality that can simply be called "thirdness"—the quality that arises when the means of perceiving an object is the impossibility of saying that the object is one thing or another.[9] Thirdness is the basis for one of Stevens's rhetorical fingerprints, the extended description that vaporizes its object with an intricate "as if" sequence or play of appositives. Elsewhere, the quality is more direct. In "Reality Is An Activity" (*OP*), thirdness compels the poet's recognition that night's moonlight lake is neither water nor air. In "A Completely New Set of Objects," it compels the reader to recognize that the poem's images are neither literal nor figurative. Stevens's river, for instance, is neither literally the Schuylkill and figuratively a visionary form, nor the reverse; and the figures in the flotillas are neither literally images of the beholder's friends and figuratively spirits of place, nor the reverse. Both the river and the figures are third things, parts of a new set of objects. Thirdness like this is the mark of fusion in Stevens; it is the way that things are perceived when the imagination has integrated itself with a local reality, the form in which a vision of mid-earth—of earth as imagination *and* reality—is a trip to Pennsylvania.

Where thirdness marks the fusion of a locality and an absolute, Stevens turns the locality into a privileged spot, a permanent threshold of fusion, by pronouncing its name as a kind of numinous formula. Set within the imaginative rhythm of the poem, the name behaves as a trope—a metonym for the transfiguration of the local scene. The essential feature of place-names in this essentially Ivesian role is that their presence is incantatory rather than referential. "Tinicum" and "small Cohansey," for instance, are names deliberately chosen for their obscurity, their lack of rich associations; and even the Schuylkill, admirable river though it is, does not have the resonance of the Mississippi or the Rio Grande. Unlike a poem such as Whitman's "Crossing Brooklyn Ferry," where the rhapsodic naming of locality forms an intimate bond between the poet and those who live after him in the places that he names, "A Completely New Set of Objects" addresses its names to unalterable strangers, readers for whom the names are essentially empty. This "emptiness" in the name is strongly in accord with the principle that reality becomes imaginative only by means of abstraction. In order to embody its fusion with an absolute, a locality is forced to make a kind of dialectical bargain: the price that a named place pays to transcend itself is its disappearance into a place-name. In turn, the name becomes less the designation of a particular locality than a signifier for locality as such, the core of definiteness over which thirdness hovers. It is in this abstract version of the local that reality and the imagination meet.

In some poems, Stevens rarefies this pattern of local abstraction still further by trading away the actual name. A place may be transformed without an imaginative christening; the mere possibility of finding a word, a name, a syllable, that belongs to it might be enough:

> [She wanted] the two of them in speech,
>
> In a secrecy of words
> Opened out within a secrecy of place,
>
> Not having to do with love.
> A land would hold her in its arms that day
>
> Or something much like a land.
> ("Two Letters," II [*OP*])

> Little existed for him but the few things
> For which a fresh name always existed, as if
> He wanted to make them, to keep them from perishing.
> ("Local Objects" [*OP*])

In "Old Man Asleep," the unspoken name is half-realized as the literal cry— or vocable—of its occasion; the "whole peculiar plot" (place/story) of the self is fused with "the earth" in "the drowsy motion of the river R." In poems like these, we might say, it is the emptiness of the name, not the name itself, that is most "pronounced."

What Stevens does with place-names, real and potential, Ives also does with the hymns, folk songs, rags, and barroom tunes that turn up continually in his music. These local melodies are almost never simply quoted by Ives; they are nearly always distorted, either in their own right, or by their placement against a dissonant or rhythmically incongruent background that leaves them sounding at once naive and defamiliarized. Perhaps the most startling instance of this occurs in "The Revival," the last movement of Ives's Second Violin Sonata. After a series of variations on "Shall We Gather at the River," the music explodes into a long coda in which the hymnody of the violin is swamped by a crashing hubbub of dissonant chords on the piano—all set firmly over a pedal point, a reiterated tone (here sounded in octaves) in the bass (example 1). The manifestation of "substance" is virtually literal, as sheer volume of sound in a jagged rhythm becomes the expression of harmonically intelligible sonority. By contrast, Alban Berg's quotation of a Bach chorale melody in the finale of his Violin Concerto is curiously free of tension, despite its intrusion of tonality into a twelve-tone texture. Not only does Berg derive the quotation from the tone-row on which the concerto is based, but the words to the chorale, "Es ist genug, Herr, wenn es Dir gefällt" ("It is enough, Lord, if it be Thy will"), are at one with the expressive purpose of the music, which is to respond to the death of a friend's daughter.

Ives almost always excludes continuities like these when he echoes a hymn tune or a traditional melody. His music is modeled on personal rather than musical memory, and a sudden, irrelevant outburst of "Dixie" against independent chromatic lines—a major event in the opening movement of his Second String Quartet—is more his style. Another treatment of "Shall We Gather at the River," in the last movement of the Fourth Violin Sonata, makes a closure out of his characteristic warping of aural perspective. The hymn does not appear without distortion, sometimes grotesque distortion, until the final measures. When it does emerge at last in pristine form, the music has to stop—and it does, pointedly cutting off the closing phrase of the hymn. Here, as in Stevens, the local makes a dialectical bargain with the absolute: in order to be heard, it reduces to an allusion to itself. Or, to generalize in a way that will cover both the local tune and the place-name: the local, in order to lend an identity to the absolute, is forced to surrender its own identity. The "local object"—the tune or the place—is not represented mimetically, but instead is translated, abstracted, into a function of the imagination—the act of naming or alluding. To vary Stevens's formula, the imagination in these cases may add only itself to the local scene, but it also takes away whatever is not itself.

EXAMPLE: Ives, Violin Sonata No. 2, finale.

Both Ives and Stevens return often to this method of forming local abstractions, but neither is entirely satisfied with the divided consciousness that it refines, half-conceals, but cannot overcome. As Stevens exclaims, it is "As if, as if, as if the disparate halves/Of things were waiting in a betrothal known/To none, awaiting espousal to the sound/Of a right joining" ("Study of Images II"). In his massive Second Piano Sonata of 1911-15, "Concord, Massachusetts, 1840-1860," Ives attempts to find that reconciling sound by forming "impressionistic pictures" (*ESB* xxv) of a moment in history that fleetingly seemed to possess a more-than-historical unity—to be "nontemporaneous" (*ESB* 52). "Perhaps," writes

Ives, "music is the art of speaking extravagantly" (*EBS* 52), and in the "Concord" Sonata he extravagantly takes the Transcendentalism of Emerson's Concord to represent an exemplary unification of place and spirit.[10]

The sonata derives its formal coherence from late nineteenth-century models of motivic transformation, but it also embodies a "program" so ambitious that Ives had to write a whole book, the *Essays Before a Sonata*, to outline it. In performance, the music is meant to be heard, not as the realization of a strictly notated score, but as the expression of a transfigured place-consciousness that is shared by the composer, the performer, the listener, and the "Concord bards" who give their names to the four movements of the work: Emerson, Hawthorne, the Alcotts, and Thoreau. Accordingly, Ives directs the pianist to establish new tempo relationships each time the work is performed. "There are many passages," he writes in a note to the score, "not to be too evenly played and in which the tempo is not precise or static. It varies usually with the mood of the day, as well as that of Emerson, the other Concord bards, and the player."

As a whole, the "Concord" Sonata is conceived as a long, erratic journey in which the music seeks out the site of its own semi-divine origin. The journey ends in a musical image of place, Thoreau's Walden Pond, irradiated by "'Transcendent Thoughts'" and "'Visions'" (*EBS* 101). This process is organized throughout the sonata by the changing relationships between a pair of primary motives. The first of these is the declamatory opening figure of "Emerson"; the second is the motive that opens Beethoven's Fifth Symphony. The significance of Beethoven's contribution is established at the close of Ives's "Emerson" essay:

> There is an "oracle" at the beginning of the *Fifth Symphony*; in those four notes lies one of Beethoven's greatest messages. We would place its translation above the relentlessness of fate knocking at the door, above the greater human message of destiny, and strive to bring it towards the spiritual message of Emerson's revelations, even to the "common heart" of Concord—the soul of humanity knocking at the door of the divine mysteries, radiant in the faith that it *will* be opened—and the human become the divine! (*EBS* 36)

The Beethoven motive is Ives's embodiment of "substance" in the sonata. As the most widely known phrase in musical history, it metonymizes the total human effort to make a music that speaks "a language so transcendent that its heights and depths will be common to all mankind" (*EBS* 8). Set against this primal musical shape is the incessant shape-changing of the Concord material, which represents the Transcendentalists' Concord as the seedbed of indigenous American "divinities" and "place-legends" (*EBS* 101), a privileged form of the spirit of place in its striving for illumination by "flashes of transcendent beauty" (*EBS* 30).

The fulfillment of this quest appears in the closing moments of the last movement, "Thoreau." Here Thoreau at Walden emerges as the composer's alter ego: he is a transcendental musician, a composer of Aeolian music (*EBS* 53), a new-world Pan who transmits the monodic "harmony" of Nature through the sound of his flute. It is through the image of Thoreau's music, intertwined with his own and with Beethoven's, that Ives will evoke "the sound / Of a right joining" that marries place to substance.

As the music draws ot a close, a melody lofts itself over a gently tolling background. Ives's essay identifies this melody with the sound of Thoreau's flute as it rises over Walden Pond at the end of an autumn day's meditation: "It is darker—the poet's flute is heard out over the pond and Walden . . . faintly echoes—is it a transcendental tune of Concord?" (*EBS* 69). The answer to that is "Yes," of course, as "Concord" assumes a double meaning. In the sound of Thoreau's magic flute, the motivic materials that form the music of place are seamlessly woven together with the oracular Beethoven motive. The movement of origination becomes mutual and continuous, as the local and absolute themes give way to each other in turn, each a momentary prelude, then postlude, to the other. Ives is willing for the listener to imagine the flute that plays Thoreau's (and his own) "transcendental tune," but his ideal performance asks for something more: the miraculous intrusion of a real flute to render the transcendental actual within the music itself. When that flute falls silent, the fusion of the local and the absolute is lost. But it has been, to borrow another phrase from Stevens, for a moment final.

Stevens's equivalent to the fusion found in Ives's transcendental tune comes not in massive ventures like the "Concord" Sonata but in poems notable for their chastened quality, a severe humility before the absolute. Yet these poems do reconcile place and spirit much as the sonata does, by bringing them into a relationship of origination. As usual, Stevens's method for this relies on the principle that the imagination works by abstraction—in this case by a pair of abstractions, one a presentation, the other a withdrawal. Stevens begins with the abstraction of imaginative naming, the act by which a local name becomes a metonym for the transfiguration of place by an absolute. He then turns to a second abstraction that disregards the place-name and identifies the absolute directly. This rhythm—we might call it naming and un-naming—at once establishes the local scene as the source of a visitation, an oracular or omphalic threshold, and finds in the absolute the ultimate ground for whatever visionary presence the local has called forth.

Stevens frequently associates naming and un-naming with rivers and river names, as if to suggest an image for the underlying rhythm by which a name will enter the poetry only to flow away as "an apostrophe that [is] not spoken." In "Thinking of a Relation between the Images of Metaphors," a local "variation" on the absolute leads to a direct intuition of the "unstated theme" as the place-name ebbs away together with the generic names appropriate to the place. The poem begins with the many-sided perception of a locality and ends with a re-perception of the same scene in the "one eye" and "one ear" of epiphany. At first, "The wood-doves are

singing along the Perkiomen. / The bass lie deep, still afraid of the Indians."
By the close, the many doves have become one dove, and the bass, the
Perkiomen, and the Indians—who gave the river its name—have been
condensed into the image of "the fisherman," an anonymous figure who
stands as "the single man / In whose breast, the dove, alighting, would grow
still." The religious overtones of the alighting dove are not casual; Stevens,
like Ives, is trying to sacralize consciousness by committing it to "place-
legends." In "This Solitude of Cataracts," the speaker desires to
transcendentalize the seeming stillness of a river that is "Fixed like a lake on
which the wild ducks fluttered, / Ruffling its common reflections, thought-
like Monadnocks." His goal is the perfect fixity found in the unnamed form
of what he sees: "a permanent realization, without any wild ducks / Or
mountains that were not mountains," a location at "the azury center of
time." And in "Extraordinary References," "The cool sun of the
Tulpehocken refers / To its barbed, barbarous rising and has peace." The
Tulpehocken fuses the violent history of place—the ancestral territory of
Stevens's family, to be exact—with the peace of the imagination that
inherits the place-legends. This fusion of barbarous origins and cool
distance is transferred from place to person as the poem proceeds:

> My Jacomyntje! This first spring after the war,
> In which your father died, still breathes for him
> And breathes again for us a fragile breath.

Fragility is paramount here, as "a second-hand Vertumnus / Creates an
equilibrium"; but even a second-hand Vertumnus is a spirit, a *genius loci* in
"the inherited garden," and the equilibrium is real. The poem closes by un-
naming Jacomyntje, turning her into a personification of the vulnerable
local self adorned with its imaginative protections: "The child's three
ribbons are in her plaited hair."[11]
    Perhaps the poem that most richly embodies the rhythm of naming
and un-naming is "The River of Rivers in Connecticut":

> There is a great river this side of Stygia,
> Before one comes to the first black cataracts
> And trees that lack the intelligence of trees.
>
> In that river, far this side of Stygia,
> The mere flowing of the water is a gayety,
> Flashing and flashing in the sun. On its banks,
>
> No shadow walks. The river is fateful,
> Like the last one. But there is no ferryman.
> He could not bend against its propelling force.
>
> It is not to be seen beneath the appearances
> That tell of it. The steeple at Farmington
> Stands glistening and Haddam shines and sways.

It is the third commonness with light and air,
A curriculum, a vigor, a local abstraction . . .
Call it, once more, a river, an unnamed flowing,

Space-filled, reflecting the seasons, the folk-lore
Of each of the senses; call it, again and again,
The river that flows nowhere, like a sea.

Stevens's river of rivers is a form of the absolute that is constantly moving
on the threshold of a locality. It is both a metaphor and a presence, an
imaginative current or "curriculum" and a flowing body of water in
Connecticut, something "not to be seen beneath the appearances that tell of
it" and a dazzling vision that flashes and flashes in the sun. Most of all, and
poignantly in such a late poem, it is a resplendent "vigor" that identifies the
transfiguration of place with the transient vigor of life itself. The banks of
the river of rivers are free of all shadows—of gaps in the light and dwellers
in the underworld. Stevens's Stygia, with its trees that lack the intelligence
of trees, suggests what he elsewhere calls the "inert savoir" of the world
without imagination. Place without spirit—really a parody of place, a no-
place stuck onto the map of the state—constitutes the gloom of the dead.
The river of rivers, translating each of the senses into folk-lore, is the
"gayety" of the living. It proffers fusion not as an episode in one's "spiritual
consciousness" but as the grateful experience of being.

Midway through the poem, Farmington and Haddam are named as
momentary sites of the river's presence, so that the two localities fuse with
the absolute that flows through them. Yet the places here are not permitted
to disappear into their names. Their appearances persist: like the river, they
glisten and shine, and the analogy constitutes a heightened blending of the
local and the absolute that verges on identification. The river is not seen
beneath the appearances that tell of it, but in them or even as them.

A responsive un-naming follows: an effort to diffuse the glistening of
transcendence over all local sights—or sites. The result is a comple-
mentarity. In the presence of its names, the local has appeared as a visible
facet of the absolute. With the names withdrawn, the transfigured
landscape returns to its visionary origin and appears only as a possibility, a
potential shape within the unnamed flowing. But the two perspectives are
continuous, intermingled, like the flashing water and the glistening steeple.
What each discloses is a river, and it is a river that we are told to call it "again
and again." The incantation itself mingles—and mingles us—with the
"flashing and flashing" that it celebrates; the vigor that sustains us "far this
side of Stygia" is this rhythm of continuities. Naming and un-naming are to
be fused in a unique epithet that resolves "the third commonness with light
and air" into a tangible singularity, a place without borders: the river that
flows nowhere, like a sea.

The rhythms of naming and un-naming in Stevens and of mutual
origination in Ives can be taken as mirror images of each other. In the flute
episode of "Thoreau," what appears is a spiralling movement in which the

local and the absolute have become partners or doubles, so that each arises constantly out of the other. What appears in Stevens's various river poems is a sort of reverse becoming, a flowing movement back into origin as the local is stripped away to reveal its ground in the absolute. Ives seems to see place and spirit as interchangeable grounds for each other, and the fusions that he creates for them are usually seamless. Sound-images in which local and absolute elements are so blended that neither seems to have any stylistic or metaphysical priority over the other recur throughout his works. In the finale of his Fourth Symphony, for example, the gradual superimposition of some half-a-dozen hymn tunes over the cantus-firmus-like melody of "Bethany" ("Nearer, My God, To Thee") produces a unique, densely layered sonority—a substance that is hymnlike but not a hymn. When the music turns toward closure, it is through a vocalise on "Bethany," so that the "cantus firmus"—and by implication the hymn sung in the Prelude, "Watchman, What of the Night"—is disarticulated into pure song. Less majestically transcendental, but equally characteristic, is the closural move in "Washington's Birthday," a fragment of "Goodnight, Ladies" that floats away in the soft, primary string and wind colors of a solo flute and solo muted violin.

Stevens, whose Concord is the home of "Mr. Homburg" as well as of Emerson (who, of course, *is* Mr. Homburg), is more cautious, more detached than Ives about such images; as Helen Vendler once observed, he ends in uncertainty more than any other major poet.[12] The fusions that Ives represents as moments of experience, of realization, of communion, appear in Stevens as tenuous glimpses, possibilities, moments in which "The point of vision and desire are the same" ("An Ordinary Evening in New Haven," III). Stevens's poems of fusion always seem to contain a reservation, however muffled; the presence of death in "The River of Rivers," a version of *et in Arcadia ego*, is no accident. Local objects can always become obstacles to the imagination or travesties of it; absolutes can become "anonymids/Gulping for shape" ("A Lot of People Bathing in a Stream"):

Gay is, gay was, the gay forsythia

And yellow, yellow, thins the Northern blue.
Without a name and nothing to be desired,
If only imagined but imagined well.
(*Notes Toward A Supreme Fiction*, "It Must Be Abstract," VI)

> The blue sun in his red cockade
> Walked the United States today. . . .
> ("The News and the Weather")

> This structure of ideas, these ghostly sequences
> Of the mind, result only in disaster.
> ("The Bed of Old John Zeller")

A clue to the sources of Stevens's "restlessly unhappy happiness" might lodge in the fact that his poetry of place is almost always steeped in solitude and often tinged with a sense of loss and abandonment, particularly by parental figures. Ives's music of place, in contrast, almost always refers to a communal or intimate occasion. The Whitmanesque ease with which he approaches fusion seems to be rooted in a secure unity with others that validates his "spiritual consciousness," and the plural, "layered" texture of his music may in part be a reflection of this primary sense of affiliation. The only hitch is that the unity is more past than present; it belongs to an American Eden that is already largely lost by the time that Ives has begun to compose. For Stevens, place is always a latent substitute for persons, native regions for parents. ("Extraordinary References" concedes the point; "The Auroras of Autumn" is almost confessional about it.) One of the notebook entries collected as the "Adagia" admits: "Life is an affair of people not of places. But for me life is an affair of places and that is the trouble."[13] The trouble is that Stevens's moments of fusion occur to a transcendental ego for whom no place is a true origin.

This ambivalence is exposed in "Our Stars Come From Ireland," a double poem that has been unjustly neglected, probably because the poet was at pains to be modest about it in a letter. In the first part, "Tom McGreevey, in America, Thinks of Himself as a Boy," Stevens tries to present the troublesome transcendental ego as an absolute that is born of place—though it is significant that he does so with a dramatic persona, a rarity in his work. The key to the poem is a remark that Stevens made in sending it to Thomas McGreevey himself: "When I look back, I do not really remember myself but the places in which I lived and things there with which I was familiar."[14] McGreevey's thoughts in the poem are of the way that his boyhood imagination turned "him that I loved" into a place-spirit, thereby "making" the place:

> Out of him that I loved,
> Mal Bay I made,
> I made Mal Bay
> And him in that water.

Place is thus an embodied denial of separation from the loved figure, for whom a subsequent couplet strongly suggests a paternal identity:

> Out of him I made Mal Bay
> And not a bald and tasselled saint.

Another late poem, "Celle qui fût Héaulmiette," follows a similar tack:

> Into that native shield she slid,
> Mistress of an idea, child
> Of a mother with vague severed arms
> And of a father bearded in his fire.

As an adult, Tom announces, "I live in Pennsylvania," and then goes on to "make" his new region with an act of imaginative naming. But it is probably

Stevens's own childhood voice that sounds here, intruding on the poem to break its narrative fiction; McGreevey lived in Ireland:

> The stars are washing up from Ireland
> And through and over the puddles of Swatara
> And Schuylkill. The sound of him
> Comes from a great distance and is heard.

As the stars wash up "through and over" Swatara and Schuylkill, they come from Pennsylvania as well as from Ireland, and as they do the paternal source of self becomes an animate presence in the new locality. The stars, visible at different times from both County Kerry and Pennsylvania, presences moving "through and over" the rivers as both distant lights and near reflections, are figures of pure continuity like the river of rivers in Connecticut, and they, too, compose a "third commonness" that identifies itself with glittering places. It is by naming Swatara and Schuylkill in the presence of this starry thirdness that Tom McGreevey connects his boyhood and adult identities as parts of a larger imaginative self. As the echo of the paternal voice confirms, he makes Pennsylvania a new birthplace "of him / And out of myself," and he succeeds in belonging there, only half in solitude.

The second poem, "The Westwardness of Everything," both re-enacts the first and deconstructs it. Tom McGreevey's fusion of place with the continuity of selfhood reappears abstractly as an absorption of both place and selfhood into a principle of pure origination. All the places that Tom has "made" are un-named and dissolved into the universal presences of sky and water. The western places, Pennsylvania, Swatara, and Schuylkill, become "westwardness"; the eastern ones, Mal Bay, Tarbert, and Kerry, become an "east" that paradoxically appears within the westwardness. No persons enter the poem at all, let alone loved ones; "he" and "I" become simply "the mind." As for the stars, they are seen here only on the edge of vanishing into the dawn—and not a natural dawn but a transcendental one that would constitute "a final change" in which "The ocean breathed out morning in one breath." This etherialized, pneumic morning would be a permanent form of beginning from which nothing would begin, an origin that produced only itself. Coming from Ireland, the stars will also have come away from place itself and faded into an absolute time, a shift that has its cost in a recognition, if not a feeling, of bereavement; the stars, says Stevens, are "Like beautiful and abandoned refugees." Their abandonment is reflected, too, in the rhetorical movement of the poem, which names the "nights full of the green stars from Ireland" only at the beginning, then piles up descriptive and appositive phrases until the object of reference becomes tenuous, almost forgotten by both the poem and the reader. But it is not clear at the close whether the second poem is a consummation of the first or a chilly retreat from it, a completion or an evasion.

The scene of fusion, the archetypal Walden Pond where the local and the absolute join in Stevens and Ives, is marked by a pervasive feeling of remoteness. It appears under the spell of a fluid, fantasy-tinged perception that both poet and composer tend to symbolize with bodies of water—a Schuylkill in mid-earth, the Housatonic at Stockbridge.[15] There is a sense of blurred edges, of life in suspension, as if this "shadowy ground," in Wordsworth's phrase, were neither a place nor a state of mind but something in between; Whitman presents the Paumanok of "Out of the Cradle Endlessly Rocking" and "As I Ebb'd with the Ocean of Life" as the same sort of intermediate space. These features perhaps explain why the use of place-names as imaginative abstractions is largely missing from the work of Stevens's American contemporaries. Neither William Carlos Williams nor Hart Crane, in particular—poets whose commanding desire is to marry the local and the absolute—is willing to accept the austerity, to make the dialectical bargains, of the fusion in Stevens.

As for Ives, his transcendental allusiveness has remained *sui generis*, though it has some points of contact with the disjunctive polyphony of Mahler and middle-period Schoenberg.[16] The music of American nationalism, represented by works like Aaron Copland's "Billy the Kid" and Virgil Thomson's "The Plough that Broke the Plains," is shaped by nostalgia and imitation, not by the will to fusion; its poetic counterpart would be found in Bryant rather than Whitman, in Sandburg rather than Stevens. Ives is probably closer to Stevens in his use of "place-legends" than to any composer, especially when the slightly hermetic, slightly fantastic side of fusion comes to the fore—say in the first movement of the Fourth Violin Sonata, where Ives mixes the hymn tune "Tell Me an Old, Old Story" with a fugue fragment written by his father, or in poems like Stevens's "Metaphor As Degeneration":

> The swarthy river
> That flows round the earth and through the skies,
> Twisting among the universal spaces,
>
> Is not Swatara. It is being.
> That is the flock-flecked river, the water,
> The blown sheen—or is it air?

It is, by the way, typical that Stevens cannot identify the "flock-flecked river" as being until he has denied it the name of Swatara, that obscure little stream just outside of Harrisburg which was his private symbol for native place.

Perhaps the best way to summarize Ives's and Stevens's approach to the problem of fusion is to reconsider two of their central images. Stevens's river of rivers and Ives's flute melody in "Thoreau,"—the epitomes of local abstraction in the two men's work—share certain primary features. Both of them trespass on the boundaries of the work of art: one by the call for an incantatory recognition beyond the close of the poem, the other by its instrumental difference from the music around it. Both, too, trespass on boundaries within the work: Ives's by combining the local and absolute themes into a single melodic line, and Stevens's by flowing nowhere, like a sea. The role of these "trespass images" is to effect a continual reversal of our perception of them. Apprehended as local—the glisten at Farmington, Thoreau's flute—they disclose themselves as absolutes, flowing nowhere, weaving-in the Beethoven motive. Apprehended as absolutes, they reverse the process: becoming Farmington and Haddam, unfolding the local theme. Their ultimate trespass, it seems, is on the boundaries of the consciousness that tries to contain them. These images, representing the end of striving, are plain and tranquil. A long way from violence, they are in both men's work the final maturity of our desire.

Notes

1. For a view of Stevens's development that takes his work in business with unaccustomed seriousness, see Frank Lentricchia, "Patriarchy Against Itself: The Young Manhood of Wallace Stevens," *Critical Inquiry* 13 (1987), 742-86.

2. From *The Collected Poems of Wallace Stevens* (New York: Alfred A. Knopf, 1954). All poems are quoted from this edition unless cited with an *OP* for *Opus Posthumous* (New York: Alfred A. Knopf, 1957).

3. From *Ralph Waldo Emerson: An Organic Anthology*, edited by Stephen E. Whicher (Boston: Houghton Mifflin, 1957), p. 238.

4. Charles Ives, *Essays Before A Sonata*, edited by Howard Boatwright (New York: Norton, 1970), p. 94 (*EBS* in text.)

5. Wallace Stevens, *The Necessary Angel: Essays on Reality and the Imagination* (New York: Vintage Books, 1951), p. 22 (*NA* in text.)

6. On the violence of Stevens's imagination, see J. Hillis Miller, *Poets of Reality* (New York: Atheneum, 1974), pp. 251-54.

7. Ives, *EBS*, pp. 75-77.

8. See Stuart Feder, "Decoration Day: A Boyhood Memory of Charles Ives," *Musical Quarterly* 66 (1980):234-61.

9. I am not alluding here to C. S. Peirce's concept of thirdness—the realm of intention, meaning, the "contingent rules" that shape experience—though Peirce's phenomenology is not incompatible with Stevens's. On Peirce's thirdness, see Richard J. Bernstein, *Praxis and Action* (Philadelphia: University of Pennsylvania Press, 1971), pp. 177-87.

10. For more detailed musical analyses of the sonata, see the original version of this essay in my *Music and Poetry*, pp. 180-191, and Wilfred Mellers's discussion in his *Music in a New Found Land* (New York: Hillstone Press, 1975), pp. 48-56.

11. Stevens's later poems of place often recollect his late-blooming interest in genealogy. For an account, see Milton J. Bates, *Wallace Stevens: A Mythology of Self* (Berkeley: University of California Press, 1985), pp. 277-96.

12. Helen Vendler, "The Qualified Assertions of Wallace Stevens," in *The Act of the Mind: Essays on the Poetry of Wallace Stevens*, edited by Roy Harvey Pearce and J. Hillis Miller (Baltimore: Johns Hopkins University Press, 1965), pp. 163-78.

13. Wallace Stevens, *Opus Posthumous*, edited by Samuel French Morse (New York: Alfred A. Knopf, 1957), p. 158.

14. Wallace Stevens, *The Collected Letters*, edited by Holly Stevens (New York: Alfred A. Knopf, 1966), p. 608.

15. "The Housatonic at Stockbridge" is the title of the finale of Ives's symphony, "Three Places in New England."

16. But Ferruccio Busoni, in a pair of important works—the *Fantasia Contrapuntistica* for piano (1910) and the Fifth Sonatina for Piano (1919)—makes structural use of material from Bach that is comparable to Ives's use of Beethoven in the "Concord" Sonata. In addition, both Richard Strauss (in his *Metamorphosen* for 23 strings, 1945) and Sir Michael Tippett (in his Third Symphony and Third Piano Sonata) draw, like Ives, on material from Beethoven.

An American Poet's
Idea of Language   Claudia Yukman*

> . . . the poem makes meanings of the rock
> Of such mixed motion and such imagery
> That its barrenness becomes a thousand things
>
> And so exists no more. This is the cure
> Of leaves and of the ground and of ourselves.
> His words are both the icon and the man.[1]

In these lines from "The Rock" Stevens conceives of reality as partaking of the nature of language, anticipating a deconstructionist and postmodernist idea of language that has come to preoccupy theoretical and critical discussion for some time. Stevens's tone, however, is surprising, and his claim that the poem (a construct of language) is "the cure of the ground and of ourselves" is all the more so. Rather than seeing language as reflecting confusion or babel or alienation, he describes language as generating a bounty of meaning. In other words, he views it as a good thing that meaning is subject to the indeterminacy of language. How Stevens comes by this experience of language and reality, given that he seems to share our postmodern view that language is all we can know, bears investigating.

Through experimentation with poetic structures, Stevens came to think about language in innovative ways. As Donald Wesling has recently argued, over the last two centuries the syntactical level of language has increasingly dominated (or at least coexisted with) poetic device as the means by which post-Enlightenment poetry escapes conventional forms of authority and meaning.[2] The dominance of syntax puts us into a different relationship to the poem and the poet than does the ascendancy of meter and rhyme. Surprisingly, that relationship is equally determined by form. Romantic and modern poetry depend on arousing, fulfilling, deferring, and even failing our expectations, through forms that do not have the conventional meanings of a hierarchical system of genres. We are affected by romantic and modern structures not because they already have meaning for us but because they compel us to make sense of poems and their

*This essay was written specifically for this volume and is published here for the first time by permission of the author.

language in problematic ways. This is a reason we think of Stevens as quintessentially modern. But Stevens's particular uses of syntax, which seem to generate his experience of language, also mark a new stage in the development of a uniquely American poetic tradition that includes Emerson, Whitman, and Dickinson—a tradition derived from the centrality of biblical poetics in American culture.

It is commonly noted that the texture of Stevens's poetry is woven with verbal units referred to in a variety of ways: aphorism, rhetorical effects, hieratic style, parallelism, apposition, verbatim repetition, lists, and so forth. Structurally, these features can be traced to an unusual degree of syntactical repetition in Stevens's poetry which, however unselfconsciously, alludes directly to Whitman's form. When Whitman, loosely imitating biblical poetry, introduced a poetics based on syntactical parallelism into American poetry, he radically separated himself from the English poetic tradition. He created a structural principle for poetry that expressed an idea of language already dominating American experience in religious and political discourses. In Whitman's poetics, syntax is the most regular unit of the line. And yet the critical controversy over Whitman's form has centered on whether he is writing metrical or nonmetrical (free verse) poetry, thus serving to point out that our questions about poetry are still informed by assumptions that arise out of a metrical poetic tradition. Whitman's use of syntax is not simply a device but a system that represents an ideology. Because syntactic parallelism is not the established structural principle in English-language poetry that it is, for example, in Hebrew poetry, this aspect of both Whitman's and Stevens's poetics—which connects them and which may distinguish an American way of thinking about language from both English and continental language theories—has not been seen as critically relevant.[3]

I

To take an otherwise stunning example of Stevens criticism, in a close reading of "The Rock," J. Hillis Miller identifies and then subsumes syntactical parallelism in advancing his view that the poem illustrates the poet's strategy of constructing in language the fiction of a referent beyond language—what Miller calls a *mise en abyme*.[4] One way in which Stevens's poem crosses its "chasm," Miller comments, "is the sequence of phrases in apposition. This is a constant feature of Stevens' poetic procedure. It is a basic linguistic resource. . . ." (p. 400). Miller cites the following lines from "The Rock" as examples:

> They bud the whitest eye, the pallidest sprout,
> New senses in the engenderings of sense,
> The desire to be at the end of distances,
> The body quickened and the mind in root.
> (*Poems* 527)

Miller goes on to say that "it seems as if [the lines] must be equivalents of one another or at least figures for one another," thereby acknowledging the implication of the syntactic rhymes. He immediately dismisses this observation, however, with the rhetorical question: "But can *eye, sprout, senses, desire, body,* and *mind* really be equivalent?" (p. 401). In a more general comment, he remarks: "This structure of not quite congruent parallelism is characteristic of all forms of the *mise en abyme.* This is one of the ways this pattern keeps open the chasm while filling it, resists the intelligence almost successfully" (pp. 402-3).

The semantic and syntactic parallelism of these lines means something other than a nonparallel list would mean—as two rhyming words are related, regardless of the logic of their association. Furthermore, it is significant that these associations are made available through language that does not depend on metaphorical hierarchy ("A," which is known, is like "B" which is unknown; "B" is more valuable). Pushed to a theoretical conclusion, this structure insists on words' semantic and syntactical relations to each other. The "chasm" created by this "not quite congruent parallelism" is located overtly inside language rather than somewhere other than—before or beyond—language.

In *Language and the Poet* Marie Borroff pays closer attention to Stevens's syntax, including verbal repetition.[5] She refers to such effects in Stevens as "didactic," "rhetorical," and at times "explicitly Christian" (p. 63). Syntactical parallelism in poetry naturally reminds us of biblical poetry, thereby inspiring "reverence" (p. 61), because it is relatively foreign in English and American poetry. Apart from its biblical associations, the repetition of words and syntax functions to create a particular kind of reading experience, which Miller somewhat ignores but which Borroff goes on to characterize in this way: "Some of the poems, indeed, consist largely or wholly of lists of appellations amounting to so many descriptive 'hypotheses' among which no choice need be made—or rather, all of which must be chosen" (p. 75). This combination of diversity and similitude is no small achievement in language. But in order to see it as such, one must consider such repetitions to be structurally there, no less than we would consider a metrical pattern or a rhyme scheme to be structurally there, with the interesting difference that the same structure that organizes the meaning of the words—syntax—also determines ordinary language and whatever language itself limits.

II

The fact that Stevens appears to say little in his prose writings about such formal features and even less about Whitman's poetics would suggest a lack of concern with them, were it not for the extensive commentary on both lines and Whitman's poetics within the poetry itself. The most striking example, though by no means an isolated one, is "Stars at Tallapoosa."[6] In this poem, Stevens, interpreting Whitman's line, "Out of the cradle endlessly rocking," as a description of the poetic line, engages in a dialogue with his precursor:

> The lines are straight and swift between the stars.
> The night is not the cradle that they cry,
> The criers, undulating the deep-oceaned phrase.
> The lines are much too dark and much too sharp.
>   (*Poems*, p. 71)

The lines of Whitman's prelude to "Out of the Cradle" do indeed "cry a cradle," in the sense that they testify to the birth of a poem and of a poet. They identify a multiplicity of sources as one, through the equivalence of a syntactical phrase:

> Out of the cradle endlessly rocking,
> Out of the mocking-bird's throat, the musical shuttle,
> Out of the Ninth-month midnight,
> Over the sterile sands and the fields beyond, where the child leaving his
>   bed wander'd alone, bareheaded, barefoot,
> Down from the shower'd halo,
> Up from the mystic play of shadows twining and twisting as if they were
>   alive,
> Out from the patches of briers and blackberries,
> From the memories of the bird that chanted to me,
> From your memories sad brother, from the fitful risings and fallings I
>   heard,
> From under that yellow half-moon late-risen and swollen as if with tears,
> From those beginning notes of yearning and love there in the mist. . . .[7]

Such lines might also be said to cry in "deep-oceaned phrases"; Whitman concludes his story about the source of his "thousand songs" by saying, "The sea whisper'd me."

Further indications of Stevens's dialogue with Whitman in "Stars" are his allusions to Whitman's central topic in the line, "The body is no body to be seen," and to Whitman's traversal of the earth and sea by way of Stevens's catalogs in the lines, "Wading the sea-lines, moist and ever mingling, / Mounting the earth-lines, long and lax, lethargic" (*Poems*, p. 72). Stevens's following two lines—"The melon-flower nor dew nor web of either / Is like to these. . ."—countermand Whitman's prose discussion of poetic form in the 1855 "Preface" to *Leaves of Grass*:

> The rhyme and uniformity of perfect poems show the free growth of metrical laws, and bud from them as unerringly and loosely as lilacs and roses on a bush, and take shapes as compact as the shapes of chestnuts and oranges, melons and pears, and shed the perfume impalpable to form.
>   (*Leaves*, p. 716)

In light of the frequency with which Stevens uses words like "lilacs" and "leaves" in his poetry, as well as his explicit homage to Whitman in "Like Decorations in a Nigger Cemetery," these indirect allusions more than resonate, indicating that, however subliminally, Stevens affiliated himself to Whitman poetically.

Perhaps because he feels so intimately tied to his predecessor, Stevens needs to portray his own poetic line as a refutation of Whitman's. His distinction between two kinds of lines suggests that he views Whitman as having collapsed the difference between word and thing. "Sea-lines" and "earth-lines" correspond intimately, mimetically, to the world they name; for Stevens, however, the poetic line is a radical alternative to the experiential world: "A sheaf of brilliant arrows flying straight, / Flying straightway for their pleasure, / Their pleasure that is all bright-edged and cold. . . ." Nevertheless, by imitating Whitman's parallelism, Stevens also calls attention to the relationship between the structure of language and what is real:

> The lines are straight and swift between the stars.
>
> The lines are much too dark and much too sharp.
>
> The mind herein attains simplicity.
>
> There is no moon, on single, silvered leaf.
>
> These lines are swift and fall without diverging.
> (*Poems*, pp. 71-72)

In relation to the enjambed lines with which they interact in "Stars," these show the sentence to be the limit of the line, calling attention to syntax as a frame of experience. Their repetition gives an image of syntax, rather than a metrical unit like iambic pentameter, as the home of the poetic line. Because the common principle, or the unit of equivalence of these lines, is a complete sentence, whatever meaning they make is allied with syntax. A syntactical pattern produces the meaning of these words, drawing a relationship between the structure of language and meaning.

The formal allusion in Stevens's lines to Whitman's prosody invokes a model of language as syntax and of meaning as inhering in language. Whereas Miller assumes in his discussion that "all poetry and all language are attempts to fill the abyss, since all language is 'based' on catechresis" (p. 420), Whitman's and Stevens's use of syntax as a unit of equivalence, in conceding that meaning is in language, concedes that the abyss is also in language. Despite their differences, both poets give primary rather than secondary status to the words they write through employing syntax as the constituent principle of lines, and conceive of language as indivisible from what is real.

III

Stevens uses syntactical parallelism strategically in his early poem "In the Carolinas":

> The lilacs wither in the Carolinas.
> Already the butterflies flutter above the cabins.
> Already the new-born children interpret love
> In the voices of mothers.
>
> Timeless mother,
> How is it that your aspic nipples
> For once vent honey?
>
> *The pine-tree sweetens my body*
> *The white iris beautifies me.*
>   (*Poems,* pp. 4-5)

The syntactical parallelism of this poem allows us to hear line endings distinctly. A parallel pattern is established in the first three lines, interrupted by the center stanza and recovered in the last "couplet." The poem, in other words, has two kinds of lines or boundaries: syntax determines the first three and last two line units. Line 4 is both syntactically parallel to the previous prepositional phrases—"in the Carolinas" and "above the cabins," and as a line unit the first in a sequence determined by parts of a sentence. Oppositions on the semantic plane are marked by this formal configuring of difference. A complete sentence structure—"The lilacs wither in the Carolinas," "Already the butterflies flutter above the cabins," "already the new-born children interpret love," "The pine-tree sweetens my body," "The white iris beautifies me,"—produces a totalizing vision of reality. These lines are generated from an other-than-human point of view. They are objective, all-knowing, and concerned with the inevitability of the natural world. By contrast, a partial sentence—". . . In the voices of mothers," "Timeless mother," "How is it that your aspic nipples," "For once vent honey?"—produces the fragmented reality of the unknowing, the human, and the subjective.

Thus, at a meta-level, "In the Carolinas" differentiates the structure of language as a system, represented by the line as sentence, from the phrasal structure of speech, represented by the line as parts of or movement toward a sentence. Line 4 not only links these two kinds of lines formally, but also semantically, since it is about voice and proceeds to establish a pattern of lines that imitate a speaking voice. The common denominator of these dichotomies is that whereas the sentence "knows," the sentence parts "question."

These formal strategies revise familiar conceptual categories. "In the Carolinas" makes an unusual claim in relation to elegy, one of the cultural occasions for poetic language, in asserting that as "the lilacs wither in the Carolinas," "Already the butterflies flutter above the cabins." In other words, before the death of spring the summer has already arrived, so there is no death. By contrast to Whitman's elegy, "When Lilacs Last in the Dooryard Bloom'd," which pauses to mark the deaths of Lincoln and the Civil War soldiers, Stevens's poem elides both loss and mourning.

Whitman's may in fact be the precise elegy upon which Stevens's poem is based. In contradistinction to Whitman's "Lilacs"—which attempts a strenuous, elegant ritual, a deferral of summer until loss has been mourned—the vantage point of Stevens's poem is one from which the break in continuity—even the minimal break of the change in seasons—does not occur.

Furthermore, the syntactical "rhymes" of "In the Carolinas" create equivalence between death and birth without making that equivalence a verbal proposition. The "already" in lines 2 and 3 can be seen as expressing semantically what is "already" stated formally. Syntactical equivalence enables Stevens to "rhyme" without the hierarchy of either metaphor or narrative sequence. The vision produced is a vision syntax would give—does give—of the moment at which the lilacs wither. The aspect of reality known through these sentences is a loss of boundaries between nature/human being, linear time/cyclical time, mother/primordial mother, and spring/summer. "In the Carolinas" is less a representation than a self-conscious use of language to see beyond the categories of experience designated by elegy: loss, and language as the monument that compensates us for loss. This suspension of the elegiac or monumentalizing function of language in turn suspends a concept of language as secondary in relation to presence and experience.

In "Metaphors of a Magnifico," Stevens explores further the generative possibilities of a syntactic poetics:

> Twenty men crossing a bridge,
> Into a village,
> Are twenty men crossing twenty bridges,
> Into twenty villages,
> Or one man
> Crossing a single bridge into a village.
>
> This is old song
> That will not declare itself . . .
>
> Twenty men crossing a bridge,
> Into a village,
> Are
> Twenty men crossing a bridge
> Into a village.
>
> That will not declare itself
> Yet is certain as meaning . . .
>
> The boots of the men clump
> On the boards of the bridge.
> The first white wall of the village
> Rises through fruit-trees.
> Of what was it I was thinking?
> So the meaning escapes.

> The first white wall of the village . . .
> The fruit trees. . . .
>
> (*Poems*, p. 19)

"Metaphors" works, poetically speaking, through syntactic parallelism. The poem states "so the meaning escapes" at the end of the fifth stanza and yet it does not end at that knowledge. Instead, it continues by repeating the earlier nouns, the parts of a previous sentence, which now reach for a future sentence: "The first white wall of the village . . . / The fruit-trees. . . ."

Syntax is not simply a system for generating a pattern in a poem, though it is that. More importantly, as "Metaphors" demonstrates, the prevalence of syntactic units in poetry gives us an image of language generating reality at its very structure, regardless of the conditions that make the speaker of this poem view "song" as having lost its meaning-bearing power. Perhaps the "old song / that will not declare itself" describes a poetic tradition that Stevens's poem challenges, a tradition such as the metrical poetic tradition of English poetry, which burdens language with the task of leading us to a metaphysical ground of being. Stevens's poem opens out the "old song," not by telling us what it means, but by showing us the possibility of generating meaning inherent in the structure of syntax.

One of the more familiar effects of syntax as a formal unit in poetry, as refrains, and villanelles show us within the metrical poetic tradition, is to create symbolic action. A poem such as Stevens's "Domination of Black" can exist at an edge between nonsense or madness and the possibility of some ultimate meaning residing in words that, recurring in slightly altered contexts, seem to reveal further meaning and capacity for meaning. Since narrative tends to prevail in our reading experience as well as experience in general over other forms of structuring experience, the parallelism of "Domination of Black" seems of secondary importance. But the poem progresses through syntactical repetition rather than a recoverable narrative cause / effect sequence. Beginning with the second stanza and continuing in every verse is the phrase "the leaves themselves turning." Besides pervading our reading experience with the motion of turning, this pattern generates a list in the middle of the poem, as Whitman's syntactic parallelism so characteristically does:

> Turning in the wind,
> Turning as the flames
> Turned in the fire,
> Turning as the tails of the peacocks
> Turned in the loud fire. . . .
>
> (*Poems*, p. 9)

Turning is thus the trace of chaos and order at once. Furthermore, turning is the function of the verse-paragraph itself, so the poem has a kind of whirlwind motion at the center of which is a particular syntactical phrase manifesting the eye of the storm as syntax itself.

Even the poem's narrative, which figures a reading experience as well as some unknown event (turning the leaves or pages of a book), reaches its climax in the near-repetition or syntactical rhyme between "And I remembered the cry of the peacocks" at the end of the first stanza and "I heard them cry—the peacocks," which is the second line of the third stanza. The entire poem is in past tense, but the last line refers to the most recent hearing of the peacocks, repeating the last line of the first stanza exactly. As in a villanelle, we are shown the shifting of signifiers in relation to their referents as a capacity of language to be reused. The repetition of words is revelatory rather than redundant.

"Domination of Black" only approaches narrative organization. Its syntactic parallelism enables us to make what sense of it we can. One of the obvious things to say of a poem like this—representative of so many of Stevens's texts in the problems for interpretation it stages—is that it is difficult if not impossible to contextualize the images. What room, what event, what meaning can the poem be seen to delimit except language itself? Like a riddle, "Domination of Black" reveals only rhetorically, as if it were telling us about something. Unlike a riddle, "Domination of Black" has no correct answer to be deciphered in puns. The more appropriate analogy in fact, given the poetics that generates this poem, would be prophetic or parabolic modes of discourse as they exist alongside a syntactical poetics in the Bible. Language goes strange, as does the language of Isaiah or Christ, in order to manifest an other-than-human reality. But as might be said of the biblical story of a God who writes and becomes the incarnate word, Stevens's poem is actually the ultimate human reality: language itself.

The use of syntactical parallelism differs from a metrical poetics most radically on just this point. The image of language Stevens creates through "Domination of Black" is of words as the creation of reality. We do not understand what this poem is about because it is about an experience only accessible as language: but another way of saying this is that the poem calls attention to its own semantic and syntactic structures in order to show us language creating rather than representing what will be real for us as we read the poem. The meta-narrative of the poem, the story of reading itself, is the activity at the center of the chaos the poem describes. "Domination of Black" is a story about language creating a reality between the writer and reader.

Our focus on syntactical parallelism leads to two hypotheses: first, that whereas conventional poetic forms such as the sonnet have only social and political significance, the constituent principle of the poetic line produces an image of language; and second, that what we think of language makes a difference in how we use it. Roman Jakobson's definition of verbal behavior and poetic discourse is crucial to my own and to most theoretical discussions of poetic structure at present.[8] His premise is that language involves selecting and combining:

> The selection is produced on the basis of equivalence, similarity and dissimilarity, synonymity and antonymity, while the combination, the buildup of the sequence, is based on contiguity. The poetic function projects the principle of equivalence from the axis of selection into the axis of combination. Equivalence is promoted to the constitutive device of the sequence.
>
> (p. 358)

As a result of the equivalence created by the repetition of some line unit, be it metrical, syllabic, accentual, or syntactical, some aspect of language is heightened. In metrical poetry, the sounds and rhythms of words—their nonsemantic, material aspect—is heightened. In syntactical poetry, or poetry in which syntax constitutes the system of equivalence of the poetic line, the heightened materiality of language is accompanied by a foregrounding of the structure of syntax and, when verbatim repetition occurs, the word as part of a sentence structure. As readers and listeners we are, respectively, less and more aware of the affectivity created by language.

As we have seen, the repetition of syntactical units is of a different order from the repetition of abstract patterns such as meter or rhyme in the image of language it creates. Abstract patterns are added to language and though they produce sensory experience for the reader, their regular repetition necessarily produces or points to something in excess of language itself. The repetition of syntax or the verbatim repetition of words points to the generative structures of language and creates an image of meaning inside rather than outside language. The relative absence of these kinds of repetition in conventional metrical poetry, as well as in free verse, reflects an equating of semantic and syntactic repetition with meaninglessness, or, as Freud sometimes characterizes redundancy, with a death wish.

By choosing syntax rather than meter as the constituent principle of his poetic line, Whitman established a formal continuity (albeit in his own fashion) between the poetry of the Bible and his book. Like Whitman, Stevens risks repeating words and syntax. Of course Stevens frequently employs the devices of meter and rhyme as well. But the parallelism he must have absorbed from reading Whitman's poetry remains a consistent aspect of his poetry, which ultimately, as his last poems articulate, challenges the metaphysics implied in the poetic tradition he inherits.

IV

Stevens sounds like Whitman discoursing on natural form[9] when he comments in *The Necessary Angel*:

> There is always an analogy between nature and the imagination, and possibly poetry is merely the strange rhetoric of that parallel: a rhetoric in which the feeling of one man is communicated to another in words of the exquisite appositeness that takes away all their verbality.[10]

Though neither Whitman nor Stevens discusses syntactical parallelism, these remarks identify its function. The phrase "words of exquisite appositeness" describes metaphor. By "verbality" Stevens refers to the denotative meanings of words. It is precisely apposition and the eclipse of verbality that Stevens achieves through his use of syntactic and semantic repetition. Through this formal device, Stevens is able to "defy / The metaphor that murders metaphor" or, in other words, to avoid creating difference—upon which metaphor is contingent—in the attempt to know similarity.

A. Walton Litz argues in *Introspective Voyager* that:

> The materials of the later poetry are there in 1937, accompanied by an accumulated repertoire of verse-forms ready for refinement. The flexible blank-verse stanzas of "Esthétique du Mal," the more formal stanzas of "To an Old Philosopher in Rome," the tercets of *Notes Toward a Supreme Fiction*, which illustrate Stevens' penchant for a relatively free verse-line controlled by a fixed stanza form—all are developed out of the poetry of the 1920's and 1930's.[11]

In light of the model of language that emerges from Stevens's early poems, his experimentation with literary forms during his poetic career appears as neither an emptying out of prior forms, parodic in its nature, nor a selection of politically significant forms. Rather, it is the backdrop to a deeper experimentation with the poetic line that enables Stevens to question the English metrical poetic tradition and the ideology it expresses.[12] I believe that syntactic parallelism is the most crucial "raw material" when it comes to reading and interpreting Stevens's descriptions of language in the late poetry. Neither the longer poems at the center of Stevens's career nor the last poems are as marked by semantic and syntactic repetition as the early work I have discussed, but the predominance of aphorism and paratactic structure is evidence that they are also influenced by the generative model of syntax. The late poetry to which I shall now turn realizes philosophically as well as verbally the aspect of language that these formal features in Stevens's early poetry reveal to him. It is more common to consider these late poems as Stevens's final view of the relationship between reality and the imagination, but they also describe what Stevens is doing with language and what his poetic practice has let him see about language.

In "The Plain Sense of Things," for example, Stevens begins yet again by recapitulating the poetic tradition he inherits, characterizing what Harold Bloom calls his and our "belatedness":[13]

> After the leaves have fallen, we return
> To a plain sense of things. It is as if

> We had come to an end of the imagination,
> Inanimate in an inert savoir.
>
> (*Poems*, p. 502)

This "after" time—after Whitman's *Leaves of Grass*, after autumn and Stevens's "The Auroras of Autumn," after the fall, after romanticism and its claims for the secular imagination—is where he finds himself both in his own life and the life of poetry. The first gesture he makes beyond this "inert savoir" is to describe composing a sentence across a figurative as well as literal blank: "It is difficult even to choose the adjective / For this blank cold, this sadness without cause."

Rather than verbalizing the blank through metaphor and thus polarizing the crisis as a hierarchy of unknown over known, Stevens goes on to explore what he has just said by creating a sequence of parallel sentences that tell the failure in related but diverse appositions:

> The great structure has become a minor house.
> No turban walks across the lessened floors.
> The greenhouse never so badly needed paint.
> The chimney is fifty years old and slants to one side.

The poignant conclusiveness of the next two lines reduces poetry prior to this poem, obviously beloved of this poet, to failure: "A fantastic effort has failed, a repetition / In a repetitiousness of men and flies."

But the usual business of repetition in poetry—formally, meter; ideologically, metaphysics—is not Stevens's project. Already present in the sequence of parallel lines cited above is his alternative to the model of language that has produced the failure he describes. Though the tone of the lines and even that of the rest of the poem is despondent to our unaccustomed hearing, ultimately what Stevens has to say of this failure is that it is a failure of imagination. In effect, we have failed to generate enough versions of reality by staking everything on a truth beyond experience and language. His list of descriptions of those failures formally suggests this. In the last lines of the poem what he learns through form is articulated: "The great pond and its waste of the lilies, all this / Had to be imagined as an inevitable knowledge, / Required, as a necessity requires" (*Poems*, p. 503).

Michel Foucault's argument that our various discourses are the instruments of political power helps us understand Stevens's relation to his poetic tradition as he sees it in these late poems. Foucault asserts that our descriptions of reality are in fact "productive hypotheses" that create the reality they seem to imitate.[14] From within the discourse of poetry, Stevens calls for a greater multiplicity of requirements or "productive hypotheses" that would challenge the idea that our culture has failed in its humanist goals. By adapting a poetics that produces an image of language as a genesis, Stevens recasts his own belatedness, and ours, as only one use of language.

"Their indigence is an indigence/That is an indigence of the light,"
Stevens writes of the "finally human" in "Lebensweisheitspielerei,"
drawing our attention to the word as multiple signifier rather than arbitrary
sign through a transit of syntactical positions. The light to which he refers in
this poem is overreaching like sunlight—or more abstractly, fate,
knowledge, imagination, divinity. These repetitions of a word anticipate a
recovery through language of language as source. Though light is a
common literary and philosophical trope for knowledge, it is also, and not
coincidentally, the first word/creation in the book of Genesis. It is through
language that the "grandeur of annihilation" becomes "stale":

> Little by little, the poverty
> Of autumnal space becomes
> A look, a few words spoken.
>
> Each person completely touches us
> With what he is and as he is,
> In the stale grandeur of annihilation.
> (*Poems*, p. 505)

Stevens's model of language is relational and mediating. It may seem
strange to say this of a poet so renowned for his obscurity and abstraction,
but this is what he himself sees about language at the end of his poetic
career. It is not nature, but the poem, "the description without place," that
makes nature accessible. "The Poem that Took the Place of a Mountain"
(*Poems*, p. 512) invents a place "even when the book lay turned in the dust
of his table." Preceding experience, sentences create a perspective from
which the world and a human relation to nature can begin; a locale where
one "could lie and, gazing down at the sea,/Recognize his unique and
solitary home."

Words are, for Stevens, "Prologues to What is Possible." In the poem to
which he gives this title, language carries the subject to the limits of
resemblance "and not beyond" (*Poems*, p. 516). At those limits he is made
aware of further meanings by language for which he feels no affinity and
yet the words indicate to him some aspect of the self as yet unknown: "The
this and that in the enclosures of hypotheses/On which men speculated in
summer when they were half asleep." These words, fictional though they
may have been ("in the enclosures of hypotheses"), have produced new
limits to the self; like the metaphor that "stirred his fear" they have pushed
the self to become what it does not yet recognize.

Stevens concludes "Prologues to What is Possible" with this description of language:

> A flick which added to what was real and its vocabulary,
> The way some first thing coming into Northern trees
> Adds to them the whole vocabulary of the South,
> The way the earliest single light in the evening sky, in spring,

Creates a fresh universe out of nothingness by adding itself,
The way a look or touch reveals its unexpected magnitudes.

(*Poems*, p. 517)

The nature of this list, "loosed" as Whitman's catalogs are, is to move from light to diminished forms of artificial light to natural light, to what in context is provocatively the most natural essential light or language: "a look or touch" that "reveals" not some other thing, some transcendental self, but the "unexpected magnitudes" of meaning possible between persons. These sentences are not metaphors but equivalent statements that exhibit the fundamental structure of language as what Whitman calls "the open road," which lies between "I" and "you" and between writer and reader. In "Long and Sluggish Lines" (*Poems*, p. 522), Stevens describes language as "this wakefulness" at the age of seventy which is "not a sleep." In "Final Soliloquy of the Interior Paramour" (*Poems*, p. 524), language is the material out of which "we make a dwelling in the evening air, / In which being there together is enough"; it is "a single shawl / Wrapped tightly round us, since we are poor, a warmth, / A light, a power, the miraculous influence."

These representations of language are in fact themselves propositions or hypotheses, but they have a ground other than rhetoric, which is the history of the use of language in America or what might be investigated further as a particularly American model of language. Inventing a syntactical poetics that alludes formally to biblical poetry, Whitman implies that language is the thing it represents; Stevens, understanding language through the same poetic structure, suggests that language invents the world it is about. The Bible, by asserting a distinction between the secondariness of humankind's fallen language and the word as creation, provides a model of language other than the dynamic of absence / presence or abyss / referentiality, to borrow Miller's terms, with which Western culture has imagined being. Absorbing the model of sacred language through Whitman's adaptation of the structures of biblical poetry, Stevens, like Whitman (and, though I have not discussed her here, Dickinson), conceives of the word as Creation rather than absence.

It could be argued that the biblical model of sacred language is subsumed by the deconstructionist argument. The Bible, in other words, is a grand rhetorical effort to make present what is absent: a disembodied God. But my point is that sacred language as it is modeled in the Bible and figured through semantic and syntactical parallelism generates and includes all reality. The biblical God is the word—in the New Testament, the word made flesh—which creates all experience. There is no history of this God before his presence as language in the command: "Let there be light." And while the void before the creation of the world might be seen as Miller's *mise en abyme*, the model of sacred language the Bible affords Whitman and Stevens (as well as other American writers) is not of referentiality that turns away from a crisis of meaning, but of referentiality

244   Critical Essays on Wallace Stevens

that self-consciously acknowledges and mediates its own production of meaning.

One might identify Americans as those for whom language has been a means by which to create the idea of a country out of the idea of a world beyond, human history out of sacred history, frontier out of wilderness, and always, political power out of texts. To appropriate lines from Stevens's "The Snow Man," on encountering a "nothing that is not there," Americans have used language to give value, to create "the nothing that is." Ironically, the model of language as creating reality that flows from the Bible to the Declaration of Independence, to the Constitution, to Walt Whitman, and to Wallace Stevens partially explains why poetry has so little political power in America: for us poetry is a discourse like any other. It affects us or it does not. We need, perhaps more than any other nation, to be reminded of what inhibited the writers of the Constitution: the future is at stake in the way we use language. This reminder is Stevens's effort and achievement.

What is perhaps the most profound revelation of Stevens's poetics appears in his very late poem "The Rock":

> . . . the poem makes meanings of the rock,
> Of such mixed motion and such imagery
> That its barrenness becomes a thousand things
>
> And so exists no more. . . .
>
> *(Poems,* p. 527)

One of the layers of Stevens's enigmatic symbol, "the rock," may well involve a renaming of the earth after Plymouth Rock, which figures being on the earth as landing on the American shore with the prospect of living out the text of sacred history. Empowered by a poetics that models language as reality, Stevens's poetic career argues that language does not fail us.

Notes

1. Wallace Stevens, *Collected Poems* (New York: Knopf, 1954), 527.

2. Donald Wesling, *The New Poetries* (New Jersey: Associated University Press, 1985).

3. Joseph Riddel's analysis in "Walt Whitman and Wallace Stevens: Functions of a 'Literatus'" exemplifies the limited grounds of comparison critics have seen between Stevens and Whitman: "They dramatize a century of change in the American conscience: which might be described . . . as the movement from so-called cosmic consciousness to an existential consciousness" (*Wallace Stevens: A Collection of Critical Essays,* ed. Marie Borroff (Englewood Cliffs, NJ: Prentice-Hall, 1963), 30. Two in-depth studies of the Whitman-Stevens relationship are Diane Wood Middlebrook's *Walt Whitman and Wallace Stevens* (Ithaca: Cornell University Press, 1974) and Harold Bloom's *Wallace Stevens: The Poems of Our Climate* (Ithaca: Cornell University Press, 1977).

4. J. Hillis Miller, *The Linguistic Moment* (Princeton: Princeton University Press, 1985), 390-422.

5. Marie Borroff, *Language and the Poet* (Chicago: University of Chicago Press, 1979), 42-79.

6. Besides verbal references to form, the presence of a semantic / syntactic poetic might manifest itself in larger structures, just as horizontal metrical lines occur in combination with vertical patterns such as fixed stanza lengths or end-rhyme patterns. So, for instance, "The Snow Man," which is one sentence, calls attention to syntax as a structure of experience. Similarly, "Thirteen Ways of Looking at a Blackbird," "Like Decorations in a Nigger Cemetery," and "The Man with the Blue Guitar" make lists—as Whitman's poems do—not arbitrarily but because the poems derive from the generative model of syntax.

7. Walt Whitman, *Leaves of Grass*, ed. Sculley Bradley and Harold Blodgett (New York: Norton, 1973), 246.

8. Roman Jakobson, "Concluding Statement: Linguistics and Poetics," *Style in Language*, ed. Thomas Sebeok (Cambridge: MIT Press and John Wiley, 1960), 350-77.

9. Donald Wesling's chapter on "Form as Proceeding" in Wesling, *New Poetries*, 70-112, accounts for such a similarity in the perspectives of Romantic and Modernist poets as a shift in the poets' perceptions of and goals for form following the eighteenth-century hierarchy of genres and styles. He argues convincingly that beginning with the Romantics, poets conceive of the self and form as part of creation rather than an imitation of nature.

10. Wallace Stevens, *The Necessary Angel* (New York: Knopf, 1951), 118.

11. A. Walton Litz, *Introspective Voyager: The Poetic Development of Wallace Stevens* (New York: Oxford University Press, 1972), 260.

12. Antony Easthope makes an instructive and interesting case for the iambic pentameter line as a discourse that expresses the ideology of Renaissance individualism in *Poetry as Discourse* (London and New York: Methuen, 1983). My own thesis, that the discourse of a syntactical poetics represents an ideology, is naturally influenced by Easthope's argument. But whereas Easthope describes the iambic pentameter line as conducive to Renaissance individualism, I am going further to posit that it also presents us with an image of language as secondary to something beyond language. Syntactical parallelism would differ from the iambic pentameter line not only in being conducive to alternative ideologies, but in presenting an image of language as meaning.

13. Bloom, *Poems of Our Climate*, 405.

14. This idea of language pervades Michel Foucault's work but is explicitly outlined in *The History of Sexuality*, vol. 1 (New York: Random House, 1980).

"The Theory of Poetry Is the Theory of Life": Bergson and the Later Stevens

Paul Douglass[*]

In 1965 J. Hillis Miller wrote, "It is impossible to find a single systematic theory of poetry and life in Stevens,"[1] and most of us have agreed. Miller and Morse, Riddel and Vendler—all have warned against a thoroughgoing philosophical approach to Stevens.[2] Some, like William Pritchard, find the poet's work often "exasperating." To read Stevens

[*]This essay was written specifically for this volume and is published here for the first time by permission of the author.

246 Critical Essays on Wallace Stevens

conscientiously means, according to Pritchard, getting "thoroughly, if not inextricably, involved in the taffy."³ But do we find no coherent theory of life *or* poetry in Stevens's work? If the poetry still "pierces us with strange relation," as Pritchard admits it does, what is that relation? Since Stevens's many statements do not simply cancel one another out, there is no need to agree with Hugh Kenner that his work expresses "nothing more profound than bafflement."⁴ Yet there is certainly bafflement in (and about) Stevens.

Precisely here, Henri Bergson offers significant help. Many have felt this: Frank Doggett has characterized Stevens's poetry as an expression of Bergsonian intuition;⁵ Samuel French Morse has termed Stevens's comedy decidedly Bergsonian;⁶ and Frank Kermode has called the poet's debt to Bergson "quite certain."⁷ Most tantalizingly, Joseph Riddel has detected sympathies between Stevens's "act of the mind" and Bergsonian psychology.⁸ All this suggests that Bergson may somehow contribute to an understanding of Stevens's preoccupations with time and process, the "chaotic order" of experience, and romantic concepts of intuition and language. Bergsonian principles certainly could underlie and unify Stevens's "prodigious search of appearance,"⁹ his labor to make poetry a *"noeud vital"* (vital tie) between "reality" and "life" ("What reality lacks is a *noeud vital* with life"¹⁰). Yet Bergson is considered the philosopher of undifferentiated *durée*. One may question how Bergsonian thought can explain a semiotically self-conscious poet like Stevens—a poet of "difference" and "decreation" (*Angel*, p. 175). Here I must lay out parallels between Stevens and Bergson, reviewing, for those unfamiliar with Bergson, a little of his thought and its history before treating some exemplary Stevens texts.

First, consider Stevens's career-long obsession with change and vitalism, his endless variations on the theme that "Life Is Motion" and "making."¹¹ Process itself becomes, as David LaGuardia has remarked, "not simply an aspect but the subject of Stevens's poetry."¹² Plainly, there are many process-philosophers to whom one could appeal here. LaGuardia is right that Stevens stands in an Emersonian and Jamesian tradition. This does not erase Bergson, however. We do not face (to paraphrase Stevens himself) a choice of exclusion. We should include those ideas "which in each other are included" so that we do not miss the whole, the "amassing harmony" of Stevens's work (*Poems*, p. 403). Bergson too posits a fluid world (he and James agreed profoundly here), and that world suits Stevens. In it, stasis ("Chaos not in motion" in Stevens's phrase) is an illusion. But we prefer "cuttings of reality" (Bergson's term) to flux and convince ourselves that those snapshots are reality, just as we agree to the deception that words "contain" our uncontainable experience. This Bergsonian tension between form and fluidity lies at the heart of Stevens's work.

The Bergsonian cosmos begins in a vital burst of energy, the *élan vital*. But this burst bifurcates immediately, troubled by the backward drag of its spent energies. Bergson compares it to a giant tea kettle shooting out steam that condenses into falling drops of water; if forms of life collectively rise, they must individually fall. Human consciousness, too, even as it unceasingly creates itself, undergoes constant "unmaking" or "decreation."[13] The living self sloughs off provisional forms of its being—for they harden and suffocate.[14] The reader may recall the opening of Stevens's "The Noble Rider and the Sound of Words," which describes the imagination's course as it rides with Plato's "Phaedrus," "traversing the whole heaven," only to "droop" and at last "settle on solid ground" (*Angel*, pp. 3-4). Stevens's vision is a Bergsonian leap to a fall.

Bergson's cosmic "tension" involves such leaping and falling: We must take things "by storm" and "thrust intelligence outside itself by an act of will" if we wish to grow: "The mind has to do violence to itself, has to reverse the direction of the operation by which it habitually thinks."[15] Stevens, too, defined all "vital reality" as "vital in the sense of being tense," and poetry he also saw as a kind of "violence from within" (*Angel*, pp. 26, 36). Conceding this, many readers will still resist the notion that Bergson can have anything to say about Stevens's poetic practice because they have been told Bergson makes *durée*—the inner nonverbal flux of psychic life— final. For Bergson (it is claimed) the poem simply returns us to the fluidity of experience. Bergson thus says little of artifice, and of language not much more—except that words kill.

But consider that *durée* remains an acknowledged abstraction in Bergson—an ideality to which we never finally penetrate:

> If this colorless substratum is perpetually colored by that which covers it, it is for us, in its indeterminateness, *as if it did not exist*, since we only perceive what is colored, or in other words, psychic states. As a matter of fact, this substratum *has no reality; it is merely a symbol* intended to recall unceasingly to our consciousness the artificial character of the process by which attention places clear-cut states side by side.[16]

Bergson thus *defines* human consciousness in terms of artifice and "difference." Michael Beehler has eloquently formulated Bergson's view: Whenever we think the artist has arrived at a final term—a "supreme fiction," in Stevens's words—there is always also the awareness of this arrival's impossibility, a "disturbance that remobilizes difference and marks these points as sites of a problem."[17] Poetry thus becomes, according to Bergson (and Stevens), the play of language tracking, and finally *emulating*, that "tensional" world. That de-creation has, for Bergson, a therapeutic value: Through laughter it corrects inflexibility; through intuition it refreshes the self's vital relation with the world. Cutting and retying constantly, poetry offers what Bergson would gladly have recognized as a "*noeud vital* with life" (*Opus*, p. 178).

I believe, then, that Bergson is more than a marginal figure for Stevens. One should question this view, but one should also question the concept of Bergson's marginality, because he was actively and deliberately "marginalized" in the 1920s and 1930s.[18] Herein lies a tale of the intellectual

248 Critical Essays on Wallace Stevens

climate of Europe and America during Stevens's lifetime—a climate Stevens knew well, having read some of the philosopher's books as early as 1912. He knew Bergson's analysis of "clock-time" and *"durée"* and saw time-consciousness having a widening circle of effects in the work of many writers, including Yeats, Eliot, Woolf, and Joyce, who had become preoccupied with experiences of a quasireligious nature. He saw this art striving toward a liberation from the "nightmare of materialism" and an embrace with "the spiritual life to which art belongs," as Kandinsky wrote in 1912.[19]

Bergson's *Laughter* and *Creative Evolution* appeared serially in *Camera Work*, and through this medium Stevens came to know Bergson's concept of "absentmindedness," which he applied in works like "The Comedian as the Letter C" and "Carlos Among the Candles." Although Bergson's theory of comedy helps us read the Stevens canon, there is more profound help in Bergson's philosophy of inner life. Joan Richardson rightly observes that Bergson's dualistic psychology ("[It] is both the unrolling and the rolling up of a coil. And it is neither."[20]) entered the heart of Stevens's writing:

> I am not certain as to how conscious Stevens was of the way he precisely exemplified, by recording in his journals, letters, and poems notations of his own movement, the ideas of Henri Bergson concerning the dual nature of our perception of time . . . . At what point Stevens became aware of his own up and down between these two elements is, in the end, not that important. But what is, is that this central notion for the century played its central part in his apprehension of his relation to the world.[21]

Stevens found many philosophers "interesting"; he apparently found none more intellectually or emotionally amenable.

Stevens did become aware of his alignment with Bergson, and late in his career quoted him often, as in "The Figure of the Youth as Virile Poet" (1943). Evidence of Bergson's direct influence may be found in Stevens's poetry and essays, which reflect Bergson's dialectical vitalism. An enduring mark of Bergsonism on Stevens may also be seen simply in his increasing drive to articulate a "theory of life" that was also a "theory of poetry." This connection between a vitalistic "life-philosophy" and poetry lies behind several major themes in Stevens's work, including a fluid universe, the apotheosis of "creative evolution," and raising the artist to the status of a "God."

Stevens used Bergson, as Riddel has said, to create a theory of the imagination "without the foundation of an idealist metaphysics."[22] He sought in his philosophical reading what Eliot had: philosophical *and* poetic truths. This activity he continued to the end:

> When I say that writing in a poetic way is not the same thing as having ideas that are inherently poetic concepts, I mean that the formidable poetry of Nietzsche, for example, ultimately leaves us with the formidable poetry of Nietzsche and little more. In the case of Bergson,

we have a poetry of language, which made William James complain of its incessant euphony. But we also have the *élan vital*.

(*Opus*, p. 187)

The *élan vital* lies behind Stevens's convictions that life means novelty—avoidance of repetition—and that this novelty manifests both value and ultimate direction: "Everything tends to become real; or everything moves in the direction of reality"; "Everything accomplishes itself: fulfills itself" (*Opus*, pp. 165, 172). The *élan vital* also contributed to Stevens's vision of a universe in and out of time, the *tensional* Bergsonian cosmos, in which "wherever anything lives, there is open somewhere a register in which time is being inscribed."[23] Stevens, too, imaged time in the dualistic mode of Bergson: "Deeper within the belly's dark/Of time, time grows upon the rock" (*Poems*, p. 171).

By 1940, Stevens was fully aware of the demise of Bergson and the ascendancy of neo-Nietzschean existentialism. He knew that from the time of Bergson's greatest popularity, prior to World War I, some had opposed "time-consciousness." After the Great War, anti-Bergsonism swept Europe, as P. A. Y. Gunter notes.[24] A brief review of this period will show how remarkable Stevens's choice to write of Bergson in the 1940s really was.

Bergson was a struggling academic who barely achieved a post at the Collège de France in 1900. By 1907, however, his reputation as a "Defender of Life" against positivism had won him international acclaim. His emergence as a philosophical "superstar" offended taste on both sides of the channel, for many felt Bergson's notoriety cheapened scholarship. Meanwhile, his books bombarded the public. In 1910 his *Essai sur les données immédiates de la conscience* (1889) was translated into English as *Time and Free Will*. In 1911, as it was about to go into its tenth French printing, *L'Evolution créatrice* was translated as *Creative Evolution*, and within two years three of his other works had been translated: *Laughter*, *Matter and Memory*, and *Introduction to Metaphysics*. Bergson had achieved the kind of fame all scholars and thinkers desire, then fear.[25] Hundreds of articles on him appeared in the British and American press. T. S. Eliot called it simply an "epidemic of Bergsonisms."[26]

Bergson's significance now goes underappreciated. He was a major transitional figure in numerous fields, from physics to biology, from phenomenology to Christian ethics. But his enduring contribution was to aesthetics. Though not particularly original, he accomplished something no one else had done, including Croce, Nietzsche, James, and Dewey. He recycled many terms, such as "intuition," "perception," "spatialization," and "tension," defining them by a metaphysics of evolutionary process: opposed streams of creation and decreation. As T. E. Hulme instantly recognized, he provided the means for a defense of art in an age of technology. Art became cultural memory; it also became a "tool" for investigating what escaped the net of science. Bergson gave Stevens the confidence to claim, with even more conviction than in Sidney's or Shelley's time, that poets are the unacknowledged legislators of the world:

There is, in fact, a world of poetry indistinguishable from the world in which we live, or, I ought to say, no doubt, from the world in which we shall come to live, since what makes the poet the potent figure he is, or was, or ought to be, is that he creates the world to which we turn incessantly and without knowing it and that he gives to life the supreme fictions without which we are unable to conceive of it.

(*Angel*, p. 31)

Stevens adopted Bergson's argument for poetry's importance, and he stuck to his Bergsonism even in the 1940s when it had become quite unpopular.

Bergson's "life-force" philosophy had always drawn a share of Anglo-American irritation—signalled in Eliot's choice of the term "epidemic." Even in 1912, Bergson's English critics had called him a "Confusions-meister" and an "aberration."[27] He was literally "pooh-poohed": "Does M. Bergson tell us that by turning away from intelligence and turning to animal instinct we shall get into touch with life? Pooh!"[28] Similarly, George Santayana's *Winds of Doctrine* (1912), called Bergson "an astute apologist . . . [with] neither good sense, nor rigour, nor candour, nor solidity."[29] All this leaves aside the now-famous attacks from Wyndham Lewis and Bertrand Russell. Lewis's *Time and Western Man* condemned Bergson for rejecting the operation of "reason." Russell, in *The Monist* (1912), made the outrageous charge that Bergson (a trained mathematician) did not understand rudimentary mathematical concepts like "number."[30]

Attacks came not merely from Anglophile Francophobes, but from the New Classicist/Scholasticist "school." Julien Benda devoted most of his career to attacking Bergson, whom he said he would joyfully have killed, would that have stopped his influence.[31] In such a climate, Bergson understandably resigned his position at the Collège de France and led an increasingly remote life as a scholar. He seems to have been constitutionally unable to engage in the internecine polemics of a Russell or a Santayana. Yet even in the absence of a response, Russell continued to cut Bergson in textbooks that had an impact on students of philosophy into the sixties: "Intellect is the misfortune of man, while intuition is seen at its best in ants, bees, and Bergson."[32] Joseph Chiari reports that T. S. Eliot found this continued hatefulness puzzling and distressing.[33]

Yet Eliot himself had vilified "creative evolution." Like Maritain and Santayana, he certified Bergsonism as heretical and dangerous because it fostered a softheaded "intuitionism" and complacency. Bergson had become the enemy to a powerful lobby including Eliot, Lewis, Winters, Maritain, Russell, Santayana, and Benda. Anglo-European anxiety to leave progressivism behind meant Bergson's "ideology," failed to get a fair hearing, as Maritain later admitted.[34] In fact, the campaign was to bury Bergson—as a scientist and philosopher, not as a person. (Only Benda sought that, and he got his wish in 1941 when an aging, sickly, and disheartened Bergson, who had registered as a Jew in occupied Paris, finally died.) This campaign succeeded. The New Classicists and the New Critics, the young existentialists and the followers of phenomenology, and the positivists and the technocrats all agreed on at least this point. And they did irrefutably "bury" Bergson.

As Leszek Kolakowski points out, *no one* who in the late twentieth century is doing serious philosophy, science, or aesthetics wishes to be publicly identified with Bergson. The man who in the first decades of this century achieved a reputation as a preeminent intellectual leader now would seem to play virtually no significant role in contemporary thought. As Kolakowski said, the mind of Europe (and one should add, of America) has changed dramatically.[35] The way it changed was not accidental, and the damnation of Bergson was no random event in that process. Many cases prove the point: Jung effaced acknowledgment of his debt to Bergson in later editions of his work.[36] Evelyn Underhill, who had greeted Bergson's visit to England with an ecstatic joy ("drunk on Bergson!"), wrote in the twelfth edition of *Mysticism* that since "the ideas of Bergson and Eucken no longer occupy the intellectual foreground," she would have chosen more "scholastic" philosophers to exemplify the hope of escaping scientific determinism.[37] One of the least recognized aspects of the New Critical revolution is its obsession with attacking, at first openly, then covertly, popularized Bergsonism as the reincarnation of romanticism.

No one understood this decline in esteem for Bergson better than Stevens. Yet he chose to support (and quote) him. In a letter of 14 November 1944, he responded to a question about this choice:

> Ordinarily, I don't write prose, and the piece in the *Sewanee Review* is an exception. A man . . . in the Department of Philosophy at Bryn Mawr, wrote me about this, objecting to my founding my view of philosophy on James and Bergson. He said . . . "Why not grapple with a philosopher full-sized?" I asked him whom he had in mind; he fell back on Plato, Aristotle, Kant, and Hegel, and then as a relief from these divinities of the Styx, suggested Whitehead, Bradley, and Peirce. I think most modern philosophers are purely academic, and certainly there is very little in Whitehead contrary to that impression.[38]

Stevens's defense of Bergson was calculated, not quirky, a part of his attempt to build up a theory of poetry and of life in the romantic tradition. Here, as in so many cases, Stevens bucks history.

He took his lumps, as when Yvor Winters attacked his "hedonism." Winters compared Stevens to Poe, accusing both of having embarked on a "quest for the new." Stevens's hedonism, Winters wrote, stemmed from his "popular romanticism" inherited from Poe, Coleridge, and the symbolists.[39] Though unnamed, Bergson is the obvious philosopher of symbolism, the "cult of the new," and romanticism so roundly attacked by Winters, Eliot, Wyndham Lewis, and Santayana. Winters no doubt read "The Figure of the Youth as Virile Poet," as confirmation that Stevens had gone wrong. But Stevens apologized for nothing, deriving ideas of language, the poet, and artistic creation from the tradition Winters caustically described as a "cult." Winters's attack was clearly a rejection of Stevens's humanism, which elevates the figure of the poet as "major man," a Bergsonian belief that "man . . . is the purpose of the entire process of evolution."[40]

Stevens gives the "poet-hero" prodigious powers and responsibilities as scion of his race, especially in his creation of practical value: "It would be tragic not to realize the extent of man's dependence on the arts" (*Angel*, p. 175). He was anxious, as Lisa Steinman has shown, for poetry to compete with science.[41] Stevens (like Pound, Faulkner, and Eliot) modeled some of his aesthetic terminology on mathematics, philosophy, physics. Such talk, as Winters charged, placed him in the tradition of the intuitive artist as defined by Bergson and Hulme.

According to Bergson and Hulme, the artist begins with the flux of "life's depths."[42] Consciousness flows like a sheet of water in "an unbroken stream of images which pass from one into another," but this "interpenetration of images does not come about by chance. It obeys laws . . . which hold the same relation to imagination that logic does to thought."[43] Bergson opposes to practical logic the science of the *form of thinking*.[44] Intuition allows study of this "logic of the imagination that is not the logic of reason."[45] The artist dives into the stream of the "immediate data of consciousness," as T. E. Hulme explained: "The creative artist, the innovator, leaves the level where things are crystallized out into these definite shapes, and, diving down into the inner flux, comes back with a new shape which he endeavours to fix. He cannot be said to have created it *but to have discovered it*, because when he has definitely expressed it we recognize it as true."[46]

The question then arises, how *does* the artist express his fluid experience? Must not the Bergsonian artist oppose words themselves, supporting instead an impossible aesthetic of "formlessness"? For Hulme, the answer is "No." If Bergson believes that words "intervene" between us and reality, and "even our own mental states are screened from us" by language, he also believes that language gave "birth to poetry . . . and converted into instruments of art words which, at first, were only signals."[47] Bergson's artist assumes the romantic pose of inarticulacy in the face of the ineffable, but his artist is also a real Coleridgean power who "cares no more for praise and feels above glory, because *he* is a creator."[48] Bergson's aesthetic extends the long tradition of viewing the artist as a secularized version of the Creator, and Stevens picks up this thread in his later work.

He does so when he says, for example, that imagination is "the way of thinking by which we project the idea of God into man," or "man's truth [should be] the final resolution of everything" (*Angel*, p. 150). One finds the underlying argument everywhere, implicitly and explicitly. In "Adagia," for example: "Proposita: 1. God and the imagination are one. 2. The thing imagined is the imaginer. The second equals the thing imagined and the imaginer are one. Hence, I suppose, the imaginer is God" (*Opus*, p. 178). But it was there in his early career as well. In "Negation," for example, published in *Harmonium* (1923):

Hi! The creator too is blind,
Struggling toward his harmonious whole
Rejecting intermediate parts,
Horrors and falsities and wrongs;
Incapable master of all force. . . .
(Poems, pp. 97-98)

This is not an indictment of God, but human usurpation of divine creation. "Negation" emerges as the "decreative" force enabling life, the necessary counterpart to creation. All creation (we see) is intuitive, and therefore inchoate *even in the mind of the Creator himself*, who is not "master" of the force he incarnates. As falsities and horrors drag back the process, the creative energy "persists" in its "struggle" toward a "harmonious whole." Later, in "Adagia," he would say simply: "Life is the elimination of what is dead" (*Opus*, p. 169). And God, the maker, is like a poet.

Renaissance aestheticians like Scaliger traced the parallel between the poet and God to Aristotle, as Spingarn long ago pointed out. Sidney recycled Scaliger's and Minturno's theories, saying explicitly that the poet may be "compared as a creator to God."[49] Bergson adapted the approach to a vitalistic teleology, saying that God ultimately wished to "create creators, that He may, besides Himself, know beings worthy of His love." Thus, for Bergson, man becomes the goal of evolution, and the "essential function of the universe [is] a machine for the making of gods."[50] This is the most helpful way of conceiving Stevens's "major man."

This "major man" is like the God in "Negation," inchoate and torn with struggle. The major man is that poet of "A Primitive Like an Orb," a composite figure, a "giant ever changing, living in change" (*Poems*, p. 443). Bergson had provided the theoretical framework for such a persona and extended his work, in *The Two Sources of Morality and Religion* (1932), to the ethical and moral sphere, treating religious dogma as the response of the creative, mythmaking power of the human race as a whole. Stevens, in arguing that "we must conceive of poetry as at least the equal of philosophy" (*Angel*, pp. 41-42), draws on this tradition of Scaliger, Sidney, Shelley, and Bergson:

> . . . If we say that the idea of God is merely a poetic idea, even if the supreme poetic idea, and that our notions of heaven and hell are merely poetry not so called, even if that poetry involves us vitally, the feeling of deliverance, release, of a perfection touched, of a vocation so that all men may know the truth and that the truth may set them free—if we say these things and if we are able to see the poet who achieved God and placed Him in His seat in heaven and all His glory, the poet himself, still in the ecstasy of the poem that accomplished this purpose, would have seemed, whether young or old, whether in rags or ceremonial robe, a man who *needed what he had created. . . .*
>
> (*Angel*, p. 51; my italics)

In this essay of 1942 Stevens quotes *The Two Sources of Morality and Religion* confidently, expressing many Bergsonian ideas, even where he does not quote, especially the creator's need for what he creates and the view that God is a creation of man. Such implications had gotten Bergson's name on the Catholic Index; they earned Winters's ire. And yet neither Stevens nor Bergson were atheists. Stevens would respond testily to Ronald Wagner's charge in 1952 that he had "surrendered all residual belief in religion."[51] Unorthodox or just plain heretical—in either case, there is an obvious parallel here between Stevens's and Bergson's God, whom we need and who (if he exists) "needs us."[52]

If Stevens often sounds areligious, we should reflect that few of his poems emphasize absurdity or nihilism ("The Course of a Particular" may be a notable exception—and it is no accident that Winters and Vendler both privilege it in the Stevens canon). The human spirit balances absurdity, and the fight goes on between immobility and play.

Finally, Stevens's world is not "sublime"—though he dwells on sublimity—nor aesthetically pure. Instead, it is *mobile*, a world of dust kicked up around the struggle between "flesh and air" (*Poems*, p. 83). The slump back to sentience as much as the airy flight of spirit colors his reality. Nevertheless, this very struggle presupposes a creative, unhuman, suprarational force. In a deeply Bergsonian way, wherever he finds "decreation" and chaos, Stevens finds also the fecund medium of our being: "The law of chaos is the law of ideas,/Of improvisations and seasons of belief" (*Poems*, p. 255). We become "connoisseurs of chaos" (*Poems*, p. 215).

In *The Auroras of Autumn* (1950), Stevens would ponder why metaphor is "degeneration," implying that it *must be* de-creation, for "being/Includes death and the imagination" (*Poems*, p. 444). Stevens records again and again his perception of a struggle between vital spirit and a materiality dragging it back. Though "memorial mosses" clog the river, it still "flows ahead" (*Poems*, p. 445). In such images, Stevens includes both the creative and destructive forces in conflict, in dialectical process:

> The mobile and the immobile flickering
> In the area between is and was are leaves,
> Leaves burnished in autumnal burnished trees
>
> And leaves in whirlings in the gutters, whirlings
> Around and away, resembling the presence of thought,
> Resembling the presences of thoughts, as if,
>
> In the end, in the whole psychology, the self,
> The town, the weather, in a casual litter,
> Together, said words of the world are the life of the world.
>   (*Poems*, p. 474)

Typically, the conflict evokes memory ("presences"), and then language embodying experience.

Stevens's embodying that experience in words demands a constant shifting of the ground of metaphor, a leaping and a falling: "Metaphor creates a new reality from which the original appears to be unreal" (*Opus*, p. 169). In "The Pure Good of Theory" (*Poems*, p. 332) he wrote of the same "soaring" he would consider in "The Noble Rider and the Sound of Words": Man "comes here in the solar chariot," but wakes "in a metaphor" and seeing the chariot is "junk . . ./Yet to speak of the whole world as metaphor/Is still to stick to the contents of the mind" (*Poems*, pp. 331-32). In "Notes toward a Supreme Fiction" Stevens also writes of Phoebus' "Invented world," of the death of Phoebus, but reminds us that "Phoebus was/A name for something that never could be named" (*Poems*, p. 381). The poems do not merely propose metaphors and demolish them. They seek to return us to "first idea" of creation (*Poems*, p. 382). The poetic here is Bergson's—a world in process of invention, a "living changingness" beyond (or beneath) which nothing can be imagined. Hints of this indeterminate, colorless substratum of being remain hints, however: "The poet is the priest of the invisible," Stevens says, and, "The acquisitions of poetry are fortuitous; *trouvailles*. (Hence, its disorder.)" (*Opus*, p. 169).

For Stevens, a proper poem "resists the intelligence almost successfully," clearing out brackish material, letting the river flow again ("Life's nonsense pierces us with strange relation" [*Poems*, p. 383]). This notion, too, is profoundly Bergsonian. According to Bergson, without automatic responses, stock ideas, and dead language, we could not function in a world of action. But we live too much in the "practical" world, and this tends to cloud our sight. The artist clears out "the utilitarian symbols, the conventional and socially accepted generalities, in short, everything that veils reality from us."[53] But remember that "reality," for Bergson, is finally self-discovery and self-creation, processes that involve *struggle*, the taking of things "by storm," and acts of will.

Most importantly for Stevens, Bergson offers techniques for shaking the veil. The first is humor. Portrayals of absurdity and mechanism crack the encrusted outer layer of "civilization," suggesting a fluid inner reality. The second technique is indirection. The higher the consciousness of the poet, the greater will be the *tension* between any partial notation of Becoming and the paradox of "constant" change. His poem resists us, just as language resists poetry. This is not merely a curse, the site of a paradoxical absence, but a triumph, for the incidental particulars of the poem can regulate our intuition by the mobility of the real, the gyroscopic "stability" of truly ceaseless change. If the poet distracts us from practical life, the border blurs, and we merge (with him) in intuitive reverie, seeing and feeling what he wishes to suggest.[54] For Bergson, the poem's unity is a "directive idea": "Above the word and above the sentence there is something much more simple than a sentence or even a word: the meaning, which is less a thing than a movement of thought, less a movement than a direction."[55] Bergson wrote to William James in 1907 to say: "I believe in the mutability of reality rather than of truth. If we could regulate our faculty of intuition by the mobility of the real, would not this regulating be a stable thing, and would not the truth—which can only be this very regulating—participate in this reality?"[56]

The logic of a poetry reaching for this "directive idea" proves to be indistinguishable from the "logic" of *durée*. The reader's memory strenuously integrates "all the ideas, all the images, all the words . . . in one single point."[57] Effort is required because the poetry Bergson envisions consists of rationally unresolvable "tensions": "By choosing images as dissimilar as possible, we shall prevent any one of them from usurping the place of the intuition it is intended to call up, since it would then be driven away at once by its rivals. By providing that . . . they all require from the mind the same kind of attention, and in short the same degree of *tension*, we shall gradually accustom consciousness to a particular and clearly defined disposition—that precisely which it must adopt in order to appear to itself as it really is, without any veil."[58] The whole poem becomes "the Name," and linguistic play becomes endless, as the poem ceaselessly evokes tensions between its partial notations and its "vector."

Bergson is thus not naive about artifice. When he says we "penetrate the veil," he still values it: "Fortunate are we to have this obstacle, infinitely precious to us is the veil." He also recognizes the illusory nature of such "penetrations." If we are filled with admiration that the poet has torn aside the veil, "the cleverly woven curtain of our conventional ego," showing us our fundamental selves in their "infinite permeation of a thousand different impressions which have already ceased to exist the instant they are named"—if we laud the artist for having known us "better than we knew ourselves," we are wrong. We have been given only another veil. "The very fact that [the poet] spreads out our feelings in homogeneous time and expresses its elements by words," Bergson reminds us, "shows that he in turn is offering us only its shadow."[59]

But according to Bergson—and Stevens wishes to agree—art may defeat this obstacle by tracking the rhythm of the *res*. We return through the *process* of disorientation and reorientation the text demands. For Bergson, art evokes living selfhood through its very artificiality, for as we peel back layers, seeking meaning, we are perpetually surprised at how meanings shift into other meanings. To become engaged, through literature, in this unending process of invention and revelation is really to confront the nature of our own being.

Stevens follows this line: "It is necessary to propose an enigma to the mind," he will say in "Adagia," for "the mind always proposes a solution" (*Opus*, p. 168). This is not as flip as it sounds, if one assumes the solving eclipses the solution. For Stevens as for Bergson, literature evokes living selfhood through its very artificiality, and one reads, as one writes, "for renewal" (*Opus*, p. 220). We *are* this transmutation, this oscillation, and whether that is a reflection of the fundamental world remains, for the poet, a matter for metaphysicians. For Stevens, poetry became more and more clearly the "spirit of visible and invisible change" (*Opus*, p. 242).

In his 1951 essay, "The Relations Between Poetry and Painting," Stevens looked back with some fondness on the previous thirty years in which, as he saw it, "a new reality, a modern reality" had been created. He quoted Paul Klee, who wrote that the preeminent artist "today comes near to the secret place where original law fosters all evolution. And what artist would not establish himself there where the organic center of all movement in time and space—which he calls the mind or heart of creation—determines every function." Admitting that this sounds almost too priestly in tone, Stevens still insists that it "is not too much to allow to those that have helped to create a new reality, a modern reality, since what has been created is nothing less" (*Angel*, pp. 174-75). No doubt Stevens's poetic is colored Crocean, Santayanian, Jamesian, and Emersonian, as well as Bergsonian. But without Bergson in that picture, Stevens's concept of a "modern reality" cannot be fully appreciated.

Bergson offers a key to Stevens's peculiar "formality," to his obsessions, his quirks of mind, his habits of writing, his conviction of the presence of the past and his belief in the freedom of the creative imagination. Stevens shared Bergson's view that art is both empiricist and sacramental. Consistent with this view, Stevens sought systematically to record the unsystematic relations between wavering forms of life and their castings. "One is always writing about two things at the same time in poetry," said Stevens, and it is this that produces the tension characteristic of poetry. One is the true subject and the other is the poetry of the subject" (*Opus*, p. 221). Behind surface contradictions in Stevens's work, we do find a "system." We also find values: The sanctity of human imagination, the ultimate "directedness" of life, divulged to us occasionally in "surprises" afforded by disinterested watching. I do not claim Stevens exhibits a faith in the salvation of human. I merely point out that he dwells on human potential and fears that, in Bergson's words, "Men do not sufficiently realize that the future is in their own hands."[60]

Stevens repeatedly discussed his theory of poetry. That theory may be inconsistently developed—or "wrong" in our terms—but it does have a ground in the "life-philosophy" of Bergson, whom he read and absorbed over a number of years. The story of Stevens's relation to Bergson and Bergsonism records in many ways the life of modernist aesthetics, sunrise to sunset. Winters was right: Stevens hung on far past nightfall. Stevens sought to believe that, in a curious but not contradictory way, language opens a door out of its own "prison house" (to use Nietzsche's phrase). For him, pure poetry is both "mystical and irrational." Contemporary discomfort with this view merely underscores our distance from an era we used to identify thoroughly with Bergson.

Notes

1. J. Hillis Miller, *Poets of Reality* (Cambridge, Mass.: Harvard University Press, 1965), 259. The quotation in the title of my essay is from Stevens's "An Ordinary Evening in New

Haven" in *Collected Poems of Wallace Stevens* (New York: Knopf, 1954), 486. See also "Adagia" in *Opus Posthumous* (New York: Knopf, 1966), 178.

2. Samuel French Morse, *Wallace Stevens: Poetry as Life* (New York: Pegasus, 1970). On pages 118-19 Morse tears into the overly philosophical reading of Stevens. Joseph N. Riddel, in *The Clairvoyant Eye: The Poetry and Politics of Wallace Stevens* (Baton Rouge: Louisiana State University Press, 1965), writes: "Philosophy may illuminate aspects of Stevens' poetics. But only his poetry illuminates philosophy. This is not to confuse either poetry or poetics with philosophy. Indeed, the only contribution Stevens' poetics makes to modern thought is the perspectives it offers on his poems" (41). Helen Hennessy Vendler, in *On Extended Wings: Wallace Stevens' Longer Poems* (Cambridge, Mass.: Harvard University Press, 1969), writes: "If I seem to neglect the poet as philosopher, it is because I believe he has often been badly served in being considered one" (9).

3. William Pritchard, *Lives of the Modern Poets* (New York: Oxford University Press, 1980), 206. Pritchard acknowledges that J. V. Cunningham expressed this idea first. See *Tradition and Poetic Structure: Essays in Literary History and Criticism* (Denver: Swallow, 1960).

4. Hugh Kenner, *A Homemade World* (New York: Morrow, 1975), 81.

5. Frank Doggett, *Stevens' Poetry of Thought* (Baltimore: Johns Hopkins University Press, 1966), 213.

6. See Samuel French Morse, "Wallace Stevens, Bergson, Pater," in *The Act of the Mind: Essays on the Poetry of Wallace Stevens*, ed. Roy Harvey Pearce and J. Hillis Miller (Baltimore: Johns Hopkins University Press, 1965), 58-91. Morse does not inquire into Bergson's metaphysics, preferring instead to introduce Pater as a counterpoint, though he admits "Bergson contributed more than Pater" (59). In *Wallace Stevens: Poetry as Life* Morse says: "What may have been the most direct debts—to Donald Evans, to Bergson, to Pater, and above all, to Santayana—will never, in all likelihood, be determined. Most of what meant most to him remains unacknowledged" (128).

7. Frank Kermode, *Wallace Stevens* (London: Oliver and Boyd, 1960), 82-83.

8. Riddel, *Clairvoyant Eye*, 275.

9. *The Necessary Angel: Essays on Reality and the Imagination* (New York: Knopf, 1951), 174; hereafter cited in text as *Angel*.

10. *Opus Posthumous*, 178; hereafter cited in text as *Opus*.

11. *Collected Poems of Wallace Stevens*, 83; hereafter cited in text as *Poems*.

12. David LaGuardia, *Advance on Chaos: The Sanctifying Imagination of Wallace Stevens* (Hanover, N.H.: University Press of New England, 1983), 126.

13. Henri Bergson, *The Creative Mind*, trans. M. L. Andison (New York: Philosophical Library, 1946), 23.

14. Henri Bergson, *Time and Free Will: An Essay on the Immediate Data of Consciousness*, trans. F. L. Pogson (New York: MacMillan, 1910), 167.

15. Henri Bergson, *Creative Evolution*, trans. A. Mitchell (New York: Holt, 1911), 193, 251; and *Introduction to Metaphysics*, trans. T. E. Hulme (New York: Putnam, 1912), 51.

16. Bergson, *Creative Evolution*, 2-4; my italics.

17. Michael Beehler, *T. S. Eliot, Wallace Stevens, and the Discourses of Difference* (Baton Rouge: Louisiana State University Press, 1987), 18.

18. One sometimes gets the eerie feeling that Bergson has been expunged from history, reading books like *Modernism Reconsidered*, ed. Robert Kiely (Harvard English Studies #11, 1983), or even LaGuardia's otherwise fine and convincing book on James, Emerson, and Stevens. Neither contains a single reference to Bergson.

19. Wassily Kandinsky, *Concerning the Spiritual in Art and Painting in Particular* (1912), trans. Francis Golffing, Michael Harrison, and Ferdinand Ostertag (New York: Wittenborn, 1970), 24, 26.

20. Bergson, *Introduction to Metaphysics*, 11-12.

21. Joan Richardson, *Wallace Stevens: The Early Years, 1879-1923* (New York: Morrow, 1986), 30.

22. Riddel, *Clairvoyant Eye*, 29.

23. Bergson, *Creative Evolution*, 16.

24. P. A. Y. Gunter, *Bergson and the Evolution of Physics* (Knoxville: University of Tennessee Press, 1969), 18-19.

25. See Thomas Hanna, ed., *The Bergsonian Heritage* (New York: Columbia University Press, 1962), 16.

26. T. S. Eliot, "Commentary," *Criterion* 12 (October 1932):74; and "The Idealism of Julien Benda," *Cambridge Review* 49, 488.

27. Sir Ray Lankester, preface to *Modern Science and the Illusions of Professor Bergson*, by Hugh Samuel R. Elliott (London: Longmans, Green, 1912), vii-viii, xvi, xvii.

28. Thomas John Gerrard, *Bergson: An Exposition from the Point of View of St. Thomas Aquinas* (London: Sands, 1913), 207.

29. George Santayana, *The Winds of Doctrine: Studies in Contemporary Opinion* (1912) (New York: Scribner's, 1926), 106-7 and 58-109 passim.

30. Bertrand Russell, "The Philosophy of Bergson," *The Monist*, July 1912, 22, 334.

31. See Robert J. Niess, *Julien Benda* (Ann Arbor: University of Michigan Press, 1956), 29, 64, 95-96, 122.

32. Bertrand Russell, *A History of Modern Philosophy* (New York: Simon and Schuster, 1945), 793.

33. Joseph Chiari, *T. S. Eliot: A Memoir* (London: Enitharmon Press, 1982).

34. Jacques Maritain, *Bergsonian Philosophy and Thomism*, trans. M. L. Andison (New York: Pantheon, 1955), 280, 337.

35. Leszek Kolakowski, *Bergson* (Oxford: Oxford University Press, 1985), 1-2.

36. P. A. Y. Gunter, "Bergson and Jung," *Journal of the History of Ideas* 43 (October/December 1982):638 ff.

37. Evelyn Underhill, *Mysticism: A Study in the Nature and Development of Man's Spiritual Consciousness* (London: Methuen, 1930), 43.

38. Wallace Stevens, Letter to Theodore Weiss, 14 November 1944, in *Letters of Wallace Stevens*, ed. Holly Stevens (New York: Knopf, 1977), 476.

39. Yvor Winters, "Wallace Stevens, or, the Hedonist's Progress" (1943), *On Modern Poetry* (New York: Meridian, 1959), 17.

40. Henri Bergson, *The Two Sources of Morality and Religion*, trans. R. Ashley Audra and Cloudesley Brereton (New York: Holt, 1935), 200.

41. Lisa Steinman, "Getting the World Right: Stevens, Science, and the American Context," *Wallace Stevens Journal* 10 (Spring 1986):18-26.

42. Bergson, *Creative Mind*, 176.

43. Henri Bergson, *Laughter: An Essay on the Meaning of the Comic*, trans. Cloudesley Brereton and Fred Rothwell (New York: MacMillan, 1911), 41-42.

44. Immanuel Kant, *Werke*, ed. Karl Vorländer et al., in *Philosophische Bibliothek*, IV, 14 ff.

45. Bergson, *Laughter*, 41.

46. T. E. Hulme, *Speculations: Essays on Humanism and the Philosophy of Art* (London: Kegan Paul, 1924), 149.

47. Bergson, *Laughter*, 153; *Creative Mind*, 94.

48. Henri Bergson, *Mind Energy: Lectures and Essays*, trans. H. W. Carr (New York: Holt, 1920), 70.

49. See J. E. Spingarn, *A History of Literary Criticism in the Renaissance* (1899) (New York: Columbia University Press, 1924), 273 ff.

50. Bergson, *Two Sources of Morality and Religion*, 200, 243.

51. Ronald Wagner, "A Central Poetry" (1952), in *Wallace Stevens*, ed. Marie Borroff (Englewood Cliffs: Prentice-Hall, 1963), 73.

52. Bergson, *Two Sources of Morality and Religion*, 243.

53. Bergson, *Laughter*, 157.

54. Bergson, *Time and Free Will*, 14.

55. Bergson, *Mind Energy*, 225; *Creative Mind*, 143.

56. Henri Bergson, Letter to William James, 27 June 1907, quoted in R. B. Perry, *The Thought and Character of William James*, vol. 2 (Boston: Little, Brown and Co., 1935), 621-22.

57. Bergson, *Mind Energy*, 195.

58. Bergson, *Introduction to Metaphysics*, 16-17; my italics.

59. Bergson, *Mind Energy*, 70.

60. Bergson, *Two Sources of Morality and Religion*, 306.

INDEX